D0587018

Sunderland College

Hylton Library

This book is due for return on or before the last date shown below
Please be aware that fines are charged for overdue items
Renew online: http://library.citysun.ac.uk
Renew by phone: call 5116231

3 1 JAN 2023

nation
ls

Author Morgan, N   Loc. Code TO.

Class. No. 338.4791   Acc. No. 0014702.

mor

21-DAY LOAN

Destination Brands
Managing Place Reputation

THIRD EDITION

Nigel Morgan
Annette Pritchard

University of Wales Institute, Cardiff

Roger Pride

Welsh Assembly Government

CITY OF
LEARNING
CENTRE
SUNDERLAND COLLEGE

ELSEVIER

AMSTERDAM BOSTON HEIDELBERG LONDON NEW YORK OXFORD PARIS
SAN DIEGO SAN FRANCISCO SINGAPORE SYDNEY TOKYO

Butterworth-Heinemann is an imprint of Elsevier
The Boulevard, Langford Lane, Kidlington, Oxford, OX5 1GB, UK
30 Corporate Drive, Suite 400, Burlington, MA 01803, USA

First published 2002
Second edition 2004
Reprinted 2005
Third edition 2011

Copyright © 2011 Published by Elsevier Ltd. All rights reserved

No part of this publication may be reproduced, stored in a retrieval system or
transmitted in any form or by any means electronic, mechanical, photocopying,
recording or otherwise without the prior written permission of the publisher

Permissions may be sought directly from Elsevier's Science & Technology
Rights Department in Oxford, UK: phone (+44) (0) 1865 843830;
fax (+44) (0) 1865 853333; email: permissions@elsevier.com. Alternatively
you can submit your request online by visiting the Elsevier web site at
http://elsevier.com/locate/permissions, and selecting Obtaining permission to use
Elsevier material

Notice
No responsibility is assumed by the publisher for any injury and/or damage to
persons or property as a matter of products liability, negligence or otherwise,
or from any use or operation of any methods, products, instructions or ideas
contained in the material herein

British Library Cataloguing in Publication Data
A catalogue record for this book is available from the British Library

Library of Congress Cataloging-in-Publication Data
A catalog record for this book is available from the Library of Congress

ISBN: 978-0-08-096930-5

For information on all Butterworth-Heinemann publications
visit our web site at www.elsevierdirect.com

Printed and bound in Great Britain

11 12 13 14   10 9 8 7 6 5 4 3

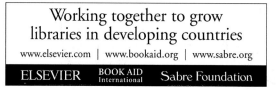

Contents

List of contributors

Malcolm Allan is Senior Director of Colliers International, a global real estate advisory company, working in its Development Solutions International Team, based in London, where he leads for the company on real estate, place and destination development, and branding strategy. He was formerly a founder and director of Placebrands (2003–2007), the world's first specialist place brand agency, and prior to that set up and ran "Thinq Global."

Simon Anholt is the leading authority on national identity and reputation, and created the field of nation branding. A member of the UK Foreign Office Public Diplomacy Board, he advises some 40 governments from America to Zimbabwe. He has written five books, edits the journal *Place Branding and Public Diplomacy*, and publishes the Anholt Nation Brands Index and City Brands Index.

Bill Baker is President of Total Destination Marketing based in Portland, Oregon, USA, and specialises in the branding and marketing of cities and regions. He held executive positions with the Australian Tourist Commission for more than a decade shaping Australia's brand identity in North America and Europe. He is the author of *Destination Branding for Small Cities* and a popular speaker on brand planning and implementation.

Tom Buncle is Managing Director of Yellow Railroad, an international destination consultancy that helps countries, cities, and regions improve their competitiveness as tourism destinations. He has undertaken branding, marketing, and eco-tourism strategies for destinations in the UK, Europe, Middle East, Africa, and the Caribbean. Tom is a former chief executive of the Scottish Tourist Board and international manager of the British Tourist Authority in Southeast Asia, Norway, and California. He produced the *Handbook on Tourism Destination Branding* (2009) for the European Travel Commission and United Nations World Tourism Organization.

Jonathon Day, PhD, MBA, recently joined the faculty at Purdue University's Department of Hospitality and Tourism Management as an assistant professor. He is also an associate of the Purdue Hospitality and Tourism Research Center. Prior to joining Purdue, Jonathon was Regional Director – Americas for Tourism Queensland (Australia) and has been involved in destination marketing in the United States for over 20 years. Jonathon's research interests include destination competitiveness, sustainable tourism, and regional branding.

Francesca d'Angella, PhD, is a researcher and consultant in the tourism industry. She is a faculty member of the Master in Tourism Management (MTM), contract researcher at IULM University of Milan, and adjunct professor at LUM University of Bari. Her research areas are destination management, stakeholder collaboration, strategic management, and decision-making processes.

Manuela De Carlo, PhD, is Professor of Strategy and Tourism Management at IULM University in Milan. She founded and directs the Master in Tourism Management (www.mtm.iulm.it) at IULM and supervises the Tourism Sector of the IULM Foundation. Her research focuses on destination management, competitive strategies, and innovation processes in the tourist industry. Manuela has led numerous research and consulting projects on destination development and tourism management for leading companies in the private sector, the Italian Ministry of Tourism, and the tourist boards of several destinations.

Keith Dinnie is Senior Lecturer in International Marketing at Breda University of Applied Sciences (NHTV) in The Netherlands. He is the author of *Nation Branding – Concepts, Issues, Practise* (Butterworth-Heinemann, 2008) and the Academic Editor of the journal *Place Branding and Public Diplomacy*. He has delivered seminars, conference speeches, presentations, and lectures in the United States, United Kingdom, France, Germany, Iceland, Portugal, Greece, China, Korea, and Japan. He is the founder of Brand Horizons consultancy (www.brandhorizons.com).

Alan Fyall, PhD, is Professor of Tourism and Deputy Dean in the School of Tourism, Bournemouth University. He has published extensively in tourism and sits on the editorial boards of many leading journals including *Annals of Tourism Research*. Alan has conducted numerous projects for clients across the UK and overseas and currently serves on the ESRC Cluster Advisory Board for Exeter University Business School.

David Gertner, PhD, joined Pace University, New York, in 2001 after visiting and serving as professor and program chair in several universities in Brazil and the USA. Throughout his extensive career, he has consulted for many companies, served on various organisational boards, and actively participated in a number of professional associations. More than 50 articles, book chapters, and essays of his have been published and presented at conferences in several countries. In addition, he has co-authored a book on Marketing Latin American and Caribbean Places and has various book projects and research projects in the works. His research interests include place marketing and brandings, and international marketing.

Michael Gould is Assistant Director of Skills and Industry Division at the Department for Employment and Learning in Northern Ireland. Prior to returning to live and work in Belfast, Michael served at several overseas locations including a diplomatic posting at the British Embassy in Washington DC and with the Swedish Ministry of Agriculture in Stockholm. Michael is a chartered marketer and a board member of the Chartered Institute of Marketing in Ireland.

Vesa Harmaakorpi, DSc (Tech.) is Professor of Innovation Systems at Lappeenranta University of Technology, Lahti School of Innovation (Lahti, Finland). Professor Harmaakorpi has his background in business life. For the last 13 years he has worked within the university community. His research interests are innovation systems and processes as well as innovation environments linked to regional development. He is a pioneer in research and development of practice-based innovation activities in Finland. The publication activities of Harmaakorpi have been extensive covering tens of scientific and other publications in international and national journals, series, and books.

Ram Herstein is Head of the Marketing Program and Associate Professor of Marketing at the Ruppin Academic Center, Israel. His research area is branding and corporate identity and his papers have been published in leading marketing and business academic journals.

Jeremy Hildreth likes to see places get the reputations they deserve. As founder and creative director of WhereBrands, he directly helps cities (like London) and countries (like Lithuania) to identify, marshal, express, and expand their reputational assets. One of the foremost practitioners of provenance-related strategy and marketing, he originated Saffron's place branding practice in 2004 and led it for 5 years. He is a Californian and a Londoner, and holds an economics degree from Wharton and an MBA from Oxford. He co-authored *Brand America* with Simon Anholt, writes regularly for *The Wall Street Journal*, and travels incessantly (and with gusto).

Soren Buhl Hornskov holds a PhD in corporate communication from the Copenhagen Business School. He has worked in research, in public sector administration, and in a private sector marketing consultancy. Soren is a project manager in regional development and lives and works in the Copenhagen area.

Eugene D. Jaffe is Professor and Head, MBA Programs at the School of Social Sciences and Management, Ruppin Academic Center and Emeritus Professor, Graduate School of Business Administration, Bar-Ilan University, both in Israel. He holds BS (Econ.) and PhD (Econ.) degrees from the Wharton School, University of Pennsylvania, and an MBA in International Business from the Graduate School of Business, New York University. He has been a visiting professor in the United States, Denmark, and Mexico and his research interests are in international marketing, business ethics, and research methodology. His latest book is National Image & Competitive Advantage: The Theory and Practice of Place Branding. His next book is *Global Marketing Strategy* (with Ilan Alon) to be published in 2011 by McGraw-Hill.

Kaarina Kari, BSc (Econ.), is Information Officer at Aalto University School of Science and Technology Lahti Center, Finland, having worked in the university community for the last 13 years.

Maja Konecnik Ruzzier, PhD, is Assistant Professor in the Marketing Department of the Faculty of Economics at the University of Ljubljana, Slovenia. Her specialist area of research is destination branding. She has published several articles on the subject, including the book *Destination Branding: Theory and Research*. She contributed to the 'I Feel Slovenia' brand development as an external brand consultant.

Philip Kotler is the S.C. Johnson Distinguished Professor of International Marketing at the Kellogg School of Management, Northwestern University, Evanston, Illinois. His *Marketing Management* (13th edition) is one of the world's leading textbooks on marketing, and he has published 40 other books and over 100 articles in leading journals. His research spans strategic marketing, consumer marketing, business marketing, services marketing, and e-marketing. He has been a consultant to IBM, Bank of America, Merck, General Electric, Honeywell, and many other companies. He has received honorary doctorate degrees from 12 major universities in the USA and other countries.

Cindia Ching-Chi Lam, PhD, is Senior Lecturer in the Institute For Tourism Studies (IFT), Macau. Her research interests range from tourist behaviour, customer choice, and quality of life to investor behaviour and accounting. Cindia has been the editor of the research notes for *Tourism and Hospitality e-Review* (Macau, China). Additionally, she is a certified accountant and enjoys researching management accounting, accounting education, and accounting history.

Weng Si (Clara) Lei, PhD, is a lecturer in the Institute For Tourism Studies (IFT), Macau. She received her PhD from University of Leeds, UK. Her research interests focus on the hospitality sector, with a specific focus on foreign direct investment.

Una McMahon-Beattie, PhD, is Head of the Department of Hospitality and Tourism Management at the University of Ulster, Belfast. Her research interests include tourism futures, revenue management, relationship marketing, pricing, and consumer trust. She has published widely in journals, books, and conferences in these areas in the UK and internationally. Una is Practice Papers Editor for the *Journal of Revenue and Pricing Management* and is the author or editor of a number of books.

Yoram Mitki is an associate professor in the Department of Business Administration at the Lander Institute, Jerusalem Academic Center, Israel. His research and consultation work are in the fields of organisational learning, system-wide transformation, and the implementation of advanced managerial approaches.

Nigel Morgan, PhD, is Professor of Tourism Studies at Cardiff School of Management's Welsh Centre for Tourism Research at the University of Wales Institute, Cardiff. A strong proponent of advocacy scholarship, he was one of the originators of the hopeful tourism perspective and is passionately interested in the multi-faceted connections between tourism, social justice, citizenship, creative destinations, and place reputation. Nigel is an editorial board member of several leading international journals including *Place Branding & Public Diplomacy, Hospitality & Society* and *Vacation Marketing* and is Joint Research Notes Editor of the *Annals of Tourism Research*.

Jon Munro is Managing Director at Cinch, an independent digital and marketing communications consultancy with experience across travel, tourism, leisure, charity, events, software, and online retail. He also heads up Digital Marketing at Visit Wales, managing a new digital marketing team and having overall responsibility for developing and taking forward Visit Wales' digital marketing strategy across UK and international markets. He focuses on strategic planning, integrated campaign planning across online and offline channels, evaluation, and measurement.

Wally Olins is 'the world's leading practitioner of branding and identity' according to the *Financial Times*. Formerly Chairman of Wolff Olins and currently Chairman and co-founder of Saffron Brand Consultants, he has advised many of the world's leading companies, including 3i, Renault, Repsol, BT, Volkswagen, Tata, and Lloyd's of London, and has also worked with many countries, regions, and cities, among them Portugal and Poland. Olins is the author of several books, including the seminal work *Corporate Identity* published in 20 languages and *Wally Olins On B®and*. His latest book *The Brand Handbook* was published in 2008. He has held fellowships and professorships at a number of leading business schools and universities around the world. The multi-award-winning Wally Olins was made CBE in 1999. He was born in London and educated at Oxford.

Can-Seng Ooi, PhD, is Associate Professor in the Copenhagen Business School's imagine.. Creative Industries Research Centre. He has been researching tourism since 1996 and has published extensively, including in the *Annals of Tourism Research, International Journal of Cultural Policy,* and *Place Branding and Public Diplomacy*. Under the auspices of *Creative Encounters*, a research project supported by the Danish Strategic Research Council, he is heading a comparative research stream on place branding, the arts, and culture.

Rachel Piggott is a freelance marketer specialising in tourism communications and destination branding. She has previously worked for a range of organisations including airlines and tourism boards and was most notably responsible for the execution of the award-winning '100% Pure New Zealand' campaign and most recently 'Share our Story' – the Northern Territory's (Australia) tourism brand campaign. Her freelance clients have included Slovenia, Auckland, and South Australia. Rachel has an MBA in strategic marketing.

Roger Pride began his career in the travel/tourism industry and worked in sales management and advertising, before joining the Wales Tourist Board in 1985. Since then, Roger has undertaken several roles within WTB and is now Marketing Director at the Welsh Assembly Government (including VisitWales). He has a particular interest in destination branding and developed a branding strategy for Wales Tourist Board that led to the award-winning 'Wales Two Hours and a Million Miles Away' campaign.

Annette Pritchard is Professor of Critical Tourism Studies and Director of the Cardiff School of Management's Welsh Centre for Tourism Research at the University of Wales Institute, Cardiff. Annette has a long-standing interest in places, representations, identities, and transformative tourism enquiry. She was one of the originators of the hopeful tourism scholarship agenda which has been the focus of much of her recent work. She has published 15 books and is currently an editorial board member of the *Journal of Tourism and Cultural Change* and *Tourism and Hospitality Research* and Joint Research Notes Editor of the *Annals of Tourism Research*.

Satu Parjanen, MSc, is a researcher at Lappeenranta University of Technology, Lahti School of Innovation (Lahti, Finland). She obtained her Master of Social Sciences degree from University of Tampere, where she studied international relations as her major, and administration and communication as minor subjects. Her current research interests relate to collective creativity in innovation activities, which is also the theme of her post-graduate studies.

Bethan Richards is Creative Director at Cinch, an independent digital and marketing communications consultancy with experience across travel, tourism, leisure, charity, events, software, and online retail. She also heads up Digital Marketing at Visit Wales, managing a new digital marketing team and having overall responsibility for developing and taking forward Visit Wales' digital marketing strategy across UK and international markets. She focuses on creative planning, executing the brand online and online user experience.

Rosanna Vitiello is a designer and strategist based in New York, focussing on spatial design and communication. She is particularly interested in the public realm, and the ability of place brands to change the perceptions (and the reality) of a place. She works with city authorities, corporate brands, and cultural organisations around the world to create exhibitions, branded environments, and communication strategies that engage and motivate the public. Rosanna holds a degree in graphic design from Central St Martins, London, and a Masters in Design for Public Space from Elisava, Barcelona.

Sheena Westwood, PhD, is Associate Professor and Director of Graduate Programs in the College of Communication and Media Sciences, Zayed University, Abu Dhabi. Her background is in the international airline industry in the UK and the Middle East. Publications include articles and book chapters on projective techniques in tourism research, tourism marketing, branding, airlines, and tourist shopping. She has a specific interest in tourism in emerging destinations, and her current research includes tourism education and tourist guiding in the UAE.

Marcus Willcocks is a designer and design researcher. His background and training is in product design (Central Saint Martins, London) and design for public space (Elisava, Barcelona). He is a research fellow with the Design Against Crime Research Centre, University of the Arts London (www. designagainstcrime.com). He also consults, mostly in London and Barcelona, on activities connected to the public realm and socially centred design and research. He has recently collaborated on projects with, among others, the City of Barcelona, CSD and INEF sports councils for Spain, URV University for the City of Tarragona, BACC cycling campaign of Catalonia, as well as with Participle service design, Sparks Projects, and multiple public and private sector agencies in London.

Lok Kei (Kathy) Wong holds a master's degree in International Public Relations from Cardiff University. Her research interests focus on destination branding, in particular the relationship between brand campaigns and the importance of local culture. Kathy is currently with Burson-Marsteller Hong Kong and primarily works on the finance and corporate communication team.

Ian Yeoman, PhD, is the world's only futurologist specialising in travel and tourism. Ian learnt his trade as the scenario planner for VisitScotland, where he established the process of futures thinking within the organisation using a variety of techniques including economic modeling, trends analysis, and scenario construction. Ian presently resides in New Zealand at Victoria University of Wellington as an associate professor of Tourism Futures.

His most recent book *Tomorrow's Tourists: Scenarios and Trends* (www. tomorrowstourist.com) looks at where the tourist will go on holiday in 2030 and what they will do. Forthcoming titles include *Tourism and Demography* (Goodfellows, 2010), *Practical Pricing and Revenue Management* (Palgrave, 2010), and *2050: Tomorrows Tourism* (Channelview, 2011). Ian is also the Editor of the *Journal of Revenue & Pricing Management* and is about to start studying for a second doctorate in Scenario Planning. When not doing the above, you will find him tramping, watching movies, trying to figure out his X-box, supporting his native football team (Sunderland AFC) and adopted one (Wellington Phoenix).

List of figures

List of tables

Tables		Page

Acknowledgements

There are many people and organisations to whom the editors are indebted for their help and support in producing the third edition of this book. We would particularly like to thank all our contributors – firstly, for agreeing to be part of our new and expanded project and secondly for allowing us to edit their hard work. We would also like to express our gratitude to all the staff at Elsevier for their assistance and guidance throughout the project, particularly Eleanor Blow, Melanie Benson, and Carole Barber.

We are also hugely indebted to many individuals in academia and industry too numerous to mention individually. Nigel and Annette would like to thank colleagues, researchers, students, and friends at the Cardiff School of Management and beyond for exchanging ideas and opinions on destination brands and Roger would like to thank all his colleagues at the Assembly Government. Finally, our thanks are due to all those readers of the earlier editions of this book who through their encouragement and feedback led us to produce this third edition. *Diolch yn fawr.*

Nigel Morgan & Annette Pritchard
Welsh Centre for Tourism Research, UWIC
Roger Pride
Welsh Assembly Government
October 15, 2010

PART **1**

Destination Brand Concepts

Do destinations really get the reputations they deserve? Not always. And it is incredibly difficult to persuade people to change their minds about places – and their notions of whether somewhere is an attractive place to live, work, study, holiday, or even travel to for treatment as a medical tourist. Simon Anholt's Nation Brands Index, which assesses perceptions of 50 or more countries, suggests that nations' reputations are remarkably stable and show very little volatility. The only significant changes since the Index was launched are the surge in the USA's popularity with the November 2008 election of Barack Obama and the collapse of Denmark's reputation among Muslims following the 2006 "cartoon incident." Today, there are 265 countries in the world (together with more territories and other administrative areas) and approximately 3400 cities. And every conceivable tourism destination – from Albania to Zimbabwe – wants to improve, reverse, adapt, or in some way manage its international image.

Despite the upsurge in books and academic papers and the explosion of consultancy firms specialising in this area, we are still far from a clear appreciation of what this actually means. In fact, there remains much misunderstanding and many commentators and some consultants and academics still interpret "place branding" as simply the application of product promotion, public relations, and corporate identity activities to countries, cities, or regions as though they are mere commodities. And not only is the notion of a place or destination brand misunderstood. Most of the relevant terms here — including 'destination', 'competitiveness', 'authenticity', 'creativity' and 'branding' itself — are contested and elusive.

The four chapters that comprise Part 1 of this book challenge and evaluate the ideas and concepts wrapped up in place and destination brands, and take a broad overview of place reputation, image, and identity. Part 1 starts with Nigel Morgan, Annette Pritchard, and Roger Pride's overview of the role of tourism in place reputation and their exploration of the DNA of creative destinations, which they summarise in the virtuous circle of destination reputation management. This is followed by Simon Anholt's review of competitive identity, which tackles how place perceptions are formed, how cities, regions, and counties can develop their competitive identities, and the link between competitive identity and strategic policy making or public diplomacy.

In Chapter 3 Philip Kotler and David Gertner shift the focus onto the link between country-of-origin effect and place brands as they see a crucial relationship between these and tourism marketing and economic development. Put it simply, they conclude that each time the name of a place is mentioned, there is an opportunity to add or subtract value to its equity. Part 1 is completed by Wally Olins and Jeremy Hildreth's contribution, which argue that branding is a manifestation of identity and that successful nation branding creates and sustains a clear sense of belonging within the nation and projects a handful of core ideas to the outside world. Their plea for everyone with a stake in place reputation management to take account of the sweep of history and the profound and subtle psychology of the human experience of place identity, and to exhibit more professionalism and reflection appropriately concludes Part 1 of this book.

CHAPTER

1

Tourism places, brands, and reputation management

Nigel Morgan, Annette Pritchard and Roger Pride

INTRODUCTION

The first decade of the twenty-first century was one of 'many perfect storms for the travel and tourism industry' (Chiesa, 2009); it began with the September 11 2001 attacks in the USA and ended amidst the worst economic crisis since the Great Depression. The decade witnessed war in Afghanistan and Iraq, the SARS and avian and swine flu outbreaks, and devastating natural and human-induced environmental disasters that are too many to list. The collapse of real estate and stock markets around the world has left consumer confidence low and unemployment high in the world's more economically developed economies and as tourism growth rates are closely correlated with economic business cycles, the coming years promise to be tough ones for the industry. Characterised by the influential writer Richard Florida (2010) as 'The Great Reset,' these are sharply transitional times, which may well prove to be a generational period of economic and social change during which individuals and places will need to find new ways of living and working.

Places compete in attracting visitors, residents, and businesses. A place with a positive reputation finds it easier to vie for attention, resources, people, jobs, and money; a positive place reputation builds place competitiveness and cements a place as somewhere worth visiting. This means that places looking to build or maintain strong reputations must consider a holistic approach to their brand which incorporates tourism, economic development, and a sense of place – all of which opens up potentially controversial questions of place authenticity, brand narratives, leadership and authorship, performativity, story-telling, and aesthetics. This chapter will:

- discuss place reputation management;
- locate tourism in its wider place reputation context; and
- introduce the virtuous circle of destination reputation model.

© 2011 Published by Elsevier Ltd. All rights reserved.
DOI: 10.1016/B978-0-08-096930-5.10001-1

PLACE REPUTATION MANAGEMENT

Tourism destination development and marketing and place reputation management have a hugely significant but complex relationship and the various connections between brand, image, reputation and identity, and creative and competitive destinations are not well understood. What do we even mean by 'destination'? It is a commonplace to suggest that tourist destinations are composites of services and natural, socio-cultural landscapes and that they exist on multiple geopolitical levels (Buhalis, 2000; Morgan, 2004; Pike, 2004). Yet, the notion of a destination is a problematic concept and is variously used by marketers and tourism professionals (as a geopolitical system with its own Destination Management Organisation or DMO) and by sociologists and cultural geographers (as a socio-cultural construction). In other words, some treat a destination as a set of attributes and others treat it as a set of cultural and symbolic meanings and contested 'realities.' Thus while Buhalis (2000, p. 98) defines a tourism destination as a 'geographical region which is understood by its visitors as a unique entity, with a political and legislative framework for tourism marketing and planning,' Saarinen (2004) understands a tourist destination as a socio-culturally produced space, the result of constantly evolving discursive practices. Arguably, the term destination is probably of most significance to marketing professionals and academics, and destinations exist only through the act of marketing. In other words, a 'place' only becomes a 'destination' through the narratives and images communicated by tourism promotional material.

Since this book was first published in 2002, the landscape of place and destination brand studies has transformed. At that time, it was the only book on tourism destination brands. Since then, Baker (2007) has published *Destination Branding for Small Cities* and several books now address the broader field of place brands and competitive identity (e.g., Anholt, 2005, 2006, 2007, 2009a; Jaffe & Nebenzahl, 2006; Dinnie, 2008; Kavaratzis & Ashworth, 2010). In 2004, the journal of *Place Branding and Public Diplomacy* was launched and today a growing number of seminars and conferences regularly attract international audiences of academics, branding consultants, and DMO professionals. This third edition of our book gathers together leading professionals, consultants, and academics to discuss the relationship between tourism and place brands; in its 25 chapters and accompanying online case studies, the contributors examine a range of tourism destinations with different profiles, reputations, markets, and resources – each grappling with the challenge of being competitive in the twenty-first century. Part 1 reviews the conceptual connections between tourism, identity, branding, and place reputation; part 2 addresses nine key challenges in tourism destination brand management (ethics, leadership, partnership, authenticity, aesthetics, tone of voice, the digital revolution, measurement, and future scenario planning); and part 3 reflects on how DMOs have confronted these challenges in 11 case studies.

We know that places compete in attracting visitors, residents, and businesses. In addition, we also know that their reputation or brand plays a hugely significant role in determining just how successful they are in this competition. According to Florida (2002) and Jansson and Power (2006), places which have strong and dynamic brands have an easier time attracting businesses and talent within the knowledge economy. But despite the recent growth in academic writing in the area of place brands or place reputation and identity management, we still lack a clear understanding of what this means in practice. The very terms 'destination,' 'competitiveness,' 'authenticity,' 'creativity,' and 'place brand' are slippery, elusive, contested, and often misunderstood.

Yet, our need for more understanding in this area is paramount. A consumer brand with genuine equity builds emotional connections and brings a powerful identity benefit, drives consumers' behaviour, and shapes their perceptions of reality; it opens doors, creates trust and respect, and raises expectations of quality and integrity. In short, a strong brand has a positive 'reputation.' In the case of a place brand, it is a powerful mediator of culture, communities, and peoples and if it has a positive reputation it will find it easier to compete for attention, resources, people, jobs, and money. A positive place reputation builds place competitiveness and creates a reservoir of goodwill. This is where a positive destination brand or competitive identity which appeals to specific tourism market segments cements a place as somewhere worth visiting. Having a strong brand is hugely important for any destination whatever its size in the fight to combat increasing product parity, substitutability, and competition. Developing a strong brand requires tenacity and commitment but if those responsible can align the agendas of tourism and investment promotion agencies, exporters, policy-makers, and cultural organisations in a long-term stewardship strategy, then they can build a real sense of purpose and vision.

Branding was applied to consumer products long before the industrial revolution, but the idea of tourism destinations pursuing formalised brand strategies as we understand them today only originated in the 1990s. Whereas earlier 'image-building' marketing activities in the 1980s by cities such as New York and Glasgow (encapsulated by the slogans 'I love New York' and 'Glasgow's miles better') foreshadowed such strategies, a strategic approach to destination branding was first introduced at a national level with countries such as Spain, Hong Kong, and Australia. Later, a host of countries, regions and cities – like the US cities of Seattle, Las Vegas, and Pittsburgh – embraced it, responding to a need to compete more effectively, to create a strategic decision-making framework and, in some cases, to increase accountability to their stakeholders. Many destinations now see place branding (which is broader than simply tourism and may encompass all or some of the following: inward investment, exports, culture, sports, events, education, and immigration) as a major part of their competitive armoury. In fact, the Destination Marketing Association International, the world's largest official destination marketing organisation designates the development of a brand strategy as one of the critical items needed for accreditation in its Destination Marketing Association Accreditation Program (Baker, 2007).

Many academics have questioned whether places can ever be brands and in a strict marketing sense they cannot, which is why some commentators talk of place reputation management or competitive identity rather than place branding (see Chapters 2 and 4). Whilst this is a more accurate description, we would say that the term 'place reputation stewardship' is even more useful, especially in the tourism sphere. In these financially strained times, DMOs face serious challenges – especially as a result of the digital revolution – and their cost, relevance, and value-for-money has come under greater scrutiny (Chapter 12). The reality for DMOs is that place reputation is derived from a host of sources, of which tourism marketing is but one (Chapter 3). The DMOs cannot control the place story or the image and they do not own the destination. Moreover, in our disintermediated world dominated by social media, it is the consumer who is increasingly shaping the brand and the media, so whilst DMOs never controlled the product, now they can't even pretend to control the message and have to think in terms of conversations and not campaigns (Epperson, 2009).

Yet, if a place's reputation exists whatever its DMO does, a place can still have a vision of how it wants to see itself and be seen and brand management can enable its key stakeholders to get there, to achieve differentiation, and secure a competitive identity (Chapter 21). In this sense, DMOs are less responsible for the 'management' and more for the 'stewardship' of destination reputations. But, theirs is still a key role in supporting and facilitating place brand management – not only speaking to the consumer alone but also to the whole tourism system, establishing, nurturing, and servicing partnerships between stakeholders (Chapter 19). In an ideal world, everything and everyone would be on brand but partnerships require encouragement and leadership. This is where the DMO comes into its own as the brand steward, leading, guiding, and coordinating the destination's online and offline 'critical promise points,' all those interactions in the material and virtual world when the destination brand promise is encountered and evaluated by its key target markets (Baker, 2007). The challenge of such stewardship should not be underestimated in today's rapidly and radically changing world.

THE NEED FOR RELEVANCE IN A WORLD OF PARADIGM SHIFT

There does seem to be something hugely significant going on out there in the world. Whatever it is, we've been in the middle of it for a while, and the recently termed 'Great Recession' has brought it into stark relief. Some say it's the end of the capitalist industrial age in America and the West and the beginning of something else. Some call it the age of globalisation, others the information age or the knowledge or experience economy. Yet others predict the dawning of a new transmodern age of planetary responsibility. Many are describing our era as one of regime change, system flip, or paradigm shift (http://www.stockholmresilience). Whilst it is a characteristic conceit of modernity to label every period as transitional, ours do seem to be particularly sharply transitional times. Indeed, this period may well prove to be one of generational economic and social change during which people, communities, and places will need to find alternative ways of living and working. Consumer confidence is fragile and many of the world's more economically developed economies are enduring recession and plummeting economic confidence, whilst volatile energy costs, political instability, and environmental disasters are global concerns. Despite the end of the Cold War, the world remains a hostile place and there are many threats to peace, of which global inequalities, food, water, and energy shortages, and transnational terrorism are just three. Moreover, there loom more gradual, insidious global threats to which most of us pay only periodic attention – human pressures on our planet's natural resources, resulting in climatic change and food, water and energy shortages (Hall, 2010).

We can perhaps be certain of only one thing about the future: that the competition for relevance and resources will be fiercer than ever. Just take the World Wide Web. Today, there are almost 250 million websites and 126 million blogs, whilst in 2009 the world's 1.7 billion internet users watched a billion YouTube videos and sent 247 million e-mails every single day. At the same time, the amount of spam in those e-mails had increased by a quarter on 2008 (royal.pingdom.com, 2010). It is becoming harder to distinguish what is significant, authentic, and worthy of our attention in our information-heavy but knowledge-light world. Ours has become a cluttered world of the long tail, where so many places position themselves as 'a great place to work, live, and play' and so many tourist destinations promise a multitude of experiences and products, that it becomes ever more important but harder to achieve stand-out (Chapter 13). Too many destinations have, in fact, become 'any country' – communicated by marketing cliché, they lack relevance or stand-out in our changing world (Table 1.1).

Over the last 50 years, tourism patterns have altered dramatically. In 1950, almost 90% of the international tourists visited the world's top 15 destinations. By 2005, things had become much more complicated and the most popular tourism destinations accounted for less than 60% of the tourist arrivals (UNWTO, 2009). Now, tourism is truly global and almost everywhere is a

Table 1.1 Any Country: Marketing clichés lack differentiation

Any Country: The Land of Contrasts

- *Any Country* is everywhere's best kept secret. It's so close to home, yet a world apart. The perfect place to escape the stresses and strains of modern life.

- Come and discover *Any Country's* many hidden gems. Step back in time at one of hundreds of heritage attractions and museums. Or just kick off your shoes and relax on one of our award winning beaches. With more than 1000 miles of coastline, you're sure to find your perfect spot.

- Whatever you're looking for *Any Country* has it all. From mountain biking or walking to surfing and sailing. *Any Country* truly is an adventure playground packed full of fun for all of the family.

- And after all that activity, what better way to unwind than to savour fresh local food at one of our award-winning restaurants. Whatever your taste, you'll find *Any Country* has the perfect ingredients for a short break or longer holiday, all year round. And wherever you go you're sure of a warm *Any Countryish* welcome.

- But don't take our word for it, come and see for yourself. What are you waiting for?

Source: walesthebrand.com

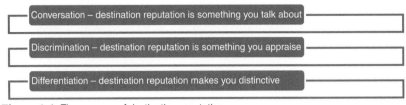

Figure 1.1 The essence of destination reputation

tourist destination so that places are engaged in a fiercely competitive battle to retain and attract not only visitors, investment, and events (Chapters 14, 15, and 17) but also talented human capital, students, residents, and even medical tourists (Chapter 16). In such a world, a positive place reputation becomes the key to place competitiveness. Further, distilled to its essence, destination reputation is the culmination of three factors (Figure 1.1). First, conversation – reputation is something you talk about; secondly, discrimination – reputation is something you critically assess; and thirdly differentiation – reputation makes you distinctive (Chapter 9).

Regardless of the quality of their reputation, today most countries have a destination brand, whether it is 100% 'Pure New Zealand,' 'South Africa it's Possible,' 'YourSingapore,' or 'Incredible India.' Even Afghanistan positions itself as the 'Last Unconquered Mountains of the World' and countries such as Iraq, Iran, and Libya have ambitious plans to grow their tourism sectors over the next decade. The top 4 destination brands as voted for by their peers are: New Zealand, India, Spain, and Australia. Research conducted for the WTO and ETC (2009) *Handbook on Tourism Destination Branding* revealed that the majority of DMOs (82%) had an official brand strategy and a toolkit explaining how to apply the brand (80%), whilst 75% think that they have a unique positioning – although we might well question whether that is truly the case. Rather startlingly, over a third of the DMOs have spent money on developing a brand strategy which they have no plans to evaluate, revealing a certain lack of professionalism and expertise (Table 1.2).

This paints an interesting picture of current DMO practice and the attitudes of their chief executives and managers to tourism destination brands. But how much do we know about the processes involved? Are these brands created by an agency in consultation with the DMO? How 'authentic' are these brands, how reflective are they of the destinations concerned, their constituencies, and their narratives? Do they move beyond the realm of marketing and public relations into the fabric of the material world, do they have resonance in the character, and personalities of the places? This survey reveals that 60% of these brands are focused only on tourism. To what extent are governments and agencies aware of the benefits of a more holistic approach to place reputation management, which speaks to (amongst others) tourists, investors, residents, and students? How many of these worldwide destinations can be described as creative destinations? Some of these questions are taken up by the contributors in this book as they consider destination brand concepts, challenges, and cases. In this introductory chapter, we offer a contribution to the debates over place brands, reputation management, and destination brand stewardship, which draw on these contributions. More than simply précising them, however, we explore

Table 1.2 Current DMO branding practice

DMO branding practice	%
Have an official brand strategy	82
Have a brand manager	37
Have a set of brand values	80
Think they have an unique positioning	75
Have a brand toolkit	80
Developed the brand in collaboration	90
Do cooperative branding	37
Are tourism-related only	60
Don't measure their brand's impact	37

Source: Adapted from WTO and ETC (2009) Handbook on Tourism Destination Branding.

the DNA of creative destinations and put forward a new model, which locates destination reputation stewardship in its broader context of place reputation management – the virtuous circle of destination reputation management.

THE VIRTUOUS CIRCLE OF CREATIVE DESTINATION REPUTATION

Places compete in attracting visitors, residents, and businesses and many of them are doing this by promoting a place brand that encapsulates the qualities that the place has in order to generate memorable positive associations and powerful place brand equity. Some have been particularly successful, for instance the 100% Pure New Zealand brand is calculated to be worth around US$13.6 billion, ranked the 21st brand in the world just behind Samsung and ahead of Dell (10yearsyoung.tourismnewzealand.com). But, whilst places which have strong and dynamic brands have an easier time attracting businesses and talent within the knowledge economy of the twenty-first century, recent research suggests that it is becoming increasingly difficult to differentiate places according to 'hard' factors such as their infrastructure, economy, accessibility, and the availability of financial incentives as so many score well in this regard (Pride, 2008).

Instead, a place's so-called 'soft' factors such as its environment, friendly local people, entertainment and leisure services, and traditions in art and culture are assuming more importance with potential investors and tourists alike. Thus, we need a more dynamic and nuanced view of the factors which create the right conditions for creativity, competitive identity, and a strong destination brand to flourish. Florida's creative class (2002) – those people who generate ideas and innovations – is attracted to places that are open to new ideas and newcomers and attaches a high value to urban facilities and cultural services such as cinemas, bars, restaurants, museums, art galleries, and upscale retail (Boschma & Fritsch, 2009). This means three things. First, that imagery traditionally associated with tourism promotion could have a significant influence on wider perceptions of the place. Secondly, that positioning and communications for economic development audiences should take full account of both rational and emotional considerations in destination or location choice. Thirdly, as tourism marketing is often the most professional part of a place's reputation management portfolio, it can lead the way in reputation management.

Whilst we have said that 'destination' is a problematic term in tourism, so 'creativity' and 'competitiveness' are equally hard to pin down for scholars and practitioners in economics, urban studies, and development and policy studies. Both are elusive, slippery terms which are often overly associated with urban areas (Clifton & Huggins, 2010). A place's competitiveness is typically measured by the ability of its economy to attract and maintain profitable firms and stable or rising standards of living for its population (Storper, 1997). While the competitiveness of places is therefore primarily coupled to their economic performance, there is a growing consensus that competitiveness is best measured in terms of the 'assets' of the local business environment, including the quality of the local infrastructure and human capital and the degree of innovative capacity (Malecki, 2004, 2007). Together with factors including the availability of high-quality cultural facilities, these 'assets' are seen to influence the ability of communities, cities, and regions to attract creative and innovative people and secure regional competitive advantage (Kitson et al., 2004). In other words, competitiveness is being increasingly discussed in relation to creativity, knowledge, and environmental conditions, rather than an accumulated wealth index (Huggins, 2003).

Just as definitions of competitiveness are being broadened in economic geography and urban studies it is time to reconsider how we judge competitive tourism destinations. Until very recently, tourism development has consistently been characterised in terms of an accumulated growth index. Success has been predicated on increased volumes of visitors and higher levels of spending; reports and strategies, whether emanating from the UNWTO or regional and national governments, measure the industry's health by its growth achievements and growth potential. Given that if everyone on earth lived like the typical European, we would need three planets to live on (http://www.oneplanetliving.org), we must question the value and long-term sustainability of such measures of success and competitiveness. We need alternative ways of measuring the competitiveness and success of destinations, such as their relevance, their capacity to provide sustainable, cohesive communities, a high quality of life, attractive and universally designed public places, their ability to embrace innovation and creativity and their stewardship of a place's culture, traditions and environment. We need to devise KPIs for mindful, syncretic growth and not mindless development.

Arguably, creative tourism destinations are urban and rural places which enhance the well-being of their populations through tourism and embrace new ways of thinking and sustainable living; places which are attractive to live in and to visit. They are change destinations which prioritise social benefit and 'mindful' development. They are also clever places which are able to command attention no matter their size or diplomatic influence. In a context of a world where stakeholders demand more for less from public sector budgets, creative destinations are those which find bottom-up, inclusive ways of enhancing and sustaining their reputation, taking advantage of the events economy, harnessing popular culture and digital platforms, delivering unique individual experiences and employing the testimonies of residents, tourists, investors, and students as place ambassadors (Chapter 18). Creative destinations are moving toward holistic place reputation management, effectively integrating the attraction of tourism, investment, and talented human capital. They are confident places which are engaging issues of social responsibility, ethical practice, and sustainable ways of living and building strong partnerships between civil society, government, and business.

The harnessing of creativity, innovation, talented human capital, and sustainable ways of living are vital for communities, cities, and regions seeking to become creative destinations. The virtuous circle of destination reputation has six elements which will mark out tomorrow's strong brands – a place's tone, traditions, tolerance, talent, transformability, and testimonies (Figure 1.2). These interconnected elements build on each other to create an (ideally) ever-improving radial cycle or a virtuous circle of creative destination reputation. Whilst we focus here on the impact of these elements on a place's tourism reputational balance sheet, it is impossible to separate tourists from all those other consumers and mediators of place identity.

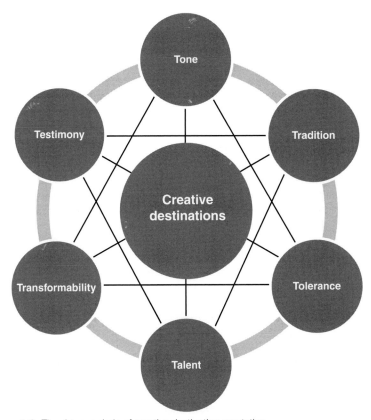

Figure 1.2 The virtuous circle of creative destination reputation

Tone

It is difficult to overstate the emotional power of a destination's tone, its identity, and sense of belonging. Vitiello and Willcocks (Chapter 22) discuss a place's ambience, its physical fabric and character and describe how some places evoke humanity and character whilst others offer anonymous, bland homogeneity or even induce fear and insecurity. A destination's ambience provides clues to its culture; a place tells its stories in its everyday fabric, communicating a message to its residents and visitors more powerfully than any marketing campaign. The public management of space is thus a key ingredient in any place reputation strategy. Creative destinations present residents and visitors with opportunities to continually rediscover and enjoy their spaces, which are designed from the bottom-up with an emotional as well as a utilitarian dimension to allow the originality of the local people to shine through in the making of place (Chapter 22, this volume).

Place tone exists in the material, symbolic, and virtual worlds but to have impact in destination reputation management it must be consistently and effectively communicated in all these worlds. Places are trying to engage visitors, residents, and other stakeholders in a stimulating conversation and place reputations must be communicated with a strong, distinctive, and engaging tone of voice in all online and offline interactions with the key target audience (Chapter 10). A place's tone (its ambience, the attitudes of its people, its heritage, and narratives) is inseparable from a destination's sense of place. Yet, communicating this is no simple undertaking and opens up controversial challenges of place authenticity, brand narratives, leadership and authorship, performativity, story-telling, and aesthetics (see Chapters 5–9).

Tradition

Of course, for many urban destinations the recognition that a place's culture and history offers unique value is not surprising and yet many destinations attach so little importance to it that they demolish their heritage to make way for sports stadia, shopping malls, and the increasingly ubiquitous and anonymous skyscrapers, which are in fact a major turn-off for tourists in search of the 'real' or 'authentic' place (Leiper and Park, 2010). Authenticity has become a hugely controversial concept amongst tourism scholars. Some argue that today's emphasis on the post-modern, the hypermediated, the global rather than the local, all suggest the redundancy of authenticity. Yet, for the creative destination, its authenticity or traditions coupled together with its tone, is a vital ingredient; for many places it is the well-spring of their reputation and identity premium (Chapter 8). Effectively and sympathetically communicated through marketing activities, tradition is the alchemical ingredient which distinguishes the bland from the unique place; it is the philosophers' stone which transforms the narratives and stories of a destination into a relevant and appealing identity (Chapters 20, 23, and 24).

This should not be a tradition which is merely static and preserved history, but one which is being constantly performed, engaged, renewed, reinterpreted, and augmented by new narratives which respond to and are engaged with making new socio-cultural forms. This is a collective authenticity, which recognises the central agency of a wide range of people in its ongoing creative production and reproduction. Without this collective authorship and support, the use of destination brand narratives in marketing activities will be doomed to failure as inhabitants at best fail to recognise and at worst reject any 'top-down' authored stories.

The difficulty in communicating tradition should not be underestimated given the need to manage and harness what Hornskov (Chapter 8) refers to as both the material (the physical) and immaterial (the marketing) realms. Even when agencies recognise the value of stewarding a successful brand, such a diverse group of actors and stakeholders are involved (with so many competing priorities and resource demands) that bringing them together is a huge task. Local authorities/municipalities, their own varied technical and infrastructural departments, government agencies, the cultural and business sectors, and the communities themselves are just a few of the interested parties we could name. All of these actors operate with very different values, goals, and operating procedures; they may be suspicious of each other and this often becomes a volatile combination (see Chapters 6 and 7).

Tolerance

Tolerance is an interesting addition to our DNA of the creative destination and our use of the term in this context is intended to convey openness to difference, to new ideas, thinking, and ways of living. Tolerant places welcome talented people of any race, religion, ethnic background, or sexual persuasion and embrace innovative and creative ways of living and working. For example, we might say how a place engages with issues of social responsibility, ethical practice, and sustainable ways of living – what we might term the global social responsibility agenda – typifies its degree of tolerance (Chapter 5). We are familiar with the notion of corporations being scrutinised and evaluated on their social responsibility records and with the power of ethically focused and socially engaged consumers to hold these corporations to account. As Anholt (2009b, p. 95) argues, 'Branding at its best is a technique for achieving integrity and reaping the reputational rewards of integrity.' We are less familiar with applying these principles to places, although there is a growing list of countries facing consumer boycotts for contravening human rights (e.g., Burma/Myanmar; Israel; Jamaica; China) and animal rights (e.g., Canada – fur seal culls; Mauritius – live exports of primates; Japan – whale hunting) (http://www.ethicalconsumer.org).

We can discern tentative indicators of sustained consumer interest in how places respond to the global social responsibility agenda and these will give rise to opportunities and threats for tourism destinations (Chapter 5). We only have to look at the recent experience of Italy. This may seem a surprising example to choose as we are all familiar with Italy's appeal as a tourism and cultural destination; indeed, it has regularly topped Anholt's Nation Brand Index in these areas. However, Italy's poor ratings for business and governance have led to a steady shift in its reputational balance sheet – particularly for its failure to act as a responsible steward of its environment and its globally significant heritage (Anholt, 2010). This loss of brand value may well have longer-term consequences for Italy's place reputation as people begin to hold more places to international account.

Talent

Supporting indigenous or incoming talented human capital is vital for any creative place seeking to enhance its economic or tourism competitiveness. Whilst Florida (2002) estimates that the creative class constitutes around a third of employment in more developed economies like the United States, service jobs in areas like tourism, hospitality, and leisure are vitally important to the growing number of countries highly dependent on tourism, especially in the less developed economies of the world. We have suggested above that creative places thrive on diversity and openness, to immigrants, to people of all sexual orientations, to new ideas, and lifestyles. In addition, we also noted that the availability of activities and services traditionally associated with tourism could have a significant influence on wider perceptions of the place and that, as a result positioning and communications for economic development audiences should take full account of both rational and emotional considerations in destination or location choice. It is instructive that Canada has recently reaped the benefits of being a welcoming place for immigrants by comparison with its larger US neighbour. When the software giant Microsoft established its new development centre in Vancouver in 2008 it cited the major reason as the city's position as 'a global gateway with a diverse population,' a place where it could 'recruit and retain highly skilled people affected by immigration issues in the United States.' The new facility is in one of the most ethnically diverse regions on the planet, whose 2.2 million residents include immigrants from dozens of countries including Asia, South America, and Europe (http://investincanada.gc.ca).

Here, a major corporation saw an ethnically diverse staff as a major asset, considering that such a range of worldviews creates innovative thinking and inspires fresh ways to interpret and solve global challenges. When Microsoft began to research locations for a new development centre staffed with experts from around the world, Vancouver's unique attributes – high scoring on all six elements in our virtuous circle of place reputation – made it an immediate choice. The city's ethnically diverse communities help immigrant employees feel at home, while its temperate climate, thriving arts scene, and high quality of life make recruitment easy and foster creativity. The city also has excellent public health care, educational, and transportation systems and scores well as an eco-city with high use of renewable energy and low pollution levels. It is also within a short drive of Whistler Blackcomb, one of the world's top ski destinations and is regarded as an attractive tourist destination. In fact, a 2010 independent study ranked Vancouver as the world's fourth best city for its quality of life – a place with a strong creative and competitive reputation (http://www.mercer.com).

Transformability

Creative, competitive destinations are agenda-setting places. Whilst stewarding and communicating the tone of a place and its tradition, a forward-looking destination simultaneously looks to embrace what is best in new practices and ways of living. Take the digital revolution, which is forcing destinations to finally realise that they never had control of their brands and that they are open to consumer scrutiny. This poses a number of challenges for the creative destination (e.g., of content, socialisation, integration, and measurement, see Chapter 11) but when DMOs strike the right note (as with Queensland's best job in the world or the YourSingapore portal and living logo) there is a conversational capital to be made, which extends beyond segment boundaries like tourism, business, and studying.

Of course, transformability in this context is about much more than embracing new technologies. It is the capacity to act and think differently and whilst in difficult times, there may be a tendency to give up on innovation and retreat into safe thinking and known markets until the worst is over, this is the time for places to examine new possibilities. Of course, changing the way we measure destination success toward mindful indicators and rejecting the cult of growth in tourism (Cater, 2010) is itself a transformative act – and ahead of the curve. There is no doubt that the pressure of climate change and human development will eventually lead to a fundamental shift in our consumption patterns as the world's population hits 9 billion in the middle of this century. These pressures may also stimulate more localised holiday-taking with the concomitant demand for high-quality, locally sourced produce. In the future, steady-state tourism consumption could lead to newer travel behaviour and a move from more distant to local and 'slower' travel could heighten the importance of the domestic market as a sustainable alternative for many destinations (Hall, 2010). For instance, Cittaslow (literally Slow City) is a movement founded in Italy in 1999. Inspired by the slow food movement, Cittaslow celebrates and supports the diversity of local town cultures and cuisines and has accredited communities in 14 countries (http://www.slowmovement.com).

At the moment, it is difficult to predict the trajectory of slow travel but moves toward more mindful, socially driven development and the resultant popularity of destinations which support local diversity seem inevitable in the long term. Similar initiatives include fair trade, carbon neutral and One Planet communities, cities and nations. There are currently Fairtrade Towns in 17 countries; carbon neutral regions are positioning themselves as proving grounds for sustainable technologies in a bid to attract new businesses and become models for sustainable living (http://www.cnr2030.org/); and One Planet Communities are designed to enable people to reduce their ecological footprint (http://www.oneplanetliving.org). Currently in the van guard, such communities, cities, and regions are opening pathways through new cultural or political terrain for other places to follow. Moreover, not only do they demonstrate transformability but this is likely to translate in the long term into a reputation which makes it easy to attract tourists and employees and foster creativity. Thus, at the moment there is a strong correlation between those cities which are in the top 50 for eco-living and the top 5 in the Mercer quality of life rankings: Vienna (1); Zurich (2); Geneva (3); Vancouver, Auckland (=4) (http://www.mercer.com).

Testimonies

The last and most important element in the cycle of destination reputation management are testimonies – those stories told by tourists, students, residents, and businesspeople of a destination, which add or subtract the real equity to a destination's reputation. If the destination experience is memorable and delivers or exceeds the brand promise then positive testimonies make the circle a virtuous one – reinforcing and enhancing a place's reputation. Of course, if the opposite happens, then equity flows away from the brand and the reservoir of goodwill is slowly drained. Despite all the marketing opportunities which exist today, word-of-mouth is still the most powerful form of communication and the digital revolution is accentuating its importance.

Digital channels have created an irrevocable change in consumer–brand relationships, which is evident in the proactive role customers take in shaping the dialogue with the brand and ultimately its reputation. This is also transforming how creative destinations perform online, with participation, openness, conversations, community, and connectedness the key words characterising this digitally inspired revolution (Spannerworks, 2007). As this conversation culture replaces our information culture (Leonhard, 2009) much of the social networking sites' content provides a wealth of 'independent' peer-produced dynamic content. Today 'the wisdom of the crowd is embodied in a wiki' and customers are 'lifecasting' their brand experiences on sites such as Wikitravel, Trip Advisor, and IgoUgo (Chapter 11). In this way, the power of testimony is magnified and as it spreads it gathers momentum.

Every person who has something positive to say about a destination – its culture, the welcome of its people, and the quality of its environment and infrastructure – becomes a place ambassador for that destination. Tourists', residents', investors', and students' testimonies are crucial to any destination's attempts to manage their reputation and it is commonplace to see place advertising which uses the testimonials of celebrities and 'ordinary people' (e.g., the 'feeling good about Newport' campaign by the host city of the 2010 Ryder Cup, used both on banners around the city http://www.newport.gov.uk). People talk about the places they have visited and it is very difficult to overstate the cultural capital of conversation about travel. At the same time, research has identified the power of friends and relatives as the number one influence on destination choice, so it is not only how 'you' talk about a place but also with 'which friends' as well (Yeoman, 2008).

Whilst in the world of the 'wiki', everyone has an opinion, those of some people are doubly important. Thus, opinion leaders and formers are highly positioned and influential individuals in their respective fields (across business, media, government, international organisations, academia, law, science, and popular culture) to whom others turn to for advice, opinions, and views and whose ideas and behaviour serve as a model to others. Communicating to a particular group and influencing their attitudes, opinion leaders have an important role in shaping markets. If they can be recruited (formerly to provide testimonials as with Newport) or simply informally as a result of positive experiences to become ambassadors for a place, then place marketers are using the opinion leader to carry and 'trickle down' its message to influence its target group. The power of opinion leaders is why DMOs place so much store on organising familiarisation visits for journalists and travel writers, why convention bureaux invest heavily in attracting conferences, seminars, and conventions, and why places strive to attract major sports, cultural, and political events, which bring leading figures from a range of fields to their cities and regions (Chapters 14, 15, and 17).

CONCLUSION

Destination reputation management might largely be concerned with enhancing how the outside world sees tourism places but it begins at home; as part of the wider process of place reputation stewardship, it depends upon building a productive coalition between civil society, government, and business which can then act as a powerful dynamic for progress. But this demands new ways of working together, building partnerships across disparate, competing, and even conflicting stakeholder groups with the DMO, an obvious coordinator. Central to the whole process is a place's vision for its future. What kind of place does its leaders, stakeholders, and communities want it to be? A place's reputation reflects how *others see it* and how *it sees itself*; its management moves its reputation forward to where it *wants to be seen*. Simon Anholt (Chapter 2) tells us that a place's symbolic actions will be central to a place's storytelling. This is as much about envisioning a place community's dreams for its future as stewarding its traditions and culture.

How can communities harness their traditions, cultures, and imagination, environment and human qualities to get where they want to be? This process involves asking fundamental questions about the kind of society its leaders, stakeholders, and communities want, the kind of environment they want to live in, the significance they place on social justice and human rights, values, family, culture, learning, immigration and desirable levels of growth and development. How can they reconcile competing needs, pressures, and desires and build consensus and an agreed platform for action? When it comes to tourism, communities must ask what kind of tourism industry they want. Do they see tourism as important in their development? If so, how will they project their traditions and culture to the outside world? Who will have the authority to tell their stories, whose narratives will be told, and whose will be excluded? These and other questions need answers if a place is to enhance its reputation and build equity in its tourism brand.

In this chapter we have seen how, in today's competitive globalised tourism marketplace, standing for something and standing out from the crowd have never been more important. This is, in fact the first of this book's three broad messages, which unfold in the following chapters. The second is that DMOs tend to be the most experienced and professional in a place's reputational management 'team' and as they move into viral marketing their role is likely to be enhanced. Tourism provides us with a unique opportunity to personalise our relationship with places either in a domestic or in an international context. Just the very act of visiting somewhere makes a place's reputation or image more significant for the visitor; once we are there our experiences will lead us to reappraise our image of that place – for good or ill. Crucially, to be truly effective place reputation management must be a holistic strategy which coheres tourism, economic development, urban planning, major event planning, and a host of other activities and sectors. And the final message – which we have summarised here in the virtuous circle of destination reputation management – is that those responsible for the stewardship of places and their reputations must embrace creativity, innovation, and sustainable ways of living – in fact, their future depends on it.

References

Anholt, S. (2005). *Brand new justice. How branding places and products can help the developing world* (2nd ed.). Oxford: Butterworth Heinemann.

Anholt, S. (2006). The Anholt GMI city brands index: how the world sees the world's cities. *Journal of Place Branding*, *2*(1), 18–31.

Anholt, S. (2007). *Competitive identity: The new brand management for nations, cities and regions*. London: Palgrave.

Anholt, S. (2009a). *Places: Identity, image and reputation*. London: Palgrave.

Anholt, S. (2009b). Editorial. *Journal of Place Branding and Public Diplomacy*, *5*(2), 91–96.

Anholt, S. (2010). Towards 'governmental social responsibility'. *Journal of Place Branding and Public Diplomacy*, *6*(2), 69–75.

Baker, B. (2007). *Destination branding for small cities*. Oregon: Creative Leap Books.

Boschma, R., & Fritsch, M. (2009). Creative class and regional growth: Empirical evidence from Seven European Countries. *Economic Geography*, *85*(4), 391–423.

Buhalis, D. (2000). Marketing the competitive destination of the future. *Tourism Management*, *21*, 95–116.

Cater, C. (2010). The growth fetish in tourism, 19th Nordic Symposium in Nordic Tourism and Hospitality Research, Akureyri, Iceland: September 22–25.

Chiesa, T. (2009). Navigating yet another perfect storm: The promise of sustainable travel & tourism. In: The travel & tourism competitiveness report (pp. 97–105), World Economic Forum.

Clifton, N., & Huggins, R. (2010). Competitiveness and creativity: A place-based perspective. Martin Prosperity Research Working Paper Series, REF. 2010-MPIWP-007

Dinnie, K. (2008). *Nation branding: Concepts, issues, practice*. Oxford: Butterworth Heinemann.

Epperson, J. (2009). DMOs in a disintermediated world, keynote. 3rd International Conference on Destination Branding and Marketing. Institute for Tourism Studies, Macau SAR, China.

Florida, R. (2002). *The rise of creative class. And how it is transforming work, leisure, community and everyday life*. New York, NY: Basic Books.

Florida, R. (2010). *The great reset: How new ways of living and working drive post-crash prosperity*. New York, NY: Harper.

Hall, C. M. (2010). Crisis events in tourism: Subjects of crisis in tourism. *Current Issues in Tourism*, *13*(5), 401–417.

Huggins, R. (2003). Creating a UK competitiveness index: regional and local benchmarking. *Regional Studies*, *37*(1), 89–96.

Jaffe, E. D., & Nebenzahl, I. D. (2006). *National image and competitive advantage*. Copenhagen: Copenhagen Business School.

Jansson, J., & Power, D. (2006). The image of the city – urban branding as constructed capabilities in Nordic city regions, Available at: www.nordicinnovation.net/_img/image_of_the_city_-_web.pdf.

Kavaratzis, M., & Ashworth, G. J., (Eds.), (2010). *Towards effective place brand management*. Oxford: Edward Elgar.

Kitson, M., Martin, R., & Tyler, P. (2004). Regional competitiveness: an elusive yet key concept? *Regional Studies*, *38*, 991–999.

Leiper, N., & Park, S. Y. (2010). Skyscrapers' influence on cities' roles as tourist destatinations. *Current Issues in Tourism*, *13*(4), 333–349.

Leonhard, G. (2009). Social media and the future of marketing and advertising. www.mediafuturist.com

Malecki, E. J. (2004). Jockeying for position: what it means and why it matters to regional development policy when places compete. *Regional Studies*, *38*, 1101–1120.

Malecki, E. J. (2007). Cities and regions competing in the global economy: knowledge and local development policies. *Environment and Planning C*, *25*, 638–654.

Morgan, N. (2004). Problematising Place Promotion. In A. Lew, C. M. Hall, & A. Williams (Eds.), *A tourism companion* (pp. 173–183). Oxford: Blackwell.

Pike, S. (2004). *Destination marketing organisations*. Oxford: Elsevier.

Pride, R. (2008). The Welsh brand – Connecting image with reality, Wales and the World Institute of Welsh Affairs Seminar, Cardiff, October.

Saarinen, J. (2004). Tourism and touristic representations of nature. In A. Lew, C. M. Hall, & A. Williams (Eds.), *A tourism companion* (pp. 438–449). Oxford: Blackwell.

SpannerWorks. (2007). What is social media. www.spannerworks.com/ebooks. In Constantinides, E. & Fountain, S.J. (2008) Web 2.0: Conceptual foundations and marketing issues. Journal of Direct, Data and Digital Marketing Practice, 9(3), 231–244.

Storper, M. (1997). *The regional world: Territorial development in a global economy*. New York, NY: Guilford.

UNWTO (2009). *Facts and figures*. Available at: http://www.unwto.org/index.php

WTO, & ETC. (2009). *Handbook on tourism destination branding*. Brussels: ETC.

Yeoman, I. (2008). *Tomorrow's tourist*. Oxford: Elsevier.

Useful Websites

http://www.cnr2030.org/
http://investincanada.gc.ca
http://www.ethicalconsumer.org
http://www.mercer.com
http://www.newport.gov.uk
http://www.oneplanetliving.org
http://www.slowmovement.com
http://www.stockholmresilience
http://www.unwto.org/index.php
www.wikitravel.org

CHAPTER

2

Competitive Identity

Simon Anholt

INTRODUCTION

I first began to write about an idea which I called *nation brand* in 1996. My original observation was a simple one: that the reputations of countries (and, by extension, cities and regions too) function rather like the brand images of companies and products and that they are equally critical to the progress, prosperity, and good management of those places. Unfortunately, the phrases *nation brand* and *place brand* quickly become distorted by ambitious consulting firms and naïve governments into *nation branding* and *place branding* – two dangerously misleading phrases which appear to imply that the images of countries or cities or regions can be directly manipulated using the techniques of commercial marketing communications. Despite repeatedly calling for it, I have never seen a shred of evidence to suggest that this is possible: no case studies, no research, and – at least in my view – not even any very persuasive arguments. Countries are judged by what they do, not by what they say, yet the notion that a country can simply buy its way into a better reputation has proved to be a pernicious and surprisingly resilient one. For this reason I coined the deliberately unsexy term *Competitive Identity* as the title of a book on the subject in 2007. It probably compromised sales of the book, but it made the point that national image has more to do with national and regional identity and the politics and economics of competitiveness than with branding as it is usually understood in the commercial sector.

Today, every place on the Earth appears to want to enhance, reverse, adapt, or otherwise manage its international reputation. Yet we are still far from a widespread understanding of what this means in practice, and just how far commercial approaches can be effectively and responsibly applied to government, society, and economic development. Many governments, most consultants, and even some scholars persist in a tiresome and superficial interpretation of 'place branding' that is nothing more than standard product

© 2011 Published by Elsevier Ltd. All rights reserved.
DOI: 10.1016/B978-0-08-096930-5.10002-3

promotion, public relations, and corporate identity, where the product just happens to be a country, a city, or a region rather than a tin of beans or a box of soap powder.

Yet the need for proper understanding in this area is crucial. Today, the world is one market; the rapid advance of globalisation means that whatever countries try to *pull in* (investors, aid, tourists, business visitors, students, major events, researchers, travel writers, and talented entrepreneurs), and whatever countries try to *push out* (products, services, policies, culture, and ideas), is done with a discount if the country's image is weak or negative, and at a premium if it is strong and positive.

In this crowded global marketplace, most people and organisations do not have time to learn much about other places. We all navigate through the complexity of the modern world armed with a few simple clichés, and they form the background of our opinions, even if we are not fully aware of this and do not always admit it to ourselves: Paris is about style, Japan about technology, Switzerland about wealth and precision, Rio de Janeiro about carnival and football, Tuscany about the good life, and most African nations about poverty, corruption, war, famine, and disease. Most of us are much too busy worrying about ourselves and our own countries to spend too long trying to form complete, balanced, and informed views about 6 billion other people and nearly 200 other countries. We make do with summaries for the vast majority of people and places – the ones we will probably never know or visit – and only start to expand and refine these impressions when for some reason we acquire a particular interest in them. When you haven't got time to read a book, you judge it by its cover.

These clichés and stereotypes – whether they are positive or negative, true or untrue – fundamentally affect our behaviour toward other places and their people and products. It may seem unfair, but there is nothing anybody can do to change this. It is very hard for a country to persuade people in other parts of the world to go beyond these simple images and start to understand the rich complexity that lies behind them. Some quite progressive places do not get nearly as much attention, visitors, business, or investment as they need because their reputation is weak or negative, while others are still trading on a good image that they acquired decades or even centuries ago, and today do relatively little to deserve.

So all responsible governments and regional administrations, on behalf of their people, their institutions, and their companies, need to discover what the world's perception of their place is, and to develop a strategy for managing it. It is a key part of their job to try to build a reputation that is fair, true, powerful, attractive, and genuinely useful to their economic, political, and social aims, and honestly reflects the spirit, the genius, and the will of the people. This huge task has become one of the primary skills of national administrations in the twenty-first century. When it comes into office, a government inherits a temporary but sacred responsibility for its electorate's most valuable asset: the good name of their country. Its task is to hand that good name down to its successors in office in at least as good condition as it received it.

HOW PLACE IMAGE IS BUILT

In an attempt to show how places communicate with the outside world, and thus create their images in the minds of certain publics (and, it should be noted, more often by accident than by design), I devised a simple model in 2002 which incorporated six channels or areas of activity that countries generally undertake:

(1) Their tourism promotion activity, as well as people's first-hand experience of visiting the country as tourists or business travellers. This is often the loudest voice in branding the nation or region, as tourist boards usually have the biggest budgets and the most competent marketers.

(2) Their exported products and services, which act as powerful ambassadors for each country and region, but only where their place of origin is explicit.

(3) The policy decisions of the region's governments, whether it is foreign policy which directly affects us, or domestic policy which gets reported in the international media. Diplomacy is traditionally the main route by which such things are communicated to the outside world, but there is an increasing closeness between the policy-makers and the international media.

(4) To business audiences, the way the region or country solicits inward investment, recruitment of foreign 'talent', and expansion into the country or region by foreign companies.

(5) Through cultural exchange and cultural activities and exports: a world tour by a national opera company, the works of a famous author, and the national sports team.

(6) The people of the country themselves: the high-profile leaders and media and sports stars, as well as the population in general; how they behave when abroad and how they treat visitors to their countries.

These six 'natural' channels of communication are shown as the points of a hexagon (Figure 2.1).

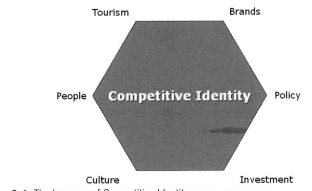

Figure 2.1 The hexagon of Competitive Identity. © 2002 Simon Anholt.

The basic theory behind managing the identity and reputation of a country or region is that if you have a good, clear, believable idea of what the place really is and what it stands for, and manage to coordinate the investments, actions, behaviours, and communications of all six points of the hexagon so that they reinforce this message, then you stand a good chance of building and maintaining a powerful and positive internal and external reputation – to the lasting benefit of exporters, importers, government, the culture sector, tourism, immigration, and pretty much every aspect of international relations.

Competitive Identity, just like any other national project, needs clearly stated and properly agreed goals. It is quite common for countries to set a mixture of precise, shorter term goals (such as a certain increase in foreign direct investment or the hosting of a prestigious international event) and longer-term changes in national image, which might be decades away. Countries with a powerful and positive identity should find the following:

- Clearer domestic agreement on national identity and societal goals
- A climate where innovation is prized and practiced
- More effective investment promotion
- More effective tourism and business travel promotion
- A healthier 'country of origin effect' for exporters of goods and services
- Greater profile in the international media
- Simpler accession into other regional and global bodies and associations
- More productive cultural relations with other countries and regions

That sounds like a lot to be asking for, and it is. But *without* a powerful and positive national identity, few of these aims are possible at all.

IMPLEMENTING COMPETITIVE IDENTITY

To develop the Competitive Identity of a country, city, or region, it is important first to understand how people's perceptions of the place are formed in the first place:

(1) By the things that are done in the country and the way they are done
(2) By the things that are made in the country and the way they are made
(3) By the way other people talk about the country
(4) By the way the country talks about itself

Most people assume that the way to change the image of a country is by talking about yourself (4). In fact, this is usually the least effective and most expensive method: it costs a lot of money because media is so expensive, and people do not pay very much attention to it anyway because advertising is always taken with a pinch of salt. Singing your own praises is not the best way to make other people admire you: it is better if somebody else does it for you (3); or, more effective still, if you can really prove your worth (1 and 2).

The country's reputation was not built through communications, and it cannot be changed through communications. Building Competitive Identity is not an advertising, design, or public relations exercise, although of course these techniques are essential for promoting the things that the country makes and does: its tourist and heritage attractions, its companies and their products and services, its music and art and other cultural products, its sport, its people, and its investment and employment opportunities. The quality of the marketing done by all of these stakeholders, and the consistency between the different messages they send out about the place, is an important factor in the way the place builds up its reputation – and of course good advertising often plays a major part in creating the positive tourism brands that many countries enjoy today.

That is not the same thing as a positive, famous, well-rounded national reputation – one that stimulates attention, respect, good relations, and good business all around the hexagon. The fact of the matter is that each stakeholder – tourist board, investment promotion agency, corporate sector, central government, and so forth – is probably not in control of all the factors that affect its business, so it is essential that they work together.

Creating more harmony in the way all of the country's companies and organisations and people do business and sell their products and services is an important part of the process of building Competitive Identity: if they are all telling the same powerful, believable, interesting story about the country, then the country has started to achieve some control over its international image.

The problem with attempting to 'market' the nation or region directly is that the propositions made are invariably abstract rather than concrete: in other words, the country is simply asking people to change their perceptions or change their behaviour without this being directly linked to a specific call to action ('buy this product,' 'call this number,' etc.). It is not telling people what it wants them to do, or giving them any good reasons for doing it; most of the time this kind of communication is doing little more than expressing an opinion (and a rather predictably self-aggrandizing opinion at that). 'Trust this country of origin,' 'we think these products are good,' 'remember this place,' 'admire our skill,' and so forth: these are simply empty requests, almost purely rhetorical, and in consequence tend to be received by the audience as rhetorical – in other words, requiring no response.

THE ART OF STRATEGIC POLICY-MAKING

But getting everybody in the country to speak with one voice, and do it well, is just part of the solution, and on its own will not achieve any dramatic enhancement of the national image. What really makes a difference is when a critical mass of the businesses and organisations in a place becomes dedicated to the development of new things: new ideas, new policies, new laws, new products and services, new businesses, new buildings, new art, new science, and new intellectual property; and when those innovations seem to be proving a few simple truths about the place they all come from, the reputation starts to move. The place produces a buzz; people start to pay attention and prepare themselves to change their minds. And the great thing about implementing the strategy in this way is that all these actions benefit the country quite independently of their effect on its reputation: they are good for the businesses and organisations and people that carry them out, so the money invested in them is also an investment in the country's economy, rather than money simply spent on marketing communications or design, and gone forever.

I would argue that governments should never do things purely for image-related reasons; no action should ever be conceived of or dedicated to image management or image change alone. Every initiative and action should first and foremost be done for a real purpose in the real world, or else it runs the risk of being insincere, ineffective, and perceived as propaganda (not to mention a use of taxpayers' money that is often extremely hard to justify). But there should be something unmistakable about the *way* in which these actions and initiatives are done; the style and method of their conception, selection, and delivery; the context and the manner in which they are presented; and the way in which they are aligned with other initiatives, which little by little will drive the country from the image it has acquired by default toward the one it needs and deserves.

Desiring a better reputation will not make a better country, but making a better country will create a better reputation. Enlightened policies alone, even if effectively implemented, are not sufficient to persuade foreign publics to part with their existing prejudices and perceptions, which in the case of national images may prove exceptionally resilient to change. This latter point has been amply demonstrated over the past 5 years through my survey, the Nation Brands Index (NBI), a major study of international perceptions of up to 50 countries. The NBI shows that, apart from two remarkable exceptions (the collapse of Denmark's image among Muslim respondents following the 2006 publication of cartoons lampooning the Prophet Mohammed, and the United States' extraordinary rise of six places in the ranking following the election of President Obama), no country's overall image has ever altered by more than about 1% per year.

Communications, clearly, are inadequate as an instrument to 'move the needle' on such a robust construct as national image: only profound, widespread, consistent, and sustained changes in national behaviour can do this. *Substance* must be coupled with *strategy* and frequent *symbolic actions* if it is to result in an enhanced reputation.

Strategy, in its simplest terms, is knowing *who* a nation is and *where* it stands today (both in reality and according to internal and external perceptions); knowing where it wants to get to; and knowing how it is going to get there. The two main difficulties associated with strategy development are (1) reconciling the needs and desires of a wide range of different national actors into a more or less single direction and (2) finding a strategic goal that is both inspiring and feasible, since these two requirements are frequently contradictory.

Substance is the effective execution of that strategy in the form of new economic, legal, political, social, cultural, and educational activity: the real innovations, structures, legislation, reforms, investments, institutions, and policies which will bring about the desired progress.

Symbolic actions are a particular species of substance that happen to have an intrinsic communicative power: they might be innovations, structures, legislation, reforms, investments, institutions, or policies which are especially suggestive, remarkable, memorable, picturesque, newsworthy, topical, poetic, touching, surprising, or dramatic. Most importantly, they are emblematic of the strategy: they are at the same time a component of the national story and the means of telling it.

Some good examples of symbolic actions are the Slovenian government donating financial aid to their Balkan neighbours in order to prove that Slovenia was not part of the Balkans; Spain legalising single-sex marriages in order to demonstrate that its values had modernised to a point diametrically opposed to the Franco period; the decision of the Irish government to exempt artists, writers, and poets from income tax in order to prove the state's respect for creative talent; Estonia declaring internet access to be a human right; or the Hague hosting the European Court of Human Rights (partly) in order to cement the Netherlands' reputation as a global bastion of the rule of law.

A building, such as the Guggenheim Museum in Bilbao or the Sydney Opera House, may have a symbolic value for its city and country well beyond its economic 'footprint' and places with no chance of being selected to host major sporting or cultural events are often observed to bid for them, apparently just in order to communicate the fact that they are internationally engaged, ambitious, and proud of their achievements. Even simple publicity stunts, such as 'The Best Job in the World', Tourism Queensland's international recruitment drive for an 'islands caretaker' in early 2009, can become symbolic acts that – in return for a remarkably small investment – create widespread 'viral' interest in places.

Often the symbolic power of such an action cannot be predicted, as its full effect derives from an imponderable fusion of the action itself, the moment and context in which it appears, the mood and culture of the 'audience,' and their perceptions of the place where it originates. The 'Best Job in the World,' by accident or by design, sat neatly at the intersection between a number of powerful ideas: the existing, positive 'brand' of Australia; the popularity of one kind of reality show that puts young adults into challenging environments and another kind where they compete for a dream job; the collapse of international financial markets and a consequent surge of interest in escape from modern urban reality; concern about climate change and the protection of vulnerable environments, especially coral reefs; and much else besides.

Such actions can also be planned, but the three most important points are as follows:

1. A single symbolic action will seldom achieve any lasting effect; multiple actions should emanate from as many different sectors as possible in order to build a rounded and believable image for the place.
2. They should never be *empty* – they must be communicative substance rather than just communication. Each symbolic action must be intrinsically defensible against the accusation of empty rhetoric, even when taken out of context and scrutinised on its own account (as commentators in a healthy democracy are bound to do).
3. They should continue in an unbroken succession for many years. Building a reputation in our busy modern world is like trying to fill a bathtub with the plug pulled out: as soon as each symbolic action is completed, its effect on public attention begins to decay, and unless it is swiftly followed

by further and equally remarkable *proof* of the kind of country that produces it, that country's reputation will stand still or move backward, and the bathtub will never fill.

It is clear that places require new and dedicated structures to coordinate, conceive, develop, maintain, and promote such an unbroken chain of proof. None of the traditional apparatus of trade or government is fit for such a purpose – at least not in a way that cuts across all areas of national activity and is capable of sustaining it for the years and decades it takes to enhance, refine, or otherwise alter the international image of a nation.

The concept of strategy plus substance plus symbolic actions is a classic 'three-legged stool' – an approach that cannot stand up unless all three conditions are met.

Strategy + Substance – Symbolic Actions = Anonymity

Countries, for example, that succeed in developing a *strategy* and are diligent at creating real *substance* on the basis of this strategy but overlook the importance of *symbolic actions* still run the risk of remaining anonymous, undervalued, or unable to change the long-standing clichés of their international reputation, because strategies are often private and substance is often boring. Without the communicative power of symbolic actions, such countries can remain trapped inside a weak, distorted, or outdated brand image for generations, and consequently fail to attract the consumers, talent, media attention, tourists, and investors they need in order to build their economies, expand their influence, and achieve their aims.

Substance – Strategy + Symbolic Actions = Incoherence

Substance without an underlying *strategy* may achieve sporadic and localised economic and social benefits, but it is unlikely to build the country's profile or influence in any substantial way. Even if the substance is accompanied by frequent *symbolic actions*, without an underlying strategic intent the messages will remain fragmented, and no compelling or useful story of the nation's progress will form in the public consciousness.

Strategy – Substance – Symbolic Actions = Spin

Strategy without *substance* is spin: it is the frequent predicament of weak governments that they make many plans but lack the willpower, the resources, the influence, the expertise, or the public support to carry them to fruition.

Strategy – Substance + Symbolic Actions = Propaganda

Strategy that is accompanied by *symbolic actions* but no real *substance* is worse still: this is authentic propaganda, a deliberate and schemed manipulation of public opinion designed to make people believe something different from reality. In today's world, where the globalisation of communications has resulted in an environment where no single message can survive unchallenged, propaganda has become virtually impossible, and such an approach will result in the destruction of the country's good name for generations.

Symbolic Actions – Substance – Strategy = Failure

Governments that focus purely on *symbolic actions* and fail to provide either *strategy* or real *substance* will soon be recognised as lightweights: carried this way and that by public opinion, and intent purely on achieving popularity, they seldom remain in power for long.

Clearly, the deliberate and planned use of symbolic actions can lay governments open to the charge of 'playing to the gallery,' and devising strategies purely or largely in virtue of their impact on national image. Such behaviour, it could be argued, is even worse than simple propaganda, as it commits more public resources to the task of creating a certain impression than mere messages do. Each case must be judged on its own merits, but it could be argued that a symbolic action can be defended against the charge of propaganda if it is based on a clear long-term *strategy* and is supported by a substantially larger investment in real *substance*.

In the end, it is largely a matter of quantity that determines such a judgment: if nine out of ten policies or investments are selected purely on the basis that they benefit the country, and one on the basis that it gets the story across too, governments may act not only with a clear conscience, but also in the knowledge that the 10 percent of symbolic actions, by enhancing the reputation of the country, are adding substantial value to the other investments and thus may ultimately contribute even more value to the country than its more weighty but less media-friendly initiatives.

What governments sometimes have difficulty understanding is that the size, ambition, or cost of initiatives may not be proportional to their symbolic value. Very large buildings which simply communicate wealth and hubris may have less power over the popular imagination than very small ones which happen to tell a story (in my other survey, the City Brands Index, the tiny statue of the *mannekin pis* in Brussels is spontaneously mentioned by 20 times more international respondents than the enormous Atomium, or even the gigantic headquarters of the European Commission; the government of Slovenia donating a few hundreds of thousands of euros to Albania, Montenegro, and Macedonia is more newsworthy than the US government donating hundreds of millions of dollars to Africa; one patient deprived of a hospital bed briefly generated more media coverage in the United Kingdom than the Labour government's injection of many billions of pounds into the National Health Service).

CONCLUSION

But any realistic discussion about the reputations of countries, cities, and regions must take another, even more significant factor into account: the level of indifference which most people appear to feel about places other than their own. As I have often noted, most people appear to feel that most other countries have little impact on, or relevance to, their own lives. What awareness and knowledge most of us do possess about other countries therefore tends to be quite abstract, and perhaps partly as a consequence of this, rarely changes. These are more like beliefs than opinions, more a series of rather simple mental images than a constantly revised or constantly assessed set of active thoughts; the images of other countries form the background to our worldview rather than being objects of direct observation or conscious appraisal. Consequently, even when we hear something new and surprising about another country, this may not affect our mental image of the country at all, which remains securely stowed in the mental compartment marked 'fundamental beliefs.'

The harsh reality is that, barring their close neighbours, most people in the world really only respect, occasionally think about, claim to know about, and generally admire a maximum of 14 or 15 countries apart from their own, and these are all major, industrialised democracies in Western Europe and the English-speaking world, plus Japan and Brazil. Most of the other countries that are well known are not much admired: they are famous because they are trouble spots (there are usually about another 15 of these at any given moment, such as Iraq, Zimbabwe, and North Korea), or because they once enjoyed a high profile, which people who do not know much about them feel they no longer deserve (such as Greece, Turkey, or Egypt), or because they are indisputably very important but not universally loved, trusted, or admired (such as Russia, China, America, or India). The remaining 160 countries on the planet largely mind their own business and are consequently ignored by everyone who is not actively planning to emigrate or go on holiday there.

So when a country asks – as so many now do – 'what can we say to make ourselves more famous?', they are really asking the wrong question. The right question is surely 'what can we *do* to make ourselves *relevant*?' Many developing countries are mystified by the fact that they have made progress and acquired wealth, and yet their image remains weak or even negative, apparently trapped in the past. The reason, as often as not, is simply that their progress is only of benefit – and consequently only of interest – to their own populations. And there is nothing wrong with that, either: for a country to focus on developing stability, good governance, prosperity, equality, and justice is impossible to criticise. But it should be understood that on their own, progress and prosperity do not equate to reputation. If a country is serious about enhancing its appeal to people *outside* its own borders, then clearly it has to start benefiting them as well as its own people.

In other words, if a country wants to be admired, it has to be relevant, and in order to be relevant, it has to participate usefully, productively, and imaginatively in the global 'conversations' on the topics that matter to people elsewhere and everywhere; and the list is a long one. Climate change, global governance, poverty reduction, migration, economic stability, human rights, weapons control, education, corruption, terrorism, and war – it is hard to imagine any country that could not pick at least one item on this list and find a way to make a prominent, meaningful, and memorable contribution to the debate and to the global effort on their chosen subject or subjects.

For the past 20 years or so, it has become more and more evident that corporations that fail to maintain high ethical standards, transparency, and 'corporate social responsibility' will soon lose the trust and respect of their consumers. Even if one is cynical and believes that 75% of organisations that preach the 'triple bottom line' are merely window-dressing, still, the fact that a quarter of all companies have fundamentally reviewed the ways, means, causes, and effects of doing business, and have cleaned up their act as a result, is revolutionary. What a revolution it would be if countries, cities, and regions, nowadays as obsessed with the value of their reputations as companies are – and justifiably so – were to follow the same principles. As I observed in an article in 2006, 'if the world's governments placed even half the value which most wise corporations have learned to place on their good names, the world would be a safer and quieter place than it is today.'

It is already clear from the NBI data that more and more people in more and more countries feel unable to admire or respect countries or governments that pollute the planet, practice or permit corruption, trample human rights, or flout the rule of law: in other words, it's the *same audience*, starting to apply the *same standards* to countries as they apply to companies. In just a few decades, consumer power has changed the rules of business and transformed the behaviour of corporations almost beyond recognition. It does not seem unreasonable to hope that consumer power might achieve a similar transformation in the way that countries, cities, and regions are run in the years to come.

CHAPTER

3

A place marketing and place branding perspective revisited

Philip Kotler and David Gertner

INTRODUCTION

At one time, in most product categories and in most markets, consumers had somewhat limited choice of products and brands. In myriad industries, a single manufacturer or service provider enjoyed a dominant market share and was the incontestable industry leader. This was the case in the automotive, appliances, electronics, beverages, personal care, financial and banking services, airlines, and consulting industries, among others. In most cases, there were also one or two strong challengers trailing the market leader. A small share of the market, left by the two or three leading brands in the category, was usually obstinately disputed by a number of much smaller market nichers.

In just a few decades, dramatic changes in the demographic, natural, economic, social, legal, and political environments, combined with unprecedented advancements in transportation and telecommunications, revolutionised most competitive environments. Suddenly, much faster than developments in past decades and centuries, the number of alternative choices available to consumers, in almost all markets, multiplied exponentially. Competition became global, rather than largely domestic. Cherished companies and brands once glorified and considered virtually invulnerable, such as GM, IBM, Coca-Cola, GE, Xerox, and Boeing, faced serious competition for the first time and experienced the erosion of market share. The assault to the supremacy of market leaders and chief brands was threatened not from their customary and predictable competitors. Instead, leading brands were defied on their own turfs by new and unfamiliar brand names originating in different parts of the world. In the automotive industry, companies such as Korean Hyundai and Kia, Indian Tata Motors, and Chinese Chery Automobile have challenged traditional market leaders; Chinese Lenovo and Taiwanese Acer in electronics; Korean LG in appliances; and Brazilian Embraer in the aircraft industry, to name a few.

© 2011 Published by Elsevier Ltd. All rights reserved.
DOI: 10.1016/B978-0-08-096930-5.10003-5

These new or hardly known contenders and brand names, with products developed and manufactured in remote and formerly improbable parts of the world, have become worthy global competitors in hard-to-enter industries, stealing positions from formerly mighty leaders. At the same time, thousands of small marketers have found a way to approach consumers with their offerings, sometimes in a global context, using novel distribution and communication channels, largely inexistent 20 years ago.

Competition among places for tourists, investors, residents, and events has not been any different. Sometime ago, a few cities, regions, and countries were the predictable and unrivaled tourist destinations of choice for travelers. Paris, London, New York, the United States, France, Italy, North America, and Europe were some of the top, dominant destinations. An incalculable number of other locations competed intensely for the share of the travel and tourism market left unclaimed by these major tourist destinations. Many of them achieved fair performances, by focusing on smaller areas of influence or on narrower target markets with specific interests, such as art, archeology, gastronomy, religion, gambling, and other markets.

Likewise, national and international conventions and conferences were more likely to be held in a few alternative and expected places. Investors would unsurprisingly cluster in certain business centres and locations close to their main competitors and markets. Particular places were the understandable preferred locations for companies in specific industries, such as Detroit for the automotive sector, Switzerland for watches and banking services, New England for pharmaceuticals, France and California for wine producers, and Italy and France for fashion designers. From the market point of view, more often than not, customers used the place or origin of the product, or the 'made in label,' as the foremost criterion to speculate about the quality of given products.

Times have certainly changed. The very same factors that allowed the supremacy of leading companies and brands to be challenged by unknown brands from distant places today also allow small communities, unfamiliar cities, faraway regions, and improbable nations in remote parts of the world to aspire, compete, and be considered by global investors, tourists, conventioneers, residents, events, and others in a wide range of industries. Nowadays, tourists not only consider but frequently choose to visit far-off locations in remote parts of the planet, to the detriment of traditional destinations. Retirees sell their homes in comfortable, safe, and valued cities located in mature economies, where they spent their lives, and venture to move to places in formerly unstable regions of the world, such as Central America, which were not even considered a choice in the past for a short vacation. Consumers are buying products made in places they had never heard of or know very little about in their pursuit for value. Top manufacturers and brands choose to produce their offerings in once unlikely places as long as they guarantee the quality they demand at a lower price, and have them distributed in the entire world, displaying the brand and the 'made-in wherever' label.

Formerly distressed and unmarketable places are improving their investment grades and are now attracting substantial investments from conservative investors seeking higher returns for their money. Similar to what has happened to top brands, the prestige and share of the world's wealth held by advanced economies, such as the United States, Germany, and Japan, is weakening.

For many years now, large emerging economies have sustained spectacular economic growth, compared to the indexes presented by mature economies. The economies of countries such as Brazil, Russia, India, and China (a group referred as the BRICs) have moved up several positions in the ranking of the largest economies.

Undoubtedly, in the new economy, transportation and communication innovations have allowed manufacturers, investors, tourists, residents, retirees, conventioneers, and event planners to consider anywhere in the globe to satisfy their needs. In a market where any community, city, state, region, nation, or neighbourhood has a shot at creating brand equity, strategic place marketing and branding may be a decisive tool to assist them in succeeding.

COUNTRIES AS BRANDS AND PRODUCTS

Products have been broadly defined as anything of value exchanged by individuals, groups, and organisations. This comprehensive description embraces tangible and intangible entities, such as goods and services, experiences, ideas, causes, faiths, people, and so forth. Virtually anything exchanged of value, such as money, time, attention, excitement, or comfort, can be considered a product. As such, it can be marketable. The proliferation of offerings and greater than ever product parity or '*commoditisation*,' however, has made differentiation much more challenging. After all, when products are perceived as being similar price becomes the major, and sometimes the only, basis for competition.

Because product attributes are easily copied, and low prices tend to erode profitability and endanger marketers' long-term survival, brands have been considered a marketer's major tool for creating value. Even when differentiation based on product characteristics is possible, consumers often do not feel motivated or are not able to analyse them in adequate depth. Therefore, the combination of brand name and brand significance has become a core competitive asset in an ever-growing number of contexts (Aaker, 1991, p. 299).

Brands allow marketers to identify and differentiate their products from their competitors'. Marketers do their utmost to build unique associations with their brand. Universally, a brand has been described as a distinctive and legally protected name, term, sign, symbol, or design, or a combination of them, used to differentiate a company's offer.[1] Additionally, and probably more important for marketers than unique names or logos, a brand creates a difference between one's and other's brands in the minds and hearts of prospective customers. In the end, brands incite beliefs, evoke emotions, and prompt behaviours. Brands encourage customers to act. Ultimately, brands represent a promise of value and performance. Marketers often extend successful brand names to new product launches, lending existing associations to them. As a result, they speed up consumers' information processing and consumers' learning.

---

[1] The American Marketing Association defines a brand as a 'name, term, sign, symbol, or design, or a combination of them intended to identify the goods and services of one seller or group of sellers and to differentiate them from those of competition.'

Beyond the utilitarian benefits expected from products, brands have social and emotional value to customers. They have personality and speak to the customer. They enhance the perceived utility and desirability of a product. Brands have the ability to add to or subtract from the perceived value of a product. Consumers expect to pay lower prices for unbranded products or for those with low brand equities. On the other hand, they pay premiums for their treasured or socially valued brands. Brands have equity for both customers and investors. Brand equity translates into customer preference, loyalty, and financial gains. Brands are appraised and traded in the market place, in some cases for billions. Brand equity has been pointed out to include many dimensions, such as performance, social image, value, trustworthiness, and identification (Lassar, Mittal, & Sharma, 1995).

Can a country also be a brand? This question has sparked much discussion over time.[2] However, for a long while now, country names have behaved as brands by helping consumers evaluate products and make purchasing decisions. They are responsible for associations that may add to or subtract from the perceived value of a product. Empirical evidence has supported that consumers are more willing to buy products from industrialised nations as a result of country equity (Agbonifoh & Elimimiam, 1999; Cordell, 1993; Wang & Lamb, 1983). In fact, products bearing 'made in Germany,' 'made in Switzerland,' and 'made in Japan' labels are commonly regarded as of high quality, due to the reputation of these countries as top world manufacturers and exporters. At the same time, 'made in Suriname' or 'made in Myanmar' labels may raise doubts about the quality of the products due to these countries' low brand equity. In one investigation, for example, researchers examined and found differences in the way consumers evaluate Toyota cars (Corolla, Camry, and Avalon) made in the United States, Japan, and Mexico (Chinen, Enomoto, & Costley, 2000). Country of origin effects have also been investigated in decisions related to the purchase of services (Berentzen, Backhaus, Michaelis, Blut, & Ahlert, 2008) and industrial products (Insch, 2003). Despite globalisation and changes in the competitive environment, place of origin continues to influence consumers' decisions in several product categories. Recent studies, for example, concluded that country of origin is still the most important decision factor for Chinese consumers when purchasing wines (Balestrini & Gamble, 2006; Hu, Li, Xie, & Zhou, 2008).

In some instances, a country may deliberately use its name to promote its products. For nearly three decades now, American consumers have regarded *Café de Colombia* (Colombian coffee) as a top quality coffee. The character of Juan Valdez helped to designate the country name 'Colombia' as a stamp of a high-quality coffee brand. This quintessential *cafetero* and his mule are portrayed in a logo created in 1981, and one introduced to advertising in 1982, to be used as a seal of guaranteed quality issued by the National Federation of Coffee Growers of Colombia (World's Best Logos, 2011). The *Café de Colombia* logo has been extensively used in advertising, promotional materials, and coffee packages, providing a good example of integrated marketing communications as well as of consistency. Consumer advertising

---

[2] The term 'country equity' refers to the emotional value resulting from consumers' association of a brand with a country (Shimp, Saeed, & Madden, 1993).

featuring the logo has paid off. Colombia is the leading exporter of coffee to the United States and *Café de Colombia* holds over 40 percent of the specialty coffee market in the United States. Research indicates that 80–90% of Americans associate the Juan Valdez logo with coffee, without any descriptive words, while around half correctly identify it as the Colombian coffee brand (FNC). In 2002, low coffee prices and the increasing popularity of coffee chains, such as Starbucks, encouraged the Colombian Federation of Coffee Producers (Federación Nacional de Cafeteros) to establish the Juan Valdez Café as the official coffeehouse of Colombian coffee. Juan Valdez stores can be found in prime New York City locations, such as Lexington Avenue, and in the Fashion District.

Even when a country does not consciously manage its name as a brand, people still have images of countries that can be activated by simply voicing the name. Country images are likely to influence people's decisions related to purchasing, investing, changing residence, or traveling. Country image can be understood as:

> the sum of beliefs and impressions people hold about places. Images
> represent a simplification of a large number of associations and pieces
> of information connected with a place. They are a product of the mind
> trying to process and pick out essential information from huge amounts
> of data about a place (Kotler, Haider, & Rein, 1993, pp. 141–143, 388;
> Kotler, Asplund, Rein, & Haider, 1999, pp. 160, 314).

A country's image derives from its geography, history, culture, famous citizens, and other important features. The entertainment industry and the media play a particularly important role in shaping people's perceptions of places, especially those viewed negatively. Not only are product categories such as perfumes, electronics, precision instruments, wines, cars, and software strongly identified with certain places, but also social issues, such as epidemics, political unrest, human rights violations, environmental degradation, racial conflict, economic turmoil, poverty, hunger, and crime. All of these have been repeatedly and strongly associated with certain locales. Of course, different persons and groups are likely to hold different stereotypes of nations since the mental phenomenon is inherently subjective. However, sometimes they are widespread and pervasive across elements of the same group; they are social cognitions, mental representations shared by members of a given society.

In this phase, each country must be able to provide accurate and reliable information. They might be dated, based on exceptions rather than on patterns, on impressions rather than on facts, but nonetheless pervasive. The simple pronunciation or spelling of a brand name in a foreign language may impact product perceptions and attitudes. Leclerc, Schmitt, and Dube (1994) found in one experiment that the French pronunciation of a brand name affects the perceived hedonism of the products and attitudes toward the brand. They also found that the French branding influence persisted even in a product taste test, that is, with a direct sensory experience of the product.

Country images, or knowledge structures related to places, or place schemata, are commonly used as shortcuts for information processing and consumer decision heuristics. People, especially in low-involvement situations, are sloppy cognitive processors. They resist changing or adjusting their cognitive structures or prior knowledge. They prefer to adjust what they see to fit what they know. They may fill in information that is not presented or distort the reality to fit their mental representations. People are also more likely to focus on information that confirms their expectations. They disregard information that challenges their knowledge structures in a process known as 'confirmation bias.' They avoid the effort necessary to reconstruct their cognitions, unless misrepresentations have a cost for them, or they find utility in the revision of a certain mental schema. Therefore, images can be long lasting and difficult to change. They can be assessed and measured, and they may be managed and influenced by place marketers as well.

THE IMPACT OF COUNTRY NAMES ON ATTITUDES TOWARD PRODUCTS

In many countries, mandatory product labeling requires marketers to disclose a product's place of origin. This legal requirement has raised the interest of marketing researchers and practitioners in understanding consumers' attitudes toward foreign products. For approximately four decades, the so-called country-of-origin (COO) effect has been the object of extensive investigation. In 1993, a book edited by Papadopoulos and Heslop, presenting only original research on the topic, was published. In 1995, Peterson and Jolibert identified 184 articles published in academic journals dealing with country image effects. By 2002, Papadopoulos and Heslop and their research group had built a database consisting of over 750 publications by more than 780 authors, published during a period of four decades dealing with 'country of origin,' or its product-country image (PCI) (Papadopoulos & Heslop, 2002). In spite of the extensive data already gathered, the impact of COO on product evaluations continues to foster interest among researchers.

COO studies have been developed for a variety of durable and nondurable consumer products, from cars, electronics, and apparel to smoke detectors and pickles. Findings consistently support that consumers pervasively use COO information as an indicator of quality. COO has become an integral part of the repertory of extrinsic cues to product evaluations along with price, brand name, packaging, and seller, as opposed to the study of the role of intrinsic qualities of the product, such as materials, design, style, workmanship, colour, and smell. The simple manipulation of the COO or 'made-in' label has been observed to influence people's attitudes, even when subjects are given a chance to see, touch, feel, or taste the very same physical product (Chao, 1989; Hong & Wyer, 1990; Jaffe & Martinez, 1995; Johansson et al., 1994; Liefeld et al., 1996; Li et al., 1997; Nagashima, 1970; Papadopoulos & Heslop, 2000; Terpstra, 1988; Wall et al., 1991). Research has also shown that national stereotypes affect relationships between manufacturers and foreign clients (Khanna, 1986).

The effect of COO has been observed through research using different methods such as survey, experiments, and conjoint analysis. In most studies, COO is used as an independent variable, while attitudes toward a product or a country's product serve as the dependent measure. Perceived quality has also been used as a dependent measure, operationalised in many ways. Some authors contend that relevant quality dimensions are different for different products, and that a given COO can be highly regarded in one dimension, such as Volvo's reputation for safety, while it may score low in another, for example serviceability (Garvin, 1987). Questions have also been raised about whether country image would really be a summary construct or should be separated into different dimensions (Han, 1989), such as country of design and country of assembly (Ahmed and d'Astous, 1999), country of brand (Hulland, 1999), country of product design, country of parts manufacture, and country of product assembly (Insch & McBride, 1998).

Another line of investigation concerns the impact of COO on highly valued global brands, such as Sony, Honda, and Daimler-Mercedes. The topic has practical implications, given the fact that, for cost or logistical reasons, global marketers constantly relocate manufacturing facilities or create new ones to better serve local, regional, or global markets. Some studies report that COO information can be less important when other indicators of quality exist (d'Astous and Ahmed, 1992; Chao, 1989; Heslop & Liefeld, 1988). For example, a global brand like Sony could provide a counterbalance to a negative COO effect (Tse & Lee, 1993). But the opposite can also happen, that is, some customers may think less of a Sony product when it is produced in a country of low esteem. The effect of COO on global brands, in multiple categories and contexts, continues to attract scholarly attention (Rosenbloom & Haefner, 2009).

Some investigators suggest that COO effects can only be understood with respect to ethnocentrism (Brodowsky, 1998). The connection between ethnocentrism and COO effects has been studied, for instance, in terms of the evaluation of food (Orth & Firbasova, 2003), and in various national contexts, such as Indonesia (Hamin, 2006), Greece (Chryssochoidis, Krystallis, & Perreas, 2007), and China (Wong, Polonsky, & Garma, 2008). Most studies using the construct ethnocentrism apply the CETSCALE developed by Shimp and Sharma (1987). One example of this is the *Malinchismo* effect (Bailey, Pineres, & Amin, 1997). In Mexico, the term *Malinchista* designates betrayers of Mexico, those who purchase foreign products and thereby devalue Mexican identity. The name comes from a Mexican woman known as La Malinche who served as Cortez's interpreter during the Spanish conquest in 1519. La Malinche became Cortez's confidant and mistress and helped him defeat the Aztec king, Montezuma II.

Expanding on the understanding of the ethnocentrism effect, Klein, Ettenson, and Morris (1998) have also researched how animosity toward a foreign nation could negatively affect the purchase of certain products. To this end, they investigated the attitudes of Chinese consumers toward Japan and Japanese products. The authors argue that ethnocentrism and animosity have different implications for perceptions of product quality. Animosity is a country-specific construct, while ethnocentrism is described as when people regard their own in-group as central and reject what is alien and unfamiliar. Examples of animosity would include Jewish consumers avoiding German products, discussed by Hirschman (1981), and Australian and New Zealand consumers who boycott French products in protest of nuclear tests in the South Pacific. In addition, researchers have studied the impact of national stereotypes on product evaluations (Chattalas, Kramer, & Takada, 2008; Liu &Johnson, 2005).

Other studies have investigated a number of possible mediators of the COO effect. Motivation has been studied as a possible one and research supports that COO effect is more likely to occur when consumers are under low motivation (Gurhan-Canli & Maheswaran, 2000a, 2000b). Researchers have also investigated the role of cultural dimensions in the COO effect. For example, individualism and collectivism have been used to explain why consumers prefer home country products over imported ones even when provided information that the foreign product is superior (Gurhan-Canli & Maheswaran, 2000a, 2000b). Expertise is another mediator studied and the impact of the COO seems to be different on experts and novices (Pecotich and Ward, 2007). In 2008, an article by Ahmed and d'Astous (2008) discussed these and other antecedents, moderators, and dimensions of the impact of COO on product evaluations supported by empirical evidence. In conclusion, extensive research has supported the impact of COO on attitudes toward foreign products. Export promotion authorities in many countries recognise that their country's reputation constitutes an important asset to be managed.

MARKETING COUNTRIES AND MANAGING THEIR BRANDS

As the world population reaches 7 billion people, living in more than 200 *de facto*[3] or *de jure* sovereign states, the challenge of building a nation's wealth has become a critical business arena. The World Bank estimated that by 2005 1.4 billion people (or one-quarter of the population of the developing world) lived on less than US$1.25 a day, considered to be below the poverty line (Chen & Ravallion, 2009). Even though poverty in the world has consistently declined in the past two decades, problems such as low living standards, population growth, job shortage, and poor infrastructure continue to plague nations worldwide (Kotler, Jatusripitak, & Maesincee, 1997, pp, 368; Kotler & Lee, 2009, pp, 368).

The challenge of national economic development has gone beyond the limits of public policy. The new economic order has transformed economic development into a market challenge as well. Nations compete with other nations and strive to devise sources of competitive advantage (Porter, 1989, pp. 855). Thus, today there are more reasons why nations must manage and control their branding. The need to attract tourists, factories, companies, and talented people, and to find markets for their exports, requires that countries adopt strategic marketing management tools and conscious branding. Place branding may provide an opportunity to reconcile the supposed conflict between ideology and economic pragmatism, especially for image-troubled places (Gertner, 2007).

Strategic place marketing concerns the enhancement of a country's position in the global marketplace. It requires understanding the environmental forces that may affect marketability, that is, the strengths and weaknesses of the country that affect its ability to compete with others, such as the size of the

---

[3] In 2009, the United Nations had 192 state members.

domestic market, access to regional trade areas, education of the population, tax incentives, skilled labour, cost of labour, security, and other indicators. It also entails monitoring the external environment; in other words, having a dynamic understanding of opportunities and threats, as well as the competitive forces in the environment. The process must involve government, citizens, and businesses, all with a shared vision. It requires setting and delivering the incentives and managing the factors that might affect place buyers' decisions, which include image, attractions, infrastructure, and people. The following subsections will deal with different tasks of country brand management – managing the image, attracting tourists, and attracting factories and companies.

Managing the image

Why do many more tourists visit Greece than Turkey? Many Turks claim that their country has longer coasts, unpolluted waters, and superb archeological sites to delight any visitor. Still, an overwhelmingly larger number of vacationers seeking sun and antiquities pick Greece instead of its Mediterranean neighbour. As a result, Turkey has tried to reposition the country and manage its troubled image. It has hired a public relations firm to promote the country worldwide as a major democracy, quite different from the image presented in the 1978 movie *Midnight Express* of a human rights violator. Tourism is a pivotal industry to Turkey's economy, and a large-scale international campaign has been implemented to get tourists to perceive the 'Turkey' brand as closer to Greece's position (Kotler et al., 1999).

Israel is another country that has made substantial efforts to change its image (see Chapter 24). Despite enjoying myriad positive image attributes, including business, intellectual, cultural, and scientific successes, the Israeli–Palestinian conflict continues to be at the heart of the nation's image. In a 35-country survey of desirable national qualities conducted in 2006, Israel ranked lowest (TheStar.com, 2007). Extensive research, which included focus groups with different segments, from ultra-Orthodox Jews to Israeli Arabs and secular yuppies, was developed to design the country's rebranding strategy. In 2008, the new branding campaign, with references to Israeli wine, art, and music, was launched in Toronto, chosen by the Foreign Ministry to be the North American test city for the new country brand (Brinn, 2008).

Assessing a brand's image and how it compares to its competitors' images is a necessary step to design the country's marketing strategy. Today there are many reasons why nations must manage and control their branding. The need to attract investment requires conscious branding strategies for different target groups. Branding may clash, for example, when Ireland wants to attract tourists (beautiful country image) and software experts (high-tech image). Kotler et al. define strategic image management as follows:

Strategic image management (SIM) is the ongoing process of researching a place's image among its audiences, segmenting and targeting its specific image and its demographic audiences, positioning the place's benefits to support an existing image or create a new image, and communicating those benefits to the target audiences (Kotler et al., 1993, pp. 141–143).

To be effective, the desired image must be close to reality, believable, simple, appealing, and distinctive. There are already too many 'friendly places' out there.

Brand managers use several tools to promote a country's image. One is a catchy slogan such as 'Spain – Everything Under the Sun,' 'Flanders – Europe's Best Business Location,' 'Miami – Financial Capital of South America,' and 'Scotland – Silicon Glen.' Visual images or symbols also play a role, such as the Eiffel Tower (Paris, France), Big Ben (London, England), Red Square (Moscow, Russia), the Statue of Liberty (New York, USA), and the Christ the Redeemer statue (Rio de Janeiro, Brazil). Events and deeds are also strongly connected to places and used to promote a country's image, such as Oktoberfest (Germany), Carnaval (Brazil), and the Wimbledon Tournament (England).

Confronting a negative image can be an arduous challenge. The brand manager has no control over environmental factors that may keep tourists and investors away, such as natural disasters, political turmoil, and economic downturns. Even more difficult can be controlling how the media and the press disseminate a country's problem, often creating or perpetuating stereotypes. A Turkish spokesperson once said that Turkey receives much worse press than it deserves. In some instances, however, managers mistakenly try to fix the country's image without fixing the problems that gave rise to it. No advertising or public relations will make an unsafe place safer, for instance. Attracting tourists to the place without fixing the problem will lead visitors to bad-mouth the country and worsen its image. To improve a country's image, it may be easier to create new positive associations than trying to refute old ones.

Attracting tourists

Tourism creates direct and indirect jobs in hotels, restaurants, consulting, transportation, and training; it increases tax revenues; and it helps the exporting of local products. In the 1990s, according to the World Tourism Organization (WTO), international tourism arrivals grew at an average rate of 4.3 percent a year (WTO, 2001). Despite the global economic crisis, in 2008, international tourist arrivals increased by 1.9 percent compared to 2007, reaching 922 million. Tourism receipts totalled US$944 billion, up by 1.8 percent from 2007 (WTO, 2009a, 2009b). The WTO forecasts that in 2020 the number of international arrivals will reach 1.6 billion (WTO, 2009b). These benefits do not come without a price, however. Tourism has been criticised for the destruction of the natural environment and threats to local cultures (Kotler et al., 1997). Nevertheless, tourism is an expanding and multisegmented market that most places seek to capitalise upon.

Country brand managers must understand that different places attract different tourists. The tourism market can be segmented by the attractions tourists seek, such as natural beauty, sun, adventure, gaming, events and sports, or culture and history. The market can also be segmented by areas, regions, or locations; by seasons; by customer characteristics; or by benefits (Kotler et al., 1993, 1999). To be successful in the tourism industry, a country must focus on what it wants to market and to whom.

Countries with natural beauty, archeological sites, or a strong culture and history will attract natural tourists, those drawn to existing features of the place. If too few natural attractions exist, the country needs to undertake investment marketing to build attractions or to promote events that will attract tourists. Money also has to be spent to build adequate infrastructure, safety, and services. Tourist managers must undertake research to understand the values tourists seek as users (performance, social and emotional values), as buyers (convenience and personalisation), and payers (price and credit). The competitive environment must also be meticulously analysed. Consumers have literally thousands of destination choices. They will be drawn to destinations that they perceive to offer the best value either because they offer the most benefits or because they are inexpensive or more accessible.

Tourism requires image making and branding grounded in the place's reality. The tourist manager can use different tools. France ran a campaign to get French people to display a warmer attitude toward tourists. Effective promotional campaigns do not necessarily require huge budgets. For example, in 1998, Foote, Cone, and Belding developed an inexpensive and effective campaign for the Jamaica Tourist Board. On its way to the 1998 World Cup in France, to promote Jamaica as a friendly place, the Jamaican soccer team – called the Reggae Boys – took the largest soccer ball ever, about five stories high, from Jamaica's capital, Kingston, to public spaces in different cities, such as New York, London, and finally Paris. In each place, people were asked to sign the ball and wish good luck to the Reggae Boys. With a modest investment – US$886,000 – the campaign received media space valued at over US$5 million. In 1999, Mediaweek granted it the 'Best Campaign Spending $1 Million or Less Award.' Jamaica received 33,600 more visitors than in the previous year and had an increase in tourist revenues of US$50 million (Consoli, 1999).

Famous residents, events, and new attractions can also help build or revamp a destination's image. The ultramodern Guggenheim Museum in Bilbao, Spain, has given a radical facelift to the industrial city of Bilbao and has helped to attract visitors and new investors. Hosting sports events or the Olympics can also give a needed lift to a country's image. In spite of tourism's importance, a country cannot expect the income generated by tourism to solve all of its problems. On the contrary, the country may first need to solve its problems to be able to generate the desired tourism income.

Attracting factories and companies

In 1996, Intel Corporation's worldwide site location team was asked to recommend a location for the company's first plant in Latin America. Numerous countries competed fiercely to receive the US$300–500 million investment, money that would bring new jobs, taxes, and secondary industries, and provide exports (100 percent of the production would be exported to the United States). It could also leverage the confidence of other global investors in the country. The analysis took several months of hard work by a number of highly ranked Intel executives. The team undertook several field trips before it was ready to recommend a short list of four countries: Brazil, Chile, Mexico, and Costa Rica. The final choice was not Brazil, then the largest

Latin American economy and market. Nor did Mexico, a member of North American Free Trade Agreement (NAFTA) and the most accessible location to Intel's headquarters, become the choice. Chile, the fastest growing and most stable economy of the continent, with one of the best and least expensive telecommunication services in the world, also lost out. Surprisingly, Costa Rica won the prize (Nelson, 1999).

Costa Rica, a country with only 3.5 million people and the smallest of the four finalists, ended up winning the Intel plant. The country was not even on the original short list. Costa Rica won because it used many of the principles of place marketing. It also counted on the great job of the officials of CINDE – *Coalición Costarricense de Iniciativas para el Desarrolo* (Costa Rica's Investment Promotion Agency). CINDE followed the recommendation of the World Bank to target the electronics industry. A consultant from the Irish Development Agency (IDA), the country's successful investment promotion agency, also assisted in Costa Rica's effort. Instead of waiting for Intel's questions, CINDE's officials anticipated them and provided the information Intel might need. The pursuit for Intel's investment dollars involved the active participation of many parties, including business professors at the *Instituto Centroamericano de Administración de Empresas* (INCAE), state ministers, and the dean of the *Instituto Tecnológico de Costa Rica* (ITCR). Even the country's former President José Maria Figueres became involved and personally discussed the business with Intel's executives. President Figueres, who was educated at West Point and pursued graduate studies at Harvard, had been committed to attracting high technology investments to Costa Rica, rather than investments based on cheap labour or the extraction of natural resources (Nelson, 1999). Costa Rica's development efforts worked hand in hand with a highly coordinated and targeted branding strategy.

One of the most interesting facets of place marketing concerns countries' efforts to attract new factories and business investments; these are expected to create new jobs and economic growth, with an overall benefit to the country's economy. Because of the dramatic improvements in telecommunication and transportation services worldwide, global companies are now searching for new locations that might bring down their costs. This has transformed supply chain management, logistics, and site selection in core competencies within global companies.

Country marketers must understand how companies make their site selection. As Costa Rica's example demonstrates, usually companies begin the process by choosing a region in which to invest (e.g., Latin America) and collecting information about the potential country candidates (see Table 3.1). In this phase, each country must be able to provide accurate and reliable information. Even better, it should anticipate informational needs, as CINDE did in the case of Intel's site selection. The country should understand the locational characteristics companies are seeking as they relate to labour, tax climate, amenities, higher education, schools, regulation, energy, communication, and business (see Table 3.2).

Today, countless countries and cities are trying to attract high-tech industries. One of the reasons Costa Rica could attract Intel investments was because of the high level of technical education in the country and the number

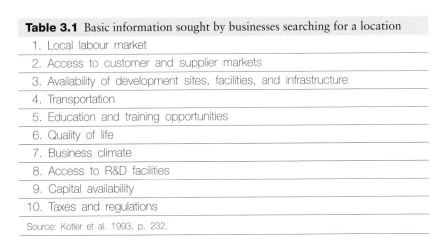

Table 3.1 Basic information sought by businesses searching for a location

1. Local labour market
2. Access to customer and supplier markets
3. Availability of development sites, facilities, and infrastructure
4. Transportation
5. Education and training opportunities
6. Quality of life
7. Business climate
8. Access to R&D facilities
9. Capital availability
10. Taxes and regulations

Source: Kotler et al. 1993, p. 232.

Table 3.2 Locational characteristics: Old and new

Characteristics	Old	New
Labour	Low cost, unskilled	Quality, highly skilled
Tax climate	Low taxes, low service	Modest taxes, high services
Incentives	Least cost production, cheap land, and labour	Value-added adaptable labour force, professionals
Amenities	Housing and transportation	Culture, recreation, museums, shopping, airport
Schools	Availability	Quality schools
Higher education	Not key	Quality schools and research facilities
Regulation	Minimum	Compatible quality of life and business flexibility
Energy	Cost/availability	Dependability/reliability
Communication	Assumed	Technology access
Business	Aggressive chamber of commerce, etc.	Partnerships

Source: Kotler et al. 1999, p. 227.

of electronics firms already located there (Nelson, 1999). As Harvard Professor Michael Porter (1998) argues, competing or complementary industries tend to form clusters of excellence that build productivity. The rivalry and competitive pressures among companies located in these clusters force them to innovate. That would explain concentrations of similar businesses in places such as the

Silicon Valley (IT and software) and New Jersey (pharmaceuticals). Countries must define the industries they wish to build and plan sites to appeal to these specific industries from the very beginning.

To compete, countries must be prepared to offer strong financial incentives to lure prospects. These incentives include tax exemption, work training, infrastructure investments, interest subsidies, and even stake participation. Attracted by the potential proceeds of new factories and businesses, some nations fail to analyse the true cost of successfully attracting a company or plant. Incentive wars have led to a situation in which each created job costs tens of thousands of dollars that might never return to the community. The inducements can far exceed the benefits that the country might get. For example, in the late 1990s, a new governor of the southern Brazilian state of Rio Grande do Sul questioned the incentives offered by his predecessor to an automobile manufacturer. Withdrawing from the deal, Ford decided to build the new facility in the state of Bahia, which offered Ford even more incentives to attract the investment. Studies have shown that although government incentives play an important role in the site decision process, they rarely determine the final result. Proximity to consumer or supplier markets and qualified labour, and confidence in the administration are likely to be more crucial aspects in the development of the decision. Numerous cases also show that the decision is also highly influenced by the market performance of the promotion agency and the commitment of local authorities.

Seeking new market opportunities

An infinite number of out-of-the-box ideas exist that places can use to take advantage of further market opportunities. In 2003, for example, New York's mayor announced the nomination of the first city chief marketing officer (Kleinfield, 2003). His job was described as being 'to offer the city and its contents and inimitable mystique as a brand available for corporate purchase.' Business opportunities envisioned by New York included having city agencies endorsing products, having corporate names associated or exposed in landmarks, franchising names of neighbourhoods to all sorts of products, sponsoring credit cards that allow holders to redeem points to be used in the city's attractions, and charging fees for people and companies willing to name public places, among other concepts. New York's example shows how with creativity places can move beyond the traditional 'marketing place' arena and replicate the market success of brands such as National Basketball Association (NBA) and National Association for Stock Car Auto Racing (NASCAR).

CONCLUSION

In our time, investors, residents, visitors, retirees, conventioneers, event planners, and others enjoy myriad alternatives when choosing places. Often, the difference between the choices available to them relies not so much on what places have to offer, but rather, on how they are perceived. Therefore, countries have progressively realised that they must expend more on conscious marketing and branding efforts to compete for their 'prospective customers.' For several decades, a great deal of empirical research has attested that country images are important extrinsic clues in product evaluations. They are familiar, elicit associations, and can influence product evaluations and purchase decisions. Country images can lend a positive reputation to a whole category, such as French wines or perfumes, or even brand it, such as in the case of *Café de Colombia* or Swatches (Swiss watches).

Likewise, a place's marketing and branding efforts can be seriously jeopardised by negative image attributes. They might be founded on rough and ready realities, or, as it every now and then occurs in fiction. Often, place images are formed or impacted by unsolicited and uncontrolled sources, such as the media and the entertainment industry. Just imagine the impact on national image by British comedian Sacha Noam Cohen's portrayal of a Kazakh reporter Borat Sagdiyev in his 2006 movie *Borat: Cultural Learnings of America for Make Benefit Glorious Nation of Kazakhstan* (see Fullerton, Kendrick, & Wallis, 2008).

Marketing and branding places entail much more than just a logo, a slogan, and the creation and implementation of advertising campaigns, public relations efforts, or even integrated marketing communications. It requires an analytical approach and strategic thinking. As other businesses in highly competitive markets, places must be acquainted with their competitive environment; understand changes affecting the market; devise market opportunities; and create, deliver, and communicate value to prospective customers in a more efficient and effective way than competitors.

Country branding requires the following strategic management approach:

(1) The country needs to carry out a SWOT (Strengths, Weaknesses, Opportunities and Threats) analysis to determine its chief strengths, weaknesses, opportunities, and threats.

(2) The country then chooses some industries, personalities, natural landmarks, and historical events that could provide a basis for strong branding and storytelling.

(3) The country should then develop an umbrella concept that covers and is consistent with all of its separate branding activities. Among the possible concepts would be a country of pleasure, quality, security, honesty, progress, or other attributes.

(4) The country then allocates sufficient national funds to each branding activity deemed to have a potentially large impact.

(5) The country creates export controls to ensure that every exported product is reliable and delivers the promised level of performance.

Marketing and branding places constitute a complex and comprehensive strategic planning process that encompasses a number of factors that have an effect on a place's magnetism. Countries will market their images, attractions, infrastructure, events, people, and other important attributes. Place marketing also calls for short-, medium-, and long-term decisions involving their brand and products, distribution, pricing, and communication. Moreover, it requires a meticulous understanding of customer behaviour and what constitutes value for place users, buyers, and payers.

After an environmental analysis, perhaps the most important aspect of the place strategic marketing process consists in segmenting the market. A place must find how to divide up the market according to meaningful variables. After analysing the relative attractiveness of the various segments identified, a place must choose the ones it wants to pursue, based on its resources and skills, and ultimately on its chances of success. As in any other arena, one shall not battle, unless it has a competitive advantage that will lead it to triumph. If not, one must develop the necessary competences first.

Having the target market(s) selected, a country then needs to decide how it is going to position itself, or how it wants to be perceived. As a rule, country names have been around for a long time. Therefore, it is almost impossible to change it, or withdraw the place from the market to relaunch it as a new, fresh, and improved brand. Still there are people who think it might be done. The Republic of Croatia, for example, was subject to a proposal to rename and relaunch itself as Republika Hrvatska. The rationale is that the name Hrvatska would not elicit the negative associations then associated with Croatia (Martinovic, 2002). In any instance, a sound marketing and branding strategy is founded in a clear positioning. A good positioning statement should clarify what the product is, to whom, and how it compares to existing alternatives.

A common mistake in place marketing and branding is to try to be everything to everyone. No matter how big and diversified a country is, it must choose a way to occupy a special place in people's minds relative to competitors. If a place acts in many competitive fields, the country name can be used as an umbrella or family brand and sub-brands developed for specific groups of customers with unique needs and interests. Each brand should focus on a particular segment. Brands should not compete among them, but rather be harmonised, to take the maximum advantage of market opportunities. The idea is to have brand managers responsible for individual brands, a category manager to coordinate several brands within the same competitive ground, such as sun and sand destinations, and someone overlooking the overall marketing and branding strategies, such as a VP of marketing, to ensure that all the brands work together, synergy is achieved, and the country makes the best possible use of its resources.

Countries have traditionally focused on what they have to offer, or the so-called product-oriented approach. The best way to succeed, however, is to be customer oriented and market driven, that is, to focus on the needs and wants of specific groups of prospective buyers, and understand particular competitive markets and external forces. Just like any other organisation or business, a place cannot be successful unless it pays close attention to customers and constantly innovates. Since the most visible part of the marketing and branding process relies on communications, all the contact points – advertising, public relations, internet, etc. – must be fully integrated and coordinated, resulting in synergy and cost savings. It is crucial to send consistent messages to the market.

A country's image is usually not built or transformed in the short run. Many times, nation marketing and branding is a work for a generation. Therefore, along with consistency, persistence is also necessary. These two – consistency and persistence – are key elements to a nation's marketing and branding success. In addition, one must understand that marketing and branding investments may take many years to yield a return. Furthermore, it can only happen if the place's value proposition is anchored in reality, not just on communication gimmicks. As with a brand name, the country brand is its greatest asset. Consequently, each time the name of the place is mentioned there is an opportunity to add value to or subtract it from country equity. In the highly competitive markets in which countries operate, most places have realised the importance of place marketing and place branding. Those who have not embraced this trend will have to do so soon or risk being left behind.

References

Aaker, D. A. (1991). *Managing brand equity: Capitalizing on the value of a brand name*. New York: Simon & Schuster Trade.

Agbonifoh, B. A., & Elimimiam, J. U. (1999). Attitudes of developing countries towards country-of-origin products in a era of multiple brands. *Journal of International Consumer Marketing, 11*(4), 97–116.

Ahmed, S. A., & d'Astous, A. (1999). Product-country images in Canada and in People's Republic of China. *Journal of International Consumer Marketing, 11*(1), 5–22.

Ahmed, S. A., & d'Astous, A. (2008). Antecedents, moderators and dimensions of country-of-origin evaluations. *International Marketing Review, 25*(1), 75–106.

Bailey, W., Pineres, G., & Amin, S. (1997). Country of origin attitudes in Mexico: the malinchismo effect. *Journal of International Consumer Marketing, 9*(3), 25–41.

Balestrini, P., & Gamble, P. (2006). Country-of-origin effects on Chinese wine consumers. *British Food Journal, 108*(5), 396–412.

Berentzen, J. B., Backhaus, C., Michaelis, M., Blut, M., & Ahlert, D. (2008). Does Made in. also apply to services? An empirical assessment of the country-of-origin effect in service settings. *Journal of Relationship Marketing. Binghamton: 2008, 7*(4), 391–405.

Best Logos. (2011). http://worldsbestlogos.blogspot.com/search?q=Juan, viewed on January 13, 2011.

Brinn, D. (2008). Israel's rebranding efforts to focus on Toronto, Jerusalem Post, in http://www.jpost.com/servlet/Satellite?cid=1205420702807&pagename= JPArticle%2FShowFull, Mar 16, 2008 21:06, viewed October 1, 2009.

Brodowsky, G. H. (1998). The effects of country of origin and country of assembly on evaluations about automobiles and attitudes toward buying them: a comparison between low and high ethnocentric consumers. *Journal of International Consumer Marketing, 10*(3), 85–113.

Chao, P. (1989). The impact of country affiliation on the credibility of product attribute claims. *Journal of Advertising Research, 29*(2), 35–41.

Chattalas, M., Kramer, T., & Takada, H. (2008). The impact of national stereotypes on the country of origin effect: a conceptual framework. *International Marketing Review, 25*(1), 54–74.

Chen, S., & Ravallion, M. (2009). The developing world is poorer than we thought, but no less successful in the fight against poverty, World Bank Policy Research Working Paper No. 4703 World Bank – Development

Research Group (DECRG). In http://papers.ssrn.com/sol3/papers.cfm?abstract_id=1259575#, date posted August 27, 2008, last revised August 11, 2009, viewed September 29, 2009.

Chinen, K., Enomoto, C. E., & Costley, D. L. (2000). The country-of-origin effect on Toyotas made in Japan, the USA and Mexico. *Journal of Brand Management*, *8*(2), 139–148.

Chryssochoidis, G., Krystallis, A., & Perreas, P. (2007). Ethnocentric beliefs and country-of-origin (COO) effect: Impact of country, product and product attributes on Greek consumers' evaluation of food products. *European Journal of Marketing*, *41*(11/12), 1518–1544.

Consoli, J. (May 24, 1999). Best campaign spending $1 million or less: foote, cone & belding. *Mediaweek and Brandweek, New York*, *40*(21), 22–24.

Cordell, V. (1993). Interaction effects of country-of-origin with branding, price, and perceived performance risk. *Journal of International Consumer Marketing*, *5*(2), 5–16.

d'Astous, A., & Ahmed, S. A. (1992). Multi-cue evaluation of made-in concept: a conjoint analysis study in Belgium. *Journal of Euromarketing*, *2*(1), 9–29.

Fullerton, J., Kendrick, A., & Wallis, C. (2008). Brand borat? Americans' reaction to a Kazakhstani place branding campaign. *Place Branding and Public Diplomacy. Houndmills: May 2008*, *4*(2), 159–168.

Garvin, D. A. (1987). Competing on the eight dimensions of quality. *Harvard Business Review*, *65*, 101–109, November–December.

Gertner, D. (2007). Place branding: dilemma or reconciliation between political ideology and economic pragmatism? *Place Branding and Public Diplomacy*, *3*(1), 3–7.

Gurhan-Canli, Z., & Maheswaran, D. (2000a). Determinants of country-of-origin evaluations. *Journal of Consumer Research, Gainesville, Jun*, *27*(1), 96–108.

Gurhan-Canli, Z., & Maheswaran, D. (2000b). Cultural variations in country of origin effects. *Journal of Marketing Research, Aug*, *37*(3), 309–317.

Hamin, G. E. (2006). A less-developed country perspective of consumer ethnocentrism and "country of origin" effects: Indonesian evidence. *Asia Pacific Journal of Marketing and Logistics*, *18*(2), 79–92.

Heslop, L., & Liefeld, J. P. (1988). Impact of country-of-origin on consumer judgments in multi-cue situations: A co-variance analysis. Working Paper No. 88–101, Carleton University.

Hirschman, E. C. (1981). American Jewish ethnicity: Its relationship to some selected aspects of consumer behavior. *Journal of Marketing*, *45*(3), 102–110.

Hong, S. T., & Wyer, R. S., Jr. (1990, December). Determinants of product evaluation: effects of the time interval between knowledge of a product's country of origin and information about its specific attributes. *The Journal of Consumer Research*, *17*(3), 277–288.

Hu, X., Li, L., Xie, C., & Zhou, J. (2008). The effects of country-of-origin on Chinese consumers' wine purchasing behaviour. *Journal of Technology Management in China*, *3*(3), 292–306.

Hulland, J. S. (1999). The effects of country-of-brand and brand name on product evaluations and consideration: a cross-country comparison. *Journal of International Consumer Marketing*, *11*(1), 23–40.

Insch, G. S. (2003). The impact of country-of-origin effects on industrial buyers' perceptions of product quality. *Management International Review*, *43*(3), 291–310.

Insch, G. S., & McBride, B. (1998). Decomposing the country-of-origin construct: an empirical test of country of design, country of parts and country of assembly. *Journal of International Consumer Marketing*, *10*(4), 69–91.

Jaffe, E. D., & Martinez, C. R. (1995). Mexican consumers attitudes towards domestic and foreign products. *Journal of International Consumer Marketing*, *7*(3), 7–27.

Johansson, J. K., Ronkainen, I., & Czinkota, M. I. R. (1994). Negative country-of-origin effects: the case of the New Russia. *Journal of International Business Studies*, *25*(1), 157–177.

Khanna, S. R. (1986). Asian companies and the country stereotype paradox: an empirical study. *Columbia Journal of World Business, New York*, *21*(2), 29–38.

Klein, G., Ettenson, R., & Morris, M. D. (1998). The animosity model of foreign product purchase: an empirical test in the People's Republic of China. *Journal of Marketing*, *62*(1), 89–100.

Kleinfield, N. R. (2003). Battery park, get ready for the bunny; branding in New York is just the beginning. *The New York Times*, April 6, 2003 A 29.

Kotler, P., Asplund, C., Rein, I., & Haider, D. H. (1999). *Marketing places Europe: Attracting investment, industry, and tourism to European cities, communities, states and nations*. Great Britain: Financial Times/Prentice Hall, December 1999.

Kotler, P., Haider, D. H., & Rein, I. (1993, February). *Marketing places: Attracting investment, industry, and tourism to cities, states and nations*. New York: Free Press.

Kotler, P., Jatusripitak, S., & Maesincee, S. (1997, July). *The marketing of nations*. New York: Simon & Schuster Trade.

Kotler, P., & Lee, N. (June, 2009). *Up and out of poverty: The social marketing solution*. Philadelphia, PA: Wharton School Publishing.

Lassar, W., Mittal, B., & Sharma, A. (1995). Measuring customer-based brand equity. *Journal of Consumer Marketing*, *12*(4), 11–19.

Leclerc, F., Schmitt, B. H., & Dube, L. (1994). Foreign branding and its effects on product perceptions and attitudes. *Journal of Marketing Research*, *31*(2), 263–270.

Li, Z. G., Fu, S., & Murray, L. W. (1997). Country and product images: The perceptions of consumers of People's Republic of China. *Journal of International Consumer Marketing*, *10*(1/2), 115–139.

Liefeld, J. P., Heslop, L. A., Papadopoulos, N., & Walls, M. (1996). Dutch consumer use of intrinsic, country-of-origin, and price cues in product evaluation and choice. *Journal of Consumer Marketing*, *1*(9), 57–81.

Liu, S. S., & Johnson, K. F. (2005). The automatic country-of-origin effects on brand judgments. *Journal of Advertising*, *34*(1), 87–97.

Martinovic, S. (2002). Branding *Hrvatska* – A mixed blessing that might succeed: the advantage of being unrecognisable. *Journal of Brand Management*, *9*(4/5), 315–322.

Han, C. (1989). Country image: halo or summary construct? *Journal of Marketing Research*, 26.2 (May 1989): 222.

Nagashima, A. (1970). A comparison of Japanese and U.S. attitudes toward foreign products. *Journal of Marketing*, *34*(1), 68–74.

Nelson, R. (1999). Intel's site selection decision in Latin America. *Thunderbird Case Series*, A06-99-0016.

Orth, U. R., & Firbasova, Z. (2003). The role of consumer ethnocentrism in food product evaluation. *Agribusiness*, *19*(2), 137–153.

Papadopoulos, N., & Heslop, L. A. (Eds.). (1993, January). *Product and country images: Impact and role in international marketing*. New York: Haworth Press Inc.

Papadopoulos, N., & Heslop, L. A. (2000). Countries as brands. London, *Ivey Business Journal*, *65*(2), 30–36.

Papadopoulos, N., & Heslop, L. A. (2002). Country equity and country branding: problems and prospects. *Journal of Brand Management, London*, *9*(4/5), 294–314.

Pecotich, A., & Ward, S. (2007). Global branding, country of origin and expertise: An experimental evaluation. *International Marketing Review, 2007*, *24*(3), 271–296.

Peterson, R., & Jolibert, A. (1995). *A quantitative analysis of country-of-origin effects*. *Journal of International Business Studies*, *26*(4), 883–900.

Porter, M. (January, 1989). *The competitive advantage of nations*. New York: Simon & Schuster Trade.

Porter, M. (1998). Clusters and the new economics of competition. November/December 1998. *Harvard Business Review*, 77–90.

Rosenbloom, A., & Haefner, J. E. (2009). Country-of-origin effects and global brand trust: a first look. *Journal of Global Marketing*, *22*(4), 267–278.

Shimp, T., & Sharma, S. (1987). Consumer ethnocentrism: construction and validation of the CETSCALE. *Journal of Marketing Research*, *24*(3), 280–289.

Shimp, T. A., Saeed, S., & Madden., T. J. (1993). Countries and their products: a cognitive structure perspective. *Journal of the Academy of Marketing Science*, *21*(4), 323–330.

Terpstra, V. (1988). Country-of-origin effects for uni-national and bi-national products. *Journal of International Business Studies*, *19*(2), 235–255.

TheStar.com (2007). Israel tried to buff its image, The Star, in http://www.thestar.com/News/article/286045, posted December 16, 2007, accessed October 1, 2009.

Tse, D. K., & Lee, W. (1993). Removing negative country images: effects of deposition, branding, and product experience. *Journal of international Marketing*, *1*(4), 25–48.

Wang, C. K., & Lamb, C. W. (1983). The Impact of selected environmental forces upon consumers' willingness to buy foreign products. *Journal of the Academy of Marketing Science*, *11*(1), 71–85.

Wall, M., Liefeld, J., & Heslop, L. A. (1991). Impact of country-of-origin cues on consumer judgments in multi-cue situations: a covariance analysis. *Academy of Marketing Science*, *19*(2), 105–113.

Wong, C. Y., Polonsky, M. J., & Garma, R. (2008). The impact of consumer ethnocentrism and country of origin sub-components for high involvement products on young Chinese consumers' product assessments. *Asia Pacific Journal of Marketing and Logistics*, *20*(4), 455–478.

WTO (2001). "Special Report Numbers 18", WTO, January 14, 2002, in http://www.world-tourism.org/newsroom/Releases/more_releases/December 2001/WTO-TTRC_Summ.pdf, viewed on July 15, 2001.

WTO (2009a). World Tourism Organization. UNWTO Tourism Barometer, June 2009. in http://unwto.org/facts/eng/pdf/barometer/UNWTO_Barom09_2_en_ex cerpt.pdf, viewed on October 1, 2009.

WTO (2009b). World Tourism Organization. Tourism 2020 vision: set of 6 regional reports and global forecast and profiles of market segments, in http://unwto.org/facts/eng/vision.htm, viewed on October 1, 2009.

CHAPTER

4

Nation branding: Yesterday, today, and tomorrow

Wally Olins and Jeremy Hildreth

INTRODUCTION

After 1945, the collapse of the great European colonial empires created a wave of new nations. Many rechristened themselves. Ceylon became Sri Lanka, Gold Coast became Ghana, and Southern Rhodesia became Zimbabwe and its capital Salisbury, Harare. The Dutch East Indies became Indonesia, and its capital Batavia was renamed Jakarta. Pakistan was quite new, carved out of India and divided into two separate bits; it had no existence before 1947. Some countries changed their names twice or more. Bangladesh has had three names in just over half a century; first it was part of India as East Bengal, then it became East Pakistan and then Bangladesh.

All of these new countries attempted to break away, substantively and symbolically, from their immediate colonial past. Many like their predecessors in nineteenth-century Europe uncovered, discovered, or invented traditions. Zimbabwe was a semi-mythical African empire located more or less where present-day Zimbabwe lies, but while the historical relationship between ancient Zimbabwe and contemporary Zimbabwe is negligible, the emotional relationship is close – it was designed by nation branding to be so.

Nations reinvent themselves as regimes and circumstances change, just as a company modulates its identity as its business develops, or a person dresses differently when he or she enters a new line of work or undergoes a personal transformation. A pertinent, plain enough definition of branding, whether of a nation or any other body, would be 'altering the outside to match the inside, with an eye toward making the inside stronger.' Another way of looking at it is to say branding is a manifestation – partially a visual manifestation – of belonging.

Clearly, branding the nation is not the same as branding a company. But people, whether they are part of a company or a nation, can be motivated, inspired, and led in the same way, using some of the same techniques. Businesses have to create loyalties: loyalties of the workforce, loyalties of

© 2011 Published by Elsevier Ltd. All rights reserved.
DOI: 10.1016/B978-0-08-096930-5.10004-7

suppliers, loyalties of the communities in which they operate, loyalties of investors, and loyalties of customers. In creating these loyalties, they use very similar techniques to those of nation builders. They create special languages, environments, colours, symbols, and quasi-historical myths. They even have heroes. Richard Branson and his famous informality, his heroic ballooning trips, and his other self-aggrandising activities; Ratan Tata, the diffident but tough family member who led Tata into global fame; and Steve Jobs, the autocratic, famously rude genius who leads Apple, to mention just three.

All of us who work with corporations and their brands understand that material objects and experiences, such as cars, clothing, gadgets, and even such apparently insignificant items as drinks or flip flops, can add real emotional and spiritual value to people's lives. They help us to identify – to belong. That is why some people are prepared to spend their own money parading around in tee shirts with the Nike logo emblazoned all over it. At another level then, it should not surprise us that flags, music, and all the other symbolic paraphernalia of the nation arouse similar emotions and help to create a sense of belonging.

Indeed, in the more successful instances of nation branding, the focus seems to be more internal than external – that is, more attention is directed to how the nation perceives itself than to how the nation is perceived by outsiders; substance and symbolism are equal, and while indirect communication and direct communication are both employed, indirect communication typically emerges as much the stronger force.

NATION BRANDING: PAST AND PRESENT

Successful nation branding creates and sustains a clear sense of belonging within the nation and projects a handful of core ideas to the outside world. These come together to create perceptions. These perceptions, both internal and external, must be broadly in line with reality. Take two examples: Britain and Poland.

Although it is no longer an imperial power, Britain still has a significant and, broadly speaking, benevolent and attractive presence on the world stage. The British identity is a quirky mixture of tradition and iconoclasm, and of conformity and anarchy. In a postimperial nation, there are just a very few and rapidly diminishing echoes of former glory still hanging about, but in contrast, Britain's youthful and highly individualistic attitudes in all areas of creativity are striking. Its [recently] somewhat wounded but still powerful financial sector also distinguishes it. Britain, without trying very consistently, presents itself as it is, in a rather disorganised but easily recognisable fashion. The most significant British legacy to the world, the English language, is now in such universal use, that, perhaps curiously, it does not seem to have that much to do with Britain alone anymore. Americans, Australians, and others share the heritage. The gift to the world of the English language is something the British could make more of – but with certain exceptions, like the work of the British Council, they take it entirely for granted.

Then look at a European country as unlike Britain as it is possible to be. Poland is not a slovenly, gray, postcommunist mess somewhere on the eastern edge of Europe. It is, on the contrary, just now as we write this, Europe's most dynamic economy, with a vigorous cultural and creative scene in everything from architecture to dance. The Polish genius does not frequently produce high levels of teamwork, but many Poles are very gifted individually – you can call it creative tension. For the first time in at least 200 years, Poland is self-confident, optimistic, and without significant enemies. It is a cohesive, dynamic modern country – the leader in Central and Eastern Europe. To the outside world and even to some Poles themselves, it does not always look like this. On the contrary, perceptions of present-day Poland are unclear, mixed, and even a bit troubled, and where they do exist are typically about 20 years out of date. The tumultuous and struggling past still dominates the calm and increasingly confident present. Poland could be to the first half of the twenty-first century, what Spain was to the second half of the twentieth century: an exemplar of dynamic change. But there is not a coherent national branding program to make it visible and palatable so that perceptions of the Polish nation are aligned with its current reality.

In order to create and sustain a clear national brand, there has to be an understanding of the country's essence. Each country is different, so the job is to find the difference and project it. But this kind of fundamental thinking does not often happen. Most national branding programs, so-called, are bland and cosmetic. They focus almost entirely on external audiences and they employ superficial advertising techniques, presenting interchangeable clichés about lovely food and welcoming natives to the tourist market. For the sake of gloss and a pretty face, they make the Red Sea, the Indian Ocean, the Mediterranean, the Pacific, and the Caribbean seem completely interchangeable. No wonder they do not work.

All this means that a lot of time and money is squandered and the idea of national branding is largely misunderstood. Governments are right to want to grapple with their nation's brands because a successful national brand encourages cohesion internally and brings huge economic and political advantages externally. They just do not do it in the right way. What is more, the contemporary context in which nation branding takes place – the internet, democracy, regionalism, etc. – is radically different from its historical context; people see more, hear more, travel more, and participate more than ever before. They are more curious and less deferential, which means that the demands on a national branding program are far greater than they once were. Most national branding efforts, such as they are, ignore this.

THE EUROPEAN UNION

Over the past half century or so, the pace at which national and regional identities and super regions and city states have emerged has increased dramatically – the nation branding scene is now complex and multifaceted. In the twenty-first century, nation branding or contemporary versions of it are all around us. In addition to the newish nations of Europe and of the postcolonial era in Asia and Africa, there are two other interesting developments. City states have reemerged. Singapore, Dubai, and the various Middle East Emirates are rich, ebullient, and pushy (see Chapters 14 and 15). Above all, they seem pretty self-confident. At the other end of the scale, there are the new shadowy super regions. In Asia, Africa, the Americas, and most particularly in Europe – in the form of the European Union (EU) – this new super region brings with it huge branding issues.

At one level, the EU is an immense success. Its expansion from 6 nations to 27 is now taken for granted, a remarkable achievement particularly bearing in mind that some of the newer entrants have reemerged from an authoritarian past. The EU has managed to help turn these uncertain entities into democratic countries which observe, give, or take a bit the rule of law. There are many other EU achievements too, including the hesitant but palpable start of a foreign policy based on the concept of soft power, the beginning of a coordinated policy on environmental issues, and so on. The Eurozone does not include all EU countries and there is continued debate about whether it is a huge potential success or another grandiose failure. But it is there and despite all the discussion about its imminent collapse, it will probably stay.

So, although nobody could truthfully describe the EU as an unqualified success, it is evidently successful enough that the political elite of many nations outside it want their nations to join. The structure of the EU, however, is generally regarded even by its own admission as dysfunctional; its bureaucracy is a byword for officious, wasteful incompetence. There is no enthusiasm for the EU among the ordinary nonpolitical peoples of Europe. Attitudes vary from mild support to indifference to hostility.

The European Parliament in Strasbourg is seen as a powerless shambles. What is more, on the world stage the EU is a bit of a farce. Nothing in the symbolism of Europe will work until the current profoundly dysfunctional and sclerotic management structure, captured by the word 'Brussels,' is changed. And that looks unlikely at the moment. Not many Europeans seem to know how the EU works. How many Europeans know the difference between the Council and the Commission? No wonder the Lisbon treaty has created so much controversy. With the best will in the world, unless you happen to be a constitutional lawyer, you cannot make sense of it. On top of all that, right now nobody seems to be in charge. There is no commanding European leader. But when we know who is in charge, where the money goes, and where the influence lies, it is just possible that a European idea may have the footing to emerge.

Despite all this profound difficulty, there is a powerful, increasingly important political need for a strong European identity – or if you prefer, brand – because each individual European state is rapidly shrinking in global influence. It is clear that even the biggest European nations, Britain, France, and Germany, will not have much individual clout by say 2050. Indeed, the only way Europe could bring real influence to bear on the world as a whole in the political sphere in the twenty-first century would be if it began to operate more cohesively, even in some situations as a single entity. For example, on issues such as global warming, energy supply, and conservation and increasingly in peacekeeping around the world, Europe needs to act increasingly as one. Which means that, at the very least, there is an urgent need for the EU to encourage European-ness, for every member state and its citizens to identify more strongly with Europe – that is, to feel European more often and in more ways – than any of them do now. So whether you happen to be a Europhile or a Eurosceptic, you have to accept that the idea of a European voice in certain global issues is vital. And that means a much stronger, less tentative, and tenuous European brand.

The right kind of branding program might – just might – enable Europeans to identify with Europe, as much, but not more, than they identify right now with their own nation and the regions or cities in which they live. Europe is the most important branding candidate in the world today, because if a successful branding program which engages its citizens begins to develop, there will continue to be significant European influence in the world. If it does not, within 50 years European influence will decline, possibly to the point of virtually disappearing. If, however, a European idea *does* clearly emerge, the economic, cultural, and even political consequences will be profound – for the world. It could also show that national identity and affiliation can coexist with something bigger.

But how to achieve this? How to get half a billion Europeans of different nationalities to emotionally identify with a whole Europe? Just to make matters more complicated, it is not only the nation to which many Europeans owe loyalty – they also owe it to their specific region. Not only do many members of the EU have fragile and quite recently created or recreated national identities (as in Slovenia, Slovakia, and the three Baltics, to name just five), but many have powerful regions which battle with the nation itself for the loyalty of its citizens.

Many Basques, Catalans, Scots, Welsh, Corsicans, Flemings, Walloons, and others are confused about whether they belong to their own region, their nation, or Europe, or some or all of these and if so in what order. (And some are not confused at all: in their minds, their region presides.) The reasons why this has happened are of course historic. Multilingual, multinational, pan-European empires were frequently and quite arbitrarily patched together from a variety of fragments, sometimes without a single or dominant language or even a single or dominant religion. National borders were arbitrarily fixed and from time to time changed. Just look at the Versailles Treaty after World War I.

Methods and approaches and benefits: How Europe can earn identity rights

Clearly both substance and symbolism will come into play in creating a European umbrella identity. There must be bottom-up, populist influences, and top-down policies. There must be an attempt to create harmony in major matters, but the EU must also accept that it has to tolerate a wide variety. Are there any precedents which are worth examining? Has anything like the EU ever happened before? Well, there were the Habsburg and Ottoman Empires. But they were a long time ago. There are also some contemporary examples. Let us take two: India and the United States. And if we look at these models closely, we can see how a mixture of symbolism and cultural blending congeals into a viable and sustainable, yet not overpowering or all-consuming, national identity.

The Indian Example

India has 28 states, and at least 14 major languages, many different from each other like Finnish is from Portuguese. People from different Indian states often cannot read each other's scripts let alone understand what the other person is saying. The only truly common language is English, which is almost exclusively spoken by the highly educated elite. India has three or four significant religious groups. It has a 40-year-old insurgency in a group of northeastern states. Regionalism of every kind is rife. For example, the Maharashtrian majority in the western city of Mumbai regularly riots against southerners and easterners who choose to live there. Two of India's prime ministers, Indira Gandhi and Rajiv Gandhi, mother and son, were assassinated by separatists. That is without mentioning Kashmir, the hideous and endemic issues of corruption, or the grotesque differences in poverty and wealth and a thousand other difficulties. So India has plenty of problems. And it is quite as diverse as Europe – if not more so. Its collapse as a single entity has been predicted with regularity since its independence in 1947. Yet it holds itself together.

Why? Because somehow or other an idea of India has emerged both internally and externally. There are a few things, a very few things, that pull the nation together. One of these, of course, is fear of the other; fear maybe of Pakistan, fear definitely of China. Another is pride in national achievement: India, the nuclear power; India, the emerging major world economy. Another unifying force is the military: the Indian army, navy, and airforce. Religion, though, is not a uniting force. Hinduism is not a state religion, although some members of the right wing political party BJP would like it to be. Another, perhaps the most important, is that there are regular elections at all levels, national and regional. They may be deeply corrupt, but they do allow people to have a say. Somehow or other, nearly every Indian seems to say and feel somewhere in his or her heart, 'It is my India.'

So although there are many factors that pull India apart, there are many more that keep it together. If India were, like Europe, trying to put itself together, nobody would believe that it could succeed. But it is there and it will not break up. So you could say that if India can stay in one piece, then it is theoretically possible for Europe to be one piece too. Another example is of course the United States.

The US example

The United States began as 13 very independent colonies, solidified into 13 rather independent states (under the Articles of Confederation in 1777), and then resolidified into 13 not-so-independent states under the Federal Constitution a short while later. The last states to join the confederation, Alaska and Hawaii in 1959, were numbers 49 and 50. It is often said about Europe 'But what do Finland and Greece have in common?' Well, how about Hawaii and Maine – a Polynesian island in the Pacific, a patch of New England with an Atlantic seacoast and a border with Canada. Yet it would never even occur to a Hawaiian or a Mainer that anything more in common were needed; that they are both American is sufficient to bind them in national interest. How could this be, and what can Europe learn from it?

In their book *Brand America: The Making, Unmaking and Remaking of the Greatest National Identity of All Time* – which was appropriately subtitled, in its first edition, 'the mother of all brands' – Simon Anholt and Jeremy Hildreth (2010) tell and comment upon the story of a country that has in many ways been understood and managed as a brand from its very beginnings (e.g., was not the Declaration of Independence, among other things, the ultimate press release for a new venture?). One of the points Anholt and Hildreth make is that the idea of 'an America' came first from abroad, before the concept was thinkable in the colonies. Part of the reason for this, according to the historian John M. Murrin, is that 'the British worried about the whole because they did not understand the parts, and they reified their concerns into a totality they called America.... In a word, America was Britain's idea' (quoted in Huntington, 1998, p. 111).

All the same, as the American self-concept grew stronger, colonists began to identify less with Britain, correspondingly, more and more non-British symbols began to appear in the colonies. Between 1735 and the early 1760s, only about 6 percent of the flags and other symbols used in America identified the population as American. After the imposition of the so-called Intolerable Acts (and there is a bit of branding in that moniker!), the use of explicitly American symbols rose rapidly in the mid-1760s to between 50 and 60 percent and remained at that level throughout the Revolution (Merritt, 1966, p. 144). And this is often the way with brands: a brand can be the sum of an observer's associations with the product or organisation. Sometimes it is external observers, with the distance and objectivity to see the wood for the trees, who discern a brand first, and later it is observers inside the organisation (or country) who take up the mantle in earnest.

In the United States, national identity and therefore national branding grew organically although even in this case there were some massive strains, like the bloody near-destruction of American unity in the Civil War. Over time, Brand America became significantly self-perpetuating, through voluntary practice and symbolism. Naturally, major national achievements (e.g., putting a man on the moon) and general success, high performance, and international prominence (e.g., continuous rise of living standards at home, garnering gold medals in spades abroad, etc.) have encouraged the process. As a result, it is the rare American who is not possessed of an enviably deep-seated and (mostly) benign patriotism.

SO WHAT ABOUT EUROPE?

So what to do about Europe? Is there a European identity, a super national identity in which somehow or other all Europeans share? Clearly there is – sort of. There is a kind of religious dimension. However willingly or reluctantly, devoutly or atavistically, most Europeans still identify themselves as deriving from a

Christian tradition. Of course, there are significant religious minorities as well as an influential body of skeptics, but Europe is still mostly Christian – kind of.

Then there are the historical roots. Although Europeans have been engaged in the most vicious internecine wars over centuries, broadly speaking they derive from a similar historical background – and give or take a bit, most countries have followed a similar political and economic trajectory over the centuries. In terms of social and cultural life, agriculture has given way to industry at approximately the same pace and so on.

In other words, although it needs detailed exploration and explanation, there *is* such a thing as Europeaness. And although 'Made in Europe' does not mean much yet, the potential exists. On the basis of anecdotal evidence, both Americans and Japanese seem to think of European products as small, beautifully designed and exuding a kind of expensive classiness. So out of that funny old mix, can a shared European identity emerge? Can a European brand be created? Here are some ideas that illustrate our thinking about how to proceed, if and when the organisational and structural mess is sorted out.

* *Look first to a new breed of Europeans.* Increasingly, there is a population of people (and enterprises also) about whose national origins and allegiances one could only say, in the words of the Facebook generation, 'it's complicated.' In this group will be the individuals who are the early adopters of a pan-European identity. Take, for example, a young woman of the authors' acquaintance. She was born in Germany to Italian parents and is equally fluent in German and Italian (she also speaks English extremely well and knows some French). She has lived in London for many years and has an Estonian partner. When asked by somebody 'Where are you from?' (while on a trip to Australia, for instance), it would be handy for her to be say 'I am from Europe' (as someone from Massachusetts would say 'I am American'). And certainly her children would be inclined to say, if such an answer were common 'My parents were European' rather than tell the whole story to every inquirer. Our point is that increasingly, national identity is becoming unwieldy for some people, and when it becomes easier, clearer, and more fun to declare themselves simply European, they probably will. This is particularly true with Schengen, the agreement that permits most Europeans to travel within most of the EU without passports.

* *Reflect the world's comprehension of Europe back to Europeans.* If Europeans grasp that non-Europeans are beginning to have a working use of a cohesive Europe, they will be more accepting of Europe as an umbrella identity. When the rest of the world talks about, say, the European attitude to climate change, this will apply a self-fulfilling prophecy toward bringing about a stronger sense of European-ness among Europeans.

* *Decrease and discourage the habitual use of national identity elements and affiliations.* In the United States, Missouri and Illinois both have state songs. Yet when baseball teams from Kansas City and Chicago meet to play, only one anthem is sung before the game begins: The Star Spangled Banner. In a Europe with a strong identity, national anthems and other identity elements, in European sports and other areas, would take a

backseat to pan-European markers. In commerce, too, national origins must be allowed to be downplayed for those who wish to operate that way. Wally Olins' own company, Saffron, has its founding offices in Madrid and London and advises clients from everywhere; it would, if it could, become incorporated, and conduct and present itself, as a European Corporation.

- *Create and/or encourage the wide use of additional and alternative new pan-European symbols.* The EU flag represents an organisation not a place. It is, therefore, unlikely to strike an emotional chord with Europeans. Other symbols – and it is perfectly okay if they are unofficial – must be available for people to use to proclaim an emotional allegiance to Europe. (Rem Koolhaas made a stab at a European flag; perhaps his interpretation should be revived.) At the same time, it would be helpful if there were Europeanised versions of national flags available for people to use to display a particular hierarchy of identity. By this we mean some visual combination or remix of a national flag with the EU identity elements (blue field, gold stars). Nobody would be forced to fly these flags, but they would out there for those who wanted to use them.

- *Promote the Euro as acceptable tender in all EU countries.* After its flag, a nation's most significant symbol of identity is its money. Dissolving the sense of separateness that results from neighbours having different currencies is a reasonable goal of those who support a more unified European identity. Of course, countries that do not wish to adopt the Euro cannot be forced to, but there is nothing to prevent retailers and other businesses from treating the Euro as 'real money' even in non-Euro regimes. A related idea would be to introduce a line of European airmail stamps, good for posting a letter from anywhere to anywhere within Europe. With communications being largely electronic, this action would be mostly symbolic – but the symbolism is important.

- *Speak English.* There are one or two other areas that are so contentious as to be currently unacceptable, like which should be the prime language of Europe. Clearly today, although quite unofficially, it is English. But nobody dares say so. The reality is that when a German and a Spaniard want to have a chat, the language they will almost certainly use will be English. Almost all pan-European businesses conduct their activities in English even when they have no UK or US operations. The French may not like it, but it is so. None of the major languages spoken in Europe, and few if any of the minor ones, are in danger of falling into disuse. Anyone who has experienced such an English-fluent society as, for example, Sweden, can see that the argument that widespread knowledge of English poses some sort of threat to national identity is a canard (and insofar as that belief inhibits local citizens from learning the international language, a pernicious canard). We are talking about English supplementing not supplanting other tongues. It will help Europeans feel like a common people if they are all *able* to speak a common language, even if that language is English and even if 90 percent of the time they are in their own country speaking their national languages and local dialects. But how to handle this?

- *Devise some kind of European pan-national service.* Another significant binding force is service. Military service has created and sustained imperial and national loyalties since before the Roman Empire. Flags, uniforms, music, languages, mutual trust, the camaraderie inspired by living and fighting together is a powerful influence in creating loyalty. Currently, Israel, a nation formed from over 100 different nationalities, derives a great deal of its cohesion from the Israel Defence Force (IDF).

  But there is not much chance of a European military force yet, even though the British and the French, currently the most powerful European military nations, are talking to each other (as we write this) about sharing a nuclear submarine fleet. Who they might conceivably use it against is, perhaps conveniently, not under discussion. So the military idea as a unifier is out, probably permanently. But what about a European version of the Peace Corps or Britain's VSO? If all Europeans between 18 and 20 could volunteer to serve in a unit which emphasised the European identity in its activities, this might act both as a unifier for generations within Europe and as a signal to the outside world that Europe does things differently. The EU being what it is, there is probably something like that already. It is just buried so deep in bureaucracy we do not know about it.

- *Teaching history.* Another issue is a common historical sense. This is difficult. Almost all history is taught with extreme national bias, in which neighbouring nations who have been fighting each other for hundreds of years are systematically vilified and demeaned. Some kind of common ground in history education at secondary and university levels would help. Dealing with this issue is going to be very difficult, but an attempt might be made to create some kind of harmony or at least to reduce national prejudice. Of course, there are very many intellectually significant pan-European activities which already exist like the Erasmus exchange student program as well as major infrastructure projects, some of which seek to deal with this issue. Those that already operate should be much more heavily promoted and a series of new cross-border educational initiatives should be introduced.

These are just a few possible initiatives, anyway – just for starters. The principal aim, behind these and other initiatives, is 'Eventually, European individuals, organisations and governments must align with, and frequently display, a common identity in which their Europeaness is as or more apparent than their nationality.'

Effective branding would make the EU more functional and more comprehensible. Many of its more acute problems would begin to disappear. Of course, special interest groups promoting one nation's interests over another would remain, but where does not that happen? Pork-barrel politics is a familiar phenomenon in the United States, too. The EU would function better as a unit and its authority would not be so thoroughly, routinely, and frustratingly questioned; this would leave it freer to do its work, with the people of Europe feeling less distanced – even slightly more involved.

Paradoxically, it is likely that regionalism would become less disruptive. Because if the EU worked properly, it would relieve many of the pressures which many European nations currently face from their own regions. Some mini regions, smaller regional groupings – some across borders already exist; an Alpine region embracing parts of Slovenia, Italy, Austria, and Germany, a Baltic region – entities which could give them the kind of outlet they seem to want. Some of the regions would have greater power and influence, particularly cultural influence, than they have now. And with a stronger extra-national identity to align with, they might also feel more comfortable relaxing the anti-national identity they currently feel duty bound to cling to as an expression of their regional identity.

What is more, an effectively branded Europe could help to ensure that Europe sustains a significant position in a multipolar world of new Great Powers. In this capacity, as we have already posited, the importance of a real brand for Europe as a focus for loyalty, complementary too and living with national and regional loyalties, cannot be overemphasised. It is one of the most important issues facing our century. And this kind of a Europe would be a model for other parts of the world facing similar identity crises, concerns, and complexities.

CONCLUSION

All this thinking is of course way beyond the vision, authority, competence, and mindset of the people who currently carry out so-called national branding programs – the politicians, but especially the advisers and functionaries. As for the consultants and suppliers, unfortunately, most of the time nowadays, those tasked or employed to 'do nation branding' (a funny way of understanding things anyway) are either local bureaux who lack the necessary perspective of the outsider, or foreign advertising, PR, or branding agencies who do not think deeply enough, who do not take into account the sweep of history or the profound and subtle psychology of the human experience of place identity. What is needed, in our view, at least to start the process is a lot more professionalism and serious thinking. It will take years. But the time to start is now (Figure 4.1).

Figure 4.1 European Union: When are you going to get on with it?

References

Anholt, S., & Hildreth, J. (2010). *Brand America: The making, unmaking and remaking of the greatest national image of all time* (2nd ed.). London: Marshall Cavendish.

Huntington, S. P. (1998). *The clash of civilizations and the remaking of the world order*. London: Simon & Schuster.

Merritt, R. L. (1966). *Symbols of American community 1735–1775*. New Haven: Yale University Press.

PART 2

Destination Brand Challenges

Those who are responsible for marketing tourism places face considerable challenges today. It is a very tough operating environment. Consumer confidence is fragile and many of the world's more economically developed economies have seen market failures, recession, and weak economic confidence, while threats to political stability, peace, and the environment are continuing global concerns. In this environment, DMOs face serious challenges and their cost, relevance, and value-for-money are under extreme scrutiny. We saw in Part 1 that place reputation is derived from a host of sources. Part 2 underlines that in our disintermediated world, where the consumer shapes the brand and the media, DMOs do not have control over the product, the image, story, the media, or the message. Thus, Part 2 comprises of chapters, which address nine key challenges in tourism destination brand management, all of which pose both threats and opportunities for tourism places: ethics, leadership, partnership, authenticity, aesthetics, tone of voice, the digital revolution,; measurement, and scenario planning.

While we have seen in Part 1 that how a place's reputation exists whatever its DMO does, a destination's communities, stakeholders, and leaders can still have a vision of how they want to see it and how they want it to be seen. Brand management can enable its key stakeholders to achieve this vision, attain differentiation, and secure a competitive identity. In this sense, DMOs remain responsible for the *management* and *stewardship* of destination reputations. In the next nine chapters, our contributors demonstrate the key role of DMOs in supporting and facilitating place brand management and the issues they face. While their place within the destination system should not be over-emphasised, they do play a key role. This involves speaking not only to the consumers, but also to all destination's stakeholders and establishing, nurturing, and servicing partnerships (as demonstrated by Chapters 7–9) and providing ethical leadership (see Chapters by 5 and 6). This is where the DMO comes into its own as the brand steward, leading, guiding and coordinating the destination's online and offline "tone of voice" (see Chapters 10 and 11) and providing research and evaluation (see Chapters 12 and 13).

Destination brand managers and DMO executives are beset by crucial challenges, the scope and scale of which may seem daunting. These challenges include the need to steward the authenticity and aesthetics of a destination in a culturally sensitive and ethical way (see Chapters 5, 8, and 9), which empowers local communities, involves relevant stakeholders (Chapter 7), avoids exploitative branding campaigns that stereotype certain communities, and ensures that the destination brand is set on a sustainable development trajectory (Chapter 5). However, those responsible for stewarding destination brand reputations must face these challenges and the next nine chapters outline how that is possible in today's rapidly and radically changing world.

CHAPTER

The ethical challenge

Keith Dinnie

INTRODUCTION

The ethical challenges in destination branding are numerous and wide ranging. These challenges derive primarily from the infinite number of groups and individuals with a legitimate claim to be considered stakeholders in the destination brand, along with the often passionately held opinions and beliefs that such stakeholders hold with regard to the manner in which the destination brand should or should not be managed. Branding a destination is a highly political activity. Those involved in destination brand management need to possess or quickly acquire skills not only in the tools and concepts of brand management, but also in the art of negotiation, change management, and conflict resolution. This skill set should, moreover, be underpinned by an awareness of the importance of managing the destination brand in such a way that it follows a sustainable development trajectory.

Numerous objections must be overcome when branding destinations. Morgan, Pritchard and Pride (2002, p. 3) have noted that many people argue that 'places are too complex to include in branding discussions since they have too many stakeholders and too little management control, have underdeveloped identities and are not perceived as brands by the general public.' Whilst these reservations regarding the practicality of branding places are certainly understandable and justifiable to a certain extent, the fact remains that if a place does not actively attempt to manage its image and reputation then it will be either ignored by external audiences or 'branded' by the media and other parties which may not always be positively disposed toward the place in question. Negative stereotypes may persist or the destination may languish in obscurity if positive steps are not taken to actively manage the destination brand. In this light, there is an ethical obligation on the relevant authorities to take action to protect the reputation of their destination. The issue of management control, or lack thereof, that is alluded to by Morgan et al. is a concern that troubles some decision makers who may be sceptical

© 2011 Published by Elsevier Ltd. All rights reserved.
DOI: 10.1016/B978-0-08-096930-5.10005-9

of the value of allocating financial resources to an undertaking as uncertain as branding a place. However, it is a characteristic of today's digital world that consumers – increasingly empowered by almost unlimited access to knowledge and information – have already wrested varying degrees of 'control' into their own hands and away from brand managers. There is no turning back the tide. The days of total management control over a brand are largely over; this applies to product and consumer brands as much as it does to place brands. A simple shift in mindset is required from the traditional but largely outmoded view that a brand can be *controlled* to a more modest but still important view that a brand can be *managed*, albeit to a lesser extent than in the pre-digital past.

The potential benefits of branding a place are so overwhelming that they significantly outweigh the objections that are routinely raised against destination branding. Baker (2007, p. 41) provides a compelling and comprehensive summary of these benefits when he states that branding a place 'creates a unifying focus for all public, private, and non-profit sector organisations that rely on the image of the place and its attractiveness... Corrects out of date, inaccurate or unbalanced perceptions... Increases the attractiveness of local products... Increases the ability to attract, recruit and retain talented people... Contributes toward a broader economic base.' Although Baker is referring specifically to the context of branding small cities, the benefits that he outlines deriving from an actively managed destination-branding strategy apply equally to other types of place such as regions or nations. The unifying force of a clearly articulated place brand strategy should, if implemented correctly, stimulate enhanced levels of stakeholder cooperation as all parties reap rewards in terms of attracting tourism, investment, and talent to the place as well as stimulating demand for the place's products and services.

A further objection that needs to be overcome concerns the ethics of treating places as brands. There is a widespread perception in society that branding is a manipulative and ethically dubious activity, which may perhaps be tolerated in the purely commercial arena of product branding but which is inappropriate for places. The irony of branding having a bad brand itself has been highlighted by Anholt (2007, p. 3), who suggests that 'there's a lot of mistrust about brands and branding these days, and this isn't helped by the fact that nobody seems to agree on what the words really mean.' In many cases, this mistrust is deserved. Hyperbole abounds in the world of branding and it is unsurprising that many people have a jaundiced view of it. For some, branding is nothing more than hype and propaganda; for others, branding is viewed more positively as a technique of reputation management and, in the context of destination branding, a means to encourage economic development in myriad forms.

Conceptually, two key issues with respect to the appropriateness of applying branding techniques to destinations arise as follows: first, who has got the legitimacy to act as the destination brand manager, and second, who should decide upon the brand values that are going to underpin the destination brand strategy (Dinnie, 2008, pp. 169–170). Both issues demand careful consideration by destination-branding policy makers, as failure to adequately address them will inevitably result in many stakeholders feeling alienated and excluded, which in turn will lead to an unwillingness on the part of those stakeholders to participate in the strategy. The need to focus on these ethical questions is one manifestation of the difference between branding a place compared with branding a product or service. This is emphasised by Avraham and Ketter (2008, p. 7), who used the term 'social-public marketing' to describe the marketing of places, and who declared that for such marketing to succeed, 'local decision makers must act democratically, not in an elitist or patronising way; they have to cooperate in the process with the place's residents and other local players; the marketing plan should not be imposed on the market as a top-down decision but evolve bottom-up; and it should be based on the benefit to the general public rather than to the decision makers or their narrow interests.' If a destination brand strategy is perceived to be nothing more than a self-serving exercise hatched by incumbent politicians and their cabals, then it is unlikely to inspire allegiance from the requisite broad range of stakeholders.

This chapter examines the various ethical challenges to destination branding outlined above, in particular it:

* examines the concept of commodification of the destination brand;
* discusses the arguments for and against this controversial phenomenon;
* analyses the importance of stakeholder mapping and citizen inclusion;
* reviews the question of sustainable development and its relevance to destination brand management.

COMMODIFICATION OF THE DESTINATION BRAND

Commodification is widely – though not exclusively – viewed in the tourism literature as a negative and undesirable phenomenon. The branding of a destination is thought by some to represent an exploitative process through which the multilayered richness of a place's culture and history is reduced to the status of a mere commodity, akin to a product in a supermarket. Authors such as Klieger (1990) and Dearden and Harron (1992) have warned that the commodification of a place's culture results in the destination appearing less authentic and therefore of less value, as local residents are turned into objects of amusement and cultural 'presentations' become increasingly detached from reality. The notion of 'authenticity' is, however, more problematic than it appears at first sight. Cohen (1988) suggests that far from having an objective quality, authenticity is socially constructed and varies according to the tourists and their point of view. This view chimes with a well-established stream of thought in the national identity literature, embodied in Hobsbawm and Ranger's (1983) seminal text, *The Invention of Tradition*. As the title indicates, the key contention of Hobsbawm and Ranger's book is that even though traditions may appear to be ancient, in reality such 'traditions' are often of relatively recent origin and rooted in a single event or short period of time. The authors also argue that there is probably no time or place that has not seen the 'invention' of tradition. Of course, the ethical justification of such invention of tradition is constantly open for debate and discussion; however, it puts into perspective the activities of destination-branding organisations whose task frequently involves the invention – or at least the heightened communication – of tradition.

The repackaging of a place brand, which in marketing terminology may in some cases approximate to the 'invention of tradition', is nothing new. It is not something that can be attributed exclusively to manipulative twentieth and twenty-first century marketers. The creation of a Scottish culture based on Highland imagery and tartanry, for example, has been challenged on the grounds that such a culture is the product of the established social order who were happy to see the invention of a Walter Scott-land based on fakelore rather than folklore, and who peddled such symbolic representations of the country even though this newly fashioned identity was bogus (Finlay, 1994). Some may feel that such criticisms are extreme. Ironically, a major challenge for those engaged in the branding of contemporary Scotland is to break out of the narrow but potent tartan-bedecked imagery that dominates external perceptions of that nation. For the purposes of branding Scotland as a tourism destination brand, such imagery remains useful and powerful; however, in terms of attracting foreign direct investment or promoting the export of hi-tech products, such imagery, redolent as it is of a mythical Brigadoon-like chimera, is less helpful.

Eloquent rebuttals to the accusation that the commodification of a place is unethical have been made by Abram (1996, p. 198), who contends that commodification can be viewed as 'part of a very positive process by which people are beginning to re-evaluate their history and shake off the shame of peasantry,' and also by Cole (2007, pp. 945–946), who states that 'understood from the perspective of the local people, cultural commodification can be positive... it needs also to be recognised as part of a process of empowerment.' Cole's claims are based on her long-term study of Eastern Indonesian villagers' experience of heritage-based tourism promotion. According to Cole, the villagers do not feel demeaned or exploited by the fact that their villages have been commodified as national heritage sites for tourists to visit. On the contrary, Cole claims (2007, p. 954) that 'tourism is bringing the villagers dignity and confidence in their beliefs... Many expressed the view that tourists make them feel proud that their culture is known to outsiders.' The commodification of their villages is thus considered to be a means of social and political empowerment for the villagers. Interestingly, prior to becoming an academic, Cole ran her own tour operating business in Indonesia. For those who vilify commodification, Cole's professional involvement in the tourism industry in Indonesia will be seen as a sign of her complicity in the commodification of the villages reported on in her study; whereas for those who share Cole's view of commodification as a benevolent and empowering force for developing places, her practitioner experience lends considerable weight to her observations and conclusions.

A particular manifestation of place brand commodification can be seen in the proliferation of festivals as a means to promote villages, towns, cities, and regions. Indeed, the ever increasing number of festivals may lead to an over-production of events and consequent loss of authenticity that has been characterised by Getz (2007) as 'festivalisation'. Festivals have been defined as 'place-contingent cultural politics' and 'political instruments and promotional products at the same time' (Jeong & Santos, 2004, p. 640). In their study of the Kangnung Dano Festival (KDF) in Korea, Jeong and Santos explore the conflicts between globalisation, tradition, and place identity that are inherent in the use of festivals as a destination-branding tool. The authors arrive at a similar conclusion to Cole above regarding the empowering potential of marketing a place, stating that 'the debate over promotion and commercialisation of place can empower marginalised groups, such as women and youth, because the values implicit in commercialisation, such as innovation and emphasis on the customer, better match their views of the meaning of the KDF than those held by the dominant group' (Jeong & Santos, 2004, p. 653). In the context of four urban ethnic festivals held in the different neighbourhoods of Toronto, the political dimension of cultural festivals is also discussed by McClinchey (2008, p. 251), who identifies 'such key realities as politics and image, social identity and reputation, cultural authenticity and neighbourhood differentiation as concerns for festival promotion and place marketing.' These complex issues represent significant ethical challenges for destination-branding organisations to manage.

STAKEHOLDER MAPPING AND CITIZEN INCLUSION

One of the key ethical challenges facing destination-branding managers is to ensure that all stakeholders with a legitimate claim to participate are included in an appropriate way in the place-branding strategy. The degree of stakeholder participation, as well as the precise stages of strategy formulation and implementation during which such participation is to be encouraged, requires careful thought by place brand managers. Insufficient inclusiveness of relevant stakeholders will lead to the strategy being either ignored or sabotaged by those who feel excluded, whereas excessive inclusiveness will lead to paralysis and inertia as different groups and individuals seek to prioritise their competing agendas. Stakeholder analysis and mapping provides decision makers with a useful means to address the challenge of reasoned and practical inclusiveness in branding a destination.

A systematic approach to stakeholder identification and salience is advocated by Currie, Seaton and Wesley (2009, p. 41), who present the argument that 'in order to produce equitable and environmentally sustainable tourism developments multiple stakeholders must be involved in the process of planning and implementing the project.' This view is also espoused by Sautter and Leisen (1999), who propose a model for the management of stakeholders in tourism planning; Simpson (2001), who stresses the need for community involvement as a key component of sustainable tourism development; and Murphy and Murphy (2004), whose strategic approach to tourism management also underlines the importance of community involvement. Decision makers should, according to Lane (2005), move from tokenistic forms of public participation to a more collaborative and partnering form. Lane's assertion rests on the assumption that there is a demand for public participation; in many cases, apathy rather than eager participation may be the norm and in such circumstances the salience of each stakeholder group needs to be evaluated.

In an excellent and insightful study that goes beyond the usual calls for automatic inclusiveness of all stakeholders, Rocha and Miles (2009, p. 445) argue that 'the sustainability of inter-organisational communities depends on how rich is the set of assumptions about human nature upon which they are based... In order to develop and sustain collaborative capabilities in inter-organisational communities, a set of assumptions that takes both self-regarding and others'-regarding preferences as ends is required to avoid any kind of instrumentalisation of collaboration, which is an end in itself.' Rocha and Miles believe that the main challenge faced by networks of stakeholders is the development of an enduring sense of membership and a solid economic base. In an earlier publication, Miles, Miles and Snow (2005) present a list of the main assumptions that underpin a successful collaborative network of stakeholders as follows: expectation that membership carries a positive economic value; mutual identification of interests; attention to the intrinsic value of relationships; information sharing; long-term commitment; continuous pursuit of equitable rewards; taking pleasure in acknowledging others' ideas; and, voluntary collaborative behaviour by independently owned and governed firms. In the context of destination brand management, such assumptions will not occur spontaneously; a core element of the strategy leadership's remit will be to nurture the development of the information sharing, continuous pursuit of equitable rewards, and long-term commitment alluded to by Miles et al.

A conceptual framework for the identification and salience of stakeholders at the level of branding a nation as a destination is presented by Dinnie and Fola (2009) in their study of the nation branding of Cyprus. Although tourism and shipping represent by far the most important elements of the Cyprus nation brand, stakeholders from other facets of Cypriot life also need to be included in the amplification and diversification of Cyprus as a multifaceted brand. The conceptual framework developed by Dinnie and Fola is constructed along two axes representing level of stakeholder participation and stakeholder salience. The framework is shown in Figure 5.1.

From the framework it can be seen that there exists a very uneven level of participation by different stakeholder groups in the branding of Cyprus. The heavy emphasis on tourism-related stakeholders needs to be complemented by enhanced participation of stakeholders from other areas of economic development such as export promotion and investment attraction. The framework is designed to serve as a useful tool for policy makers to assist them in their management of the various stakeholder groups who can potentially play a contributory role in building the Cyprus destination brand. The ethical dimension of the framework resides in the evaluations that need to be made in assigning degrees of salience to different stakeholders, which is a politically sensitive issue that needs to be handled carefully.

Stakeholder mapping can be applied not only within a place but also between places. In destination branding there often exist opportunities for

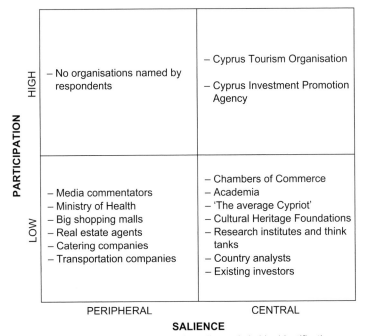

Figure 5.1 Conceptual framework for nation branding stakeholder identification. Source: Dinnie and Fola, 2009.

collaboration between different places, usually neighbouring places which may traditionally have viewed each other as rivals rather than allies. One example of such collaboration at international level is the 'European Quartet One Melody' co-branding initiative launched by the national tourism organisations of the Czech Republic, Slovakia, Hungary, and Poland. This campaign aimed to stimulate tourism to the Central Europe region and to encourage tourists to visit each country rather than just one country.

In other contexts, stakeholders can also be identified at subnational regional level. For example, a network of stakeholders from seven different administrative areas within three bordering prefectures of Japan have come together to forge a collaborative strategy designed to simultaneously promote their individual place brands as well as their joint region brand. The seven administrative areas are Tokamachi, Uonuma, Minamiuonuma, Tsunan, Sakae, Yuzawa, and Minakami. The three prefectures to which the seven areas belong are Nigata, Nagano, and Gunma. It is highly unusual for administrative areas from three different prefectures to collaborate on such an initiative. The basis for this unusual collaboration lies in the common geographic and climatic characteristics shared by the seven areas – each area is mountainous and receives extremely heavy snowfall, which has until now stifled economic development due to the inaccessibility of the areas for half of every year. A prime driving force behind the collaborative campaign is to transform the consistently heavy snowfall from a weakness into a strength. The lack of industrial development has a plus side in that the region can still offer an experience of 'old Japan' through its unspoilt nature and traditional culture. A simple but powerful name has been chosen for the campaign: 'Snow Country.' For domestic tourists, this name is extremely evocative because it is also the title of a very famous book of the same name written by Yasunari Kawabata, the first Japanese writer to win the Nobel Prize for Literature. The book *Snow Country* is based in what has now been called the 'Snow Country' tourism zone.

The benefits of a collaborative approach to regional destination marketing amongst convention and visitors bureaux (CVBs) have also been demonstrated by Naipaul, Wang and Okumus (2009, p. 462), who conclude that 'forming partnerships among neighbouring destinations is beneficial for all participating CVBs in terms of enhancing product portfolio, cost reduction, and efficiency.' Collaborative activities by neighbouring destinations in a region can diversify a region's product mix (Palmer and Bejou, 1995), whilst the likelihood of success is greatly increased by the presence of a collaboration champion (Little, Leverick, & Bruce, 1995). Numerous pitfalls must, however, be avoided if the fruits of a collaborative process are to be enjoyed, chief among which are mistrust and suspicion amongst collaborative partners as well as the failure by certain stakeholders to recognise the real value of collaboration (Fyall & Garrod, 2004).

Citizen inclusion, or public participation, appears widely in the literature as a prerequisite for successful destination branding. Lane (2005, p. 283) declares that '... public participation has made a comeback... participation has become a central feature of making and implementing policy.' It has, however, been emphasised that public participation must be meaningful and that 'there is a critical difference between going through the empty ritual of participation and having the real power needed to affect the outcomes of the process' (Arnstein, 1969, p. 216). There are many different stages of the decision-making process at which the public may make interventions. Painter (1992, p. 24) outlines a number of possible points where public participation may occur, '... from setting the agenda, defining problems, collecting information and analysing it, identifying and selecting possible options, legitimising the preferred option by a formal decision, through to implementation and evaluating outcomes.' When grappling with the challenge of citizen inclusion, policy makers need to bear in mind that local residents are not necessarily a homogeneous group; in reality, residents are likely to hold diverse perceptions and attitudes toward tourism (Andriotis & Vaughn, 2003). Policy makers need to be aware of the range of residents' attitudes toward tourism as such attitudes will likely affect residents' behaviour toward tourists (Nicholas, Thapa, & Yong, 2009). In their case study of the Pitons Management Area near Soufriere on the island of St. Lucia in the Caribbean, Nicholas et al. (2009, p. 390) point out the danger of failure to achieve citizen inclusion when they state that 'the notable lack of involvement of residents presented critical implications for the sustainability of the site.'

In some cases, there may be a conscious and deliberate decision to exclude certain groups from the development of the destination brand through a rewriting of history in societies undergoing dramatic transformation (Goulding & Domic, 2009). Goulding and Domic's analysis is focused on the case of Croatia in the aftermath of the brutal disintegration of the former Yugoslavia. In a study of the less traumatic context of Australia's Gold Coast, Marzano and Scott (2009, p. 247) present a riposte to the conventional wisdom that the destination-branding process can only occur through an inclusive and collaborative process, stating that 'despite numerous conceptualisations of destination branding as a collaborative process, this paper finds that power is exerted in various forms and a destination branding process can have a positive outcome even if there is a lack of unity and collaboration amongst stakeholders.' Marzano and Scott's assertion may well be greeted with relief by destination-branding policy makers who feel assailed on all sides by conflicting demands, inconsistent support, and political in-fighting.

SUSTAINABLE DEVELOPMENT

Perhaps the most significant ethical challenge in destination branding is to adhere to an approach that will lead to sustainable development. Tourism is an essentially ambivalent phenomenon characterised by the well-known paradox that the more popular a destination becomes, the more degradation it suffers due to the influx of excessive numbers of visitors, to the point that the original attraction of the destination may be destroyed. Even eco-tourism is not immune from this potential spiral of degradation. Eco-tourism has been vividly disparaged as 'ego-tourism' (Wheeller, 2005), whilst Hjalager (1999, p. 4) asserts that in a tourism context, '... symbolic consumption is predominantly connected to activities such as trekking in wild mountains or river areas, expeditions to the Arctic or to tropical rain forests, etc... Tourism experiences of this kind are often characterised as eco-tourism in spite of the fact that, if expanded to include larger numbers of guests, environmental problems would probably be created or worsened.'

The environment-tourism nexus is further explored by Holden (2009, p. 373), who states that 'environmental policy has to date had little influence upon the workings of the tourism market, the supply and demand elements of which determine the "use" or "non-use" of nature.' Holden goes on to identify the two main approaches that policy makers can adopt in order to reduce the negative environmental impacts of tourism upon the environment, namely price control and quota control, exemplified by the tourism policy of Bhutan in which a quota of twenty thousand tourists per annum is set. These tourists are all required to pay a fee of US$200 per day during their visit. However, Holden acknowledges that this approach involves government interference in the workings of the free market and therefore it is unlikely to be embraced in today's neo-liberal political economy. Nonetheless, others have called for an interventionist approach in the belief that 'from a social point of view, taxing tourism can be welfare-enhancing, as externalities of rapid tourism growth should be internalised' (Sheng & Tsui, 2009, p. 627). A different perspective on sustainable tourism development is adopted by Koutsouris (2009, p. 577), who concludes that '... the success of area-based sustainable tourism development... largely lies in providing local actors with the means to engage in a process of managing complex and potentially risky situations; the collective learning of stakeholders, supporting multiple-loop learning, is a key mechanism for arriving at more desirable (sustainable) futures.'

One of the most compelling reasons for policy makers to address the ethical challenge of sustainable development is the potential for destination brands to use sustainability as a differentiator. Chang (2009, p. 121) states that 'with increasing awareness of environmental issues, sustainability has become an important element of destination management,' whilst Insch (2009) develops a conceptualisation of green destination brands based on the ways in which destinations highlight their green credentials as part of their brand identity. Further impetus to the use of sustainability and green credentials as destination brand differentiators will in future be required through the development of appropriate scales to measure objectively the 'greenness' or sustainability of destinations, so that consumers can compare different destinations on the basis of objective data rather than on potentially misleading or exaggerated claims made by the destinations themselves through their own marketing communications. Such indices have been developed to measure the social responsibility performance of corporations (Fowler & Hope, 2007). There is no reason why similar indices cannot be developed to measure the sustainable development performance of destinations.

CONCLUSION

Ethical challenges abound in destination branding. These challenges include the need to manage the destination brand in a culturally respectful manner that empowers rather than demeans local residents; ensuring that all stakeholders who are willing to make a positive contribution to the destination-branding strategy are invited to do so; avoiding the exploitation of branding campaigns that benefit only certain cliques rather than the community as a whole; establishing a structure and process to facilitate a collaborative process amongst stakeholders, with the caveat that it may not always be possible or even desirable to adopt a fully inclusive approach in circumstances where some stakeholders are apathetic; and the immense and urgent task of ensuring that the destination brand is set on a sustainable development trajectory. The scope and scale of such challenges may seem daunting. However, the onus is on policy makers to face up to these challenges, as the outcomes of a destination-branding strategy can have a significant impact for better or worse on the lives of the people who live, work, study, invest, buy from, or visit there.

References

Abram, S. (1996). Reactions to tourism: a view from the deep green heart of France. In J. Boissevain (Ed.), *Coping with tourists. European reactions to mass tourism* (pp. 174–203). Oxford: Berghahn Books.

Andriotis, K., & Vaughn, R. (2003). Urban residents' attitudes toward tourism development: the case of crete. *Journal of Travel Research, 42*(2), 172–185.

Anholt, S. (2007). *Competitive identity*. Basingstoke: Palgrave Macmillan.

Arnstein, S. R. (1969). Ladder of citizen participation. *Journal of American Institute of Planners*, *35*(4), 216–224.

Avraham, E., & Ketter, E. (2008). *Media strategies for marketing places in crisis: Improving the image of cities, countries and tourist destinations*. Oxford: Butterworth-Heinemann.

Baker, B. (2007). *Destination branding for small cities*. Oregon: Creative Leap.

Chang, T.-Z. (2009). Sustainability as differentiation tool in destination branding: An empirical study, 3rd International Conference on Destination Branding and Marketing, Institute for Tourism Studies, Macao SAR, China, December 2–4, 2009, 121–129.

Cohen, E. (1988). Authenticity and commoditization in tourism. *Annals of Tourism Research*, *15*(3), 371–386.

Cole, S. (2007). Beyond authenticity and commodification. *Annals of Tourism Research*, *34*(4), 943–960.

Currie, R. R., Seaton, S., & Wesley, F. (2009). Determining stakeholders for feasibility analysis. *Annals of Tourism Research*, *36*(1), 41–63.

Dearden, P., & Harron, S. (1992) Case study: tourism and the hill tribes of Thailand. In B. Wheeller & M. Hall (Eds.), *Special interest trourism* (pp. 95–104). London: Belhaven.

Dinnie, K. (2008). *Nation branding – Concepts, issues, practice*. Oxford: Butterworth-Heinemann.

Dinnie, K., & Fola, M. (2009). Branding cyprus – A stakeholder identification perspective. 7th International Conference on Marketing, Athens Institute for Education and Research (ATINER), Athens, Greece: July 6–9, 2009.

Finlay, R. J. (1994). Controlling the past: Scottish historiography and Scottish identity in the 19th and 20th centuries. *Scottish Affairs*, *9*, Autumn, 127–142.

Fowler, S. J., & Hope, C. (2007). A critical review of sustainable business indices and their impact. *Journal of Business Ethics*, *76*(3), 243–252.

Fyall, A., & Garrod, B. (2004). *Tourism marketing: a collaborative approach*. Clevedon: Channel View Publications.

Getz, D. (2007). *Event studies: Theory, research and policy for planned events*. Oxford: Elsevier.

Goulding, C., & Domic, D. (2009). Heritage, identity and ideological manipulation: the case of Croatia. *Annals of Tourism Research*, *36*(1), 85–102.

Hjalager, A. -M. (1999). Consumerism and sustainable tourism. *Journal of Travel & Tourism Marketing*, *8*(3), 1–20.

Hobsbawm, E., & Ranger, T. (1983). *The invention of tradition*. Cambridge: Cambridge University Press.

Holden, A. (2009). The environment-tourism nexus: Influence of market ethics. *Annals of Tourism Research*, *36*(3), 373–389.

Insch, A. (2009). Green essence or green wash? Conceptualisation and anatomy of green destination brands. 3rd International Conference on Destination Branding and Marketing, Institute for Tourism Studies, Macao SAR, China: December 2–4, 2009, 190–198.

Jeong, S., & Santos, C. A. (2004). Cultural politics and contested place identity. *Annals of Tourism Research*, *31*(3), 640–656.

Klieger, P. (1990). Close encounters: 'intimate' tourism in Tibet. *Cultural Survival Quarterly*, *14*, 2–5.

Koutsouris, A. (2009). Social learning and sustainable tourism development; local quality conventions in tourism: A Greek case study. *Journal of Sustainable Tourism*, *17*(5), 567–581.

Lane, M. L. (2005). Public participation in planning: an intellectual history. *Australian Geographer*, *36*(3), 283–299.

Little, D., Leverick, F., & Bruce, M. (1995). Factors affecting the process of collaborative product development: a study of UK manufacturers of information and communications technology products. *Journal of Product Innovation Management*, *12*(1), 16–32.

Marzano, G., & Scott, N. (2009). Power in destination branding. *Annals of Tourism Research*, *36*(2), 247–267.

McClinchey, K. A. (2008). Urban ethnic festival, neighborhoods, and the multiple realities of marketing place. *Journal of Travel & Tourism Marketing*, *25*(3–4), 251–264.

Miles, R., Miles, G., & Snow, C. (2005). *Collaborative entrepreneurship: How networked firms use continuous innovation to create economic wealth*. Stanford: Stanford University Press.

Morgan, N., Pritchard, A., & Pride, R. (2002). *Destination branding: Creating the unique destination proposition*. Oxford: Butterworth-Heinemann.

Murphy, P., & Murphy, A. (2004). *Strategic management for tourism communities: Bridging the gaps*. Clevedon: Channel View Publications.

Naipaul, S., Wang, Y., & Okumus, F. (2009). Regional destination marketing: A collaborative approach. *Journal of Travel & Tourism Marketing*, *26*(5), 462–481.

Nicholas, L. N., Thapa, B., & Yong, J. K. (2009). Residents' perspectives of a world heritage site. *Annals of Tourism Research*, *36*(3), 390–412.

Painter, M. (1992). Participation and power. In M. Munro-Clarke (Ed.), *Citizen participation in government* (pp. 21–36). Sydney: Hale & Ironmonger.

Palmer, A., & Bejou, D. (1995). Tourism destination marketing alliances. *Annals of Tourism Research*, *22*(3), 616–629.

Rocha, H., & Miles, R. (2009). A model of collaborative entrepreneurship for a more humanistic management. *Journal of Business Ethics*, *88*(3), 445–462.

Sautter, E., & Leisen, B. (1999). Managing stakeholders: a tourism planning model. *Annals of Tourism Research*, *26*(2), 312–328.

Sheng, L., & Tsui, Y. (2009). Taxing tourism: enhancing or reducing welfare?. *Journal of Sustainable Tourism*, *17*(5), 627–635.

Simpson, K. (2001). Strategic planning and community involvement as contributors to sustainable tourism development. *Current Issues in Tourism*, *4*(1), 3–41.

Wheeller, B. (2005). Ecotourism/egotourism and development. In C. M. Hall, & S. Boyd (Eds.), *Nature-based tourism in peripheral areas* (pp. 263–272). Clevedon: Channel View Publications.

CHAPTER

6

The leadership challenge

Malcolm Allan

INTRODUCTION

This chapter explores the concept of brand leadership as it applies to places which have recognised the need for and value of a place brand strategy. Increasingly these are places which have an extensive and sophisticated offer for residents, workers, businesses, and visitors. Commonly they are major tourist attractions, centres of culture and heritage, centres of learning, and places of leisure and entertainment. Place brand strategy involves more than the design of a memorable logo and a catchy tag line; it plans, provides for, and tells consumers the story of the offer and experience of the place, as it has been, as it is, and as it will be in the future. The chapter:

- Discusses place brand leadership as a new concept which describes how the brands of places are developed and led by the key stakeholders of the place;
- Demonstrates the importance of 'shared leadership';
- Outlines good practice in place brand leadership;
- Examines new skills and behaviours for brand leadership.

PLACE BRAND LEADERSHIP

Place branding is a collective endeavour and rarely the province or responsibility of just one stakeholder alone, such as the local or national government. It is most effectively practiced when the key stakeholders of a place come together to plan and manage their investments in its offer and the experience they want people to have there. Typically, as individual organisations, they will have very different purposes, responsibilities, goods, and services, with very different and potentially competing service and product brands. But what unites them is

© 2011 Published by Elsevier Ltd. All rights reserved.
DOI: 10.1016/B978-0-08-096930-5.10006-0

their shared desire to improve their place, how it operates, and what it offers to consumers and investors. The offer of a place is commonly quite complex. It is often a combination of products and services on sale, events, and programs of activities, combined with the physical features of the place – buildings, spaces, streets, architecture – and the culture and history of the people who live there and their forbearers. In other words it is a complex mix that they need to make sense of for people who know the place and for those who do not. And, in words that bastardise a very well-known saying attributed to Abraham Lincoln – 'You cannot describe everything about your place and all that it offers to all people, everywhere, all of the time'. You have to choose carefully and selectively, what you are going to say about your place and to whom, with style, clarity of, and economy of language, if you are to describe it in ways that will catch and hold interest, be memorable and be action orientated, stimulating people to find out more about it or to visit it. For such simplicity to be achievable agreement between the principal stakeholders about the brand that describes the offer and experience is necessary and shared leadership of the implementation of brand strategy is necessary if it is to become a reality.

Brand leadership is a common expression in the lexicon of brand development and management. It is commonly held to mean the brand that leads a particular market or product or service segment of a market. It can also be applied to brands that are innovative and creative. Place brand leadership, in comparison, is a new concept which describes how the brands of places – the offer and experience of countries, cities, towns – are developed and led by the key stakeholders of the place, often in partnership with each other.

Unlike fast-moving consumer goods brands, place brands are not limited to the qualities and features of their products, and principally expressed through logos and strap-lines; rather, they describe to consumers the offer of services and experiences that a place has to offer them and where and how to access them. Increasingly, their success is dependent upon the involvement of the people who provide those services and experiences in building the brand of the place – the key stakeholders of the place, those who are active investors in what it has to offer.

Places, like political parties and companies, need leadership – not in the traditional sense of elected leaders of majority parties in town halls or in parliaments, but leadership by and from the key stakeholders of the place working in close partnership with each other to realise its potential and, where desired, to create a brand that describes its offer and experience in ways that will attract and captivate the interest of the consumers and investors whom they wish to attract. So, why is leadership so important for the brands of places? The leaders of places – elected politicians and business and community leaders – can have a significant influence on how people think about their place. What they say and what they do can attract or repel people, institutions, companies, investors, and tourists. And, increasingly in the political sphere, especially at the level of the nation and in major metropolitan cities, the elected leaders of places are having an impact on their image and reputation; witness the range of responses from business leaders to the policy statements and pronouncements to elected mayors, for example, in places like London, New York, and Paris.

In parallel, more people are realising that the reputation of their place is important to them as residents or workers, in terms of the strength of association that they have with it and their comfort with the way it is governed, how administrations treat them, how the place describes itself and their personal 'fit' and comfort with such descriptions, in particular with their view of the place and how it operates, especially in relation to their own standards and values. And people are not alone in this regard; increasingly private companies and major institutions regard the reputation and identity of the places where they choose to operate as important to their own reputation and well being. These factors can have an impact on the attraction and retention of labour and on the conditions which support their successful operation.

It is no surprise then that in an increasingly competitive global economy that countries and major cities are recognising that they need to effectively distinguish themselves from their competition if they are to develop, attract, and retain human talent, investors, companies, and tourists, and successfully export their products and services, values, and lifestyle opportunities. Many places and their leaders have also recognised that they also need to distinguish themselves through their culture and heritage; witness the intense competition to be a European Capital of Culture with its attendant legacy of potential new jobs, enterprises, and cultural institutions, all of which can help attract and retain people, businesses, and investors. Place branding, then, helps places to differentiate themselves, to establish distinctive identities, and to be clear on what their offer is to the rest of the world and to be clear on the kind of experience people will have when they live or work in or visit the place.

As noted above, place brands are a lot more complex than product brands as they are usually an expression of a range of offers and experiences, facilities and services, many of which can be in competition within the place in the attraction of customers and visitors. Place brands can be an aggregate of this mix or they can feature one or a few dominant elements in the offer that they feel sufficiently differentiates them from their competition. And it is this potential internal competition for the attention of customers and visitors that drives the need for shared leadership of the process of developing and managing a brand strategy for the place. While it is common, at least in Western Europe over the last 10 years, for place brand initiatives to be initially led by the public sector, it is most unusual for all the principal services and attractions of a place to be the responsibility of that sector. It is far more likely that the major owners of, and investors in, the offer of services and facilities that the brand covers will be in the private sector. Hence, the need for the creation of some form of shared leadership of the development of a brand strategy for the place.

In my experience over the last 10 years it has become very clear that such initiatives need to be undertaken by a partnership of complementary interests, who are dependent on each other as key stakeholders in the development and delivery of the brand offer of the place, charged with creating the distinctive brand identity that will set the place apart from its competition. I term this approach a 'place brand partnership.' This is a form of partnership that is dependent on what is known as 'shared leadership.'

THE IMPORTANCE OF SHARED LEADERSHIP

Also apparent over the last 10 years has been the growth of interest in leadership generally. This has been seen not just in the private sector but also in the public and community or not-for-profit sector as it is referred to in North America. Leadership and its effectiveness has been recognised as having an impact on the performance of companies in particular, their profitability, their market share, and their influence in their markets and more widely in society. The quality of its leadership is increasingly being recognised as being one of the important intangible assets of value to companies and their shareholders, which contributes to their brand, perhaps their most important intangible asset, and are major determinants of their reputation and value to investors.

The importance of leadership development for companies can be seen not least in the proliferation of courses, seminars, and conferences on the subject, hosted by universities, business schools, and leadership institutes. This growth in private sector interest has been paralleled, at least in the UK, by a similar, if slower, growth in the public sector of leadership development programs for senior civil servants and senior local government officers and elected members; witness the establishment and growth of the leadership development work of the Innovation and Development Agency in the local government in England and Wales and the leadership programs of the Civil Service College at Sunningdale in Berkshire. Leadership development has also been recognised as being of importance to the community/third sectors, especially so in North America where it has been championed by the Drucker Foundation.

The point of this discourse is that potentially all the key sectors that need to be involved in cooperatively leading the development of brands for places should have a familiarity with, if not a good understanding of, the value of leadership and its effective practice. However, the challenge for place branding really lies in the area of cooperative or *shared* leadership, as opposed to the development of the personal leadership skills of those who lead individual institutions, organisations, and companies, often likened to and termed 'hero' leadership after the writings of Joseph Campbell (2008).

Shared leadership, which is what is required for effective place branding, essentially requires a great deal more give and take from leaders from these different sectors, than they are probably used to in their own spheres of influence. They need to move from the exercise of 'hard power' (we will do it my way) to the exercise of 'soft power' (let us find mutual benefits through agreement). Joseph Nye (2004) makes a powerful case for a more balanced use of hard and soft power in the conduct of public and civic affairs and concludes that soft power – getting others to want the outcomes that you want and your sharing theirs – is a far more effective use of power that will bring others to your cause and create common cause and purpose. Nye suggests that the positive exercise of soft power – through consultative policy making and respectful behaviour – can stimulate the positive involvement of other key stakeholders, from the private and community sectors, in the framing of public policy initiatives. In my view a prime candidate for the use of soft power is in the leadership of brand development for places.

The behaviour and policies of our political leaders, be they presidents, prime ministers, mayors, or party leaders in local government, what they do and how they do it, all impact on our perceptions of the places that they say they lead and govern. In the latter half of the twentieth century the actions of a number of political leaders had a number of serious consequences for their brand and reputation which had a number of grave economic costs, for example, the consumer boycotts of products from Greece under 'the Colonels' and similar boycotts of South African products during the years of Apartheid. Similarly, in the early years of the twenty-first century, a number of commentators (principally Anholt and Hildreth, 2010) have written on the effect on US trade as a result of the country's foreign policies and the consequent damage to its cultural reputation. This can produce feelings of discomfort, distress, disenchantment, and detachment among populations, or feelings of satisfaction, depending on personal points of view. And, as we have seen in Europe and in Southeast Asia in recent years, people are prepared to take to the streets to express their anger when they become concerned about the effect of the actions of their governments, which in turn affects external perceptions of their place and its offer, which can have significant implications for the travel and tourism sectors in those countries.

What this also illustrates is that the way that national governments conduct what is now referred to as 'public diplomacy' (being a combination of foreign and domestic policy) can have a significant impact on their brand – especially on their image and reputation. Public diplomacy is now recognised as having a major impact on the brands of nations and major cities, as witness the efforts of both the current Mayor of London, Boris Johnston, and his predecessor, Ken Livingstone, to cultivate potential inward investors through the promotion of their policies for the development of the UK capital as a centre for innovation, research, higher level skills, and a great place to do business. This is in line with national policies that help to establish reputations of a particular nature – witness the positive 'country of origin' effect of Japan on the perceived quality of its electronics and computer industry products and the desire of European regions and cities to import this effect and reputation in to their places through inward investment by Japanese companies (see Kotler and Gertner, Chapter 3).

A powerful place brand can therefore be of considerable competitive advantage for a place in a world where countries, regions, and cities actively compete with each other to wield influence, attract, and retain talent, businesses, cultural institutions, and major international events. A well-led place brand strategy offers more of a chance of capturing those potential assets. The way that the place is led and the behaviour of those who lead it can make a significant difference to the attitude of potential investors, who are more likely to value a place whose leadership is at one with each other and which has got its act together working in partnership, sharing responsibility for its development.

SHARED BRAND LEADERSHIP

Place brand strategy brings together and integrates public diplomacy, private corporate investment, community action, and personal investment in the fabric and service offers of places through effective marketing and communications practices. Effective place branding coordinates all the messages about the place, particularly those directed at particular target populations, both internal and external, through its people, its businesses, its institutions, and its organs of government. To do so successfully all those who can carry the message about its offer and all those who are responsible for its creation need to participate in and share responsibility for the creation and delivery of the brand. Using a form of partnership as a vehicle for doing so enables individual leaders to move from a position of focus just on their own agenda, goals, and objectives to balance that with a greater understanding of those of others and creating an opportunity to devise and implement a common agenda that engages more talent and resource in the development of the brand. A place brand created in partnership enables all the stakeholders involved to move in a common direction and provides clarity of shared purpose which can be a powerful differentiator for the place distinguishing it from its competition and rivals.

We can look at a number of recent examples of place brand initiatives to see varying forms of partnership being used as the basis for groups of key stakeholders sharing the leadership of brand strategy development and implementation. In 2005 in Southampton, a major port on the south coast of England, an informal place brand partnership was created under the wing of the city's formal Community Partnership, a statutory body responsible for the disbursement of public sector expenditure, to create and implement a brand strategy for the city. Composed of representatives of the Community Partnership, the city council, further and higher education, the health sector, the business community, and the media, the brand partnership was composed of two bodies, a brand leadership team and a brand development team. The latter team was responsible for the research required to understand what the current and proposed offer of the city was and the options for the development of a brand while the former team was responsible for leading the process, advocating for the selected brand strategy, and helping to secure resources for its implementation, responsibility for which is led by Business Southampton, a new body created in 2006.

A similar form of partnership was created in 2009 by Sefton Borough Council in Lancashire to guide the review of an existing brand strategy for the coastal resort town of Southport which had been devised by the borough council some years before. That brand strategy had been developed to help revive the town as England's classic resort. To carry out the review the Council invited around 20 representatives of the major stakeholders of the town to come together with it to form a brand strategy partnership to guide the council and its brand consultants on the key challenges being faced by the town and how to refocus and better develop its offer of services to new key audiences as well as more traditional ones. These stakeholders included local hoteliers and their managers, the operators of attractions, food and beverage operators, the operators of public transport services, the managers of major retail stores, representatives of the North West regional development agency and representatives of the council's tourism, marketing and culture departments. This partnership, in addition to guiding the review on the existing brand strategy, was also responsible for devising a new vision for the future offer of the town and the identification of new markets and new offers.

A further variant on this theme of partnerships for new visions, the 'Paisley Vision Board' was formed by Renfrewshire Council in the west of Scotland, to bring the key stakeholders in the town of Paisley together to develop a vision for its regeneration, an important element of which has been to assess the scope for re-branding the retail offer of the town centre. A traditional shopping centre serving both the town and surrounding settlements, its retail core has been significantly and negatively affected by the development of two large out-of-town shopping centres, Braehead and Silverburn. The council retained destination development and property consultants to advise it on the possibilities for redefining the offer and brand of the town centre as one of value retailing and their recommendations for attracting retailers of this nature are now being considered.

A further variant on this approach – creating a brand partnership of professional real-estate experts – was used by the Irish developer, Treasury Holdings, for the development of a brand strategy for its Babylovsky Park golf resort at Tsar Skeloe near Pushkin, about 25 km from St Petersburg in Russia. The company formed a Brand Development Team in partnership with its consultant advisers, which brought together destination development, landscape and building architecture, sports, cultural and marketing, and promotion expertise to help develop a brand strategy for the offer of the place and to describe the experience of living there and playing golf in a former imperial forest and park.

Another variant on the theme of partnership for the development of a brand strategy can be seen in the cross-border ecotourism development initiative being led by the tourism Ministry of Singapore and its counterpart of the south Malaysian Iskander Region which lies across the waters of the Straits of Johor from the island of Singapore. This initiative is designed to create a new brand strategy for the integration and joint marketing of the offer of four ecotourism sites, three in Iskander and one in Singapore. This unique cross border partnership is currently exploring the potential to market and promote the improved offer of these four sites under the uniting theme and concept of 'Waterland' and is exploring a marketing concept to integrate it with the more established and traditional tourism attractions of Johor Badhu and Singapore. None of this work would have been possible without the willingness of the leadership of the two countries to work together in partnership and to devise a development strategy of mutual benefit.

The final example of a partnership being put together to create a new place brand and a new offer is the London Development Agency's initiative, the East London Green Enterprise District (ELGED), covering Thames riverside areas of Tower Hamlets, Newham and Barking and Dagenham in London. Reporting to a partnership of the four public bodies, a team of consultants devised a brand vision and strategy for the area, identified a wholly new offer, and identified ways of implementing the strategy through, initially, a series of showcase projects. The brand vision for the ELGED area envisages it as being a place which exemplifies a green and sustainable urban settlement, a place that welcomes and showcases a range of businesses which make or use green and sustainable technologies and processes, and who run their businesses on green principles.

We can see from this short list of examples that there is no one form of partnership that needs to be used as the basis for groups of leaders from key place stakeholders to come together to devise and implement place brand strategies. What is common to each of the initiatives is a desire to involve people and organisations and a desire to share responsibility and leadership within a realisation that the ambition for each of the places will not be realised without a collective endeavour.

GOOD PRACTICE IN PLACE BRAND LEADERSHIP

A number of lessons can be drawn from the initiatives outlined above that are of relevance to existing and future place brand partnerships. These are:

- Place brand leadership is not what one powerful local leader provides for all of his or her fellow stakeholders but is what emerges from the reciprocity of the relationships between them, from their interactions, and what they create jointly.
- In brand partnerships the right vision is not that of the most powerful or vocal stakeholder, no matter how attractive, but rather it is what emerges from a genuine dialogue between the stakeholders.
- Place brand partnerships need to be led by someone who is skilled at building relationships, skilled at building partnerships that bring organisations together in common purpose, able to build win–win relationships.
- Brand partnerships of this nature need to work in new ways, ways that are probably quite different to the ways of working of individual stakeholders, requiring new behaviours such as extended teamwork, extensive consultation, openness, and clarity of communication.
- Brand partners need to create a culture of trust and reciprocity and a willingness to 'give to get' to secure progress.
- Place brand partners need to work hard at breaking down traditional barriers between themselves and to become accountable to each other.

Leadership and partnership is therefore as important to the development of places as is its history, culture, investment, businesses, architecture, built environment, educational institutions, and population. The way leadership is practiced says a lot about the way the place is governed, its values, and what it wants to do for and in the rest of the world, how it wants to be seen by the rest of the world.

The process of leading the creation and implementation of a place brand must be led at the highest level within each stakeholder organisation and have the active involvement of or the blessing of the most senior elected or appointed official or office bearer, such as the president, the leader of the council, or the mayor. And, as touched on above, to be effective, place brand leadership should not be confined to the public sector alone, it needs to include business and community leaders. The challenge facing those from the public sector is to be willing to share power with business and community leaders. The challenge facing business leaders is to recognise that playing a role in the leadership of their place is part of the CEO job description and a crucial element of their corporate social responsibility. The challenge for community leaders is to demonstrate to the other two sectors the value of their grassroots knowledge and the activists they can mobilise in support of shared vision and shared goals.

CHALLENGES FACING PLACE BRAND LEADERSHIP

Leaders of place brand partnerships face a number of challenges if they are to operate effectively and if they are to devise and implement an effective brand strategy. These include:

- The identification and recruitment of people with the required mind set and abilities from the key stakeholders – people who are willing to subordinate their organisation's vision to a greater common good.
- Being able to successfully negotiate and agree on a shared purpose for the partnership and a uniting vision for what it wishes to achieve for the place that is credible, memorable, inspiring, and attainable.
- Align their organisation colleagues and fellow citizens to the vision.
- Being able to devise and manage an affordable brand strategy that will achieve the agreed vision, managing in line with change to avoid being blown off course.
- Agree and implement actions that will bring the brand alive.
- Behave in line with the brand and its values in what they do and what they say.
- Effectively communicate the brand in action to stakeholders, citizens, media, and potential investors.
- Grow the value of the place for its citizens, businesses, investors, and potential visitors.
- Be able stewards of the assets of the place – increasing their attractiveness and worth – and the value of its human capital – the people who live and work and perform there.

NEW SKILLS AND BEHAVIOURS FOR BRAND LEADERSHIP

To meet the challenges listed above those involved in sharing the leadership of brand partnerships will need to learn new skills and behaviours, as follows:

- The ability to use power 'softly';
- The ability to think creatively and 'out of the box';
- The ability to actively listen and suspend bias;
- A willingness to 'give to get' a shared common purpose;
- A willingness to balance personal and organisational objectives with those of other partner stakeholders;
- The ability and a willingness to negotiate outcomes for the greater good;

- A willingness to create a shared vision that is greater than that for their own organisation, albeit one that could potentially benefit it;
- Be accessible and open in their conduct of the partnership's affairs;
- Live the values of the brand of the place;
- Actively gather or create the resources the place requires to implement its brand strategy.

CONCLUSION

If it is accepted that place branding is of value to countries, regions and cities, to their citizens, businesses, institutions, to their image and reputation, then resources of time and finance, knowledge, and skills need to be invested in the creation of effective, relevant, memorable, inspiring, and attainable brand strategies by those who represent the key stakeholders of the place. If it is accepted that this is not a job for the public sector alone then partnerships of the key stakeholders need to be created as a way of mobilising and focussing the knowledge and resources required and as a vehicle for their work together. If it is accepted that this form of partnership cannot be led in traditional ways then new forms of shared brand leadership need to be devised and practiced among the stakeholders. Those involved need to understand and develop the values, knowledge, and skills of effective shared leadership and partnership working. This does not usually happen naturally or by chance. It needs to be learned and practised until it becomes second nature.

Those in government will face the biggest challenge of all as some may not be able to recognise that they do not have all the people, knowledge, and skills required to lead the process of creating the brand strategy for their place and that they will need to work in much greater partnership with stakeholders from the private and community sectors. Those in the rest of the community, in the private and voluntary sectors, will need to actively demonstrate to the public sector the worth of their being involved in such partnerships. Once accepted as partners they need to work effectively with the other sectors and not be reliant on the public sector. Finally, whoever is involved in shared leadership and partnership, they need to constantly remember who they are leading on behalf of, namely their community, fellow citizens and businesses, institutions, and organisations, all of who need to be regularly communicated with, consulted, and involved in the development and implementation of the brand strategy, responded to rather than just listened to, and treated with dignity rather than disdain.

References

Anholt, S., & Hildreth, J. (2010). *Brand America: The making, unmaking and remaking of the greatest national image of all time* (2nd ed.). London: Marshall Cavendish.

Campbell, J. (2008). *The hero with a thousand faces* (3rd ed.). Novato, CA: New World Library.

Nye, J. (2004). *Soft power: The means to success in global politics*. New York: Public Affairs.

CHAPTER

The partnership challenge

Alan Fyall

INTRODUCTION

Irrespective of their type, location, and scale, destinations represent an amalgam of many industrial services, such as accommodation, transportation, attractions, entertainment, recreation, and food services. This fragmented and highly disparate 'product' clearly does not make the management of the visitor experience an easy task. As competition becomes more intense the ease with which many destinations are substitutable and struggle to seek differentiation in crowded markets represent formidable challenges for their future management and marketing. It is a fact that destinations are far more multidimensional than consumer goods and other types of services. It is also true that the geographical and political boundaries that dissect many destinations often render considered management theory irrelevant, while the consistent lack of funding and the need to maintain a healthy balance between the demands of visitors and residents introduce challenges that are outside the scope of more traditional consumer- and business-marketing challenges (Pike, 2005, pp. 258–259).

Above all, however, it is the heterogeneous omnipresence of the market interests of the diverse group of active stakeholders that constitute the destination. This point was reinforced by Manente and Minghetti (2006, p. 230) in that the 'presence of a wide range of stakeholders who interact with and within the resort, each one with diverging interests and different perceptions of the destination, make it very hard to plan coherent development of the destination'. They went on to add that the 'key issue is to harmonise the variety of interests/perceptions on the one hand and of tourism products on the other with the identity of the destination, in order to create an integrated system of tourism supply'.

This widely accepted view of destinations as being difficult to manage has in recent years led to much closer scrutiny of the relationships among actors and stakeholders within destinations and the means by which they can collectively

© 2011 Published by Elsevier Ltd. All rights reserved.
DOI: 10.1016/B978-0-08-096930-5.10007-2

manage better the destination 'experience' for consumers (Dredge, 2006; Fyall & Garrod, 2005; Sheehan & Brent Ritchie, 2005). There is little disagreement both professionally and academically with regard to what needs to be done *vis-à-vis* the management of destinations (Wang & Fesenmaier, 2007). The perennial challenge, however, is how?

This chapter therefore:

- Introduces collaboration in the specific context of destinations, i.e., partnerships;
- Discusses those factors that underpin, and provide a rationale for, future partnership structures for the effective management of destinations;
- Introduces the emerging trend toward the adoption of 'corporate' approaches to branding and emerging partnership structures that are facilitating the adoption of a more inclusive, integrated, and professional approach to the branding of destinations;
- Offers some thoughts for the future collaborative management of destinations.

DESTINATION PARTNERSHIPS

The need to 'collaborate', 'partner', or simply 'work together' is not unique to tourism. What is particular to tourism, however, is the interdependencies of its different actors, the generally small scale of those actors, and the fragmentation of its markets (Soisalon-Soininen & Lindroth, 2006, p. 187). As early as the 1990s, Selin (1993, p. 218) commented that 'on an international scale and locally, tourism planners and operators are discovering the power of collaborative action' with rapid economic, social, and political changes 'providing powerful incentives for tourism interests to recognise their interdependencies and to engage in joint-decision making' (1993, p. 217). Notwithstanding, to counter and manage more effectively the inherent complexity of tourism, many sectors within the wider industry have turned to various forms of collaboration; the assumption being that the management of destinations in the context of this chapter is likely to be more effectively dealt with by inter-organisational collaboration and the formation of partnerships.

The move toward the need for greater collaboration in the context of destinations is referred to by King (2002) as the 'network economy', in that those entities responsible for the management and marketing of destinations (often referred to as Destination Management Organisations or DMOs) will probably enter into strategic relationships with industry partners who can together provide a seamless experience for the customer. This is because it will be the 'relevance of the experience they offer the customer, rather than the destination they promote, which will be the key ingredient for success in the future' (King, 2002, p. 108). Bennett (1999) shares this viewpoint as do Fyall and Garrod (2005) who call for much more collaboration between all those involved in the destination product in order to take destinations forward. Collaboration is not considered a luxury in this instance, but as a necessity for destinations to survive in the face of considerable competition and environmental challenges (Pearce, 1992).

Partnership approaches to the management of destinations bring many benefits. For example, there is often a reduction in risk through strength in numbers and interconnectedness within and across destinations as is there the efficient and effective exchange of resources for perceived mutual benefit. Partnerships can also help counter the threat of channel intermediary powers while in peripheral locations, destination partnerships serve as a vehicle to broaden the destination domain. They can also help counter greater standardisation in the industry through the use of innovative collaboration marketing campaigns and offer the potential to develop destination-wide reservation systems and two-way dialogue with customers through technological collaboration. In addition, Hill and Shaw (1995, p. 26) argue that 'co-operative marketing may be particularly advantageous when a country's tourism product is underdeveloped or when existing products are in an advanced stage in the product life cycle and it is desirable to attract new markets and/or formulate new products'.

However, destination partnership activity is far from widespread. For example, there remain a number of constraints and drawbacks to collaboration both within and between destinations. These include general mistrust and suspicion among partners due to governance or structures that are inappropriate for moving the shared project forward; inability of various sectors within the destination to work together due to excuses of a political, economic, or even inter-personal nature; instances where particular stakeholders fail to recognise the real value of the partnership and remain closed to the benefits of working together; the frequent disinterest in partnerships from 'honey-pot' attractions, and competition between municipal authorities that administer separate geographical regions within a recognised destination resulting in inertia (Fyall & Garrod, 2005, p. 290).

Despite the above, inter-organisational collaboration in the form of public–private sector partnerships remains a popular strategy for destinations. In a recent study conducted by Fyall, Fletcher, and Spyriadis (2010, pp. 21–25) on the future management of destinations in England, 12 key lessons were drawn from an extensive review of destination partnership practice. These can be summarised as follows:

1. Each destination operates in a unique wider environmental and political context and thus no blueprint structure exists for the generic management of destinations;
2. Many destinations are facing considerable pressure on both capital and revenue budgets;
3. Large capital funds appear more likely to be available when tourism is more closely allied to wider regeneration programs;
4. All destinations are beginning to adopt a more commercial focus;
5. Partnerships appear to work less well in mature destinations (particularly where financial inducements are less forthcoming);
6. Considerable trust is required from the trade to 'buy in' to new structures;
7. Key industry players are essential members;

8. A longer-term evolutionary approach to change is recommended rather than radical change;

9. A positive and genuine approach to partnership working is necessary as is the ability to continually reinvent within a constant cycle of change;

10. Local authorities are deemed to be, and are to remain, an essential player in maintaining the neutrality of new organisational structures;

11. A strong political will which encompasses the need to continue investment in tourism is required for alternative structures to succeed;

12. A holistic view of the management of the destination is considered paramount for the future successful management of destinations.

The following section develops some of the above themes further in an attempt to explain more fully those core propositions that underpin, and provide a rationale for, future partnership structures for the effective management of destinations.

FACTORS UNDERPINNING FUTURE DESTINATION PARTNERSHIP ACTIVITY

Destinations as collaborative networks

As evidenced in the beginning of this chapter, the amalgam nature of the destination product (in that they contain multiple components, multiple suppliers and multiple stakeholders, and represent multiple meanings to multiple markets and segments) is such that a singularly competitive 'free market' solution is seldom, if ever, recommended as a *modus operandi* for the management of destinations; the criticisms advanced initially by Palmer and Bejou (1995) on the surface appearing to stand the test of time. To best manage the complexities and imperfections inherent within destinations it is, therefore, widely accepted that destinations need to bring together all parties to collaborate rather than to compete, and to pool resources toward developing an integrated management and delivery system as evidenced in work by Buhalis and Cooper (1998), Prideaux and Cooper (2002), and Pavlovich (2003) among others. A more recent study by Wang and Fesenmaier (2007, p. 863) merely confirms the notion that the continued need for a 'substantial degree of co-ordination and collaboration among the variety of different players within destinations is a natural response to the industry's inherent fragmentation'.

Confirmation of the above in England is widespread although it is not solely the nature and characteristics of destinations that underpin the surge in activity in recent years. Collaboration within destinations has evidently been taking place for many years and most notably over the past decade. For example, the First Stop York Tourism Partnership (FSYTP) in the North of England was launched in 1995 as a public–private sector partnership while Marketing Manchester began life in 1996. The more recent interest in the development of collaborative arrangements in England is, however, attributed to a number of other drivers. The most significant perhaps is political devolution more broadly and the devolution of responsibility to the regions more specifically where devolution has served to galvanise the regional strategists, and the funding that follows, in support of new collaborative arrangements for the management of destinations. In addition, the considerable pressure on funding and year-on-year decreases in many destination budgets, the desire for a more holistic approach to counter poverty and urban deprivation in both coastal and urban destinations, and the view that the current devolved agenda really does represent a 'last chance' for the development of tourism, all lead to a greater sense of urgency and commitment to new arrangements for the management of destinations not witnessed for a number of years (Fyall, 2008).

One particular issue worthy of scrutiny is the extent to which in some destinations individual components do not wish to collaborate. This raises two similar but separate questions. Firstly, to what extent do all individual components within the destination collaborate? Due to the 'geographically limited area' of destinations, von Friedrichs Grängsjö (2003, p. 427) argues that different enterprises exist side by side and are 'obliged to collaborate with others with whom they may or may not wish to have close contact'. A follow-on question can then be asked as to whether all components are aware of their wider 'networked' role in the destination? This issue was identified in the study conducted by Manente and Minghetti (2006, p. 229) who argued that not only are individual components 'not aware of their role in the creation and management of local supply, of their influence on the destination image and then on the customer's experience' but neither are they 'conscious of being a system or of the importance their interactions have in organising the product and then determining the destination competitiveness on the market'. With regard to the two questions raised, evidence suggests that not all components do in fact collaborate.

With regard to the first question, there are instances where individual components within the destination clearly do not collaborate. For example, one key challenge for destinations is the means by which new corporate-branded entrants to destinations can be enticed to participate in local and subregional destination marketing rather than operate as stand-alone entities. In some destinations, new hotel groups and major corporations of longstanding have been slow and to some extent openly hostile to participation in the partnership approach to destination management and marketing. This can be explained, in part, by the centralisation of decision making by major corporations and the lack of delegation of authority to managers at the local level. One solution designed to compensate for the loss of income to the DMO is to broaden the scope of membership further and to develop more effective cross-border initiatives to extend the reach of the destination. Although the centralisation of decision making for major corporate players represents a core component of this argument, for some destinations it is their historically weak efforts at partnership activity that have done little to inspire confidence and engagement of some of destination's key private sector players.

The above discussion leads on to a more fundamental question as to how those charged with the management of destinations actually define the destinations they purport to manage. In short, what is the destination? For the majority of cases, destinations demonstrate different contextual backgrounds, have distinct product offerings and boundary issues to deal with, have contrasting capital and revenue budgets, and are varied in the degree to which the public sector intervenes. These differences alone make comparison difficult and question the overriding methodology of comparison. For the most part, destinations continue to represent 'well-defined geographical areas within which the tourist enjoys various types of tourism experiences' as defined by Vanhove (2006, p. 102). For example, the extent to which Bournemouth on the South Coast of England incorporates Poole and Christchurch in future years in the context of tourism will impact greatly on arrangements advanced to manage the broader destination.

Interestingly, while Buhalis (2000, p. 97) argues that destinations are often 'artificially divided by geographical and political barriers, which fail to take into consideration consumer preferences or tourism industry functions', where consumer preference was taken into consideration, such as in the South West of England, this only exacerbated an already delicate situation (SWT, 2005). Ultimately, the view of consumers is only one part of a complex equation. Where destination boundaries are also considered to be 'manufactured', the boundaries of the destination serve political rather than destination objectives with a resulting hesitancy among many components to adopt an inclusive collaborative approach.

Despite the definitional haze that often suffocates the academic scrutiny of collaboration more generally (see Himmelman, 1996), ultimately all definitions of collaboration represent variations on a theme. Evidence clearly suggests that collaboration is widespread within and among destinations if one accepts the broad definition posited by Wood and Gray (1991, p. 146) whereby collaboration occurs 'when a group of autonomous stakeholders of a problem domain engage in an interactive process, using shared rules, norms, and structures, to act or decide on issues related to that domain.' Not only is collaboration, as defined above, no longer considered a luxury, it is in fact viewed as a necessity that brings with it considerable benefits (Poetschke, 1995). For destinations, however, no single approach is universally applicable to their effective management while all destinations are faced with a reasonably common set of problems and challenges and that a variety of structural options exist for adoption and implementation by those managing destinations.

Mechanisms and management processes for collaboration

For partnership activity to succeed in the longer term it is critical that mechanisms and management processes evolve continuously and adapt if they are to remain current and of value to destinations seeking to achieve effective collaboration among various stakeholders. Marketing Manchester represents a suitable example in that while starting life as a Promotions Agency in the mid-1990s (something that was deemed appropriate at the time), it has now matured into a fully inclusive DMO. The example of the YFSTP in York is also appropriate while the recognition among stakeholders in Bournemouth that collaboration has always existed, albeit under a variety of guises, is testament to the fact that arrangements to manage destinations continue to evolve in an attempt to meet the changing internal and external forces impacting upon them (Fyall, 2008). This is also true for Visit Peak District in that it has evolved from previous collaborative relationships among the Peak District National Park Authority, Derbyshire Dales District, High Peak Borough and Staffordshire Moorlands local authorities, the University of Derby, and the Derbyshire Chamber of Commerce. Although new mechanisms and management processes are highly relevant, most notably in the current devolved context of tourism in England, collaboration represents a dynamic and evolutionary phenomenon which continues to be moulded by a variety of internal and external forces whereby the significance of each varies over time. Perhaps most fundamental is that effective collaboration is simply difficult to achieve and that no single form of collaboration lasts forever; as evidenced by Caffyn's life cycle analysis of collaboration (2000).

Although the above discussion relates to appropriate structural arrangements suited to the effective management of destinations, in their study conducted over a decade ago, Jamal and Getz (1995) argued that this was insufficient in isolation and that tourism organisations more broadly needed to develop a new managerial 'mindset', namely one that rejects the notion of business relationships shaped by constraints, choice, and competition, and embraces the potential of collaboration to counteract the turbulence that tends to intensify as the industry develops. Hence, rather than explore mechanisms and management processes, is there sufficient evidence of a change in mindsets among those managing the destinations featured in this study?

In many destinations, private sector disinterest and the inability to see the wider destination picture suggest that the bigger picture is most definitely not being recognised. This then begs the question as to how can a change in mindset be cultivated? In England, a myriad of extreme external events such as Foot and Mouth Disease and the attacks on New York in 2001 contributed much to a need to refocus and review existing approaches to the management of destinations. Likewise, the changing political context of the United Kingdom broadly and England more specifically has driven forward the regional agenda and the need for all destinations to work more holistically with their sub-regional neighbours while in some destinations, most notably the North East, the historical dependency culture of external funding sources is making way for a more realistic and visitor-driven approach to the management and marketing of destinations.

For any destination, collaboration more often than not refers to a coming together of the public and private sectors (Bennett, 1999). Carter (2006) suggests that destinations will only succeed when they harness the talents of both sectors and that while governance options are many and varied no one solution fits all in that different circumstances will require different solutions. For the most part, solutions can either be 'top down' or 'bottom up' or indeed a mix of both. The destination management arrangements put in place by the Northwest Regional Development Agency represent a clear example of a 'top down' approach where the local authorities have been encouraged to 'buy-in' to the subregional DMOs (Cooper, Fletcher, Fyall, Gilbert, & Wanhill, 2008, p. 494). The model adopted by the South West can also be regarded as 'top down' although it is less prescriptive than that advocated in the North West (SWT, 2005).

The South West's approach is less strategic than that implemented in the North West in that very little prescription is evident with no clear guidelines in existence to frame the destination arrangements for its subregions. This in itself has on occasions hindered 'buy-in' while the lack of resources made available to fund change has continued to hinder the creation and development of superior destination management arrangements. Evidence of this is most stark in the report published by the South West Regional Assembly. This report raised explicitly the concern that DMOs appear to be 'one of the more contentious and less-understood aspects of Towards 2015' (SWRA, 2005, p. 23). In contrast, the strategy adopted in the South East of England represents a good example of a 'bottom up' approach in that it recognises that the region does not in itself represent a destination in the minds of visitors and, in turn, destinations have been encouraged to develop themselves with a focus on product quality, wider visitor economy, and overall provision of high-quality services.

Collaboration and organisational longevity

One key question for all destinations is the extent to which organisations or individual components within destinations are sustainable in the long term if they remain outside of collaborative relationships? For example, a number of major attractions or hotel corporations frequently decide to work outside of destination partnership structures. Many indeed thrive and prosper outside of the public arena of tourism and for the foreseeable future little evidence exists to suggest that the situation is likely to change. The perceived weaknesses of destination management arrangements, in some instances, are well entrenched historically while the perceived quality of people in the public sector would appear to represent a future barrier to inclusion for both organisations (Fyall, 2008).

One interesting alternative view is the extent to which the Darwinian view of collaboration comes into play: described by Bleeke and Ernst (1991) as when the 'strong' acquire the 'weak'. This stance is built on the notion that collaboration is merely an alternative form of competition and a temporary and continually evolving one at that. As outlined by Manente and Minghetti (2006, p. 230), destinations represent 'systems' or a 'group of actors linked by mutual relationships with specific rules, where the action of each actor influences those of the others so that common objectives must be defined and attained in a co-ordinated way'. This highlights the need for individual components of the system to be aware of the interactions among different destination stakeholders as well as the need to understand more fully the impact exerted by the competitive environment on the destination system. Notwithstanding, organisations often collaborate with alternative objectives in mind with longevity often a long way down the list of priorities.

Clearly, the specific context of destinations is crucial in determining the extent to which organisational performance is in fact truly dependent on the establishment and maintenance of effective relationships in meeting the expectations of visitors. The numerous drawbacks of collaboration in many destination contexts are such that they collectively serve as a major barrier to collaboration. Issues such as general mistrust and suspicion among collaborating partners, the inability of various sectors to work together due to excuses of a political, economic, or even inter-personal nature, and instances where particular stakeholders fail to recognise the real value of collaboration and remain closed to the benefits of working together all exist and are, on occasions, perhaps understandable.

Collaborative success

One of the challenges when discussing collaborative success is in the identification and clarification of what actually constitutes success as the means of measurement are seldom agreed upon. For example, although various partnerships can be held up as models of good practice, many are successful in the particular context of their own destination with success in one destination not always a precursor to success elsewhere. One of the principal lessons for destinations for the future is the need to be inclusive and for the development of a holistic mindset *vis-à-vis* the management of destinations. In this context, DMOs represent a recent conceptualisation of the organisation function for the management of destinations, where the 'M' emphasises total management rather than marketing. This refocused philosophy represents a more holistic approach to the management of destinations whereby the DMO is responsible for the well being of all aspects of the destination. According to Ritchie and Crouch (2003, pp. 73–74) it 'emphasises the provision of a form of leadership in destination development that makes extensive use of teamwork in all DMO-led initiatives. Destination promotion is no longer the sole purpose of the DMO. While this modified role presents many new challenges, it also provides a much broader range of opportunities for ensuring destination competitiveness'. Haati and Komppula (2006) argue also that the DMO is the most appropriate organisational entity to meet the experiential needs of visitors, despite the fact that the principal links of the 'experiential chain' are virtually always outside the control of those managing destinations.

One final point related to the above is the need for an understanding of how in the future DMOs can be structured in a manner that will enable them to create value and deliver collaborative advantage. While King (2002) is very critical of many existing DMOs, he develops and adds weight to his criticism by advocating that the customer is now very much an active partner in the marketing process. He goes on to add that for destinations to be a success, marketers need to engage the customer as never before, as well as to be able to provide them with the types of information and experience they are increasingly able to demand. Talk of creating a holistic 'destination' or 'visitor' experience is an easy task. The more challenging aspect is to incorporate the ideas of King (2002), Pine and Gilmore (1999), and Ryan (1991; 1997), among others, more fully into the management of destinations. Finally, although the scope of DMOs varies, in most cases they exist to build the destination, to support and bring together the trade, to help minimise business failures, particularly among SMEs, to manage the public realm, to build and develop the destination brand, to represent the interests of the trade at national, regional, and subregional organisations, to develop skills and training for the trade, and to deliver an input into the planning process and wider economic development plan. Ultimately, the role of a DMO must be to 'enhance the long term competitiveness of the destination' (Pike, 2004, p. 39).

CORPORATE BRANDING AND ITS INFLUENCE ON FUTURE DESTINATION PARTNERSHIPS

To achieve long-term competitiveness there is an increasing trend among destinations to move away from simply 'more of the same' local authority structures and to be more receptive to stakeholder needs, just as there is a need in many destinations to develop genuinely stronger partnership working with a greater sense of engagement and 'buy in' from all parties. One of the areas in which many destinations are finding common ground is in their gradual adoption of more 'corporate' branding techniques and the destination management structures necessary for this higher profile umbrella approach to destination reputation building to succeed. Hankinson (2007) and Leith and Richardson (2003) highlight many similarities between corporate and destination branding. Firstly, both require high-level management in that they are both required to reflect, and are reflected by, a set of sub-brands and consumer experiences. Secondly, both are reliant on effective internal coordination and external compatibility. Finally, both brand types need to be managed and communicated with a broad spectrum of stakeholders.

This migration towards 'corporate' branding techniques reflects recognition of the growing maturity of branding in destinations, the need to more professionally dovetail strategic visions, organisational culture and brand image, and the personal interest and recognition in the power of branding by senior management. For destinations to succeed in their adoption of corporate branding techniques, Hankinson (2007) proposes that destinations demonstrate strong visionary and effective leadership; a brand-orientated organisational culture where the brand is built internally from senior management down and is embedded across the organisation; effective internal coordination; consistent communication; and strong compatible partnership structures.

One recent example of the above trend is the Destination Edinburgh Marketing Alliance (DEMA), Ltd, which was launched in April 2009. A public–private partnership, DEMA was established to lead and facilitate the promotion of Edinburgh, Scotland's capital city and magnet for both domestic and international visitors. Consistent with the earlier discussion in this chapter, DEMA was established in response to the fragmented coordination of previous activity, the recognised need for clarity of common purpose, the need to bring stakeholders together and to speak with a single, coherent, and unified voice, and the need for a definitive destination promotion strategy. Above all, DEMA was deemed to be the most appropriate vehicle for Edinburgh to fully capitalise on its assets and the potential for cross selling across the four themes of *visit*, *invest*, *live*, and *study*. What distinguishes DEMA from so many 'me too' DMOs across the United Kingdom is its remit to bring together a diverse mix of businesses and organisations to promote the city through fresh coordinated planning and to enhance Edinburgh's reputation as a place to visit, invest, live, work, and study. The Destination Edinburgh Marketing Alliance is custodian of the Edinburgh *Inspiring Capital Brand* (see http://www.edinburgh-inspiringcapital.com) and works in close collaboration with national stakeholders which include VisitScotland, Scottish Development International, and Scottish Enterprise to ensure that all its activities complement national promotion activity.

Although a highly successful destination, like many other destinations, Edinburgh faces growing competition for visitors, inward investment, students, and immigration. In response, rather than adopt a piecemeal approach to branding, DEMA has developed a compelling city proposition and clear audience-targeting plan to fully leverage benefits from the *Edinburgh Inspiring Capital* corporate brand. Through a combination of market research, the use of a mix of digital platforms, public relations, and promotion, DEMA is evidence of a proactive approach to working in partnership with public and private agencies to fully maximise the destination's assets through shared marketing campaigns and budgets.

CONCLUSION

According to Pike (2004, p. 2) the vast majority of DMOs, irrespective of where they are in the world, share 'a common range of political and resource-based challenges not faced by private sector tourism businesses'. The most notable challenge is that of year-on-year reductions in contributions from the public purse, something that has been hastened with the onset of financial crisis throughout much of the world. This factor alone represents a significant catalyst for change which single-handedly may change how the industry and general public view destinations, especially with regard to boundaries. Above all, it will force all destinations to reflect on past practice, confront head on the severe resource challenges they are facing, and encourage destinations to be more radical in the mechanisms and management processes adopted to develop destinations to their full potential and to build reputations that are sustainable in the minds of all stakeholders and their respective markets.

References

Bennett, O. (1999). Destination marketing into the next century. *Journal of Vacation Marketing, 6*(1), 48–54.

Bleeke, J., & Ernst, D. (1991). The way to win in cross-border alliances. *Harvard Business Review, 67*(6), 127–135.

Buhalis, D. (2000). Marketing the competitive destination of the future. *Tourism Management, 21*(1), 97–116.

Buhalis, D., & Cooper, C. (1998). Competition or co-operation: the needs of small and medium sized tourism enterprises at a destination level. In E. Laws, B. Faulkner, & G. Moscardo (Eds.), *Embracing and managing change in tourism* (pp. 324–346). London: Routledge.

Caffyn, A. (2000). Is there a tourism partnership life cycle?. In B. Bramwell, & B. Lane (Eds.), *Tourism collaboration and partnerships: Politics, practice and sustainability* (pp. 200–229). Clevedon: Channel View Publications.

Carter, R. (2006). Destination management and governance: A framework paper for discussion. UN WTO Ulysses Conference, June 1.

Cooper, C., Fletcher, J., Fyall, A., Gilbert, D., & Wanhill, S. (2008). *Tourism principles and practice* (4th ed.), London: Prentice Hall.

Dredge, D. (2006). Policy networks and the local organisation of tourism. *Tourism Management, 27,* 269–280.

Fyall, A. (2008). *Managing destinations: a collaborative approach. The emergence and development of sub-regional destination management arrangements in the south west of England. Unpublished PhD Thesis.* UK: Bournemouth University.

Fyall, A., Fletcher, J., & Spyriadis, T. (2010). Diversity, devolution and disorder: The management of tourism destinations. In M. Kozak, J. Gnoth, & L. Andreu (Eds.), *Advances in tourism destination marketing: Managing networks* (pp. 15–26). Abingdon: Routledge.

Fyall, A., & Garrod, B. (2005). *Tourism marketing: a collaborative approach.* Clevedon: Channel View Publications.

Haati, A., & Komppula, R. (2006). Experience design in tourism. In D. Buhalis, & C. Costa (Eds.), *Tourism business frontiers: Consumers, products and industry* (pp. 101–110). Oxford: Elsevier Butterworth Heinemann.

Hankinson, G. (2007). The management of destination brands: Five guiding principles based on recent developments in corporate branding theory. *Brand Management, 14*(3), 240–254.

Hill, T., & Shaw, R. N. (1995). Co-marketing tourism internationally: Bases for strategic alliances. *Journal of Travel Research, 34*(1), 25–32.

Himmelman, A. T. (1996). Rationales and contexts for collaboration. In C. Huxham (Ed.), *Creating collaborative advantage* (pp. 19–43). London: Sage.

Jamal, T. B., & Getz, D. (1995). Collaboration theory and community tourism planning. *Annals of Tourism Research, 22*(1), 186–204.

King, J. (2002). Destination marketing organisations: Connecting the experience rather than promoting the place. *Journal of Vacation Marketing, 8*(2), 105–108.

Leith, S., & Richardson, N. (2003). Corporate branding in the new economy. *Journal of European Marketing, 37*(7/8), 1066–1079.

Manente, M., & Minghetti, V. (2006). Destination management organisations and actors. In D. Buhalis, & C. Costa (Eds.), *Tourism business frontiers: Consumers, products and industry* (pp. 228–237). Oxford: Elsevier Butterworth Heinemann.

Palmer, A., & Bejou, D. (1995). Tourism destination marketing alliances. *Annals of Tourism Research, 22*(3), 616–629.

Pavlovich, K. (2003). The evolution and transformation of a tourism destination network: the Waitomo Caves, New Zealand. *Tourism Management, 24*(2), 203–216.

Pearce, D. (1992). *Tourist organizations.* Harlow: Longman.

Pike, S. (2004). *Destination marketing organisations.* Oxford: Elsevier.

Pike, S. (2005). Tourism destination branding complexity. *Journal of Product & Brand Management, 14*(4), 258–259.

Pine, B. J., & Gilmore, J. H. (1999). *Experience economy: Work is theatre and every business a stage.* Boston, MA: Harvard Business School Press.

Poetschke, B. (1995). Key success factors for public/private sector partnerships in island tourism planning. In M. V. Conlin, & T. Baum (Eds.), *Island tourism* Chichester: Wiley.

Prideaux, B., & Cooper, C. (2002). Marketing and destination growth: A symbiotic relationship or simple coincidence?. *Journal of Vacation Marketing*, *9*(1), 35–51.

Ritchie, J. R.B., & Crouch, G. I. (2003). *The competitive destination: A sustainable tourism perspective*. Oxford: CABI.

Ryan, C. (1997). *The Tourist Experience: A New Introduction*. London: Cassell.

Ryan, C. (1991). *Recreational tourism: A social science perspective*. London: Routledge.

Selin, S. (1993). Collaborative alliances: new interorganizational forms in tourism. *Journal of Travel and Tourism Marketing*, *2*(2/3), 217–227.

Sheehan, L. R., & Brent Ritchie, J. R. (2005). Destination stakeholders exploring identity and salience. *Annals of Tourism Research*, *32*(3), 711–734.

Soisalon-Soininen, T., & Lindroth, K. (2006). Regional tourism co-operation in progress. In L. Lazzeretti, & C. S. Petrillo (Eds.), *Tourism local systems and networking* (pp. 187–196). Oxford: Elsevier.

SWRA. (2005). *The report of the regional strategic review on tourism in the south west*. Taunton: South West Regional Assembly Scrutiny Panel.

SWT. (2005). *South west tourism: Destination management organisation delivery plan*. Exeter: South West Tourism.

Vanhove, N. (2006). A comparative analysis of competition models for tourism destinations. In M. Kozak, & L. Andreu (Eds.), *Progress in tourism marketing* (pp. 101–114). Oxford: Elsevier.

von Friedrichs Grängsjö, Y. (2003). Destination networking: Co-opetition in peripheral surroundings. *International Journal of Physical Distribution & Logistics Management*, *33*(5), 427–448.

Wang, Y., & Fesenmaier, D. R. (2007). Collaborative destination marketing: a case study of Elkhart county, Indiana. *Tourism Management*, *28*, 863–875.

Wood, D. J., & Gray, B. (1991). Towards a comprehensive theory of collaboration. *Journal of Applied Behavioural Science*, *27*(2), 139–162.

CHAPTER

The authenticity challenge

Søren Buhl Hornskov

INTRODUCTION

It is no coincidence that Copenhagen's logo includes a badge. A badge is something you wear to tell the world who you are. A badge is an individual statement. And because Copenhagen is an open city the badge is also an open playground for our members and others to make their statement and tell their story about Copenhagen… (www.opencopenhagen.com).

Authenticity has, for some time, been looked at with considerable scepticism; as a result of the pronounced interest in strategic thinking concerning the global rather than the local, some argue that the concept has even lost its relevance, that our hyper-mediated culture has created a world in which the specific, historical characteristics of places have moved into the background, that we have somehow moved beyond authenticity.

This chapter contends the opposite: that authenticity continues to be strategically vital. We may even argue that in a cluttered market with many different destination offerings, authenticity has become even more important because it can make the difference between bland and unique (Pine & Gilmore, 2007). Correspondingly, considerations of authenticity should be part of any destination branding strategy, and will continue, if treated the right way, to be a vital source of value. This chapter therefore:

- Discusses how any authenticity strategies need to consider two interconnected dimensions of authenticity: material and immaterial. While the material is concerned with physical reality, the immaterial dimension of authenticity is concerned with social and cultural aspects of destinations. Both, as we will see, are important to the authenticity challenge;
- Presents a case study of Copenhagen in order to highlight the importance of this aspect of destination branding.

© 2011 Published by Elsevier Ltd. All rights reserved.
DOI: 10.1016/B978-0-08-096930-5.10008-4

ORIGINS OF THE ORIGINAL: AUTHENTICITY IN MARKETING

Branding has always been concerned with authenticity. There is a deep current of interest within the branding field in what *lies behind*; in what is persistent, real and enduring. In a sense, this has been the raison d'être of branding since the surge of branding theory in the late 1990s: branding has sold itself and argued its case from the basic assumption that what sells and succeeds is always that which is honest, no-nonsense and somehow evidently and in itself valuable. In fact, what marketing considers to be the first examples of branding were driven by authenticity strategies as these early branding campaigns were aimed at authenticating goods according to their origin. Goods were branded to communicate a certain symbolic guarantee of quality. Kelloggs Corn Flakes is an example of this: at the beginning of the twentieth century, Kellogg's launched the slogan 'original and best' to distance the brand from a surge of generic variations of the same product. Consumers were encouraged to believe that Kellogg's was in fact better because it was original and because it was authentic; it was the original, more seasoned product, the thing in keeping with the essential property of a particular generic good and has since been widely believed to be, well, just somehow *better*.

Even though marketing theory and history tells us that authenticity is about the properties of a product, there is every reason to be aware that people make authenticity (Knudsen & Waade, 2010). It is the belief that a product is authentic that makes it so. Therefore, we need to take a look at how authenticity is made.

THE PERFORMATIVITY AND STRATEGIC POTENTIAL OF AUTHENTICITY

From this basic assumption begins the strategic interest in authenticity. The authenticity challenge is thus the strategic task of communicating the lasting and site-specific qualities of goods, people and destinations. It is about telling the world how the histories of things such as cereals and destinations represent a unique source of value – a source for value likely to have a lasting character. The authenticity challenge is thus based on a particular infatuation with the historical origins of things – and not least how these origins are constantly reinterpreted.

The assumption that the original is somehow better also implies that if you can establish the experience of authenticity in the minds of consumers (tourists, buyers, investors, followers alike), you have tapped into a lasting resource of true, appealing narratives of the destination. We can call this the performativity of authenticity. By 'performativity' we mean to focus on what happens when we talk about authenticity; when we call things authentic and try to make people accept them as such. The force of this kind of performativity lies in its promise to transcend the trivia of day-to-day experience. It carries with it the promise of cutting through the bulk of mundane and ordinary marketing messages, which, compared to the call for authenticity, leave the consumer at best disinterested and, at worst, hostile and irritated.

The performativity of authenticity is very closely linked to concrete, earthly things such as historical buildings and monuments. These things are the evidence of authenticity. Our experience of the authentic depends on them. Therefore, material things and the practises of making them, such as architecture and design, move to the forefront in strategies concerned with authenticity. The manipulation of the physical environment becomes a key strategic tool and understanding the physical dimensions of places (and their narratives) becomes a crucial area of strategic effort (Graham et al., 2000; Olins, 2004, p. 23).

In the case of destinations, this trend is evident in the current surge of interest in heritage. This extends beyond merely attention to conservation and historical knowledge as such, but to the communication and continual redefinition of historical authenticity for commercial purposes. Cities from Bilbao to Riga are concerned with finding ways to express how their histories may provide valuable and appealing identities. This work is most often based on broad strategies, making use of both traditional marketing channels and the physical environment (Pedersen, 2006).

We are thus strategically interested in authenticity for at least two reasons. First, authenticity carries with it a particular kind of performativity. There is a power to it. In other words, if we experience things as authentic, it makes a difference that we talk about. Secondly, authenticity is no constant. It may appear to be given, such as in the case of roman cisterns, New Yorker art deco or the original recipe of Corn Flakes. Yet, authenticity is always open to interpretation. It thus needs, paradoxically, to be renewed and reinterpreted. We will take a closer look at the case of Copenhagen to provide an example of this dynamic nature of authenticity. Copenhagen is a city with 1000 years of history and a number of institutions and sights that claim to be authentic. As we will see, the Copenhagen brand, however, has been designed to allow the emergence of new forms of cultural, social and business authenticity.

ORIGINS OF AUTHENTICITY: THE CONCEPT OF AUTHORSHIP

'Authenticity' comes from the Latin word 'auctor,' which means 'founder' or literally 'one who causes to grow.' The word shares its etymology with the Greek *poetes*, which means 'maker, author or poet' from the verb *poein*, meaning 'to make or compose.' Authenticity, then, is what comes out of – and continues to stand from – an original act of making. The concept of authorship is a recurring problem in the arts and humanities. Walter Benjamin, a German writer and philosopher, discussed the problem of authorship in the essay 'The work of art in the age of reproduction' (1935). Benjamin's challenge was to understand what happens, with the onset of modern media and reprinting techniques, when authorship in the hands of an individual creator is no longer an immanent trait of the artistic medium. What happens, in other words, when art is not identified as a particular and unique work of art, say, a painting, but with a quality of an expression that may be copied and distributed endlessly (much like the case of the current problem of authorship in digital music.)

Benjamin's analysis has become progressively more relevant as authorship has become increasingly complex. Today, with collective authorship in online media (Wikipedia being a case in point), it has become evident that authorship is, in many cases, distributed among a host of different actors. This means that responsibilities as well as creative agency is spread out and shared by many actors. In addition, as the case of Wikipedia illustrates, contemporary media encourages the constant rewriting of messages and even artworks.

Now, even though the authenticity of art – as the relation between author and work of art – is a complex matter, we may argue that the authenticity of a place is even more complex for the following two reasons:

1. In destination branding, the distribution of authorship is becoming a prerequisite for production. In modern liberal societies with highly critical and reflexive publics, a lasting and legitimate brand identity can never be carried by a coherent, single, individual 'author' of brand narratives.
2. Authorship is an ongoing and dynamic process rather than a signing of messages or works that stand through time. In the branding of places and destinations, in other words, messages and narratives are constantly made and remade.

These characteristics of authorship in the case of destination brands set specific challenges for the making of authenticity. At the strategic level, it is clear that authenticity is constructed in ongoing social processes. Strategy, then, is the activity of working out how to reinvent authenticity in a joint venture in which a number of actors participate.

THE IMPORTANCE OF THE MATERIAL: PAST AND PRESENT IN THE BUILT ENVIRONMENT

The planning and execution of an authenticity strategy thus works on two levels at the same time. First, it organises the broad constituency of authenticity in social networks (the immaterial level of the strategy). Secondly, it aims to harness the performative power of the crucial material dimension of authenticity. Authenticity strategies need to construct an appealing sensory experience of authenticity, which can be communicated in material media. An authenticity strategy aims to understand that destinations, even in the globally mediated reality of today, are in important ways *physical*. Branding strategies therefore often refer to the physical environment as the basis or the reality that supports or lends credibility to the pay-offs and narratives. This may explain why heritage is becoming increasingly important for the strategic development of destinations (Koolhaas, 2004). It is about defining the past as relevant to contemporary identities, thus showing its continuing relevance to today's audiences and markets.

The importance of heritage and built environment underlines the radical demands for cross-sector cooperation in any authenticity strategy. While a purely immaterial strategy (a marketing campaign say, or an effort to involve and include citizens) may be managed by agencies from one sector of urban management, a strategy working on both material and immaterial levels requires the cooperation between different sectors of government. For instance, the technical-infrastructural departments of a municipality who manage heritage and the built environment will have to work together with cultural and business sector actors. As we will see, the case of the Copenhagen brand provides evidence of the difficulty of such cross-sector cooperation.

ORGANISING AUTHENTICITY: COMPLEXITY AND RISK OF CONFLICTS

We will briefly return to the challenges of the immaterial level. Here, too, we are confronted with the necessity of cross-sector cooperation. As we have seen, the practical organisation of authenticity, in light of the notion of distributed authorship, is about making different people work together to produce a collective product; in this case a brand. When we are dealing with corporate brands, the structures necessary for people to work together may already be in place. The board of directors may require different parts of the organisation to work together and while discipline is of course sometimes a problem, it can be overcome through the top-down structures of businesses. In destination branding, however, the situation is more complex. Different sectors are not used to working together and there may be deep, politically determined differences between how things are done. In destination branding, the building of structural connections between separate institutions and agencies is made difficult by what social scientists call 'functional differentiation' (Luhmann, 2000, p. 54). Social science argues that it is a trait of advanced societies that they form mutually segregated systems dominated by different logics, values and even different ways of making sense. Thus, when, for instance, voluntary sector organisations cooperate with state institutions, we cannot expect them to understand each other very well.

In fact, we can expect a certain measure of conflict in most cross-sector cooperation. A study of a dance festival in the Øresund Region, which was thought to support the development of a regional brand, showed that cooperation between the local dance scene and the strategic actors was fraught with conflict (Hornskov, 2007). People who work with art and culture in the partly voluntary sector are often quite sceptical of the motives of what they perceive as illegitimately commercial and political actors. We may speculate that this tension is even more pronounced when claims are made to authenticity. If someone makes a claim for the original meaning of a city, nation or region, someone else is bound to oppose or even take offense. There is an often inescapable conflicting logic at work. These differences might make for a creative potential but in most cases they carry with them the risk of conflict. This phenomenon is emphasised in destination branding, where commercial, administrative, artistic, and more broadly cultural actors are expected to cooperate.

COPENHAGEN: EMERGENT AND USER-DRIVEN AUTHENTICITY

Copenhagen, capital of Denmark, is at the same time a historically rich city and a modern, global, and ambitious place. From a branding perspective this ambiguity represents both opportunities and particular challenges to do with the fundamental issue of balancing a focus on history and on the future within complex institutional structures. While blessed with a very long period of tranquillity and prosperity, Copenhagen is characterised by being, at the same time, very modern and traditional. As a home to one of the oldest monarchies as well as the most computer-literate population in the world, Copenhagen is a composite historical artefact and a highly self-reflexive and critical public will make certain that any half-baked and naïve narratives of identity and meaning will live short and ridiculed lives.

This means (as it does in most other Western urban centres) that authenticity is a contested issue. The claims to authenticity are many and varied and arguably, defining a brand for a historically rich and multisignificant reality is in itself a negotiation of what counts as authentic. At the same time, Copenhagen is characterised by its complicated institutional structures: tourism, for example, is an intricate business in which a range of organisations compete for funding and political backing to further their particular agenda. The metropolitan area of Copenhagen is governed by more than 20 municipalities, some with less than 30,000 inhabitants, and two regional administrations with relatively little political power. Even though there are long and fruitful roots of political cooperation, the political reality is that changes are hard fought and even slight political and institutional change requires long and costly negotiations and networking.

In such an institutional structure, branding is difficult. Everybody seeks recognition of creating a successful brand, yet nobody wants to run the risk of wasting their budget to benefit others more than themselves. In complicated political systems there is a 'catch 22' impeding shared brand identities – even if most people can see that everyone would benefit. The strategic development of tourist organisations, municipalities, corporations and others is made difficult by this situation. When key actors first began working on a branding strategy for foreign investment in 2006, their work soon became dominated by the idea that in order to work, the brand would have to have a sufficiently broad appeal and be, as it were, seen as the outcome of decentred decisions rather than imposed from a perceived 'outside'.

The city's main tourist organisation, Wonderful Copenhagen, and its foreign investment agency, Copenhagen Capacity, joined forces to create a new brand to further their common agenda of attracting attention to the city. From the outset, the strategy was to develop the brand identity as well as a brand ownership association. The association was a way of securing funds to finance campaigns for the brand, while at the same time a way to build ownership in the business community of Copenhagen. One of the first steps was the establishment of an analytical basis. To do so, the research agency, Red Associates, was hired to find out what made Copenhagen attractive to foreign investors and multinationals. The research led to the recommendation that 'advanced lifestyle, team-focused work culture and lean culture' should be emphasised in all strategic communications. The study also showed that investors based their decisions largely on irrational factors such as personal experience and relationships to locals.

Copenhagen Capacity and Wonderful Copenhagen issued a public tender for the development and implementation of a new brand, attracting proposals from more than 30 communications and advertising agencies bidding for the prestigious assignment. In this preliminary phase, the focus was on winning over reluctant business leaders to join a common strategy to develop a flexible, yet inspiring, narrative for Copenhagen. The objective was to find the agency most likely to encourage the multiple institutions, organisations and business interests in the city to engage in the branding process. The successful agency, the locally based People Group, put forward a proposal focused on the value of openness and suggested a strategy foregrounding Copenhagen as an inherently democratic, tolerant and hospitable city.

THE ELEMENTS OF THE COPENHAGEN BRAND

The Open brand consists of three elements: the name 'Copenhagen', of which the letters 'open' are printed on the background of a circle shape (referred to as 'the badge') and, thirdly, the pay off 'Open for you'. The brand book suggests a range of variations, tailor-made for various particular purposes. The variations have different colours and patterns on the badge and transform the pay-off according to a particular purpose: 'open for business', 'open for inspiration', 'open for shopping', and so on (Figure 8.1).

The basic premise of the brand is that the badge may be used to communicate a range of different messages and thus further many different strategies. Yet, in all these different contexts, the brand communicates the basic value of 'openness'. The brand ownership association puts it this way: 'The new brand, Copenhagen – Open for you, supports Copenhagen's openness, accommodating attitude and accessibility and simultaneously implies a vision of becoming the most open capital in the world' (www.opencopenhagen.com). The founding agencies of Wonderful Copenhagen and Copenhagen Capacity

Figure 8.1 Variations of logo design. Source: Copenhagen Capacity

Figure 8.2 Open for destination branding

were thrilled to get what they perceived as a dynamic and engaging brand identity, perfectly balancing a key, yet controversial political value with an inclusive esthetic. The brand, the people behind it believed, would be crucial to developing a truly open urban culture. Lars Bernhard Jorgensen, managing director of Wonderful Copenhagen, said in an interview on national radio that 'even though the city may not be the most open city just yet, the brand will be key to realise this vision in the future'.

From the point of view of the creative agency, the Copenhagen brand has two major advantages: it is campaignable and unpretentious (campaignability in this context means having the qualities that make the brand easy to incorporate in existing campaigns). With the relatively small budgets involved, both brand owner and creative agency knew that they would have to create something the users would find easy and attractive to adopt and use within their existing strategies. To be attractive in a Danish business context, a brand had to convey the right measures of a salient, yet non-controversial message, and the flexibility of form. Moreover, the consensus was that the brand would have to be aligned with dominant self-images of Danish business culture. The people behind the brand believe that it has, as a core component, the idea that Denmark is a small country and that the Danish business community should therefore rather promise too little than too much. Danish businesses often emphasise their unpretentiousness and therefore the brand had to be realistic and align with their values of pragmatism, professionalism, modernity, liberalism, and the absence of pretense.

The ambition to align the brand with these prudent business values stands out as an effort to express an authentic value base for the Danish business environment – a base stretching well beyond business and into broader cultural and political strands of life. The Open brand is thus based on an idea of emergent and self-expressed forms of authenticity. Among the tactics to further convey this self-expression is an interactive tool on the brand website. Here, visitors can design their own Open-logo and write their own pay-off. The interactive tool allows people to combine a range of colours and patterns with their own text. The result is a unique, customised logo. Figure 8.2 demonstrates how this may look.

CREATING OWNERSHIP

With the brand in place, Wonderful Copenhagen and Copenhagen Capacity could step up the effort to expand the brand ownership association. The strategy was to follow a three-step plan:

Figure 8.3 Visualisation of the Brand at Copenhagen Visitors Centre. Source: Copenhagen Capacity.

1. Expand the association member base, thus raising funds for future campaigns while establishing and maintaining ownership in key audiences.
2. Making the brand visible and available at key events and key infrastructural nodal points, such as cruise ship facilities and outdoor advertising at urban hot spots (see Figure 8.3).
3. Show the brand to international audiences and establish ownership with the Copenhagen public.

Step one, the expansion of the member base, is deemed crucial to the success of the brand. First, membership generates funds to use for campaigns and activities and, secondly, membership generates new brand designs and a thus constantly transforming brand design. The brand association was founded with 18 member organisations in May 2009. By September 2009, it had acquired an additional 10 members, towards its goal of 50 member organisations by the end of 2010. The principle of the member association is a key dynamic of the brand strategy: membership does not merely generate user-rights and formal influence on how the brand is managed; it generates the right and desire to develop the brand. This is the case not only in terms of the ongoing redesign of the graphic identity (adding new surfaces and colours to the badge), but also in terms of the ongoing reinvention of the brand narrative. The pay-off is a highly flexible matrix as 'Open to...' may be combined endlessly with ideas, people, products, initiatives and values Copenhagen is open to – and of course, the brand narrative may spread beyond the original intentions of the association.

The brand association is aware that inviting participants to interpret and transform the brand does not merely create possibilities, but also carries risk. The strategy of openness means that interests with which the association does not want to be associated may find it beneficial to design its own badge and reinterpret its own 'open for...' pay-off. What if, for instance, the extreme right or some violent organisation would choose to make the brand its own? In the case of such a crisis, the brand association will claim the rights of the brand and thus legally impede any abuse of the brand. The marketing director of Wonderful Copenhagen considers this as a last resort. He admits that there is an inherent risk to this sort of brand design, but there is also a world of possibility.

THE FUTURE OF THE COPENHAGEN BRAND

Steps two and three of the implementation plan – enhancing the visibility and physical presence of the brand and reaching out to international audiences – are yet not fully developed. There are several barriers to the realisation of steps two and three. First, Wonderful Copenhagen and Copenhagen Capacity have based the strategy on building the strength of the brand association. Having members is a prerequisite for the expansion of the plan. The risk aversion of public as well as private organisations, which followed the onset of the financial crisis in 2008–2009, means that it has become more difficult to recruit members. Secondly, related to the difficulties of increasing the member base, the brand association encountered some difficulty in engaging the municipalities of the Copenhagen Area as a result of the political realities of a metropolitan area organised around many different political units. The consequence of this lack of support at the municipal level is that the original intention to use the built environment as a strategic platform may be under threat as the municipalities are responsible for the planning and control of most aspects of built environment and hence their cooperation in this issue is crucial.

CONCLUSION

This chapter argues that authenticity strategies have the potential to combine and align the immaterial and material aspects of destinations. More specifically, the authenticity challenge requires focus on the *performativity* of authenticity and the complex relations of *authorship*. When we talk about and make claims to authenticity, the effects are unpredictable. I have argued that authenticity is very often a contested issue. When applied to destinations with long traditions and rich political histories, the destination branding strategist thus need powerful and appealing tools of communication. The case of Copenhagen provides an example of a campaign, based around an appealing, inviting narrative and a design philosophy that has accessibility and self-expression as key components. In terms of authorship, there seems to be a formal as well as an informal approach. Formally, dealing with distributed authorship is about negotiating viable agreements between actors from a broad field of relevant sectors. Informally, the engagement of this host of people is about creating motivation and ownership beyond and by other means than the formal organisation of interests.

In the case of the Copenhagen brand, the brand association provides an example of a formal approach, while the brand narrative and flexible form of the logo show us how to work with informal and even playful forms of engagement. In the Copenhagen brand the notion of openness is both method and message. The campaign aims to issue an open invitation to use and define identities from a simple plot: Copenhagen is open in all the ways you can imagine. The success of the campaign hinges on the combined tactics of motivating the use of this narrative and communicating in all the media of the city. At the time of writing this chapter, the use of the built environment is still not resolved. It remains to be seen if the brand association can cooperate with the often public actors in control of buildings and infrastructure. It is worth keeping in mind, however, that the authenticity challenge requires focus on long-term goals. The work of constructing perceptions of authenticity requires time, and so does the strategic use of the built environment. The notion of distributed authorship is just another way of saying that we are dealing with the challenge of linking and engaging interests and investments that are spread out and not easily conjoined. The authenticity challenge is a long-term effort to build relations between different functional sectors of the society.

The example of Copenhagen discussed in this chapter has introduced a set of themes that may guide those facing local authenticity challenges. The following are recommendations for the authenticity strategist, who will need to:

- Organise emerging, not predefined, forms of ownership and involvement;
- Be prepared to mediate conflicts over claims to authenticity;
- Avoid the temptation to control and seek short-term effects. Goals should be realistic and long term since perceptions of authenticity change very slowly;
- Provide appealing and flexible brand narratives and media that allow for self-expression;

- Create synergies of the material and the immaterial;
- Combine the development of social relations (in the form of cooperation, civil engagement, etc.) and the performative constituents of the physical environment.

References

Graham, B., Ashworth, G. J., & Turnbridge, J. E. (2000). *A geography of heritage. Power, culture and economy*. London: Arnold.

Hornskov, S. B. (2007). On the management of authenticity: Culture in the place branding of Øresund. *Place Branding and Public Diplomacy, 3*(4), 327.

Koolhaas, R. (2004). Preservation in overtaking us. *Future Anterior, 1*(2), 1–3.

Knudsen, B. T., & Waade, A. M. (2010). *Re-investing authenticity*. Bristol: Channel View Publications.

Luhmann, N., (2000). *Sociale systemer*. Copenhagen: Hans Reitzel.

Olins, W. (2004). Branding the nation: The historical context. In N. Morgan, A. Pritchard, & R. Pride (Eds.), *Pritchard and pride: Destination branding. Creating the unique tourist destination* (2nd ed.). Amsterdam: Butterworth-Heinemann.

Pedersen, S. B. (2006). Trains, planes, billboards and people at Kastrup airport station: Branding a territorial transformation from 'Local' to 'Global'. In S. R. Clegg, & M. Kornberger (Eds.), *Space, organizations and management theory* (pp. 183). Advances in Organization Studies. Copenhagen: Liber and Copenhagen Business School Press.

Pine, B. J., & Gilmore, J. H. (2007). Authenticity: what consumers really want. Boston, Massachusetts: Harvard Business School Press.

Useful Website

www.opencopenhagen.com

CHAPTER

9

The aesthetics challenge

Satu Parjanen, Vesa Harmaakorpi and Kaarina Kari

INTRODUCTION

The competitiveness of cities and regions has been much discussed lately. Although territorial competitiveness is a disputed concept (see, e.g., Krugman, 1998), it is widely accepted that territorial units play a crucial role in economic transformation (see, Camagni, 2002; Harmaakorpi, 2006; Storper, 1997). The competitiveness factors of cities and regions have been defined in many studies. For example, Silander, Tervo, & Niittykangas (1997) define regional competitiveness factors to include: (i) business factors, (ii) cost factors, (iii) labour costs, (iv) infrastructure, (v) R&D environment, (vi) living environment, and (vii) grants and attitudes. Later, Linnamaa (1999) suggested that the competitiveness of an urban region consists of six basic elements: (i) human resources, (ii) companies, (iii) infrastructure, (iv) embeddedness in networks, (v) institutions and development networks, and (vi) quality of living environment. Linnamaa introduces image as a seventh element supported by combinations of the basic elements.

According to Florida (2002), a creative class is a key driver of urban and regional growth. It is the nature of the population that makes the difference. Regions with a high share of creative people will perform better economically because they generate more ideas and innovations and attract creative business. The creative class is attracted to places that are characterised by, for example, an urban climate that is open to new ideas and newcomers. The creative class also attaches a high value to urban facilities and small-scale cultural services, such as movie theatres, bars, museums, art galleries, restaurants, and trendy shops (Boschma & Fritsch, 2009).

Cities compete in attracting visitors, residents, and businesses. They do this by creating a city brand that encapsulates the qualities of the city and generates powerful and memorable positive associations. According to Florida (2002) and Jansson and Power (2006), places which have built strong and dynamic

© 2011 Published by Elsevier Ltd. All rights reserved.
DOI: 10.1016/B978-0-08-096930-5.10009-6

brands have an easier time attracting firms within the knowledge industries. This chapter explains the following objectives:

- It discusses the importance of the built environment and aesthetic matters in the debate on the competitiveness of cities.
- It introduces ideas of city design management as a way to ensure a city's uniqueness and to further develop an interesting brand.
- It discusses the range of possibilities to involve the people of the city in the design management. The creativity of inhabitants is vital in each city's efforts to attract new businesses and people to fuel their prosperity. Participation of the people makes the brand more original, holding a higher perceived user value. Users are widely acknowledged as a valuable source of creativity and knowledge in the development of new products, services, or ways of operating.

AESTHETICS IN PLACE BRANDING

Branding is the process of designing, planning, and communicating the name and identity of a product, service, or organisation in order to build or manage its reputation (Anholt, 2007). In fact, branding places is different from branding products, and it is not possible to approach these tasks in exactly the same way (Anholt, 2004). While all products are affected by external change, places like cities are particularly vulnerable to international politics, economics, terrorism, and environmental disasters (Morgan & Pritchard, 2002). The purpose of place branding is to increase the attractiveness of a place and to find a combination of unique attraction factors for each place to make it different from other places (Rainisto, 2003).

The experience economy is an important concept in understanding what makes one city different from another. It goes beyond the simple institutions a city offers. The experience economy consists of the whole range of associations and emotions that people experience when they spend time – or consider spending time – in a particular place (Cities of the Future, 2006). The experience economy has changed the focus of our economy away from its traditional emphasis on articles, industry, and production to an economy in which consumers are willing to pay an extra price for products and services that hold certain qualities, feelings, values, meanings, identities, and aesthetics (Stigel & Friman, 2006). Aesthetic matters are often regarded, especially in public discussion, as something only having to do with how things look. In fact, aesthetics is about surfaces and their effects on our senses and aesthetic value is often connected with pleasurable experiences. But aesthetics is not limited to the surface qualities of objects surrounding us. There is also so-called deep aesthetics, which often truly constitute the aesthetic quality of life (Haapala, 2009). The aesthetics and the built environment are affecting many elements, which in turn are seen as sources of the competitiveness of cities (see Figure 9.1).

At most, the environment affects people's well-being when it presents itself as a natural living environment. Humans recognise in the landscapes, flora, and fauna the same structures and processes, which also form their own

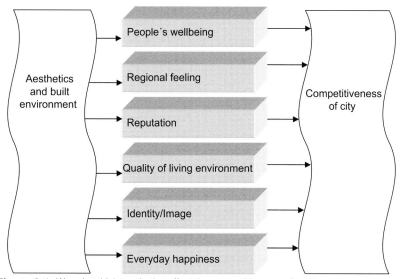

Figure 9.1 Ways in which aesthetics affect the competitiveness of a city.

identities. This is also realised in city communities, because people have a natural desire to imprint themselves on their environment and a need to mark their own territory by getting attached to the familiar elements. People who have been born and bred in cities, as well as people who have lived for a long time in cities, are not necessarily aware of the visual city; they experience their environment through phases in their own life and the important occurrences in the city (Maula, 1999).

Karisto (2004) for his part inspects the city from the perspective of everyday happiness. He divides the development of the cities into an administrative-economic city (where the focus is on increased competitiveness and efficient production of services) and a home city (where the focus is on the environment and everyday happiness). People's quality of life is also affected by the public space, which can be a happiness factor and also act as a collective resource for the inhabitants. We can talk about everyday aesthetics and according to Karisto (2004, p. 31), forms of city culture, which emphasise space culture and everyday happiness are increasing. The objective is to increase versatile city experiences that emphasise happiness.

In a territorial context, internal identity is used with feeling, a need to belong somewhere, a regional feeling, which means identification and commitment to a certain place or region (Virtanen, 1999, p. 7). Internal identity reflects a common history, a spiritual home. The development of inner identity is affected by both visual and linguistic issues. External identity, that is, image, is the common idea of an object, whether it is positive, nondescript, or negative. The visual aspect is stronger than the linguistic aspect: the intensity of the identity is essentially affected by an attractive environment offering aesthetic pleasure. An environment which is friendly, safe, secure, and aesthetic is imperative for modern civic pride.

Image usually means the public view formed of a person, company, or community, which is often purposefully developed and directed at selected target groups. The image of a place is the sum of the beliefs, ideas, and impressions that people have of that place (Kotler, Asplund, Rein, & Haider, 1999). Places that create a brand image can effectively attract customers and since every place has to compete with every other place unless a place can come to stand for something, it stands little chance of being remembered for long enough to compete for attention (Anholt, 2004). The objective of the image is to personalise the city, how it is experienced, and what it is known for as the city's image can be decisive in decisions taken by companies or individuals looking for a place to settle or visit. To maintain and increase their attractiveness to target groups, cities must consider what sort of image they should have. The image of a place is the result of many activities, which can build the unique character of the place; thus, the image is not easily copied by other places (Rainisto, 2003, p. 75).

Symbols of the city image include a unique milieu and nature, the cultural environment, architecture, sights, commercial and industrial architecture, cultural and sporting events, and the profile of the city and its inhabitants. Image is only partially based on the physical environment and its perceivable characteristics. It is also related to the abstract: cultural connections, history, internationalisation, economic weight, the whole spectrum of the parameters acting in the background. It can be built on an event like the Richard Wagner Festival in Bayreuth or the Opera Festivals in Savonlinna and Verona. Architecture has always been a significant emblem of city images and prominent examples include the Guggenheim Museum in Bilbao, Gaudi and Barcelona, Niemayer and Brazil, and in Paris the fine architecture of the Arab World Institute on the banks of the River Seine, or the modern glass pyramids at the Louvre. Public construction has, through the ages, produced facades of power: the Pyramids, the Great Wall of China, the Aztec cities, and the vast construction projects of Hitler, Stalin, and Ceausescu.

The characteristics of the built environment and the quality of residential environments are key factors in the successful functioning of communities. The quality of their residential environment can affect economic opportunities and the competitiveness of communities, as well as the health of their residents. Raunio (2001) emphasises the quality of the living environment as an important factor in creating competitiveness for places. The power of place, as Florida puts it, plays an increasingly strong role when the creative class chooses where they work. According to Florida (2002, p. 232), the quality of a place has three dimensions: (i) *what is there*: the combination of the built environment and the natural environment; a proper setting for the pursuit of creative lives, (ii) *who are there*: the diverse kinds of people, interacting and providing cues that anyone can plug into and make a community, (iii) *what is going on*: the vibrancy of street life, café culture, arts, music, and people engaging in outdoor activities; in other words, a 'scene' or 'buzz.' The combination of these three dimensions creates an image and a reputation for a place being able, in the best case, to attract the creative class to a region.

In the business world, the concept of reputation has been one of the eye-openers in recent times. On average, business reputation has been regarded as a strategic issue comprising extended impressions of the organisation built around images and actions. This view includes the argument that reputation is positively related to companies' competitive advantage (Fombrun, 1996).

However, reputation is not limited to corporations and other organisations. Regional reputation can be conceptualised as the composition of the images and experiences emerging from the encounters of the city and its interest groups (Aula & Heinonen, 2002; Aula & Harmaakorpi, 2008; Aula & Mantere, 2005).

Reputation can be based on three principles. Firstly, reputation is something that can be discussed and told about. From this perspective, reputation is produced and re-formed through storytelling or in other kinds of culturally bound representations. It is thus always linked to a communicational dimension, which is called 'the communication principle of reputation,' Secondly, reputation is related to an assessment of its object, which is called 'the evaluation principle of reputation.' Thirdly, reputation has something that makes a difference between one object and the other, which is called 'the distinction principle of reputation.' Although it is based on these three principles, a good reputation necessitates functional communication networks both inside a city and between a city and its co-operation partners. A city must endeavour to manage its reputation and thus affect the evaluations made of it. Moreover, a city must develop something unique, distinguishing it from other cities (Aula & Harmaakorpi, 2008).

The significance of a good reputation is often described through the concept of emotional appeal (Fombrun, 1996). In the same way an organisation's reputation affects how good it is considered to be; a city's reputation affects its appeal. The more attractive a city is, the better its potential for economic success. From the perspective of a city, a good reputation affects local operational preconditions. Reputation builds trust and brings esteem. It affects the opinions of the important interest groups and evaluations of the city, and is significant in, for example, placing or investment decisions (Aula & Harmaakorpi, 2008). A high-quality reputation cannot exist without genuine substance; thus, to acquire and maintain a good reputation, a well-designed city must exist in reality. This 'reality' arises from actions requiring active initiative and careful planning. A well-designed city is a platform for potential reputation and an attractively built urban environment develops a reputation, which in the long term can lead to the improved competitiveness of the city.

ENSURING AESTHETICS IN CITY BRANDING

The framework of city design management

City design or aesthetics is a catalyst for a strong identity and thus success and growth; moreover, successful city design will increase the comfort of the inhabitants, the quality of the living environment, and the city image. It takes into account the city's history and culture, the needs of individual residents and the city's companies, the infrastructure of the region, and the external interest groups. City design or aesthetics is a more extensive concept than town planning as it also includes implementation – indeed city design management means the all-inclusive managing of city design (see Harmaakorpi, Kari, & Parjanen, 2008).

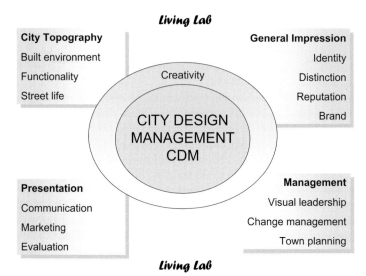

Figure 9.2 The framework of city design management.

The framework of a city design management is depicted in Figure 9.2. The elements of the framework are: (i) city topography, (ii) general impression, (iii) presentation, and (iv) management; creativity being the over-arching element, which binds these elements. The *city topography*, meaning the physical elements of the city, is an essential part of visual city design. It covers architecture, streets, parks, water systems, lighting systems, signposting, street fittings, and the general cleanliness of the city. The functionality of the built environment facilitates and enables the development of an active street life with its various activities. However, the physical part of place attraction is not enough to create a city brand since buildings and architecture are easily imitated by other places (Rainisto, 2003, p. 73). An essential part of the *general impression* and the building of territorial image is the identity and to distinguish itself from other cities, the city needs to emphasise its own uniqueness (always recognising that it is important that the image of the city matches reality). But it is insufficient to only invest in urban facilities and general impression as such; cities have to *present* their existence, that is, communicate their attractiveness to target groups. This image-forming or marketing will contribute to making the city known and improving its reputation.

The image of a city is positively influenced by the extent to which the city is known and the reputation of any city is good or bad only if it is evaluated as such. In constructing an image of a city, people will use whatever knowledge they possess and if the marketing of an urban image is untruthful, it will negatively affect the reputation of the city (Hospers, 2003). Finally, nothing will happen if the re-formation process is not *managed*. Besides the actual city design, essential parts of the design process are the elements of visual leadership and change management. The changes cannot be achieved if a vision of city design cannot be formed and the necessary measures for change are not applied (see, Kotter, 1988). Success of branding is mainly the responsibility of the senior management and involves all levels of stakeholders of a place

(Rainisto, 2003, p. 218). The uniqueness of a city brand lies primarily in its form as a network rather than an organisation with clear boundaries and internal structures as a city is a network of individuals, businesses, public services, local government, and partnerships with varied and often competing interests (Parkerson & Saunders, 2005, p. 245).

Creativity is the key ingredient of successful city design management and cities that succeed in developing creative strategies locally have the opportunity to grow to become competitive, creative cities. For cities to be competitive in a globalised environment, simply reducing the cost of doing business is not sufficient. Cities should also take actions aimed at adding value to local businesses, by creating an environment that provides incentives for local firms to innovate and learn from each other.

Place branding should find, release, and help direct talents and skills, and promote their creative use in order to achieve innovation (Anholt, 2004). Place can be a resource of visual materials and stimuli; for example, creativity of workers or locality-based intensive social and cultural activities may be a key source of inspiration, meaning that inspiration and new ideas can be gained from intensive activity in localities (Drake, 2003). Urban creativity is encouraged by concentration and diversity and concentration is not so much a matter of the number of people but rather the density of interaction. A dense concentration of people in a certain place favours frequent meetings and happenstance contact between individuals, and thus makes new ideas and innovations more likely. Diversity means variation between the inhabitants, their knowledge and skills, and the activities they pursue, as well as the variation in the built environment, which means a mix of buildings with differing functions. A functional and aesthetic built environment gives people the opportunity to meet one another on the streets, parks, or cafés, and exchange ideas and knowledge, pick up new ideas, and generate innovations (Hospers, 2003, pp. 262–264).

User-driven place branding

The competition among cities is intense, and a strong city brand is a potent weapon to maximise the visibility of a city's qualities and allows it to differentiate itself from its competitors. Cities have become nodes of dense networks exchanging investment, information, goods, and people. They have also become poles of innovation and knowledge management through access to information technology. Many cities have initiated strategic projects to develop cultural or lifestyle qualities: a broad spectrum of cultural events and institutions, sporting arenas, festivals and diverse forms of urban recreation, new residential areas, aesthetic upgrading of the city's public spaces, and the conservation of important building environments. The question is, when cities follow almost identical strategies, can they all enjoy the same level of success? (Cities of the Future, 2006).

Cities that succeed in attracting visitors, residents, and businesses do so by creating a city brand that encapsulates the qualities that the city has and generates powerful and memorable positive associations. Nowadays, cities are facing growing demands on budgets, combined with diminishing revenue bases. The demands, for example, on a city's infrastructure change and expand constantly. Cities have to ensure that their physical and technological assets can support the changing needs of their inhabitants. There is a need for new perspectives, ideas, knowledge, creativity, and motivation in order to find new ways to develop the city and its brand. To sustain a competitive edge for the city, more attention must be given to meeting the needs of the stakeholders. This means that people in the city must be involved in the design management of a city and in doing so they will feel the strengthening of local identity and will be willing to disclose the external network outside the city about it, thus realising the communication principle of reputation. The city design management team should attempt to actively involve all stakeholders (e.g., employees, partners, customers, and inhabitants) in the design process.

New services, processes, and models depend on an individual or group coming up with innovations and developing them. In order to foster development and originality, it is important to integrate different types of knowledge and experiences into a cooperative perspective. Networks can be considered as sources increasing the innovative capabilities of organisations and regions (Reagans & McEvily, 2003) and as actors are seldom capable of innovating by themselves, networks play an important role as channels for new knowledge (Florida, 1995). It is widely accepted today that users or user networks are often a major source of innovation and have even been proven to be the principal driving force of many innovations in different industries (Lettl, Herstatt, & Gemuenden, 2006). This phenomenon has many names: user-driven innovation (Von Hippel, 2005), user involvement (Alam, 2002; Magnusson, 2003), co-creation (Prahalad & Ramaswamy, 2004), or participatory innovation (Buur & Matthews, 2008). Understanding the role that users can play in innovation has been the focus of different strands of research in economics, organisation and management science, social sciences, design and engineering, and systems development. Many of these studies differ radically in their aims, methods, findings and, especially, implications for the management and organisation of user-driven innovation.

There is no universal agreement on whether user involvement is beneficial or not, and the research findings are contradictory. But there is a consensus about the valuable input of users in the early phases of innovation processes – especially in incremental innovations (Lettl et al., 2006). At least two main benefits of involving users in the ideation phase have been identified: users can bring in ideas with a higher perceived user value and, furthermore, they can bring in more innovative ideas under certain circumstances (Kristensson & Magnusson, 2005). Bitner, Brown, & Meuter (2000) recommend that, particularly in the design process of technology-based services, close involvement of customers is useful. Being asked to come up with ideas without any restrictions can stimulate creativity. The creative potential of the users may actually be dependent on not knowing exactly what is possible. This enables them to think outside the box. This theory is supported by psychological experiments, the results of which have shown that priming can, in fact, reduce creativity, as participants tend to be preoccupied with already-known solutions (Dahl & Moreau, 2002; Marsh, Ward, & Landau, 1999).

An important question is how user involvement is actually conducted in user-driven place branding. Modern communication technologies facilitate new ways for users and inhabitants to become more active and powerful as user involvement can take place, for instance, in on-line communities (Jeppesen & Molin, 2003), but users can also be involved in different kinds of brainstorming and workshops. According to Lundkvist and Yakhlef (2004), ideas do not just exist; rather they take shape in and through conversational engagement between actors. Formal and informal conversation between stakeholders cross-fertilises perspectives, and generates new insights and ideas. Lettl (2007) also suggests that the interaction dimension of user involvement is important, and face-to-face interactions are needed to develop an understanding of the complex information that users transfer.

One possibility to bring different stakeholders together in city design management is using different kinds of Living Labs (Figure 9.2). A Living Lab is a system for building a future in which real-life user-driven development and innovation will be a normal co-creation technique for new products, services, and societal infrastructure. A Living Lab offers services and methods, which enables the users to take active part in development and innovation. The Living Lab laboratory is located where the people are, that is, at home, in school, in the workplace, in town, and among hobbyists. Products, services, and solutions are developed and tested in real surroundings and end-users actively participate in development. The Living Lab believes that the needs of the user and the consumer are paramount in developing products, services, and solutions, and at the same time, new solutions and business opportunities are sought among rising trends and weak signals.

CONCLUSION

City design or city aesthetics management aims to increase competitiveness by distinguishing the city from others. City design management consists of four basic elements: city topography, general impression, presentation and management, creativity being the bond that binds these elements together. A city brand needs all these elements to be successful. An attractive city needs a functionally built environment with diverse street life and effective identity, image, reputation, and branding in order to absorb important human flows. The measures of city design need to be presented by communication, marketing, and evaluation, and the change must be envisioned and managed in a creative and distinctive way. One way to do this is to involve the inhabitants and other stakeholders in city design management as using networks for sharing both personal and municipal intelligence is one of the most effective ways of keeping pace with changing times. Therefore, urban aesthetics developed by means of city design management could create a basis for the distinction principle of reputation, whilst the communication principle is extremely important in the realisation of city aesthetics as a competitiveness factor.

ACKNOWLEDGEMENT

The authors wish to thank the European Regional Development Fund and the Regional Council of Päijät-Häme for the opportunity of presenting their research in Destination Brands.

References

Alam, I. (2002). An exploratory investigation of user involvement in new service development. *Journal of the Academy of Market Science*, *30*(3), 250–261.

Anholt, S. (2004). Branding places and nations. The economist series In R. Clifton, J. Simmons, & S. Ahmad (Eds.), *Brands and branding* (pp. 213–226). Princeton, NJ: Bloomberg Press.

Anholt, S. (2007). *Competitive identity. The new brand management for nations, cities and regions*. Basingstoke: Palgrave Macmillan.

Aula, P., & Harmaakorpi, V. (2008). Innovative milieu – a view on regional reputation building: a case study of the Lahti Urban Region. *Regional Studies*, *42*(4), 523–538.

Aula, P., & Heinonen, J. (2002). Maine: Menestystekijä. Helsinki: WSOY.

Aula, P., & Mantere, S. (2005). Hyvä yritys: Strateginen maineenhallinta. Helsinki: WSOY.

Boschma, R., & Fritsch, M. (2009). Creative class and regional growth: Empirical evidence from seven European Countries. *Economic Geography*, *85*(4), 391–423.

Bitner, M. J., Brown, S. W., & Meuter, M. L. (2000). Technology infusion in service encounters. *Journal of the Academy of Marketing Science*, *28*(1), 138–148.

Buur, J., & Matthews, B. (2008). Participatory innovation. *International Journal of Innovation Management*, *12*(3), 255–273.

Camagni, R. (2002). On the concept of territorial competitiveness: Sound or misleading? *Urban Studies*, *39*(13), 2395–2411.

Cities of the future – global competition, local leadership. (2006). PricewaterhouseCoopers. Available: http://www.pwc.com/gx/en/government-public-sector-research/pdf/cities-final.pdf

Dahl, D. W., & Moreau, P. (2002). The influence and value of analogical thinking during new product ideation. *Journal of Marketing Research*, *39*(2), 47–60.

Drake, G. (2003). This place gives me space: Place and creativity in the creative industries. *Geoforum*, *34*, 511–524.

Florida, R. (1995). Towards the learning regions. *Futures*, *27*, 527–536.

Florida, R. (2002). *The rise of creative class. And how it is transforming work, leisure, community and every day life*. New York, USA: Basic Books.

Fombrun, C. (1996). *Reputation: Realizing value from the corporate image*. Boston: Harvard Business School Press.

Haapala, A. (2009). The aesthetic quality of life. The Future of Aesthetics Annual Conference of the Nordic Society for Aesthetics, June 11–14, 2009, Trondheim.

Harmaakorpi, V. (2006, September). The regional development method as a tool for regional innovation policy. *European Planning Studies*, *14*(8), 1085–1104.

Harmaakorpi, V., Kari, K., & Parjanen, S. (2008). City design management as a local competitiveness factor. *Place Branding and Public Diplomacy*, *4*(2), 169–181.

Hospers, G. -J. (2003). Creative cities in Europe. Urban competitiveness in the knowledge economy. *Intereconomics*, *38*(5), 260–269.

Jansson, J., & Power, D. (2006). The image of the city – urban branding as constructed capabilities in Nordic city regions. Retrieved from: www.nordicinnovation.net/_img/image_of_the_city_-_web.pdf

Jeppesen, L. B., & Molin, M. J. (2003). Consumers as co-developers: Learning and innovation outside the firm. *Technology Analysis & Strategic Management*, *15*(3), 363–383.

Karisto, A. (2004). Arkiviihtyvyyden aika, kaupunkipolitiikan pehmeä puoli. 14/2004 In *Kaupunkiseutujen kasvun aika* (pp. 31–36). Sisäasianministeriön julkaisuja Helsinki: Alueiden kehittäminen.

Kotter, J. P. (1988). *The leadership factor*. New York: Free Press.

Kotler, P., Asplund, C., Rein, I., & Haider, D. (1999). *Marketing places Europe*. London: Pearson Education Ltd.

Kristensson, P., & Magnusson, P. (2005). Involving users for incremental or radical innovation – A matter of tuning. Paper presented at 12th International Product Development Management Conference proceedings in Copenhagen, Denmark, June 12–14. Retrieved from http://www.mangematin.org/MCOI/Textes%202005-6/KristenssonMaggnusson-MatterOfTuning-2005.pdf (accessed 17.12.08).

Krugman, P. (1998). *Pop internationalism*. Cambridge, MA: MIT Press.

Lettl, C. (2007). User involvement competence for radical innovation. *Journal of Engineering and Technology Management*, *24*, 53–75.

Lettl, C., Herstatt, C., & Gemuenden, H. G. (2006). Users' contributions to radical innovation: Evidence from four cases in the field of medical equipment technology. *R&D Management*, *36*(3), 251–272.

Linnamaa, R. (1999). Kaupunkiseudun kilpailukyvyn rakenteelliset ja dynaamiset elementit. In M. Sotarauta (Ed.), *Kaupunkiseutujen kilpailukyky ja johtaminen tietoyhteiskunnassa, Suomen Kuntaliitto* Helsinki, Finland: ACTA No. 106.

Lundkvist, A., & Yakhlef, A. (2004). Customer involvement in new service development: a conversational approach. *Managing Service Quality*, *14*(2/3), 249–257.

Magnusson, P. R. (2003). Benefits of involving users in service innovation. *European Journal of Innovation Management*, *6*(4), 228–238.

Marsh, R., Ward, T., & Landau, J. (1999). The inadvertent use of prior knowledge in a generative cognitive task. *Memory and Cognition*, *27*(1), 94–105.

Maula, J. (1999). Eurooppalainen kaupunki. Lecture on 11th January 1999 by Professor Maula, Tampere University of Technology, Department of Architecture, The Institute of Urban Planning and Design.

Morgan, N., & Pritchard, A. (2002). Contextualizing destination branding. In N. Morgan, A. Pritchard, & R. Pride (Eds.), *Destination Branding. Creating the unique destination proposition* (pp. 11–41). Oxford: Butterworth Heinemann.

Parkerson, B., & Saunders, J. (2005). City branding: Can goods and services branding models be used to brand cities? *Place Branding*, *1*(3), 242–264.

Prahalad, C. K., & Ramaswamy, V. (2004). Co-creation experiences: the next practice in value creation. *Journal of Interactive Marketing*, *18*(3), 5–14.

Rainisto, S. (2003). Success factors of place marketing. Helsinki University of Technology, Institute of Strategy and International Business, Doctoral Dissertations 2003/4, Espoo.

Raunio, M. (2001). Asuin- ja elinympäristön laatu kaupunkiseutujen kilpailuetuna. In M. Sotarauta, & N. Mustikkamäki (Eds.), *Alueiden kilpailukyyn kahdeksan elementtiä* (pp. 129–150). Helsinki: Suomen Kuntaliitto: ACTA No. 137.

Reagans, R., & McEvily, B. (2003). Network structure and knowledge transfer: the effects of cohesion and range. *Administrative Science Quarterly, 48*(2), 240–267.

Silander, M., Tervo, H., & Niittykangas, H. (1997). Uusi aluepolitiikka ja yritysten sijaintikäyttäytyminen Keski-Suomen taloudellisen tutkimuskeskuksen julkaisuja 142, Jyväskylä.

Stigel, J., & Friman, S. (2006). City branding – all skoke, no fire? *Nordicom Review, 27*(2), 243–266.

Storper, M. (1997). *The regional world: Territorial development in a global economy.* New York, USA: The Guilford Press.

Virtanen, P. (1999). *Kaupungin imago. Mikä tekee Pariisista Pariisin ja Pisasta Pisan.* Helsinki: Rakennustieto Oy.

Von Hippel, E. (2005). Democratizing innovation. Cambridge: The MIT Press. Retrieved from: http://web.mit.edu/evhippel/www/democ1.htm.

CHAPTER

10

The tone of voice challenge

Roger Pride

INTRODUCTION

The Oxford English Dictionary defines 'reputation' as, 'the beliefs or opinions that are generally held about someone or something'. In the case of Wales, these beliefs and opinions have not always been positive. Moreover, they have been fashioned over many years and many are firmly entrenched. It can be argued that countries – like people – have individual reputational balance sheets – a wide range of positive, negative, and neutral characteristics, assets, resources, and features that collectively determine whether the overall reputation is in credit (positive) or in deficit (negative). This chapter will:

- Outline the Wales brand context;
- Discuss the tourism brand and marketing strategy;
- Consider the brand ambition for Wales.

THE WALES BRAND CONTEXT

Like most professional Destination Marketing Organisations (DMOs) the former Wales Tourist Board (WTB), regularly undertook qualitative research among current and potential visitors to the country. The aim was to better understand the way in which Wales was viewed as a holiday destination. During the 1990s, the research revealed that the perception of Wales was very different for those who had been on a holiday compared to those who had not visited the place. In the main those who had visited Wales were able to formulate their perceptions based on their holiday experiences, whereas, the perceptions of non-visitors seemed in the main to be influenced by images of Wales received through non-tourism communication and experiences.

© 2011 Published by Elsevier Ltd. All rights reserved.
DOI: 10.1016/B978-0-08-096930-5.10010-2

Put another way, the image of Wales as a tourism destination had been 'contaminated' or 'polluted' by a wide range of factors not directly related to holidays. Much of this research had been conducted with residents from the rest of the United Kingdom. It is not surprising, therefore, that the majority of them will have had multiple contacts or 'touch points' with Wales and Welsh people. These influences would range from images of Wales conveyed on television news and drama to observations of Wales generated through sport and some would even be influenced by recollections of Welsh people they might have known or might have seen in the media.

In previous years, many of those non-tourism communications could be regarded as being negative. News content involving stories about industrial unrest in Wales, particularly within the mining industry, created associations with heavy industry. From time to time, there were stories of minor acts of terrorism, such as the burning of second homes in Wales. No doubt these and other factors would have contributed to the overall impression of Wales held by those researched. It followed, therefore, that the task of improving the perception of Wales as a tourism destination could not be completely isolated from the need to influence the wider reputation of Wales as a country. If reputation is the beliefs or opinions that are generally held about someone or something, in the case of Wales these beliefs and opinions were not always positive. Moreover, they had been shaped over many years and for many were firmly ingrained.

I have said above that places – like people – have individual reputational balance sheets – a wide range of positive, negative, and neutral characteristics, assets, resources, and features that collectively determine whether the overall reputation is in credit (positive) or in deficit (negative). The conventional tourist board, of course has very little influence over these 'non-tourism factors'. However, we were aware that some of our competitor destinations were more able to overcome the negative aspects of their reputation. A good example would be Ireland. At the time Ireland was often in the news because of the political troubles in Northern Ireland. Stories relating to anti-British sentiments and even acts of violence perpetrated by the IRA and other republican terrorist organisations were prevalent in the media. However, it appeared that potential visitors were more able to isolate these non-tourism factors (see Chapter 23). We concluded that their reputational balance sheet was in credit – the positive associations of Ireland as a destination were strong enough to enable many to ignore these negative political stories or at least to put them to one side when considering holiday destination choice.

At that time we believed that our role was to influence and enhance those tourism factors that were, to some degree, under our control, both in terms of product and experience enhancement and in terms of brand communication. If we could improve the positive aspects of Wales' reputational balance sheet it would act as a strong counterpoint to those negative elements beyond our control. In other words, we believed that our role was to strengthen and accentuate the positives of the tourism experience so that Wales as a destination could more easily overcome the non-tourism 'pollutants'.

In recent years many countries have come to recognise the value of a strong brand image for the country. They have recognised the benefits of an identity premium not just for tourism promotion, but also for the marketing of the country as a place to invest, a place to study, a place that offers high-quality food produce, and so on. Governments have also begun to appreciate the interdependency, in image terms, of these various sectors. As argued above, a country's competitiveness within a particular market is to some extent dependent on its reputation as a whole. For this reason, many countries have tried various ways to devise brand and organisational architecture to influence and guide the marketing of the place to their various target sectors.

Wales was no exception. Shortly after the establishment of the Welsh Assembly Government (WAG) in 1999, the then First Minister, Rhodri Morgan began to turn his attention to the development of a brand strategy for Wales. This evolved in various ways until eventually in 2004 he announced that the WTB and Wales' economic development agency – the Welsh Development Agency – would be merged directly into WAG. This presented the opportunity to bring more coherence to the promotion of Wales and to bring more of the levers of brand control under the influence of WAG. Although governments in other countries had sought greater control over brand policy, few had taken the step to ensure closer management of brand delivery for the major external marketing programs.

At that time the brand and marketing work that the WTB had undertaken had received widespread praise for its originality and results. Consequently, I was given the task of building on the brand work developed for tourism and for developing the wider place brand architecture and framework for the Wales brand. The main aspects of that work are explained in the remainder of this chapter. It is important to point out that the destination brand for tourism had already been developed and therefore had a major influence on the wider brand development. Under normal circumstances, the domain or overarching brand would be created first and it would direct the development of the positioning for the various sectors. Nevertheless in Wales it was felt important to build on existing successes rather than start with a blank sheet of paper – after all, a lot of research and analysis, which had led to the development of the tourism brand, were very relevant for the other sectors.

THE TOURISM BRAND AND MARKETING STRATEGY

Figure 10.1 illustrates the core components of our tourism plan. It is based on an analysis of the brand, an understanding of our existing and potential customers, and an appreciation of the marketing environment in which Wales competes. It also highlights the importance of the tone and content of communications to our target market segment.

The brand is based on the core pillars of Real People, Human Place and Magical Culture and History:

- Real People – The Welsh are down to earth, open-minded, grounded, approachable, and genuine. They are also proud and passionate, straight talking, and possess a wry humour.

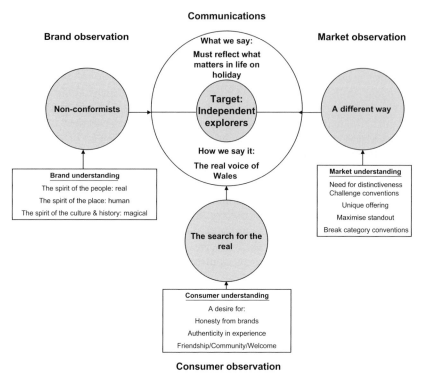

Figure 10.1 The core components of the tourism plan

- Human Place – Wales is inclusive and welcoming; it offers simple powerful experiences. There is a strong sense of belonging and an egalitarian tradition. Wales is not remote. It is lived in and enlivened. It is compact and accessible.
- Magical Culture and History – Wales is a place with undeniable magic. There is a deep history with layer upon layer going back into the mists of time. It is a land of legends and stories, which interweave fact and fiction, which blur the lines of myth and reality. It is the place of King Arthur, of the Mabinogi of deep Celtic tradition. It is a country of unusual customs and traditions, whose place names go beyond mere identification to capture a human story.

However, we needed a strong core idea at the heart of the destination brand. One of the key insights was that the Welsh could be regarded as 'The Original Non-Conformists'. A quote from the celebrated Welsh travel writer Jan Morris supports this: 'Wales has generally set itself against the Powers and Potentates, against the pretensions of authority, against snobbery and arrogance'. Wales has had a long tradition of challenging the status quo in the fields of politics and religion. This healthy disregard for the conventional way of doing things is a great asset for a challenger brand (see Morgan, 1999) and it was felt that we could use this to build a compelling point of view on holidays based on a strong set of values for leisure and life.

This 'Different Way', we summed this up as 'The Real Alternative' and this became the idea at the brand core. We would communicate Wales as the Real Alternative to more conventional tourist destinations; a real, living, breathing, working country that presents our independently minded visitors with a genuine welcome and authentic, imaginative, and unpacked experiences; a country that visitors can explore and enjoy in their own individual way. Therefore, at our brand core was the idea of a different way of doing things – a Welsh order of things, an amalgam of character, temperament, climate, and history. We wanted to convey a Welsh way of looking at the world.

Consumer research had suggested that consumers were increasingly expecting more honesty from brands. People were becoming more marketing savvy and could spot inconsistencies and false claims in brand communication. There was also an increasing desire for more authentic experiences. Our target visitors wanted to be part of the place they were visiting. They wanted genuine friendship and welcome and wanted to feel part of the community they were visiting, if only for a short while. We summed this up as 'the search for the real' and we described our target visitor as an 'Independent Explorer'. Independent explorers are in search of new experiences and places. They shun over commercialised tourist honey pots. They are free minded and do not follow the herd. They are free spirited, they look for places that allow them to be themselves, that enrich them, and challenge them. They like to interact with the place, to understand its culture and to meet its people.

We further segmented this group into the following categories:

* Family explorers – Families with young children looking for holiday opportunities and destinations, which allowed them to spend time with one another and to learn and grow as a family.
* Active explorers – People whose holiday and leisure decisions were often driven by a desire to pursue outdoor interests and activities.
* Personal explorers – Potential visitors who were seeking opportunities, which help them learn and grow as individuals or those looking for quality products and experiences for sharing with close friends and partners.

In terms of market environment in which we competed we observed that most destinations were very unadventurous in terms of their marketing and communications. Those responsible for marketing destinations are often under pressure to play it safe and to satisfy the complex structure of stakeholders, places, and products that make up the destination. As in most market categories, conventions and norms around the style and tone of marketing communications start to build. There was clearly a need for distinctiveness and to challenge those conventions and norms. We felt that it was important to promote a unique offering and to maximise the standout of our marketing communications from those of our competitors.

The ultimate and, perhaps for us, the most crucial additional ingredient for the Wales brand was the creation of a distinctive tone of voice for our communications. This tone of voice stemmed from the personality of the Wales brand. In seeking a marketing agency to work with us to implement our marketing communications we had prepared a marketing brief, which went into great detail about the brand, our target customers, and the marketing environment. We eventually appointed Wieden and Kennedy who had developed a strong reputation for creativity and cutting-edge work – most notably for campaigns they had created for Honda. In responding to the brief, the Creative Director Tony Davidson was skeptical about the whole idea of applying traditional branding techniques for countries. He fully supported the need to have a strong 'Welsh' point of view, but he argued passionately that this point of view needed to be communicated with a distinctive and engaging tone of voice. He felt that it was this tone of voice, which would set Wales apart from its competitors. We then worked together to discover and cultivate the real 'Voice of Wales'.

We wanted the Wales advertising and communication to sound natural, approachable, and honest. We sought a conversational approach with short uncomplicated sentences. We wove a humorous, wry thread through each communication piece in keeping with our brand personality. We preferred clipped, straightforward headlines with no unnecessary words. We had to be original and intriguing – this is easier if we avoid the general and vague. So, in our communication we embraced the personal, the specific, and the anecdotal to highlight the human and real aspects of the Wales brand. Figure 10.2 illustrates examples of the Wales tone of voice, which were included in the original brand guidelines. We compare how other destinations might talk about aspects of the destination to the Welsh tone of voice. The Welsh tone of voice is in italics.

The Wales tourism brand had very strong value set, a clear point of view, a close understanding of the market in which we competed and our potential visitors, and a distinctive style and tone of voice. So it was from this very solid foundation that we began to look at the wider brand architecture and strategy for Wales.

(i) Other countries would say – 'or try one of the many vast stretches of white beach with only the sound of crystal clear water lapping on to the shore...'

Wales would say – *Tenby Beach stretches for three miles. This year it won the award for having the best sandcastle sand in Britain.*

(ii) Other countries would say – 'the bustling market town of xxxx, with its famous Abbey, lies at the heart of the area. There is also a very attractive park, and a leisure centre. The town has a modern, attractive shopping centre and is host to a weekly Monday market which provides a colourful focal point and draws crowds from a wide surrounding area.'

Wales would say – *Jane Morgan has been setting up her cheese stall in the Monday market for 27 years. 'Tastes have changed' she said. 'Now they want their Caerphilly with Chocolate chips in it.'*

(iii) Other countries would say – The xxxx also has excellent visitor attractions, and offers great activity options from world-class golf and fishing to horse-riding, walking, cycling, and water sports.

Wales would say – *Hole 17 at Celtic Manor is the longest in European golf. It is 679 yards and you are supposed to do it in five strokes. Peter Smith has just taken an 11.*

Figure 10.2 The distinctive Welsh tone of voice

THE BRAND AMBITION FOR WALES

In devising the wider brand strategy for Wales we recognised that we needed a framework, which was clear and focussed enough to give direction to all relevant communications relating to the Wales brand, yet it had to be flexible enough to accommodate the messaging needs of many sectors. The strategy would fail if, through seeking more consistency, we actually dilute the communication to specific audiences.

Our solution needed to satisfy the following criteria:

- It needed to be broad and flexible enough to drive and inform all strategies, communications and behaviour. This of course is a huge challenge; but if the overall framework just focussed on communication it would fail to influence future strategy and behaviour, which we felt was important.
- The brand needed to motivate potential customers, stakeholders and to enthuse the people of Wales. It was critical to ensure that the solution met with widespread support within Wales as well as among our target markets.
- The brand needed to ensure that over time it would help build an identity premium for Wales.
- The brand would add value to all communication.
- The brand would reflect the idea of Wales being a small, clever country – something that many key politicians were strongly supportive of.
- Finally, we wanted to ensure that the brand reflected the challenger brand principles that seemed so relevant for Wales and which had worked so well in previous tourism campaigns (see Pride, 2004).

The framework would need a domain brand, which would drive all strategies, communications, and behaviours. It would need to allow for the creation of specific positioning for key sectors. There would be a core value set, which allowed some flexibility for each sector. There would be a common and distinctive tone of voice for all communication. Finally, there would be one brand identity or logo.

The initial development work involved interviews with key stakeholders in the sectors outside of tourism. We needed to understand the relevance and applicability of the Wales tourism brand to these sectors and to identify those elements, which were common and where we needed to adapt in order to enable suitability beyond tourism. We concluded that communicated in the right way the core components, 'Real People' and 'Human Place', were right to support the wider brand. However 'Magical Culture and History' seemed to be specific to tourism. We decided, therefore, to retain 'Human Place' and 'Real People' as core components. The third component focusing on culture, beliefs, or attitude could change to allow greater relevance.

Research also suggested that the central idea of 'a Different Way' was valid in a wider context. It would allow Wales to have a clear point of view and to challenge conventions. It would also encourage us to develop a distinctive offer in sectors we were targeting. Consequently, the first phase of the brand development work centred on the interpretation of 'A Different Way' as the core positioning for the domain brand and for Foreign Direct Investment (FDI) for Wales. We also looked for a third component to support 'human' and 'real'.

The role of the domain brand is subtly different to the positionings and propositions within specific sectors. It needs to steer the direction of all strategies, behaviours, and communication linked to the brand. Its purpose can be seen as a kind of national compass giving direction, guidance, principles, and values to inform decision making. As such 'A Different Way' in this context, should be about defining the national approach to solving problems and developing policy and strategy. In searching for the overall domain brand positioning we revisited the idea of the 'Original Non-Conformists' for our insight and inspiration. Research had also shown that Wales was a home to a good number of 'firsts' – inventions and ideas, which stemmed from the desire to challenge the status quo. However, Scotland had already positioned itself as the Land of Innovation and Inventions. We needed something that was deeper and routed in the national psyche. Ultimately, we decided on 'Original Thinking.' We also decided on 'challenging' as the third component to support 'real' and 'human.'

So what should 'Original Thinking' say about Wales? It suggests that Wales is a nation prepared to follow its own patch; a nation, which is not unduly swayed by outside influence. Wales should look for Welsh solutions for Welsh problems. It reflected the fact that the Welsh are passionate people, not afraid to speak their own minds. The positioning underpinned the fact that Wales is a land, which cherishes culture and creativity. As a result, it supports and nurtures the creative industries and positively encourages artistic and cultural expression. The domain brand needs to help mark out the ambition for the nation. As such, while being rooted in reality, it needs to be visionary and have a degree of stretch and ambition attached to it. 'Original Thinking' encourages the development of a country, which prides itself on being different, alternative, innovative and thinking laterally. The kind of behaviours inspired by the idea of 'Original Thinking' might be bold, pioneering, goal-orientated, entrepreneurial, creative, resourceful and imaginative (Figure 10.3).

Figure 10.3 Neolithic man, glaciers, or Merlin?

THE TRADE AND INVESTMENT BRAND

Apart from tourism, the other main external marketing of Wales was focussed on the promotion of Wales as a location for FDI. Research work among potential inward investment decision makers sponsored by the Welsh Development Agency demonstrated that, increasingly, investment decisions were being strongly influenced by perceptions of the place rather than other 'hard' factors such as access to markets, the availability of appropriately skilled labour, the provision of land and premises, and the potential for relocation grants. These place-related 'soft' factors such as an agreeable climate and environment, friendly local people, tradition in art and culture, and entertainment and leisure provision were becoming increasingly important. It could be argued that the 'hard' criteria had become hygiene factors – criteria that needed to be satisfied but were not necessarily differentiating.

This research and analysis, therefore, suggested two things: first, the imagery more traditionally associated with tourism promotion could have an important influence on wider perceptions of the place. Second, it implied that the proposition and communication for FDI should take full account of both the rational and emotional considerations in destination or location choice.

Again initial consultation suggested that 'real' and 'human' were relevant in FDI promotion. 'Real' would demonstrate that Wales always treated its customers and business partners with honesty and integrity, that we would never over-promise and under-deliver. 'Human' reveals that being a small country Wales treats every business as vitally important, regardless of its size. It also respects and is sensitive to the needs of an individual business, taking time to understand the issues it faces and find appropriate solutions. The third component chosen for the FDI positioning was 'inventive.' We needed to demonstrate that we were creative, imaginative, and resourceful in our approach to business and that we were willing to embrace new and innovative ways of working. It suggested that we needed to be tailor-made in our approach, delivering bespoke solutions that best suit our customers' or business partners' objectives and aspirations.

Initially for business marketing, we interpreted 'A Different Way' as 'The Real Opportunity.' However, we recognised that if we were to break through a very crowded market place we needed to be very original in our actual campaign delivery. Many competitors were talking about 'opportunity' but once again we detected a great deal of similarity and conformity in the way these competitor destinations were marketed. The communication was littered with clichés – it tended to be very inward looking and the tone was corporate and cold.

Early creative ideas linked to new positioning were fresh and sat very comfortably alongside the tourism communication (Figure 10.4). In reality, however, it needed to be more audacious and challenging in order to stand out from those competitors. There are literally hundreds of special development countries/regions/zones across Europe and further afield all seeking to attract FDI. At the time of writing we are in the process of evolving the business proposition and developing a new campaign, which celebrates the Welsh Way of doing business. It will turn the idea of being a small country into a positive

We believe in making stuff that lasts.
We believe in good old-fashioned service.
We believe in sport.
We believe in trying to have some fun.
We believe the environment needs a few more friends.
We believe in making people think as well as buy.
We believe the glass is half full.
We believe higher quality means lower impact.
And we believe tea should always be made in a pot.
But hey that's just our way.
We're howies? Cardigan Bay's 3rd biggest clothing company.

Figure 10.4 Howies, Cardigan Bay's 3rd biggest clothing company

and celebrate the energetic and can-do ambition of Wales. Above all, it will break with sector norms and we want it to be talked about.

CONCLUSION

The challenge of ensuring that nation brand strategies provide a framework for the successful integration of tourism, business, food, and study communication is a real one, which all places are going to have to consider. The solution we devised for Wales was a good one for the time and place and circumstances we were in at the time. However, there is still a long way to go. We need to develop a clearer narrative around the brand to make it more accessible and understood by all stakeholders. Wales has a great story to tell. The individual chapters which relate to the different sectors in which we compete need to add up to a compelling read – a compendium of persuasive reasons to engage with Wales.

We need to find better ways of communicating the brand story internally – to the people of Wales. Too often the brand communication is focussed exclusively on external markets. Without solid foundation of support for the brand story within Wales, it will be difficult to find ambassadors who will help us convey the Wales brand story to outsiders. Like all good stories, the story of Wales needs to be well told. This is where a distinctive tone of voice and engaging style will help to ensure that there are more people willing to listen to the Wales brand story and to act as a result.

References

Morgan, A. (1999). *Eating the big fish: How challenger brands can compete against leader brands*. Chichester: John Wiley & Sons.

Pride, R. (2004). A challenger brand. Wales: Golf as it should be. In
N. Morgan, A. Pritchard, & R. Pride (Eds.), *Destination branding: Creating the
unique destination proposition* (2nd ed.). Oxford: Elsevier.

Useful website

http://walesthebrand.com

CHAPTER

11

The digital challenge

Jon Munro and Bethan Richards

INTRODUCTION

Don't let anybody tell you anything different. We are all still learning. Most marketing professionals now agree that what we are experiencing is a fundamental and revolutionary change. Digital channels have driven a radical shift in customer behaviour and this is no more evident than in the customer's relationship with a brand and the active role the customer takes in shaping the dialogue with that brand and ultimately its reputation. When it comes to deciding where to go on holidays our friends' recommendations are frequently quoted as being the most influential factor and when researching those recommendations the information derived online occupies a critical role in destination choice.

Digital channels have grown up and no longer represent 'new' media. Just when marketers were starting to understand traditional 'push' media such as display and email, the balance of power changed. At the same time response through traditional channels has fallen, on and offline, as consumers are becoming increasingly turned off by one way dialogue. Advertising clutter is driving down returns as marketers grapple for attention in an increasingly crowded and ambivalent market. The now infamous Web 2.0 brings with it a collection of open source, interactive, and user-controlled online applications that support the creation of informal networks and facilitate the flow of ideas and knowledge by allowing the efficient generation, sharing and editing of informational content (Constantinides & Fountain, 2008). The terms social media and Web 2.0 are often used as interchangeable but social media is associated with the social aspects of Web 2.0 applications – participation, openness, conversations, community and connectedness (SpannerWorks, 2007).

The marketing environment we work in has changed beyond all recognition and relentlessly pushing our destination brand to an increasingly skeptical audience is becoming less effective in driving brand equity. Our customers are engaging in more meaningful relationships with brands and demanding

© 2011 Published by Elsevier Ltd. All rights reserved.
DOI: 10.1016/B978-0-08-096930-5.10011-4

that brands humanise and personalise their communications with them. It is now possible to collaborate on an unprecedented scale with anyone and everyone involved in shaping your destination brand. For destination brands and the Destination Marketing Organisation (DMO) this state of play creates a serious and exciting challenge. This chapter:

- Considers the tools, technologies and channels that are driving significant change in customer behaviour and how destinations are currently using them;
- Discusses the key challenges facing destination branding – content, socialisation, integration, and measurement;
- Considers what this means for destination brands, the DMO website and digital marketing strategy.

TOOLS, TECHNOLOGIES, AND CHANNELS

So what are the key tools and technologies within the tourism and travel space and how are DMOs currently using them? Blogging is becoming synonymous with the Internet and is seen as particularly important within tourism and travel. Corporate blogs are published by organisations in pursuit of their organisation goals and personal blogs by individuals based on their own personal experiences. There is an opportunity to reach out to the blogging community and influence what they are talking about in much the same way as traditional PR does to travel journalists. By utilising a syndicated blogging platform such as that used by Tourism British Columbia (www.hellobc.com) a DMO can aggregate and provide filtered search across blog contributions from a variety of contributors; the organisation itself, its marketing partners, the tourism industry and the visitors themselves. The recently launched Visit Wales blog award 'Wales in words' incentivizes the provision of quality content on third party blogs, facebook, flickr and myspace and builds links between those and the Visit Wales blog (http://blog.visitwales.co.uk) thus supporting the link building and SEO (Search engine optimisation) strategy.

Microblogging based on a stream of short text updates, currently in the form of twitter, has got to be the most talked about online application of the moment. One of its most powerful facets is its immediacy and mobile application – for your customers, it provides a powerful real-time search engine, which can be accessed on the fly and instantly tuned to interest and specific need. @VisitBritain publishes a relevant and useful commentary of events going on across the UK and @visitlondonweb provides a stream of last minute style things to do across the capital. Often lacking strategic direction, a destination's current approach to twitter is typically organic with similar feeds competing for the same followers.

Social networking means people can come together and create relationships online, often forming communities around specific interests. Destinations can create their own online communities within existing platforms or engage in dialog with an existing community. Visit Sweden have gone one stage further by creating their own social networking platform (www.communityofsweden.com)

as well as a Visit Sweden page on facebook. To what extent visitors and potential visitors can be expected to join communities on multiple specific platforms rather than engage with them through their trusted and favoured platforms remain to be seen. Much of the content across social networking sites, and increasingly that accessed directly through search results, originates from the users themselves and as such provides a wealth of peer-produced dynamic and relevant content untouched by marketing people.

An interesting and often politically sensitive issue for the DMO is exactly how to present user reviews of tourism products such as accommodation alongside existing quality grading systems. Some drive an integrated approach to product review but many opt for a user review platform such as that offered by Digital Visitor and used by Visit Britain (www.visitorreview.com/visitbritain) or their own bespoke solution such as that developed by the Canadian Tourism Commission (www.localsknow.ca), which focuses on destination content in the form of video and pictures, often with supporting commentary and ratings.

Exactly why is user-generated content so important? Quite simply because people trust other people more than they trust those trying to peddle their destination or hotel. People increasingly subscribe to people and that wisdom of the crowd is embodied in a wiki. Wikitravel (www.wikitravel.org) aspires to be the most comprehensive and up-to-date free worldwide travel guide and relies on successive iterations from travellers around the globe to maintain the content and its accuracy. Dedicated photo and video sharing sites enable channel development that corrals content in one place often under the banner of a destination brand (www.youtube.com/user/purenewzealand). Content can be organised using the tags created by the content creators (www.flickr.com/photos/tags/newzealand/) as well as the content consumers themselves. Social bookmarking sites do the latter and harness the power of the community through allowing the user to tag, save, share and manage their bookmarks.

Real Simple Syndication (RSS) means the user can subscribe to specific content and receive updates directly rather than having to visit that specific website. Widgets provide mini applications that can be downloaded to a user's desktop or embedded in third party sites. The end result is that increasingly it is the user that retains control of their own personalised online experience and it remains their choice about what content they interact with and from whom it comes. One feature of travel-related content is that it is generally associated with place – it can be georeferenced. Google mapping has been a Web 2.0 success story and none more than in travel and tourism. The ability to integrate Google maps in a website and overlay with navigation and product information has become the standard for product search. The ability to 'mashup' travel product with an endless array of user-generated georeferenced content is extremely powerful and more recently Google Street View has enabled another level of virtual experience for the potential visitor.

Don't forget traditional search, however. For most DMOs it is likely to continue to be the biggest driver of traffic to your website in the foreseeable future. With over one billion searches per day carried out on Google, where exactly you sit on the left or the right-hand side of this most important Internet real estate for your priority search terms is critical. There appear to be three key challenges facing the DMO. Firstly, which keywords should the organisation, its marketing partners and the industry it supports be bidding for – the long tail of tourism content might provide part of the answer. Secondly, how to build visibility on the left through SEO rather than continue to rely on paid for listings on the right-hand side – and which keywords to target through natural and paid search. Thirdly, how to take a strategic and integrated approach to SEO that coordinates and harnesses the efforts made through social media and online PR – the disciplines are inexorably linked and success in search engine marketing is correlated to the power of your brand online.

Supporting everything digital is the explosion in high speed Internet access – increasingly accessed through wireless networks. Rich audio visual content is no longer limited to the traditional broadcast channels we have worked with for so long and those very same channels are available online and can be accessed on demand to supplement an increasingly personalised online experience. Add to this the huge development in mobile technology and the inevitable convergence across media, channels, and devices, and you are faced with an environment in which not only can consumers consume content anywhere but they can also create and share from anywhere.

Customers are taking control of their relationships with brands, and the system of values, beliefs and attitudes that shape and influence customer behaviour has changed. Information culture has been replaced by conversation culture (Leonhard, 2009). Conversations, whether a review on tripadvisor, a picture on flickr or an interaction on twitter, drive the informal exchange of thoughts, opinions and feelings between customers who are increasingly listening to each other. Those conversations ultimately shape your brand and, at its most extreme, your brand becomes its reputation online defined through the conversations customers are having about their real brand experiences. Those conversations are seamlessly conducted across the real and virtual worlds as multitasking becomes a way of life; discussing, reading, browsing, contributing whilst eating and drinking. Our customers are lifecasting; they are sharing their personal life experiences online driven by the question 'what are you doing,' and at the same time creating a wealth of real-time experience. Whilst the decision to take a holiday might be an entirely rational one, the decision about where to take that holiday is likely to be an emotional one and influenced by the wealth of conversational content associated with that destination.

THE DIGITAL CHALLENGE

So what are the key challenges facing destination branding within the context of a changing digital media landscape and changing customer behaviour? We suggest that the challenges lie in four key areas – content, socialisation, integration, and measurement.

Content

We are all publishers – content is king and right now user-generated content reigns supreme. In the old destination marketing world, most content was locked up in the brochures that the DMO and their marketing partners were producing on a seasonal or annual basis. When more of that content resource moved online marketers suddenly realised that what could be saved in print production wasn't nearly enough to fund the provision of content across a more dynamic presence on the Internet. Marketers are never going to keep up and they need to find another way to fuel that content hungry web presence. Our destination and destination brand occupies a particular online space and within that space exists a network of content creators and content consumers (see Figure 11.1).

The Internet provides a truly collaborative environment and the challenge therefore is how does the destination harness that resource and mobilise it to help fulfill their marketing goals? The Visit Wales *wales10000things* campaign, run from March to October 2007, provides an early and interesting example. Supporting the '10 minutes in Wales' communications strategy by providing a virtual experience of what Wales has to offer through user-generated content, the campaign revolved around a platform for uploading, rating and sharing pictures and video content with supporting descriptions. This was the first time Visit Wales had relinquished total control of what appears on its website and relied on the contributions of others to support key messages such as the variety and wealth of things to do in Wales. The campaign put some of that control in the hands of the people of Wales and the tourism industry in Wales, relying on them to upload suitable content alongside user-generated content from visitors, thus providing a basis for collaboration.

Communities need something to lineup against, and the campaign line 'Real adventure holiday ideas' was a credible proposition and something that the network of content creators and consumers could get behind and support. The Visit Wales blog was launched in January 2008. Since then, customer commentary, in response to specific posts has not always been one

Figure 11.1 The network of content creators and consumers

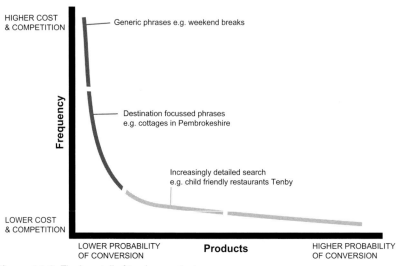

Figure 11.2 The long tail of tourism content

hundred percent positive. The point being though (and the same applies to user reviews) is that the rational consumer is capable of making a reasoned judgement. Where that commentary is concerned the fact that it was not entirely positive adds to the content's credibility and most people viewing that content will come to their own, invariably positive, conclusions. In the pursuit of reputation management and brand equity online the organisation can listen to these conversations and it can engage in the conversation for its own benefit if it so decides. The content itself lasts well beyond the life of the campaign or blog post. Any destination has a wealth of content associated with it – a long tail of content covering the spectrum of place content from country, through regions, cities, and towns and ultimately specific businesses (see Figure 11.2).

Relevance, quality, and appropriately linked content drive search traffic. Destination marketing should be concerned with both making sure that the customer experience is serviced appropriately by the destination's content network as well as ensuring that the content network handles search traffic efficiently. This might also provide a framework for defining keyword territories for DMOs, their marketing partners and tourism businesses themselves.

Socialisation

Socialisation can be defined as 'the process of learning one's culture and how to live within it' – for an individual it provides the skills and habits necessary for acting and participating within their society (Wikipedia, 2009a; 2009b). Destination brands have to learn about conversation culture, how to position themselves and how to apply an appropriate set of tools and approaches to participate in this new world. No longer can they rely on shouting from the rooftops or buying an audience – they have to find new and innovative ways

Figure 11.3 Owned, earned, and bought media

of attracting an appropriate audience and orientate themselves with that audience. Customers can arrive at your website from almost anywhere but generally that covers three key types of digital media: owned, earned, and bought (see Figure 11.3).

Owned media includes your own website, all of your other websites and your communications with your existing customers. Optimisation in this area should be concerned with your own web presence and eCRM strategy. Bought media covers anything for which you pay for a presence in and success in this area relies heavily on good media planning, efficient buying and the ongoing reporting and optimisation of that media presence. Earned media is much more about engaging with communities, listening to them and seeding conversations in those communities. To be successful in the earned media space, a brand needs to orientate its web presence within both the network of user-generated content that exists beyond its own site as well as the conversational content that surrounds it (see Figure 11.4). Your web presence then becomes a platform from which the brand can listen to, facilitate, and engage with the conversations going on around them as well as drive traffic from them.

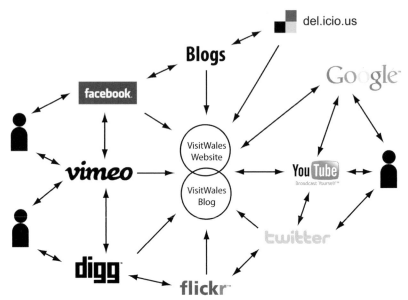

Figure 11.4 Your web presence within the earned media space

Integration

The occasions when a customer comes into contact with your destination brand, in the real or virtual world, are almost limitless. Integration really matters. Destination marketing needs to support the customer journey from inspiration, through booking and planning, catering for customers' needs at the destination, as well as building advocacy and creating return visits. The fragmented nature of the tourism product has always made coordination of this effort across different marketing partners and the industry a complex challenge. The same marketing objectives still apply – the destination still needs to acquire new customers, convert them, retain and grow business as well as measure and optimise what it is doing. The development of Web 2.0 and social media is indeed a fundamental and revolutionary change but the extent to which it currently dominates marketers' conversations should not mask the fact that what it provides is another set of channels that should be approached strategically, evaluated like any other channel and planned as part of an integrated digital marketing strategy.

The same argument extends to offline channels and broadcast media – digital does not replace offline communications, it works alongside them, enhances them and adds value to them. When Visit Wales launched *the wales1000things* campaign it did so across online and offline channels coordinating the message between them. Later on the content created through the campaign was used to develop a further direct mail piece based almost entirely on visitor contributions – thus taking online content back offline. Destination marketers need to remain cognizant of their target market's media habits and a multichannel strategy, at its best, can deliver stronger brand performance and customer loyalty (Bruce, Bondy, Street & Wilson, 2009).

Broadcast media, traditional or in the broadband era, will continue to support inspirational content and provide the vehicle for mass distribution of inspirational messages. It provides the opportunity for the brand to define its position and its opinion on something – over and above the noise created through social media. It amplifies that noise, drives awareness, and brings the brand front of mind, supporting other channels and increasing demand for your search terms. Get the basics right and it will support everything you do. Your website still needs to support your user experience and site conversion goals, thus increasing loyalty and conversion. Your eCRM strategy still needs to build strong and valuable relationships with your existing customers. Although social media is often hailed as being a brand crusader in times of reducing resources, destination brands must take account of or at least be aware of the opportunity cost associated with developing new channels and new approaches.

Measurement

New ways of doing things require new approaches to measurement. Destination marketing activities are often concerned with campaigns and measurement typically focuses on campaign awareness, response and conversion with an indicator to the effect on destination awareness and emotional proximity to that destination. Where online is concerned we measure success through things such as site traffic, numbers of unique users, the amount of content viewed, and on site conversion. In our new environment our success is much more dependent on things like the quality of our content network and the amount and sentiment of conversations carried out within the community of people with which we connect. Platform-specific metrics (such as the number of twitter followers or facebook friends) should be used in combination with other digital marketing benchmarks, such as SEO rankings, conversation sentiment, and behavioural outcomes (Econsultancy, 2009a; 2009b).

Whilst social media and online PR will drive traffic to your site, it is the attention to your brand and the 'buzz' it creates around it that is particularly important. However, measuring sentiment and the overall affection towards a brand is perhaps one of the more challenging measurement activities. Where measuring the social web is concerned, Weber (2009) suggests taking an approach that covers four key areas; involvement, interaction, intimacy, and influence. Involvement relates to the number of people in your network or community, interaction measures the number and type of action taken by those people, intimacy relates to the overall affection or aversion to your brand and influence measures the level of advocacy within your network. Most importantly the set of metrics you use to measure your efforts needs to be closely tied to what success looks like for your destination brand and drive the right strategic and tactical decisions.

WHAT DOES THIS MEAN FOR DESTINATION BRANDS?

It's fair to say that destination branding online has become more complex. We have to relinquish control and we need to understand that in the online space our brand's reputation is molded and defined by conversations and dialog, networks, and communities. If our reputation is 'the result of what we do, what we say, and what other people say about us' (Wikipedia, 2009a; 2009b), then how do we relinquish control whilst behaving in a way that will positively affect our brand's reputation in the mind of the consumer? The challenge, therefore, is fundamentally about reputation management and influencing collective opinion in the new networked environment. Adding to our woes, there seems to be no one coherent answer or strategy amongst DMOs as to how we affect collective online opinion and how we engage across multiple channels in an integrated way.

However, in the absence of a 'set piece' solution the new marketing environment is producing unprecedented levels of creativity, technical convergence, and some great storytelling. Tourism Queensland's 'Best Job in the World' contest provides a good example. We are in uncharted 'test and refine' territory and for now that feels right. Reassuringly, if we go back to the beginning, we'll find the basics have not changed. Our starting point is a unique brand position, a set of brand values, a target audience, a well defined look and feel, a tone of voice, and now more importantly than ever in this new conversation culture, a unique 'point of view'. Supporting that point of view requires a more interactive approach to marketing. Brands need to listen to all the information provided by customers (both explicit and implicit), understand the past and present to determine the best possible course of marketing action and communicate in a manner that is compelling, timely, and relevant (Anderson, 2009).

Perhaps then, the art and science of marketing in this new environment is fundamentally about deciding when to listen, when to take part and when to stimulate and cultivate conversations. That depends on the tools you are using as much as what you are trying to achieve. Twitter, for example, is a conversational tool whereby consumers expect to engage directly with brands. In this respect the destination brand conveyed by a DMO is considered an objective authority and therefore a valued source of opinion. The informal rules of engagement on twitter dictate that the brand should engage in a two way conversation. This should be done in an open, honest, and approachable way or brands risk damaging their perceived integrity and transparency. Being open to scrutiny is a sign of a brand's confidence and consequently engenders trust. Consumer opinion and sentiment can make or break a business and crisis management, the appropriate manner in which to respond to a 'tweet-storm,' for example, is an important consideration for destination brands. However, if a destination brand has built trust and support with the wider community over time by engaging with the network and activating brand participation then in times of crisis that same loyal army of brand evangelists can quickly counter balance and neutralise negative commentary.

Deciding which stories to tell and which conversations to cultivate requires an understanding of past and present perceptions of the destination. DMOs are privy to a vast amount of consumer research highlighting the perceived destination negatives and commonly propagated stereotypes and misconceptions. An effective social media strategy should therefore tactically deploy and instigate stories that address these destination negatives and support them with examples of 'best in class' product.

Challenger brand thinking (Morgan, 1999) resonates as strongly today as it did 10 years ago; be ruthlessly focussed; overcommit to what you do; stand out and stand for something unique in category; communicate this constantly, consistently, and saliently. Going big and communicating a consistent story becomes an even more exciting possibility when we consider harnessing and engaging our network of content creators. During the prelaunch phase of *wales1000things* Visit Wales mobilised the content network to assist in pre-populating the website with images, video, and commentary. Staff, friends, family, journalists, bloggers, and the tourism industry all uploaded content driven by a passion to change the perceived wisdom and encourage early engagement in the new website. It is generally accepted that the best online PR campaigns come from collaboration across different disciplines within the organisation and among multiple external agencies (Econsultancy, 2009a; 2009b) and you can add to this the opportunity to leverage the brand equity of authoritative brands through appropriate partnerships and bought media. Successful destination branding in the new world relies on a collaborative approach and harnessing the power of the content network, the community, and like-minded brands where the overall effect is greater than the sum of the individual parts.

CONCLUSION

Awareness and use of DMO websites is lower than that of commercial websites in the same space. Whilst perceived as an authoritative site by those that use them, their role as the 'official' site for the destination brings with it some less attractive connotations – limited and mainstream information, a biased view of the destination where the negatives are often overlooked and providing nothing 'off the beaten track' (Visit Britain, 2009). A perceived lack of objective and comparative information means their usefulness where initial destination choice is concerned is less than it might be. They score more highly for the provision of information that has no commercial motive – weather, security, visas, currency, museums, attractions, and background information on the destination's culture, history, and geography. Within the context of the customer journey DMO websites are currently used primarily at the planning and pre-visit stages (see Figure 11.5).

Taking into account the changing media landscape, the effect that has had on customer behaviour and the challenges outlined above, the DMO needs to think carefully about how to reinvent and reposition their web presence alongside that of commercial websites. The Internet has driven the move from a world of scarcity to one of abundance and this in itself provides an

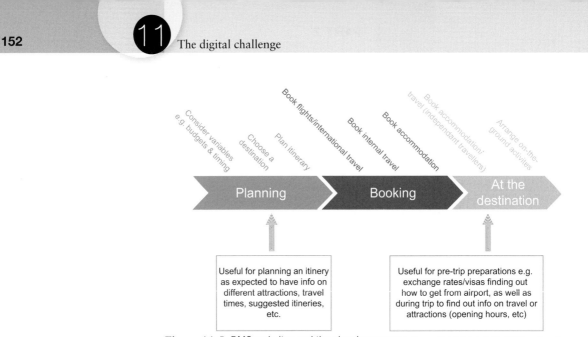

Figure 11.5 DMO websites and the planning process Source: Visit Britain Insights (2009) produced by Brands in Action.

opportunity. Providing a filter, being a curator and aggregator of content and conversations, and wrapping them up in the destination brand is one way the DMO website could add value and provide a valuable user experience. If socialising your web presence equates to opening up your website and providing a platform from which to monitor, link, and engage with content and communities that exist outside your own that necessarily means the flow of information and content should be two way.

The opportunity is as much about syndicating your content as well as pulling in relevant professional and user-generated content to your site. The challenge then becomes one of building on the DMO's existing authority, both in the eyes of Google and the consumer, adding the real and authentic credibility you need to compete and drive trust and wrapping the destination brand around all digital content and communications. By closing the loop between inspiration and advocacy through appropriate integration of user-generated content the destination can add real credibility to its inspirational messages. With the right toolset, rising to this challenge is more about the application of the tools rather than the technicalities of the tools themselves – much of which is possible for a small team of informed individuals not constrained by process or a one size fits all platform.

However, embracing the opportunities created by Web 2.0 and social media has been slow at the DMO level with many still in the early and experimental stages. So, what are the barriers? DMO websites are often built on a Destination Management System that powers the front end, as well as providing product search, retrieval, and backend functionality. Web 2.0 and socialisation brings with it a new set of tools that need to be integrated with existing systems and platforms. The relationship with stakeholders and the industry can be a very different one in this new environment; potentially hugely collaborative, but roles and responsibilities need to be redefined and as such it represents a significant cultural change. However, it is perhaps internal organisational change where the greatest barriers exist. Digital marketing strategy needs to be particularly responsive to a changing market and the organisation needs to be able to respond more quickly to the opportunities and threats this brings. DMOs are not typically strategically agile organisations but if they are going to survive in an environment of rapid and constant change they need to engage in strategic analysis, development, and implementation on a more continuous basis and over shorter cycles than they have ever done in the past. Success requires the right people, the right mindset, the right internal structures, and the right stakeholder and industry relationships where, across all of those things, innovation, decentralisation, and collaboration are all important.

References

Anderson, E. R. (2009). Next-generation campaign management: how campaign management will evolve to enable interactive marketing. *Journal of Direct, Data and Digital Marketing Practice*, *10*(3), 272–282.

Bruce, L., Bondy, K., Street, R., & Wilson, H. (2009). Channel evolution: how new multi-channel thinking can deliver competitive advantage. *Journal of Direct, Data and Digital Marketing Practice*, *10*(4), 329–335.

Constantinides, E., & Fountain, S. J. (2008). Web 2.0: conceptual foundations and marketing issues. *Journal of Direct, Data and Digital Marketing Practice*, *9*(3), 231–244.

Econsultancy (2009a). Online PR and social media trends briefing – june 2009 http://econsultancy.com/reports/online-pr-and-social-media-trends-briefing

Econsultancy (2009b). Online PR trends briefing – january 2009 http://econsultancy.com/reports/online-pr-trends-briefing-january-2009.

Leonhard, G. (2009). Social media and the future of marketing and advertising www.mediafuturist.com.

Morgan, A. (1999). *Eating the big fish: How challenger brands can compete against leader brands*. Chichester: Wiley.

SpannerWorks (2007). What is social media. In Constantinides, E., & Fountain, S.J. (2008) Web 2.0: conceptual foundations and marketing issues. *Journal of Direct, Data and Digital Marketing Practice*, *9*(3), 231–244 (www.spannerworks.com/ebooks).

Visit Britain (2009). To understand information needs, expectations and usage in the holiday planning process in order to guide the development of the new Visit Britain website, Visit Britain Research Debrief, February 5, 2009

Weber, L. (2009). *Marketing to the social web: How digital customer communities build your business*. New Jersey: John Wiley & Sons.

Wikipedia (2009a). http://en.wikipedia.org/wiki/Socialisation (retrieved 03/07/2009).

Wikipedia (2009b) http://en.wikipedia.org/wiki/Reputation (retrieved 03/07/2009).

Useful websites

www.hellobc.com
http://blog.visitwales.co.uk
www.communityofsweden.com

www.visitorreview.com/visitbritain
www.localsknow.ca
www.wikitravel.org)
www.youtube.com/user/purenewzealand
www.flickr.com/photos/tags/newzealand/

The measurement challenge

Jeremy Hildreth

INTRODUCTION

We all like to know how we're doing. And feedback, note psychologists and educators, is a vital component of learning, growth, and development. So when a place is making specific, dedicated efforts to alter or improve its image, the desire to find out what people really think – and whether that thinking is shifting in some hoped for way – is understandable. The good news is it's actually easier to get valid and useful feedback than people might assume. The bad news is, for whatever reason, most of the methods commonly used to gain feedback are flawed, resulting in feedback that is of limited value or, worse, is even misleading.

Importantly, before we can do any effective counting, we must know which factors are the ones to count. Although rarely expressed so tersely, the ultimate purpose of any place branding activity, in my considered opinion, is simple and threefold: (1) for the place to become better understood in various facets; (2) and more attractive to, or appreciated or trusted by; (3) more people. Therefore, what we seek and what this chapter will discuss are:

- Ways to notice, monitor, and measure whether and to what extent one or more of these is happening;
- Some thoughts on how we can achieve the best odds of successfully counting the things that count.

HOW PLACE BRANDS WORK:
A DECONSTRUCTION

Awareness: it all starts with awareness, the customer's (or any stakeholder's) awareness of perceptual, mental, and emotional associations with a place and its various real or imagined aspects. So let's begin by contemplating a textbook definition of awareness as it's used as a marketing term (i.e., brand awareness).

© 2011 Published by Elsevier Ltd. All rights reserved.
DOI: 10.1016/B978-0-08-096930-5.10012-6

'There are three classical measures of brand awareness in a given product category:

1) Spontaneous awareness: consumers are asked, without any prompting, to name the brands they know, even if only by name, in a product category; the spontaneous awareness of [a] brand is the percentage of interviewees indicating they know the brand.

2) Top-of-mind awareness: using the same question, the top-of-mind awareness of [a] brand is the percentage of interviewees who name [it] first.

3) Aided awareness: brand names are presented to interviewees; the aided awareness of [a] brand is the percentage of interviewees who indicate they know the brand' (Laurent, Kapferer, & Roussel, 1995, p. 170).

Now, what the authors of this definition mean by brand is 'brand name,' or more accurately 'product name.' In a place branding sphere, what is the equivalent of product names? I would say 'Barcelona' is a product name – very similar to a corporate brand name – and 'Gaudi,' 'city beach,' 'La Rambla,' 'enormous Mediterranean port,' 'Catalan language and culture,' '1992 Olympic games, and that photo of the diver,' 'economic transformation/conducive to business,' 'that Woody Allen film with what's her name and the other gal,' 'classy and affordable weekend break destination,' and so on we can consider to be constituent sub-brands of Barcelona of which various individuals and audiences may be aware.

Ascertaining spontaneous, top-of-mind or aided awareness – referring to our textbook definition – regarding Barcelona is bound to involve both the corporate name, 'Barcelona,' as well as some metaphorical product sub-brand. For example, a survey question might be put out to a certain target audience of London professionals: 'Name some European cities that are fun and stylish and warm and where you can eat well for a few days – in other words, cities really worth a visit come spring.' Various cities might be mentioned – Cannes, Naples, Athens, etc. – with Barcelona amongst them. This question, one suspects, would show Barcelona has high general awareness of some its most relevant traits as a tourist destination (and, by extension, I submit, as a nice place for business, study or conference organising).

As this chapter will argue later, trying to measure the overall image of a place is typically folly – and comparing the overall images of a number of places is hopelessly problematic. But, having said that, it does seem worthwhile to realise that the overall brand strength – if it is anything at all – is merely a summation of the number, type, quality, and positivity of associations people have of the place. Which relates, of course, to the bottom line of place brands: Barcelona is more thoroughly known and understood and appreciated, by more people, than Naples; thus, we say – with unnecessary and distracting jargon, frankly – that its brand is stronger.

BRANDING IS TEACHING, RESEARCHING IS TESTING

The above discussion leads straight on to a worthwhile insight: branding can be thought of as teaching, and researching can be regarded as testing. This simple metaphor holds up surprisingly well; I'll give an example. I once sat next to a voluble young GE employee for the duration of a 13 hour flight. One of the many subjects we chanced to discuss was the brand identity of GE, whose core component is the well-known 'GE' script-lettered monogram, or roundel, known within the company affectionately (but highly unofficially) as 'the meatball.'

GE has been in the Dow Index for 113 years. With more than 300,000 employees, it is the largest company in the world. It operates everywhere, and in nearly every way. Yet despite its prominence, GE does not, apparently, take its recognition remotely for granted. In fact, said my long-haul seatmate, whenever GE enters a new market or segment it deploys its logo only in baby blue. The company then conducts periodic research into the awareness of the logo in baby blue, and only when that awareness has reached 50% does GE allow the monogram to appear publicly in pink, black, beige, or any other hue of the brand's prescribed colour palette.

To carry the metaphor further, a brand strategy might be thought of like a classroom curriculum. The subject of study is you – 'you,' in this case, being the place concerned with its image and promotion – and the students represent your marketplace. As the teacher, you must assess what the students already to know, consider what you want them to know, and decide upon a process of leading them stepwise from relative ignorance to relative enlightenment, or even mastery, of the subject. Along the way, naturally, you will test them. And you will test them not only as a way of gaining feedback on their and your progress; if you are a clever teacher, you will also use testing as an aid to teaching – in other words, as a pedagogical technique in itself (more on this below).

If you're a place and you're 'doing some branding,' you'll need to make judgements about your audiences' knowledge. 'Their knowledge' is another way of saying *what they think they know* which is bound to include correct perceptions as well as misperceptions along a continuum. Importantly, you will give some thought to sorting audiences by how much they know about you already, and possibly even decide to ignore groups who, for now, haven't heard about you at all or who don't already have a certain notion of you.

For example, when working with East Timor a few years ago, I advised that country to confine its entire communications strategy, more or less, to 'people visiting Bali, Indonesia, who have already heard of East Timor.' The assumption was that this group was in the best position to *take action* on an appeal to visit East Timor, since logistically it's via Bali that most people get to the storied half-island of East Timor; so, these individuals are physically nearby, and since Bali is a place people often settle in for a month or six, they may have time on their hands. Given those facts, along with part two of our premise (that they'd already heard of East Timor), what we felt we needed to teach them next was that Timor was (a) easily accessible (indeed, uniquely so) from where they were right now; (b) perfectly safe to visit and explore; (c) a scene of momentous human triumph which demanded a visit from anybody who considered himself or herself a *real* traveller. If memory serves, 'The meek stay in Bali' was the headline we dreamed up (Hildreth, 2005).

So, in place branding, you must choose your audiences with discernment not only, obviously, regarding their validity as 'targets' (which like 'brand' is an obfuscating and overused bit of marketing jargon), but also regarding their level of knowledge. Some people, you'll find, just don't know enough about you right now, or have too many misperceptions, or aren't in a position to act in a way that's helpful to you. Give them a miss, for now, is my earnest advice.

This process of place branding – of teaching others about your place one audience and one metaphorical chapter (or paragraph) at a time – is never complete. It is literally endless. The United States, undoubtedly the strongest nation brand in the history of nations, which is better known in more facets than the next 10 countries put together, still struggles with misperceptions in many quarters around the world (and I'm not talking about the ways in which America may actually *deserve* a bad brand, but the areas in which it is genuinely misperceived) (Anholt and Hildreth, 2010).

In Sweden in November 2009, I happened to meet with the Brand Sweden office of the Swedish Institute. It is responsible for keeping up and dusting up Sweden's reputation amongst foreigners. My ignorance-feigning but genuinely curious query of 'But what could you possibly want to improve about Sweden's image?!' was answered with an acquiescent and appreciative 'Of course we're very pleased to be so well regarded as a country...' followed by a list of things for which Sweden has decided it would like to be *even* better known, and roughly ranked by priority. As Sweden apparently grasps, in place branding, there are never any laurels to rest on. Such is the nature of the beast.

HOW TRUSTED, UNDERSTOOD, ATTRACTIVE, AND POPULAR ARE YOU? FIFTEEN GUIDELINES FOR OBTAINING FEEDBACK ABOUT PLACE IMAGE

At the heart of research is a conundrum: if you ask too much of it, it will give you nothing; but paradoxically, if you ask rather little, it can give you a lot. The key, I've come to believe, rests in recognising the profound difference between finding evidence for something and proving it beyond doubt – and in being satisfied with the former. Indeed, if you want to know exactly what people think about you (and what percentage improvement has occurred in their perceptions across the last two quarters), you will be thwarted; it's inevitable. But if you are content simply to notice interesting and positive trends, and you seek telling feedback rather than ironclad answers, research will serve you well.

In the final analysis, I believe, what a place wants and needs, and all it can legitimately ask for, frankly, is to become part of the consideration set of an increasing number of relevant audiences who are making various types of decisions (e.g., where to visit, where to invest, where to go to school, where to buy things from, where to put their attention when they read the newspaper, etc.). Research certainly can verify if this is happening or not. Toward that end, I offer below 15 pointers for undertaking research. Many of these are informed or inspired by actual advice I have given to clients. The majority of examples in the list below are from the work Wally Olins and I did with the Lithuanian Development Agency in 2008 and 2009 (Hildreth & Olins, 2009); some are from the work we did with the Brazilian state of Rio de Janeiro in 2007 (Hildreth, 2007); and others I have either invented or found elsewhere.

1) *Ask questions that force a truthful, gut-level response.* Perceptions, in contrast with factual associations, are not necessarily held in the conscious mind. Therefore, to find out what they are, like a doctor rapping the hammer beneath the kneecap, you need to prod them directly. Exhibit A of this comes from Mantas Nocius, head of the Lithuanian Development Agency and well-travelled former World Bank officer, who mentioned in the course of our work for Lithuania that one way he personally judges a country is by asking himself 'Would I go to the dentist there?' So in the survey we wrote for Lithuania, we asked that very question (detailed in Number 2 below). We also asked, bluntly, 'If (God forbid) you needed an artificial limb, would you rather have one that was made in China or made in Lithuania?' This kind of question, I submit, is more likely to elicit useful feedback about how trusted Lithuania is as a manufacturer, as a place of origin, than 'On a scale of one to five, how much would you value a product that was made in Lithuania over the same product made in China?'

2) *Ask questions that match the way people actually think.* The other problem with 'On a scale of one to five…' is who amongst us regularly thinks on a scale of one to five? Not me, anyway, and I do this stuff for a living. So when you press people to evaluate something on a one to five basis (technically known as a Likert scale), they must pause and put real effort into coming up with an accurate answer (I do believe, by the way, that people do try to answer survey questions accurately, but they will only work so hard for you before they give up and start spouting nonsense – just as you would!). When we asked 'Would you go to the dentist in Lithuania?' we did not offer simple 'Yes' or 'No' as the options. Instead, we fleshed out 'yes' and 'no' to match the way we imagined would be the thought process of somebody who came down with tooth pain whilst visiting a foreign country: '1 = no, not if I could help it; 2 = yes, sure, why not?' Because the real question is not would you or wouldn't you go to a Lithuanian dentist, it's how would you feel about going if you had no choice. (Come to think of it, that would have been an even better way of wording the question.) Anyway, do yourself a favor: make it easy for your respondents to give feedback by structuring and wording your questions in ways that align with normal human decision-making processes and internal dialogue.

3) *Ask questions people can actually answer.* Related to Number 2, the last step you should take before going live with a survey is to run through it and double check that the every question is answerable as stated. I have been surprised, when I have chosen (as I do now and then) to answer telephone surveys for my mobile operator or my bank, for instance, how many 'one to five' questions are asked that are actually just 'yes/no' questions. But in all instances, you cannot assume you will get a valid answer to a question just because it's on your survey. You must take care the question as stated can easily and fully be answered using the response options offered. By way of hyperbolic example, imagine being on a first date and inquiring: 'So how much do you fancy me, on a scale of one to five? And would you fancy that person at the next table more than you fancy me if that person were sitting here in my place?' Two things will probably happen: (1) you'll get an answer that doesn't mean much and (2) the respondent will lose some amount of interest in talking to you. Ergo, the rule: don't ask stupid questions.

4) *Write survey questions that are fun and which teach people something.* I like it when some survey questions have a secondary pedagogical purpose and/or contain interesting tidbits. For example, 'Lithuania was recently ranked 22nd in the world in the International Quality of Life rankings. That's ahead of countries like Sweden, the United Kingdom, Ireland, and Monaco. Are you surprised to learn Lithuania has such a high quality of life?' Or, 'Lonely Planet says the second best beach in the world is in Lithuania. Does knowing that make you more interested in visiting the country than you otherwise might be?' Or: 'It is a fact that Lithuania, when it was part of the Soviet Union, was one of the USSR's major technology centres. If you were a CEO looking to outsource to a research lab in Lithuania, would knowing this fact make Lithuania more attractive or less attractive, or wouldn't it make a difference at all?' (Significantly, all three of those claims – the quality of life, the beach, and the technology prowess – are true.)

5) *Leave surveys of reasonable length where people have time to fill them out.* Many are the times I've sat in a restaurant after ordering my food, or in an airport lounge waiting for my flight, and realised *this* is the moment when someone should ask me the questions I know they're dying to ask. Of course, there's no need to ask 27 questions every time. What's wrong with picking three or four (or even one or two?) vital questions and posing them to individuals who are in a context that makes them receptive to questioning? Even leave-behind surveys, such as those that could be supplied to hotels and distributed in rooms, needn't be long and arduous. Remember: people are glad to give you feedback if it's no trouble for them, but you do yourself a disservice by asking people more than they want to tell you: you damage the quality of the feedback you're likely to get, and you miss the chance to offer the good customer service experience that allowing people to help you affords.

6) *Sometimes ask open-ended questions.* 'Tell us what you know or feel, if anything, about Kamchatka?' Questions like this are called open-ended because the respondent is entirely free to answer as her or she wishes. As the conversational expert Wayne Elise points out, this is actually the most respectful way to frame a question. Elise gives the example of the 'bad waiter' who asks: 'Is everything all right?' Obviously it is much easier to say 'Oh yes' than to reply 'Well, actually, it isn't.' Better, he argues, for the waiter to say 'How is everything?' in a sincere tone of equanimity that suggests any one of a range of responses truly is acceptable to him. My only caveat here is that an open-ended question can require more work to answer than a multiple choice or yes/no. So take care to heed pointer Number 3 above and pose open-ended questions for which most people will have a ready answer, and might even enjoy proffering an opinion on (e.g., 'Please tell us something you hate to encounter within the first hour of arriving in a new country.').

7) *Use research to test hypotheses.* Although open-ended questions have their place, leading questions can be easier to answer and readily lend themselves to confirming things you think you know already. For example, if you have had bad news circulating about your place, you may suspect that enough time has passed and that the bad news no longer is a major turnoff for people; almost certainly your bosses will want this to be the case anyway, and so finding corroborating evidence in research is politically helpful. How would you approach this? Several years ago I gave a news interview which included my comments about how the high-profile reports of children being found locked in Austrian cellars would affect Brand Austria (World Business, 2008). I said: 'As long as it's not in the top five things that you know about a place, then [bad news] is not really affecting the brand. But Austria we don't know much about, so they find a girl locked in a cellar that impacts the brand. For a little while. Till it falls out of the top five.' More or less, I think this is correct, and if the Austrian Tourist Office later wanted to find out if this unfortunate news item had indeed fallen out of the top five or not, and had ask me how to formulate a survey question, I might have suggested: 'Crime is generally very low in Austria, but some time ago there was widespread coverage in the media about the arrests of several Austrians for kidnapping children. Would this negatively impact on your desire to visit Austria as a tourist now, however? Yes or no.' Or something along these lines.

8) *Ask fact-checking questions in order to deduce familiarity (and thereby segment your audiences).* Some people know more about you than others, and I advocate asking a bellwether question in every survey: those who know the answer to that question shall be counted as familiar with you, and those who don't, won't. For instance, if you were doing a survey about Brazil, you could ask: 'What's the favourite sport in Brazil?' Anybody who didn't say football obviously knows very, very little about Brazil. In a commercial context, and of an audience you assume to be more informed, you might ask 'Which Brazilian city is the nation's commercial capital?' as a way to double check familiarity. You can then parse your data with this in mind (because, frankly, if somebody does not know that Sao Paulo is Brazil's commercial capital, you might want to discount his or her opinions about more detailed matters of Brazil as an investment destination or place for doing business).

9) *Put yourself in a relevant peer group.* As I hope I've made clear throughout this chapter, realism and reasonableness are essential ingredients in any research effort. One of the places where this most comes to bear is on the peer group in which you place yourself for making comparisons: you've got to be honest with yourself here if you really want valuable and valid feedback. With Lithuania, we asked: 'In what order would you like to visit the following countries? Latvia, Estonia, Lithuania, Poland, Slovenia, Serbia.' This question was designed simply to reveal the relative prominence and attractiveness of Lithuania within the Baltic region and another New EU country in southern Europe (Slovenia), a country similar to Lithuania insofar as it too has a weak yet weakly positive reputation amongst Western Europeans. As a bookend

or control, we also threw in a non-EU country (Serbia) with a hazy yet not-so-good image. In another question, which obliquely regarded manufacturing or place of origin, we asked: 'What is your reaction to the following countries? (5 = extremely positive, 4 = very positive, 3 = neutral, 2 = negative, 1 = extremely negative): Czech Republic, Spain, Hungary, Poland, Estonia, South Korea, Romania, Estonia, Latvia, and Lithuania.' Not bad, but in hindsight, a narrower range – or at least a smaller number – of countries might have yielded a more attentive response from those answering the question.

10) *Don't attempt to measure an overall image.* One of the common mistakes in this place branding game is trying to measure an aggregate rather than aggregating a measurement. Whilst there may be, in some abstract way, such a thing as an overall image of a place, I dispute its measurability. And if it is measurable, I would dispute its usefulness to place marketers and its comparability to the overall image of another place (as is done in rankings, which I'll discuss shortly). This is down to the individuality of places, which I regard as ultimately sacrosanct. If, as I maintain, one of the purposes of place branding is to abet a place's endeavour to become its best self, I fail to understand how comparing perceptions of Sweden and Canada 'on the whole' is any more pertinent than comparing the images of Mohammed Ali and Picasso 'on the whole.' It might, of course, be a pleasant diversion, but at the cost of introducing a dash of mindlessness to an arena it's best excluded from.

What you can do, however, is put countries in groups based on some perceptual facet that is likely to have registered amongst the surveyed pool. For instance – again, regarding Lithuania – we asked: 'If you were to indicate the power of certain countries in setting trends in Europe, where would you place Lithuania with regard to the following areas? (5 = far ahead of European trends, 4 = just ahead of European trends, 3 = same as other European countries, 2 = a little behind, 1 = quite a bit behind) Film, Painting, Art, Literature, Music (pop and jazz), Sports, Cities, Fashion, Nature and ecology, Business and commerce, Overall quality of life.' Two of these in particular – music and quality of life – were chosen deliberately on the assumption that they would indicate a massive under-appreciation of Lithuania in these respects, as Lithuania scores surprisingly highly in both areas.

11) *Discover perceptions of your people.* There is research which concludes that one of the primary motivators of a positive decision taken to invest in a country is the fact that the decision maker is acquainted with one or more citizens of that country (van de Laar & Neubourg, 2006). All this does, really, is confirm what we all already know intuitively: that how we rate a place is connected to how we rate the people we know who are from there. So, ask: 'How personally familiar are you (or have you been) with any Korean/Basque/Alaskan person?' Answer choices: I have [had] a good friend (or more); I know [have known] someone slightly; I don't think I really know any. Separately, the 'rap' on a given populace is intimately tied to the reputation of the place they occupy, so it is important to find out (or confirm or disconfirm, if you think

you already know) what stereotypes, prejudices, expectations, etc. are prevalent amongst relevant groups of foreigners. On behalf of Lithuania, we inquired: 'To what degree do the following characteristics describe a typical Lithuanian person? Energetic, daring, stubborn, trustworthy, eccentric, thoughtful, fashionable, hardworking, disciplined, educated, skilled, Eastern European, lively, tolerant, Scandinavian, creative.' (Note: since the brand strategy called for conveying Lithuanians as some of these things, this question also was intended to help reveal, in time, how well the strategy was achieving its aims.)

12) *Get a baseline* before *undertaking branding activity*. In addition to focussing the mind on what the branding program intends to accomplish, undertaking a first pass at periodic research is just good practice. I'm not talking here about research that informs the development of the strategy, although that's good too. I'm talking about research that will later be used to gain feedback, and doing it before you need the feedback. Designing your research methods after you've started to implement your strategy isn't damaging – it's just missing an opportunity, as you will never again have a chance to get a pre-branding-effort baseline. For a host of reasons, the sooner you have valid research to help you formulate communication tactics and – far more importantly – to encourage and suggest particular policy changes, the better.

13) *Use a modern-day clipping service*. Although it's perhaps unorthodox, I believe you should make casual, passive noting a mainstay of your ongoing research. It is far better to draw a reasonable inference from one or two pieces of real qualitative information than to jump to scientific (but wrong) conclusions based on faulty quantitative research. In 2007, we told Rio de Janeiro: 'Arguably the most effective way to gauge and monitor improvements and changes in Rio's image is noting and analysing the way in which Rio is covered in newspapers, magazines, TV shows and websites in Rio, in Brazil and internationally. Fairly sophisticated 'coding' techniques exist for this sort of activity, so that it can be discerned (by hypothetical example) that the share of stories about Rio devoted to Carnival and crime has fallen 10% in the last year whilst the share of stories associating Rio with creative enterprise has increased 20%. This kind of monitoring can be done in an ongoing fashion – almost in real-time – and with a high level of confidence in the meaningfulness of the results.' Nowadays you'll need to include, even emphasise, Twitter, Facebook, and the blogosphere, or whatever mediated technologies prevail by the time you read this.

14) *Look for imaginative ways to measure indirectly*. Related to Number 13, to gauge the success of your efforts you will have to be both creative and interpretive in noticing the derivative effects of improvement to image. One place to look is changes in actual behaviour patterns. As we advised Rio, 'The idea of people 'voting with their feet' comes up in many contexts, and it is certainly true in place image. The sorts of things for which data might be available, and from which conclusions about Rio's attractiveness might be drawn, include: business class tickets sold to Rio (also versus to Sao Paulo); people moving to Rio versus to Sao

Paulo (from abroad and from elsewhere in Brazil); number of conference attendees, and number of conferences, held in Rio; expatriates moving back to Rio; foreign and national student enrolment as well as number of graduates in certain fields (e.g., design, IT, business, etc.); business permit applications and growth in employment (particularly in certain sectors, and particularly versus Sao Paulo); patent registrations from Rio (growth, and as a percentage of Brazil's total international patent filings).

15) *Create research that is PR-able in itself.* Some research that you do can be 'buzz worthy' in and of itself. In explaining what I mean, let me give credit to my friend Deroy Murdock, a syndicated columnist and political PR specialist in New York, who introduced me to this method. Years ago, whilst working on behalf of a policy group devoted to reforming the American public pension system, Deroy devised a survey to be undertaken amongst a particular demographic of wage earners. Most of the questions were straightforward, but one – about belief in extraterrestrials – was offbeat. However, after commissioning the survey, the advocacy group that was Deroy's client was able to report: 'More young workers believe in UFOs than believe they will receive their full public pension at retirement.' Did that get headlines? Did it ever! Years later, when the subject of pension reform arises, one still sometimes finds this 'statistic' cited. I have yet to engineer as perfect a survey question result as that one, but I shall keep trying, and I recommend you do the same.

In Lithuania, we included at least two questions meant to be inherently newsworthy: 'Lithuania either is in the EU or it isn't. How much money would you bet that it is? (1 = 0 euros, 2 = 10 euros, 3 = 50 euros, 4 = 100 euros?') and 'True or false: the inventors of Skype were Lithuanian.' The point of the first question (in addition to being posed to align with actual human thought processes, in accord with point Number 2 above) was to find evidence which would drive home to an internal Lithuanian political audience the extent to which Europeans did not even recognise Lithuania as EU brethren. The point of the second question was to stir up the rivalry Lithuania has with Estonia; the founders of Skype were, in fact, Estonian, but we were betting that given a 50–50 choice, a lot of respondents, ignorant or uncertain of this fact (which Estonia is only now beginning to fully capitalise on, in my view, as the PR coup it is), would take the bait. We imagined indignant headlines in Estonian papers: '45% of Europeans think Lithuanians invented Skype!' Who says mirthfulness has no place in brand research?

A WORD ABOUT RANKINGS AND VALUATION

Without making myself judge, jury, and executioner on the subject of the validity of various rankings and valuations, I feel duty-bound to weigh in with a few thoughts. After all, this is a chapter about noticing, monitoring, and measuring place brand strength and there are a number of notable published surveys which purport to do just that.

My summary judgment of rankings is that they are fun, and although they do yield, here and there, definite insights, they are far from uniformly useful and must be interpreted carefully and critically. My summary judgment of place brand valuation is that it yields far fewer actual insights than the various rankings do, and is, to boot, dangerous in its misleading precision and flawed in its basic method.

The giant, and as far as I'm aware, the progenitor, of the place brands ranking is the Anholt-GfK Roper Nation Brands Index™ (and its sister city brand index). Begun in early 2005 by Simon Anholt and GMI (Global Markets Institute), for a while it came out quarterly; however, now it's done only annually because results don't change dramatically enough from quarter to quarter to justify the expense of surveying 'our panel of over 20,000 ordinary people in 20 different countries' at that frequency.

To its credit, the Anholt index does ask provocative questions that people know the answer to without having to think too much (e.g., 'If you were going to be falsely arrested for a crime you didn't commit, in which country would you prefer this to happen?' I *love* that one). The individual countries' spider plots – which map to Simon Anholt's widely utilised and accepted competitive identity hexagon (which posits people, governance, exports, culture and heritage, tourism and investment, and immigration as the 'vectors' of a nation brand) can be very revealing, and they are comparable to each other. As a whole, the NBI inevitably suggests both a precision and hierarchy that just aren't there, but used wisely, the index is undeniably a valid and useful tool.

The rankings of the East West Global Index, put out quarterly and annually by East West Communications and 'powered by' Perception Metrics seem to change significantly each time, although Singapore seems to do well regularly, often placing first. I like that some fairly low-profile countries like Ghana, Fiji, and Kuwait often fare quite well on this index, and I appreciate that the methodology is simple (although it surely relies on judgements and assumptions to carry it out). The index is what it is: 'Quarterly and annual rankings of 200 countries and territories, including all 192 UN members, based on how they are described in major media' (East West Global Index, 2010).

The consultancy FutureBrand also has an entry into the annual surveys with their Country Brand Index, undertaken annually and first issued in 2006. Again, as with all rankings, I dispute on principle the final, aggregated results. However, the FutureBrand methodology is interesting and yields insights country by country: 'Our approach incorporates a global quantitative survey, expert opinions and external statistics. These factors are compared and combined to better understand drivers, preference, importance and relativism of country brands' (Plapler, 2006). Fair enough. In the survey, 'Respondents answered questions about behaviour around destination selection, country associations with particular attributes, as well as overall awareness/familiarity, past visits, intent to visit, and willingness to recommend destinations to others.' The statistics deemed relevant, and somehow incorporated into the algorithm, include 'Travel services import and export data, and growth rates by country; beach availability/length of coastline; crime per capita; exchange rates; tourism related marketing expenditure; FDI confidence index; language fluency; fast food expenditure per capita' and several others. My main quibble here is that most of these, valid though they may be, speak to a country's actual assets and not to how the country is perceived.

In any case, in 2008, I told journalist Randall Frost, writing for Interbrand's BrandChannel portal: 'Anholt's index looks at perceptions of nations from one angle, the East West index from another. Both ways are interesting. Both ways are valid. Both ways are limited. Both ways are helpful as far as they go' (Frost, 2008). I stand by that, and add a ditto for FutureBrand's offering. I read all of these surveys with interest whenever they fall over my transom. Yet I must reiterate: whatever insights may be gleaned from the outcomes and findings of rankings and indexes – and there are plenty – I insist that the hierarchical ranking of 'overall images' per se must be regarded as entertainment not scholarship.

And finally, let me offer a harsh word or two about place brand valuation. To value a commercial asset, according to financial valuation precepts, you must first be able to assign to it two things: a stream of cash flows, and a discount rate. Never mind a discount rate; I do not understand how you can figure out with any accuracy which cash flows to a place are due entirely to the place's brand. I am skeptical of this even in the case of corporate brand valuation, but in the circumstance of a place it strikes me as a fool's errand.

In the Q4 2005 edition of the Nation Brands Index, when the survey was still in its infancy, a Brand Finance valuation ranking also was included. It was later dropped, but the method, called 'royalty relief,' was explained in the full report for that quarter: 'This approach assumes a country does not own its own brand and calculates how much it would need to pay to license it from a third party' (Anholt & GMI, 2005, p. 3). The elegance of this is undeniable, as is its abstract validity; but on what grounds do they deem sound the numbers they plunk into the equation? This is not detailed.

The danger of using an unreliable method like brand valuation to evaluate place brand strength is twofold: (1) it provides a false sense of certainty. And as Mark Twain said, 'It ain't what you don't know that gets you into trouble. It's what you know for sure that just ain't so' and (2) it provides a false substitute for better ways. If you find a way of isolating the brand-related cash flows to a place, then by all means strike up the valuation calculator. Until then, I'd steer clear.

CONCLUSION

This chapter has reviewed noticing, monitoring, and measuring place brand strength, and with respect to those three notions, I offer the following conclusions:

- You can certainly notice changes, if you're both realistic and astute about what those changes are likely to look like.
- And you can often, at least regarding certain aspects of place image or particular audiences, engineer more formal ways of monitoring changes in perceptions over time. I have provided 15 pointers herein for how to do this.

- And sometimes, when a certain monitoring technique turns out to have exceptional vividness and stability, you might even achieve something approaching a genuine quantitative measurement of the way people regard you.

Beyond that, I have put forth the view that brainless research is useless research, and that too much research in the area of place branding strikes me as brainless. This is understandable, if unnecessary. So strong is the desire to 'find out how we're doing' that the temptation to latch onto anything that seems to offer this feedback, especially if it's positive feedback, is hard to resist. Unfortunately, wishing won't make it so. Likewise, as Einstein famously said, 'Not everything that can be counted counts, and not everything that counts can be counted.' Luckily, I believe that in place branding, the things that *really* count – specific perceptions rather than vague overall images – can in fact be counted. It just requires some thoughtfulness and imagination to do it right; an acceptance of realistic limits helps, too.

In sum, active and passive research, done properly and mindfully (and this chapter has attempted to give some guidance as to what that entails in practice), will indicate whether the ideas and messages of a legitimate, toothed place brand strategy are getting across, and whether people's views of you are changing in line with your hopes and ministrations. Furthermore, if, as I have elsewhere stated (Hildreth, 2010, p. 27) that 'making a place better for those who live there – or helping a place become the best it can be in this competitive world – is the true moral purpose behind place branding,' then, indeed, obtaining feedback about your progress is a laudable, worthwhile, and achievable venture.

References

Anholt, S., & GMI. (2005). How the world sees the world: the Anholt Nation Brands Index Powered by GMI. Fourth Quarter.

Anholt, S., & Hildreth, J. (2010). *Brand America: The making, unmaking and remaking of the greatest national image of all time* (2nd ed.). London: Marshall Cavendish.

East West Global Index 200 (2010). Accessed on 11.05.2010 at http://www.eastwestcoms.com/global.htm.

Frost, R. (2008). Rating nation brands: what really counts? Accessed on October 6, 2008 at http://www.brandchannel.com/features_effect.asp?pf_id=443

Hildreth, J. (2005). Destination Timor-Leste: Human triumph, cultural fusion and a land untamed. Produced by Saffron Brand Consultants for the East Timor Development Authority.

Hildreth, J. (2007). 1Rio: So far, so good: comments and recommendations in the early days of Rio's image, reality and identity development programme. Saffron Brand Consultants, October.

Hildreth, J. (2010). Place branding: a view at arm's length. *Place Branding and Public Diplomacy*, 6(1), 27–35.

Hildreth, J., & Olins, W. (2009). Selling Lithuania smartly: a guide to the creative-strategic development of an economic image for the country. Saffron Brand Consultants, March 2007, accessible at jeremyhildreth.com.

Laurent, G., Kapferer, J. -N., & Roussel, F. (1995). The underlying structure of brand awareness scores. *Marketing Science*, *14*(3), 170–179.

Plaper R. (2006). FutureBrand Country Brand Index 2006: insights, findings and country rankings. Available online, see http://www.ontit.it/opencms/export/sites/default/ont/it/documenti/files/ONT_2009-06-23_02036.pdf.

van de Laar, M., & Neubourg, C. (2006). Emotions and foreign direct investment: a theoretical and empirical exploration. *Management International Review*, *46*(2), 207–233.

World Business (2008). State Sponsored Spin 31 October 2008, interview with Jeremy Hildreth, http://www.youtube.com/watch?v=kpwk8n5nLY0&feature=related.

CHAPTER

13

The future challenge

Ian Yeoman and Una McMahon-Beattie

INTRODUCTION

Destination branding is one of the hottest topics amongst place marketing professionals and politicians, from Scotland to Kurdistan to New York to South Africa and every other place on the planet. Today, choice of holiday destination is a significant lifestyle indicator for aspirational consumers and the places where they choose to spend their squeezed vacation time and disposable income. With every country in the world offering a tourism proposition, the environment has become extremely competitive. In fact, the only place one can't visit as a tourist is outer space, but Richard Branson's Virgin Galactic is set to change that.

Holidays, whether a short break in Marrakesh or 2 week safari vacation in Kenya is increasingly permeating the discourse of everyday life and is now considered a necessity rather than a luxury. Every country has a destination brand, whether it is *Live it, Visit Scotland, 100% Pure New Zealand, Uniquely Singapore,* or *Incredible India.* Even Afghanistan positions itself as the *Last Unconquered Mountains of the World* (Yeoman, 2008). More and more, nations, cities, and villages are increasingly spending more on advertising in order to compete for the tourist pie. So, what does the future hold? This chapter:

* Sets out to understand the changing nature of destination brands by examining the real value of destination brands;
* Discusses the outlook for them using a range of scenarios.

© 2011 Published by Elsevier Ltd. All rights reserved.
DOI: 10.1016/B978-0-08-096930-5.10013-8

THE REAL VALUE OF BRANDING

What is a brand? According to Nicholas Ind (2005: 3):

A brand is something that is owned by buyers and other stakeholders. The argument is this: just as capital is a concept, so is a brand. Although a brand is related to a physical product or service it is itself immaterial. It is a transforming idea that converts the tangible into something of value....

What has changed in recent years is that the power has shifted from the manufacturers of the brand to the consumers of the brand. Ind (2005) states that brands are 'owned' now by their buyers. The shift is a result of greater consumer empowerment – as choice proliferates, the consumer gains more control of the marketplace. Additionally, as communication is made comprehensively networkable through the internet, it is easy for consumer voices to be heard – voices which are often as powerful as corporate advertising.

Consumers' responses to brand propositions are constantly changing. Twenty years ago, we conspicuously consumed. Today, consumption is far more discrete. This in no way demonstrates the demise of brands, but rather an evolution of consumers' relationships with them. Aspirational marketing has been the cornerstone of so much advertising and promotion but consumers are increasingly tired of seeing unattainable images. Lately, certain brands have become successful by becoming 'reality' brands, which reflect the everyday lives of their consumers. This does not mean that there is a diminished place for aspirational marketing, rather that brands must understand where they must stand in the aspiration / reality spectrum. Aspirational marketing is what tourism marketing is all about (Morgan, Pritchard, & Pride, 2004). So is the tourist in danger of tiring of destination branding?

There are certain growing challenges to brands which companies cannot afford to ignore. Firstly, over the years distrust towards corporations and institutions has been growing. As every country, place, and region offer a tourism brand today, tourism has become saturated with choice, and there are greater pressures for brands. There is even an argument that tourism brands today don't actually make any difference as they have no price point – it's the influence of the low cost airlines that are the driving force behind consumer destination choice (more on this below).

The rise of the brand since the late 1980s and early 1990s has been nothing short of phenomenal, to the extent that super brands such as Coca-Cola, McDonalds, and Nike have become victims of their success. The super brands have been heavily criticised by the anti-brand movement as advocated by Naomi Klein (2001) and Neil Boorman (2008) who vocalise a certain collective hangover felt by a generation enthused by over-marketed images of freedom and self-expression. The baby boomer generation grew up against a background of social unrest, changing attitudes, and massive wealth creation whereas generation Y is now in its first consumer recession (Yeoman, 2008). Looking to the future, brands have always had to engage with consumers' agendas in order to survive and that will be true in the future, in that respect some things don't change.

THE CHANGING NATURE OF BRANDS AND DESTINATION BRANDING

The brand as a guarantor of quality

One of the world's leading tourism brands is 100% Pure New Zealand, but like other destination brands it doesn't own any product, therefore a fundamental weakness of all destination brands is that it is not a guarantor of quality. For example, when one stays at Gleneagles, Scotland's premier resort, one has a perception of high prices reflecting high quality. Peter Lederer, Chairman of Gleneagles, understands that price acts as a quality-guaranteeing device as it is being conspicuously evaluated – that is why Gleneagles will never sell below a certain price as it impacts on the perceptual value (Yeoman & Lederer, 2004). Research by the Future Foundation found that nearly half of consumers feel that premium goods are usually or always worth paying for (Yeoman, 2008). In the UK food retail industry, the quality–price perception is illustrated by Tesco who offer Tesco Finest and Tesco Value; it is understood that the first offers luxury while the second offers the most basic goods at rock bottom prices. From a tourism perspective, destinations such as Norway, Dubai, and Switzerland position themselves as premium brand destinations, whether it is conspicuous consumption and luxury in Dubai's case or a more authentic, pristine destination such as Norway or Iceland (Lennon, Smith, Cockerell, & Trew, 2006). Destinations that position themselves as premium destinations will have to be strong on quality assurance, ensuring that they deliver on the proposition they promise to the consumer. The worst thing they could do is overpromise, so implementation and guaranteeing quality is essential. In the future, destinations could decide to be more exclusive – only promoting businesses that match the brand promise or use legislation to ensure that if hotels or restaurants want to operate they must meet quality assurance standards.

The brand as a shortcut

Today, there are no undiscovered places as every country and place on earth has a Lonely Planet Guide including Afghanistan, the Falkland Islands, Libya, and Eritrea. Many of these destinations didn't exist as countries 20 years ago or were thought of as terrorism hot spots but today, you can take a holiday at the North or South Pole and everywhere in between. Today's tourist has a paradox of choice (Schwartz, 2004) when it comes to deciding where to holiday; thus if a typical British tourist is looking for a cheap sunshine holiday, it would make sense to go to Spain rather than fly across the world to Fiji as Spain is associated with safety, value, access, sunshine, and families. Each destination has a different set of associations wrapped up with its brand, whether it is '*what happens in Vegas stays in Vegas*' and its reputation as a 'bit sexy, a tad alluring' and 'safely dangerous,' or the *Live it, VisitScotland* brand which is 'enduring, human and dramatic' (Yeoman, Durie, McMahon-Beattie, & Palmer, 2005). In a cluttered world of the long tail, where destinations offer a multitude of experiences and products, it becomes even more important for destinations to portray a clear image that saves people time on having to gather complex information on destination choice. Hence, it is important that brands convey a clear, congruent image as any contradictions or inconsistencies in brand image will leave the potential tourist unsure of what is being offered.

The role of Destination Marketing Organisations (DMOs) is to act as the guardian of the brand, ensuring it is delivered and not spoiled. As destinations can no longer be everything to everybody, DMOs must be able to segment visitors by willingness to purchase against lifestyle and geographical location. In addition, they must ensure an easy and clear pathway for visitors in understanding the brand through the exploration of information, including the use of internet sites or other technology intermediaries that facilitate both exploration and purchase.

The cultural capital of conversation

In advanced capitalist societies, consumption has become intrinsic to self-expression and tourism is a prime example of this; as our affluence has grown, so too has our cultural and social knowledge and people's expectations (and the way in which this informs consumption) have become more important. The cultural capital of tourism is expressed in how tourists talk about the places they have visited, the food they have eaten, the museums they have visited, and the people they have met. Today, consumers 'tick off' which countries they have visited and to a certain extent boast about it with friends, hence the cultural capital of conversation becomes very important. At the same time, research has identified the power of friends and relatives as the number one influence on destination choice, so it is not only how 'you' talk about a place but also with 'which friends' as well (Yeoman, 2008).

Celebrity branding

For decades destinations have been using celebrities as brand endorsers. According to research by the Future Foundation (Yeoman, 2008), close to a fifth of the UK population openly agrees that if a famous person endorses a product they would be more likely to buy it (see Figure 13.1).

However, it is most likely that a sizable proportion of the population would be positively influenced without realising or admitting it (Jayadeva, 2007). More than any other time, we are living in a celebrity culture and modern society consumes a bottomless amount of celebrity news. But at the same time, to a certain extent, consumers are tired of the constant exposure in advertising of unattainable lifestyles. However, this does not mean that there is no longer a place for selling these aspirational images and the success of celebrity branding in many cases attests to that.

Unsurprisingly, young adults are the most directly influenced by celebrity endorsement. Approximately a third of people under 34 admit their purchasing behaviour can be influenced by celebrities but once people enter the 35–44 age

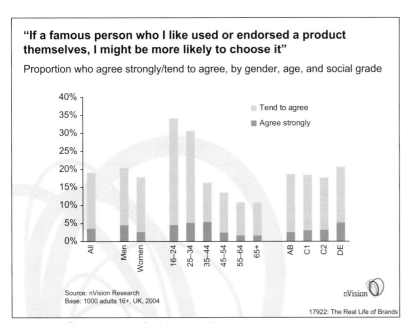

Figure 13.1 The importance of celebrity branding. Source: Yeoman/Future Foundation 2008.

group they report to be less influenced by celebrities. This can be attributed to many factors and we do know that the young are far more interested and influenced by famous people as they are still building identities of their own and are more immersed in popular culture.

Celebrity endorsement can work phenomenally well. For example, since the UK Top Shop retailer launched its Kate Moss fashion line, its sales have increased overall – with the success of her clothing line have a knock-on effect. However, celebrity association it is not a quick fix for a brand struggling with identity. If the celebrity who endorses the brand is not completely congruent with the brand image, the endorsement will have a detrimental impact, sending out mixed brand messages. From a tourism perspective, celebrity endorsement is likely to continue to be an effective shortcut for destination brands and an excellent example of this is Arnold Schwarzenegger and other Hollywood stars appearing in the California *Find Yourself Here*© campaign – in this case the association between the enviable California lifestyle and glamorous film stars is a close fit.

The truism of trust

As markets become more advanced and new products and brands are born every day, aspirational marketing will have to work harder to grab tourists' attention and interest. Destination branding is all about aspiration and emotion, and one way to maintain this appeal to emotion is through authenticity and simplicity. In an economic downturn, Flatters and Wilmot (2009) observe how consumers turn to simplicity. Even prior to the current recession, many consumers were feeling overwhelmed by the profusion of choices and 24/7 connectivity and were starting to simplify. The US publisher Time Inc. recognised this trend early and capitalised on it by launching its highly successful back-to-basics magazine *Real Simple* in 2000. In the same way, Apple was responding to the trend when it launched the elegant and spare iPod in 2001. However, the recession is accelerating this maturing trend.

Consider, for example, the rise of edited retailing (where consumers are offered limited collections of coordinated product choices), the growing demand for trusted brands and value, the increasing desire for advisers (ranging from social networks to product ranking web sites) who can simplify choice making, and it seems that enthusiasm for less complicated, more user-friendly technologies, products, and services abounds. From a tourism perspective, 100% Pure New Zealand is a simple brand that represents purity, unspoilt landscapes, and an authentic experience – and celebrated its tenth anniversary in 2009. The uncomplicated manner of the brand has residency with today's tourist and as such, many other countries have tried to copy the many virtues found in 100% Pure New Zealand, whether it is *Norway : Powered by Nature* or *Enjoy Turkey*. Many destinations have returned to basics and presented an image based upon an arrangement of simple values, which are true to the destination.

However, the truism of trust is a double-edged sword. Most DMOs are a function of government and most consumers are less trusting of government (Yeoman, 2008) amidst a worldwide scramble for social responsibility and ethical behaviour. Hence, brands must appear simple and transparent to the consumer with no contradictions. Nicolas Ind (2005) argues that in interactions between people and organisations, there has to be a congruency between what is being offered and what is being delivered. In today's society where no one can hide and where information is freely available, the same is true about brands (Yeoman, 2011). As Yeoman (2009) points out:

> In the expectation economy which is inhabited by experienced, well-informed tourists from Germany to South Korea who have a long list of high expectations that they apply to each and every good service and experience on offer. Their expectations are based on years of self-training in hyper-consumption, and on the biblical flood of new-style, readily available information sources, curators B*** S*** filters and the rise of mistrust in destination brands.

And in relation to 100% New Zealand, Yeoman (2009) writes:

> Don't take 100% Pure New Zealand for granted. If the tourist doesn't like you, they will simply tell the world via YouTube or the dedicated website for 'green washing' at www.greenwashingindex.com. That is why 100% New Zealand has to be backed by quality assurance, Qualmark is even more important today than ever before. One of the key roles of quality assurance is to embed a green way of life into daily life for the tourism industry.

In other words, destination brands can't pretend to be something they aren't and promise something they can't deliver on.

Brands and loyalty

Re-visitation is central to all destination brands. Whilst is it easy to entice tourists once, how does a brand ensure that they keep coming back? Malcolm Roughead, Cheif Executive at VisitScotland states that:

> ... the key is understanding the values that the consumer lives by, knowing what their attitudes and beliefs are; their perception of Scotland and understanding how to tap into that potential; then converting to travel patterns and purchasing through loyalty ladders and segmentation. Organisations like VisitScotland haven't got the budget to market all of Scotland to everybody, they must decide who their consumers are and match the product they have got on offer ... it's all about return on investment (Roughead, 2009).

It is imperative to identify the reasons why consumers keep coming back to a brand in order to retain a grip on this behaviour just as it is essential to understand consumer motivation in order to ascertain their relationship with any brand proposition. Hence, looking closer at a segmentation model on consumers' purchasing attitudes and behaviours can offer valuable insight for brands. Scotland, like many other destinations, has undertaken sophisticated marketing segmentation research in order to understand who their tourists are. An understanding of those UK tourists who holiday in Scotland is set out in the publication *Know Your Market* (Tourism Intelligence, 2009) based upon the attributes of loyalty, attitudes, and emotions. Figure 13.2 shows a representative sample of the UK population in which 10% of the UK population regularly holiday in Scotland and 27% who will never holiday in Scotland.

Vital statistics: the loyalty ladder

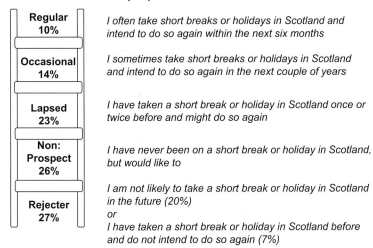

Omnibus survey Jan 2006; base 1050 representative of UK

Figure 13.2 VisitScotland loyalty ladder

Further analysis by the VisitScotland Research Branding team segmented the UK population according to visitation to Scotland. Six segments were formulated which describes a range of attributes, emotions, socio-demographics, and likelihood of visiting Scotland on holiday. Warm segments are people who already come to Scotland and VisitScotland would like to encourage to stay longer, spend more, and repeat visits. Cold segments are those tourists who might like to visit Scotland but it is not yet on their radar. One of the warm segments (Figure 13.3) are those termed 'Affluent Southern Explorers' – people who have strong connections to Scotland through family and friends. Their lifestyle is not materialistic, they want authentic experiences and travel is important to them.

By segmenting and quantifying this market, VisitScotland was able to decide how to communicate to them and what offers to make. As a result, VisitScotland's *Perfect Day* campaign targeted this group through a coordinated campaign in cinemas, glossy magazines, and satellite TV. Further details of the campaign highlights can be seen at http://perfectday.visitscotland.com and an illustration of the media is shown in Figure 13.4. By understanding the tourist market, VisitScotland has found out how tourists interact with the brand and, as a result used this research to drive marketing strategy and industry partnerships.

Price pressures

In normal circumstances, the price of a product is a major determinant of how the consumer sees the brand and its position within the market. However, from a destination branding perspective, the challenge is an interesting one as DMOs don't own any of the products and therefore have no control over price. Yet price has been a major success factor for many destinations over the last decade as the phenomena of the low-cost carrier has transformed many destinations. The success of Edinburgh as a destination on one hand can be attributed to successful marketing by VisitScotland, but on the other it is the connectivity with other UK and European cities that has been the key. For example, Easyjet has transformed air travel and consumers' expectations on how much air travel should cost. This has forced many other airlines, who do not necessarily see themselves in the low-cost market to drop their price, resulting in the continued downward spiral of the price paid by passengers per airline kilometre travelled (Kuhlman, 2004).

In the future, as consumers become more sophisticated, price is likely to become decreasingly important. However, in a competitive globalised market, tourism product parity is becoming more of the norm as, for example, the UK consumers can purchase low-cost adventure holidays in Eastern Europe, compared to similar but more expensive products in Western Europe; thus this will result in increasing pricing pressures.

Consumer boredom and the desire for new experiences

In our postindustrial affluent society, access to material goods no longer promises the status that it once did. Indeed, the vast majority of those in an affluent society can afford to indulge from time to time – and our advanced

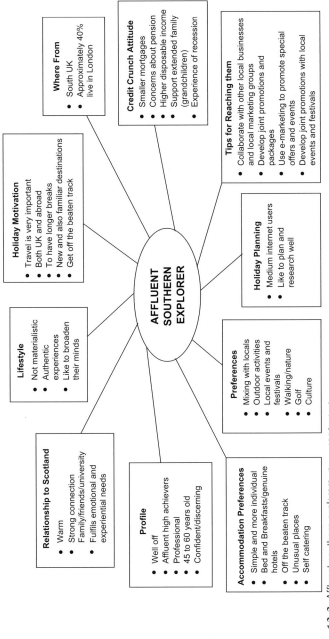

Holiday Motivation
- Travel is very important
- Both UK and abroad
- To have longer breaks
- New and also familiar destinations
- Get off the beaten track

Where From
- South UK
- Approximately 40% live in London

Credit Crunch Attitude
- Smaller mortgages
- Concerns about pension
- Higher disposable income
- Support extended family (grandchildren)
- Experience of recession

Lifestyle
- Not materialistic
- Authentic experiences
- Like to broaden their minds

AFFLUENT SOUTHERN EXPLORER

Tips for Reaching them
- Collaborate with other local businesses and local marketing groups
- Develop joint promotions and packages
- Use e-marketing to promote special offers and events
- Develop joint promotions with local events and festivals

Holiday Planning
- Medium internet users
- Like to plan and research well

Relationship to Scotland
- Warm
- Strong connection
- Family/friends/university
- Fulfils emotional and experiential needs

Preferences
- Mixing with locals
- Outdoor activities
- Local events and festivals
- Walking/nature
- Golf
- Culture

Profile
- Well off
- Affluent high achievers
- Professional
- 45 to 60 years old
- Confident/discerning

Accommodation Preferences
- Simple and more individual
- Bed and Breakfasts/genuine hotels
- Off the beaten track
- Unusual places
- Self catering

Figure 13.3 Affluent southern explorers. (Source: VisitScotland).

Figure 13.4 A perfect day. (Source: VisitScotland).

economy is bursting to the brim with products to satisfy our every whim – hence, the movement from conspicuous to inconspicuous consumption (Yeoman, 2008). In such environments, it is becoming increasingly harder for a brand to excite and entice consumers. Although tourists are as engaged as ever with the products and experiences that brands offer, they are increasingly becoming bored with the market in general as destination offerings become very homogeneous – one marketing campaign seems similar to another. Indeed, in a society where new brands and products are born every day, novelty soon wears off. From a tourism perspective, this means brands need to create new experiences by continuously striving for innovation and invention through stretching the brand.

An immediate society and technological revolution

In a time-scarce society where dial-up internet service is a thing of the past, today's consumer expects instant and accurate information. Our patience can be measured in nano-seconds rather than seconds. Think of today's average generation Y (born 1974–1994) consumer. Aged between 19 and 36, they have grown up connected, carry ipods and mobile phones, they choose between hundreds of TV channels, skip commercial advertising using TiVO technologies.

They multitask and never stay on one task for long. They live in an instant and global society, happy using SMS or twittering, they have more friends on Facebook than real friends. This is a generation of skimmers who speed read and write in cryptic. Their identity is embedded in Facebook or MySpace. They have very short time spans and are very demanding (Green, 2007; Yeoman and McMahon-Beattie, 2006). As a result, the interface between DMOs and tourists has completely changed; no longer is the traditional marketing mix about product, promotion, path, pricing, packaging, and push. It is consumer 2.0 marketing mix, content and context, conversations and context, connectivity, collaboration due to transparency, creativity and collaboration, and cooperation. Basically, marketing has moved the 'P' to the 'C'. The nature of consumer decision making and the growing hunger for social interaction has been a catalyst to alter the marketing mix. No longer can DMOs focus on the tourist, the tourist has assumed the driving seat in brand identity (Green, 2007).

LOOKING TO THE FUTURE

The branding literature is littered with predictions about the end of the brand, such has been the impact of Naomi Klein's book *No Logo* (2001), which argues that rebellion is in the air and brands are a vision of corporate multiculturism merely intended to create more buying options for consumers. She contends that, as a consequence, brands have become ubiquitous and out-of-step with an ethical, inconspicuous consumption future world in which brands will be abandoned. Klein's interpretation of the future is a single and exact version, one which is doomed to fail because no one can predict an exact future. In fact, the prediction of multiple plausible futures or scenarios is recognised as a more useful and appropriate way forward. Scenarios are like fairy tales or stories as they provide an internally consistent view of what the future might turn out to be. A good set of scenarios are plausible in that they can be 'imagined' in terms of current, visible, events or trends that might cause them to happen. The core purpose of scenarios is not to predict the future but to help organisations think about possible futures.

Figure 13.5 highlights four scenarios about the future of destination branding based upon two core drivers, *the role of trust* and *relationship*. The role of trust is central to destination marketing and two bipolar outcomes are advocated, *influential* and *distrust*. The second driver relates to the type of relationship the brand has with the tourist, namely, *affair* or *conversation*. Four scenarios are then constructed and explained.

- Scenario 1: Marriage
    - The tourist trusts your brand and considers your influence as statesman-like.
    - Word of mouth advertising and recommendation are high. The destination has high social cachet and cultural capital amongst consumers.
    - The brand is backed by a strict quality assurance program that delivers on brand promise; hence the brand is a guarantor of quality.

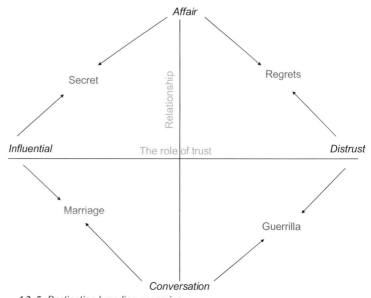

Figure 13.5 Destination branding scenarios

- The relationship with the tourist is a lifetime one based upon open dialogue and confidence. The relationship is about recommendation not short-term opportunity or selling.
- Independence and integrity are core values.
- The brand knows the tourist and offers advice about activity, timing, and availability.

- Scenario 2: Guerrilla

  - The tourist only visits your destinations once, and never returns after a bad experience. The brand promise is not delivered.
  - The tourist doesn't trust your brand as she/he presumes you are a liar; the information and marketing imagery are not underpinned by truth and are merely glossary imagery.
  - The key characteristic of this scenario is that the tourist posts video clips on www.youtube.com and messages on social networking sites such www.facebook.com telling people not to visit your destination.
  - No cultural capital is found in this scenario only negative vibes.

- Scenario 3: Regrets

  - The tourist only visits your destination once and regrets the experience.
  - The brand is not a guarantor of quality – it is patchy and inconsistent.
  - The tourist tries his/her best to ignore future contact with the brand, switches off and skips all messages from you, she/he doesn't return your calls and sees the brand as a pest and reports your behaviour to the authorities. Your relationship verges on harassment.

- ○ Your brand is distrusted and not credible.
- ○ The tourist goes out his/her way to avoid you and is embarrassed when friends and relatives speak about the destination brand.

- • Scenario 4: Secret

  - ○ The relationship between the brand and the tourist is based upon an affair where the brand has got to make offers based upon price and availability.
  - ○ The brand always has to work hard and be tempting.
  - ○ The tourist is not loyal and has many relationships with other destinations which are not meaningful.
  - ○ The brand works hard to deliver on quality and wants to make the relationship more permanent.
  - ○ The brand has little influence over the tourist: it is an affair of convenience.
  - ○ The tourist tells certain friends about you – but no personal recommendations.
  - ○ The brand has some social cachet but no cultural capital.
  - ○ The brand is like a bar of chocolate – not good for you but desirable.

CONCLUSION

Will all brands be burned as suggested by Neil Boorman (2008) and Naomi Klein (2001)? We think not. In a society where paradox of choice has become the mainstream, those destinations with high resonance with tourists will become shortcuts to purchase. This doesn't mean brands can become complacent with a degree of narcissism, neglecting their tourist market and guaranteeing quality. In the future, destination brands will face a set of challenges based upon trust, competition, cultural capital, celebrity, relationships, and loyalty. Brands will fail if those factors don't have appropriate investment.

Although brands may be as needed and relevant as ever, tourist promiscuity and boredom should shake destinations out of any complacency. In order to respond to these challenges, DMOs will have to respond as guarantors of quality by matching demand with supply. This means moving towards the *Marriage* scenario in which trust and lifetime conversations are the cornerstones of success. The *Marriage* scenario is also a process of finding the right partner; knowing what they want; being proactive; making suggestions to ensure an enduring relationship of trust, love, and emotional connectivity. It also means being selective in how you target your potential tourists and how you talk to them (if you are too eager – you will scare them away). This scenario reminds us of Mel Gibson in the film *What Women Want*, in which he can read their minds and make the right decisions. A marriage is about understanding each other.

In a world where tourists are inundated with advertising and personalised communication, it is vital to build a relationship in order to find out who they are. A relationship is extremely important, as affairs quickly go wrong and tourists will become hostile towards your brand, as seen in the *Guerrilla* scenario. The power of social media means that today's tourist can tell the world about your destination through a posting on YouTube or Facebook instantly. Whatever the future holds for destination brands, marriage is not a 'bed of roses' and requires investment, communication, time, and trust.

References

Boorman, N. (2008). *Bonfire of brands*. Edinburgh: Canongate Book.

Flatters, P., & Wilmot, M. (2009). Understanding the post-recession consumer. *Harvard Business Review*, *87*(7/8), 106–112.

Green, C. (2007). *Sales and marketing in a web 2.0 world*. Jacksonville: HSAMI Foundation.

Ind, N. (2005). *Beyond branding: How the new values of transparency and integrity are changing the world of brands*. London: Kogan Page.

Jayadeva, J. (2007). The real value of brands. www.nvisiononline.co.uk (accessed 2.03.07).

Klein, N. (2001). *No logo*. London: Flamingo Press.

Kuhlman, R. (2004). Why revenue management is not working. *Journal of Revenue & Pricing Management*, *2*(4), 378–387.

Lennon, J. J., Smith, H., Cockerell, J., & Trew, J. (2006). *Benchmarking national tourism organisations and agencies: Understanding best performance*. Oxford: Elsevier.

Morgan, N., Pritchard, A., & Pride, R. (2004). *Destination branding: Creating the unique destination proposition*. Oxford: Elsevier.

Roughead, M. (2009). Personal communication with author on the future of destination branding, June 26.

Schwartz, B. (2004). *Paradox of choice: Why more is less*. London: Harper Collins.

Tourism Intelligence (2009). Knowing your markets…Scotland's visitors. (accessed August 1), at http://www.tourism-intelligence.co.uk/guides.aspx.

Yeoman, I. (2008). *Tomorrow's tourist*. Oxford: Elsevier.

Yeoman, I. (2009). Why 100% Pure New Zealand brand is even more important for the future. (accessed on July 12, 2009) at http://www. tomorrowstourist.com/why100.php

Yeoman, I. (2011) 2050: Tomorrows tourism. Bristol: Channelview Publications In press.

Yeoman, I., Durie, A., McMahon-Beattie, U., & Palmer, A. (2005). Capturing the essence of a brand from its history – the case of marketing Scottish tourism. *Journal of Brand Management*, *13*(2), 134–147.

Yeoman, I., & Lederer., P. (2004). Back to the future? Directions for revenue management. *Journal of Revenue & Pricing Management*, *2*(1), 81–82.

Yeoman, I., & McMahon-Beattie, U. (2006). Tomorrow's tourist and an information society. *Journal of Vacation Marketing*, *12*(3), 269–291.

Useful website

http://www.tomorrowstourist.com

PART ❸

Destination Brand Cases

The first part of this book discussed key concepts of destination brands and place reputation, image and identity, while Part 2 specifically discussed nine essential challenges in contemporary tourism destination brand management. The third part examines these broad issues through in-depth analysis of 11 case studies. They discuss a range of destinations with different histories, reputations, resources, markets, and levels of tourism development – each confronting the challenge of being competitive in the twenty-first century. The case studies are drawn from Asia and Australia (Australia, Macau, Singapore), Africa (Namibia), Europe (Barcelona, Belfast, London, Milan, Slovenia), the Middle East (Abu Dhabi, Jerusalem), and the Americas (New York, San Antonio).

While these 11 case studies reinforce and complement the themes of the earlier parts of the book, their writers each provide their own unique insights into destination brand management. Part 3 opens with Can-Seng Ooi's exploration of what he terms 'the accreditation approach' to destination branding. Taking the example of Singapore, Can-Seng discusses how destinations leverage globally recognised events, branded tourist attractions, and landmark projects to boost their reputations. This raises an interesting paradox – that places seek to host well-known branded events and attractions to gain 'accreditation' as a world-leading city (or country), and in the process become more like other world cities, each with their F1 circuits, Guggenheim museums, theme parks, mega-malls, and casino hotels. Indeed, the next three chapters discuss destinations, which have pursued this strategy – Abu Dhabi (Chapter 15), Macau (Chapter 16), and Milan (Chapter 17), while later Rosanna Vitello and Marcus Wilcocks (Chapter 22) focus on New York, London, and Barcelona – all established world cities with these types of attractions.

As this 'accreditation' approach may lead to a homogenisation of destinations, to make it an effective reputation-enhancing strategy, places must retain their authenticity and distinctive 'tone of voice,' something which Bill Baker shows us can be projected organically through film and popular culture. His chapter (Chapter 18) illustrates how an integrated marketing program can be developed to link a film's themes (in this case *Australia*) to enhance a destination's approach toward branding. Authenticity, culture, and a distinctive sense of place are at the heart of the Namibia (Chapter 19), San Antonio (Chapter 20), and Slovenia (Chapter 21) destination brands, just as they are in those of Belfast (discussed by Michael Gould as a post-conflict destination) and Jerusalem (analysed by Yoram Mitki, Ram Herstein, and Eugene Jaffe as a destination repositioned following crisis). Following these discussions of places with reputational 'issues,' Annette Pritchard, Nigel Morgan, and Roger Pride's epilogue (Chapter 25) reflects on this very point and considers destination reputation management and tourism futures.

CHAPTER

14

Branding and the accreditation approach: Singapore

Can-Seng Ooi

INTRODUCTION

Branding aims to make a destination stand out in the global tourism market. The brand asserts the place's uniqueness. The assertion of uniqueness has become an institutionalised global practise for celebrating destination identity. This uniqueness often emphasises the historical, social, and cultural values of the host society (Boniface & Fowler, 1993; Hall, 1999; Lanfant, 1995; Oakes, 1993; Richards, 1996). The emphasis on uniqueness in the destination brand however overshadows an important and complementary strategy in destination branding: the accreditation strategy. This chapter

- Describes and discusses the accreditation strategy;
- Presents a case study of Singapore in order to highlight the importance of this aspect of destination branding.

THE ACCREDITATION APPROACH

There are many reasons why destinations are branded (Ooi, 2002). The brands are meant to modify the perceptions of global audiences. They also selectively package the positive elements of the destination into an attractive story. Destination brands are also place identities, around which various tourism industry players rally. Tourists and residents may use destination brands as gaze lenses, through which they selectively interpret and acquire an understanding of the place. Regardless, tacit behind these brands is how the brands are formulated in relation to the ways global audiences perceive the place. The world is heterogeneous. This also means that different people will have different perceptions of the same destination. As mentioned, a destination brand attempts to focus people's minds and provide a coherent and attractive

© 2011 Published by Elsevier Ltd. All rights reserved.
DOI: 10.1016/B978-0-08-096930-5.10014-X

story of the destination. This is easier said than done. The attempt to focus minds through a unique brand story is increasingly being complemented by the accreditation approach. There are at least three levels in the accreditation approach, all of which make use of readily recognisable events and attractions to brand the destination.

At one level, the accreditation approach makes use of significant and popular events (e.g., the Olympics and World Bank meetings) to draw attention to the place (Brown, Chalip, Jago, & Mules, 2002; Burgan & Mules, 1992; Green & Chalip, 1998; Smith, 2004). An example of this first level of accreditation approach is the 2009 International Olympic Council (IOC) congress, during which Rio de Janeiro was selected for the 2016 games. It was held in Copenhagen. Because of the significance of the event, many famous personalities from competing candidate cities came to the capital. They included entertainer Oprah Winfrey, US President Barack Obama, Brazil President Luiz Inacio Lula da Silva, King Juan Carlos of Spain, and footballer Pele. Thousands of journalists descended onto Copenhagen. The announcement of the result was telecasted 'live' to more than a billion people, during which a promotional clip of Copenhagen was presented. Subsequently after the event, non-Olympic features and stories of Copenhagen were published, broadcasted, and telecasted as journalists returned home with a new collection of stories. For instance, Oprah Winfrey made a feature on why Danes are 'the happiest people on earth,' using Copenhagen as the backdrop (Oprah Winfrey Show, 2009). The hosting of important and popular events, like this IOC meeting, creates awareness of the destination because of the global publicity. These events provide globally transmitted stories that are linked to the place. The destination also gets associated with famous celebrities. Just as importantly, the organisational capabilities of the destination are showcased and the place is given international recognition. In other words, besides generating awareness and stories, these renowned events give recognition and credibility to the destination at various levels.

Complementing the significant events at the first level, the second level of the accreditation approach makes use of globally recognised and branded tourist attractions like Legoland and Guggenheim Museum to build up the appeal of the destination (Braun & Soskin, 1999; Nilsson, 2007). These attractions do not make the destination unique but they give a tacit badge of approval to the place. So, for instance, a Guggenheim Museum will increase and ascertain the cultural attractiveness of the destination, like for Bilbao. So, paradoxically, destinations want to host certain choice attractions that are also found in other destinations. In the context of destination branding, these 'branded' attractions accredit and vouch for the destinations.

A third level of the accreditation approach taps into promoting established and well-tested types of tourist attractions because these attractions communicate specific positive messages to global audiences (Dybedal, 1998; Florida, 2003; Harmaakorpi, Kari, & Parjanen, 2008; Knox, 2008; Mossberg & Getz, 2006; Slater, 2004). Unlike the first and second levels of the accreditation approach, the third-level approach refers to events and attractions that are not already 'branded.' Nonetheless, people are familiar with these types of products (Kim & Jamal, 2007; Prentice, Witt, & Hamer,

1998; Weaver, 2005). For example, many attractions have taken on similar formats, such as film festivals, art biennales, and pedestrian shopping streets. Using a similar formula and following the footsteps of the Eiffel Tower and the Statue of Liberty, structures are built with the intention to symbolise places and become icons themselves, e.g., the Pearl Tower of Shanghai and Guggenheim Museum of Bilbao. By following popular heritage village strategies, Finnish tourist authorities branded Lapland as 'Santa Claus Land' and created a 'Santa Claus Village and Workshop' (Pretes, 1995). These attractions and events are best practises in the tourism industry, one may argue as they are readily appreciated and recognised by many tourists. By having these attractions, they also communicate certain images of the place and promote certain activities in local society, such as generating more bubbly street life, celebrating local film culture, and generating a more vibrant art scene. They thus contribute to and accredit the place with certain characteristics.

I have discussed the search for uniqueness by the Singapore Tourism Board (STB) when branding the city-state (Ooi, 2004). This chapter looks at how the authorities use two of the most significant tourism projects to brand Singapore as a vibrant and exciting destination. Singapore has a clean, efficient, and modern image. Such an image is a double-edged sword. The Singaporean government has been successful in transforming a small former British colony into an efficient business and financial city in the last five decades. The stable social and political environment, modern infrastructure, controlled industrial relations, no-nonsense approach to enforcing civic behaviour, pro-business policies, and single-minded drive toward economic prosperity have led to the view that the country is sanitised and sterile. In other words, Singapore has a dull image. The new 'YourSingapore' destination branding of the city-state wants to change that.

'YOURSINGAPORE'

Over the decades, the destination brands, Instant Asia, Surprising Singapore, New Asia – Singapore and Uniquely Singapore, had celebrated the city's multicultural population and embraced the city's blend of the exotic East and efficient West (Ooi, 2007). Its population is made up of three official ethnic groups: Chinese, Malay, and Indian. Singapore is also the most economically developed country in Southeast Asia. Southeast Asia is an exotic region for tourists of other parts of the world. But Singapore faces competition. 'Malaysia – Truly Asia' and 'Amazing Thailand' are only two of the many successful tourism campaigns by competitors in Southeast Asia.

In March 2010, the STB launched the 'YourSingapore' destination brand (STB 2010) to replace the former 'Uniquely Singapore.' Singapore has changed its tourism positioning five times since 1964. In the 1960s and 1970s, Singapore was 'Instant Asia,' where one could find an array of Asian cultures, peoples, festivals, and cuisine conveniently exhibited in a single destination. In the 1980s, 'Surprising Singapore' positioned Singapore by placing contrasting images of modernity and Asian exoticism together. The coexistence of East and West, old and new were highlighted. And in the 1990s, Singapore has promoted itself as 'New Asia – Singapore.' There was a subtle shift in the focus from 'Surprising Singapore' to 'New Asia – Singapore.' 'Surprising Singapore' promised pockets of unexpected diverse and distinct ethnic cultures in a modern city, whereas 'New Asia – Singapore' offered ethnic cultures fused into modern development. Metaphorically, 'Surprising Singapore' described a smorgasbord of various ethnic cultures in a modern environment, 'New Asia – Singapore' presented Singapore as a 'melting pot' of eastern and western cultures (Ooi, 2004). The story of 'Uniquely Singapore' followed 'New Asia – Singapore' as the latter was found to be too abstract for many visitors.

Regardless of the successive destination brand stories, the authorities have always pursued the vision of an exciting and energetic Singapore, for instance, in the last decade, the government has relaxed its regulations to encourage a livelier cultural scene and more vibrant nightlife (Ooi, 2005). In March 2010, the STB launched YourSingapore. This campaign moved from the old approach of presenting Singapore as a unique destination to emphasising personal travel experiences. With the launch of yoursingapore.com, visitors can build their own itinerary and decide what they want to do (STB, 2010). The unique aspects of Singapore are still accentuated but the YourSingapore approach frames Singapore as a supermarket with a wide range of products; the visitor can pick and choose what he or she likes. If Singapore was to be an exciting and comprehensive supermarket, it must brand itself as such.

Communicating the image of Singapore as vibrant and exciting is important and STB has done so over the years using a number of strategies. One, various government authorities are actively searching for, and bidding to attract, major events to the country. Two, following from the active canvassing, besides hosting pop concerts by international mega stars, popular musicals, and blockbuster exhibitions, Singapore hosts big events, for example, the 2006 World Bank and IMF meetings, the 2009 APEC summit and the first-ever Youth Olympics in 2010. Such events generate extensive international media publicity, not because Singapore is unique but because these events are globally important. Three, to 'accredit' the promoted lively images of Singapore, the Singaporean authorities seek investments and endorsements from international firms. Besides searching for events, state agencies actively seek out opportunities to make Singapore into the hub of global and regional organisations, including those in the media, design, telecommunication, pharmaceuticals, and financial sectors. Singapore is already a regional hub for the global media industry. MTV, Discovery, HBO, and BBC have made Singapore their regional headquarters. These setups endorse Singapore as an innovative, cultural, and creative place by just being there. Four, to become a respected arts and cultural city, Singapore has also established a number of cultural institutions. Three national museums were established in Singapore in the mid-1990s, and in 2002, Esplanade – Theatres by the Bay was opened. The Singaporean government wants the city-state to be the cultural capital of Southeast Asia (Ooi, 2007). Many of these events, attractions, and recognitions are not unique to Singapore but they would increase the credibility of the lively cosmopolitan city brand. Thus, there will always be something exciting for visitors to choose, experience, and create in their own YourSingapore.

In the last few years, two major tourism development projects were launched – the Formula One races and the opening of two casinos. They are tourist attractions but more importantly, they contribute important brand messages about the destination. I will look at these case projects in some detail to highlight the dynamics in the accreditation approach to branding.

FORMULA ONE (F1) AND BRANDING SINGAPORE

In the 1960s, car races were popular in Singapore. These races were stopped in 1973 because they were thought to promote reckless driving. There were seven deaths over 11 years in the races along public roads (Lim, 2008). With limited physical space in Singapore, the island-state did not want to dedicate a racing course for car races. Furthermore, car races are for the masses and they do not make Singapore into a culturally refined city. That was the view of the prime minister then. In 2005, the Minister Mentor (MM) Lee Kuan Yew, the aforementioned former prime minister, revealed that he regretted the decision to ban car races (Lee, 2005). He said that the Singaporean Government has come to consider popular culture, including F1, as big business today (Koh, 2005a):

> [Pop singers and MTV programmes attract] millions of young viewers around the world, and there is big business in this. So from a business point of view, whether I like it or not, I should be – the Government should be – interested in this.

Singapore staged its first F1 races in 2008. It was also the first night race in F1's history. Each season costs S$150 million (US$100 million) to stage, 60% borne by tax payers. Public roads in the middle of the central business district have to be closed for weeks, roads have to be upgraded before the start of each season, and because the races take place in the middle of the city centre, pedestrians and vehicle traffic flows are severely disrupted. While there are reports of brisk business during the F1 races, shopping centres surrounding the circuit area suffer because it is inconvenient for people to visit them (Lim, J., 2009; Lim, L., 2009; Tan and Lim, 2008). In addition the noises are deafening and because the races are held at night, strong lighting is needed which consumes massive energy and is not environmentally friendly.

Regardless of these costs, STB and the government take up the races. S. Iswaran, senior minister of State for Trade and Industry, stated the importance of the races for Singapore (Straits Times, 2009):

> The F1 continues to improve Singapore's international branding and improves mindshare. It also serves as a very good platform for business networking, innovative activities and the creation of new opportunities.

STB declares that the F1 races 'will help to put us firmly in the global spotlight ... the buzz will boost Singapore's efforts to be the entertainment and events capital of Asia' (Foo, 2008). How does F1 contribute specifically to the destination branding of Singapore? One, F1 is part of the popular culture strategy for Singapore in branding itself. Popular cultures draw global masses. Singapore may not be unique in hosting these events but the island-state is associated with the fun and exciting images of popular cultural events (Figure 14.1).

Two, F1, besides being popular, is glamorous. Celebrities visited Singapore to perform, to visit, or to be seen. In 2008 and 2009, famous persons who were

Figure 14.1 Part of the Singapore Grand Prix F1 race circuit, with the Singapore skyline as the backdrop. Source: URL http://www.f1-site.com/wallpapers/2009/f1/singapore/practice/singapore-photo-f1-wallpaper-2009-1.jpg.

at the F1 events included singer Beyonce, actress Lindsay Lohan, businessman Richard Branson, and actor Jackie Chan (Chee, 2009; van Miriah, 2009). Media stories about celebrities at F1 events give attention to Singapore and Singapore is glamorous by association. Three, the telecast of F1 races makes Singapore sights familiar. The intangible benefits are considered invaluable; Singapore would move away from its dull image as millions of people could see speeding cars racing round the city centre. The races will also remind F1 fans of Singapore annually. The illuminated and spectacular night skyline has also made their way into new editions of computer racing games – *F1 2009* and *Need for Speed: Nitro* (Loh, 2009).

So, in sum Senior Minister Goh Chok Tong, former prime minister, reiterated that the races are money well spent by STB (Lim, 2009a; 2009b): 'We want to have a reputation that this is a good place to work, to live, to play. F1 helps us to acquire that reputation.' While F1 is constantly talked about in the branding of Singapore, holding F1 races does not make Singapore unique. Instead, F1 is popular and familiar to international audiences; F1 has a given image and reputation which by association accredits Singapore as a glamorous, exciting, and trendy city.

CASINOS AND BRANDING SINGAPORE

In 2010, Singapore opened its first casinos in two Vegas-styled 'integrated resorts' (IRs) – Marina Bay Sands and Resorts World at Sentosa. The former is located in the middle of the central business district and is run by Las Vegas Sands. The latter is on the resort island, Sentosa, and this IR is managed by Genting, a Malaysian casino operator. In March 2004, the then Minister for Trade and Industry George Yeo mooted the idea of hosting a casino in Singapore. Many religious and civil groups voiced strong objections against any casinos in Singapore emerged. The casino discussion became a lively money-versus-values debate; Singaporean society was polarised into those who take an economic pragmatic position and those who take an unbending moral stance against gambling. The government cabinet was not unanimous and the casino debate was one of the most heated public discussions held in Singapore ever.

A STB officer, voicing his own view, was exasperated and complained to me about those members of the public who were against the casino. Not only has a tourism project become a focal point for criticism, he was alarmed that naysayers are ignoring the reality that Singapore is losing foreign exchange – Singaporeans were and are travelling overseas and taking cruises just to gamble. The social conservatism prevalent in Singapore is giving the destination a boring image.

But eventually, the government decided to have two casinos, not just one, in late 2005. It was and is considered that the casinos are important for tourism and the destination branding of Singapore. As part of the process to shape public opinion and appease civil society, the Ministry of Information, Communications and the Arts (MICA) issued a brochure – *Why Integrated Resorts?* – to convince the general public of the decision (MICA 2005). The decision was a pragmatic one – Singapore tourism, while still healthy, is losing market share; Singapore is facing strong tourism competition in the region; the casinos will give a S$1.5 billion (US$1 billion) annual boost to the economy and create 35,000 jobs. The casinos will not only change the image of Singapore but show that Singapore is changing with the times.

The oft-recognised founding father of Singapore MM Lee Kuan Yew explained why he had banned casinos in the past, 'I did not want to undermine Singapore's work ethic and breed the belief that people can get rich by gambling, something that is impossible' (Lee, 2005). But now, he found that old 'virtues are no longer sufficient' because international professionals and executives want an economically vibrant and exciting city to visit and live in. Casinos and integrated resorts will eventually be built in competing destinations in the region and, like it or not, Singapore has to address the competition. The goal now for Singapore then is to make the city 'more lively and exciting, a fun place and, at the same time, retain its virtues – clean, green, safe and wholesome' (Lee, 2005). But how would the integrated resorts and casinos brand Singapore?

One, the IRs are important because they would boost the array of tourism attractions and facilities on the island. The reputation of Singapore as a congress centre, a family-friendly destination, and an eventful city would be enhanced. For instance, Las Vegas Sands won the bid because it would provide a 120,000 m² convention centre. It will also have an 'ArtScience' museum, exploring the connections between art and science. As for Resorts World at Sentosa, a winning point is the Universal Studios theme park. There will also be concert halls, restaurants, and theatres in both IRs. Although these are not unique in the world, these are facilities and attractions that make a tourism destination attractive as a whole.

Two, the casinos allude to a less strait-laced aspect of Singapore. This is part of the bigger strategy to change the image of Singapore. For instance, Members

Figure 14.2 The Sands Marina Bay integrated resort defines Singapore's skyline. © Marina Bay Sands Pte Ltd., 2009. All rights reserved.

of Parliament voiced their worries about the loosening up of regulations in Singapore to attract foreigners and to present a livelier image of Singapore. The then Minister of State for Trade and Industry Vivian Balakrishnan replied (Singapore Parliament Hansard, 2004):

> *There was an article that Professor Richard Florida wrote, entitled 'The Rise of the Creative Class.' [...] His research found that cities, which are able to embrace diversity, are able to attract and foster a bigger creative class. These are key drivers in a knowledge-based economy. The larger lesson for us in Singapore is that we need to shift our mindset so that we can be more tolerant of diversity.*

Three, the two projects will become physical icons of the city. Prime Minister Lee Hsien Loong pointed out that the resorts will change the city's skyline (Koh, 2005b). For instance, the Marina Bay Sands resort features the 'Sands SkyPark,' a garden larger than two football fields, connecting three 55-storey hotel towers at roof level, 200 m above ground (Figure 14.2). The image of an unusual floating garden will come to symbolise Singapore.

The IR and casinos will market and brand Singapore, not by making Singapore more unique but by offering products and images of Singapore that global audiences can relate to. They increase the credibility of Singapore as a congress hub, a family-friendly destination, and a vibrant city. These attractions and facilities are found in many other cosmopolitan cities and Singapore wants to be considered one. In other words, these attractions and facilities accredit Singapore as an(other) cosmopolitan city.

CONCLUSION

In the academic and practise literature, there is an accepted claim that uniqueness is all important in destination branding. In reality, however, there are many strategies used to make the destination less unique in the branding process.

Instead, 'branded' attractions that are not unique to the country are pursued because the destination can be positively associated with these attractions. Some of the events will create awareness of the place. Events, attractions, and facilities are also enhanced to make the city more cosmopolitan. The issue is then not being more unique but more similar to other destinations.

To reiterate, there are three levels in the accreditation approach. At one level, the accreditation approach makes use of significant and popular events (e.g., the Olympics and World Bank meetings and F1 races) to draw attention to the place. At the second level, 'branded' and familiar attractions, such as Universal Studios theme parks and the Guggenheim Museum, are lured to set up in various destinations. These attractions inadvertently vouch for the place. At the third level, destinations use tested formulas and offer *similar* attractions to global audiences (e.g., film festivals, rock concerts, art museums).

There are some lessons from the accreditation approach to destination branding. One, in the branding of a destination, while a unique selling proposition is important, branding and tourism authorities are tapping into global audience perceptions and trying to draw visitors' attention through popular and readily recognised attractions. These attractions readily draw attention and awareness to the destination. They are more accessible to mass international audiences than local stories, heroes, and cultural practises, which foreigners have to acquire local knowledge to appreciate. The uniqueness of local elements may be too exotic and difficult to communicate. A unique destination brand story can thus be 'too' unique and inaccessible to visitors.

Two, the accreditation approach to destination branding accentuates how tourism and destination branding authorities follow certain 'models' of destination development. Destinations learn, even copy, from each other, in the name of best practises. Art biennales, music festivals, observation towers, physical icons, museums, and staging of blockbuster musicals are just some examples. But as a result, tourism destinations will become more alike rather than unique. Regardless, tourists are not necessarily looking just for the unique, rather they also seek attractions that they are familiar with and want to reaffirm their preconceived ideas of what a particular destination is like (McIntosh & Prentice, 1999; Prentice, 2004; Ritzer & Liska, 1997; Weaver, 2005). Thus, a destination which has an aspiration to be recognised as a cosmopolitan city will use available formulas to enhance the local night life, cultural scene, and street buzz.

Three, the accreditation approach also demonstrates the dynamics amongst tourism destinations. As mentioned, DMOs are actively seeking to associate their places with and be endorsed by branded tourist attractions. They innovate from tested formulas found in other destinations, as in the case of Singapore. Essentially, destinations not only compete, authorities in these places also interact and respond to the competitive tourism industry through strategies and policies. In the context of destination branding, the challenge is to find a way to protect ideas and products. The only solution is probably to innovate and be more creative than competitors.

In contrast to the branding-through-uniqueness approach, the accreditation approach highlights a different perspective to destination branding. The uniqueness and accreditation approaches complement one another. The accreditation approach reminds us that destinations are becoming more akin to, rather than more unique from, one another. That would also explain why so many destinations branded as unique are also becoming similar. For the case of Singapore, the authorities have decided the uniqueness of Singapore will come from how individual tourists experience Singapore, as a tourist creates one's own 'YourSingapore.'

DEDICATION

This chapter is dedicated to Professor Richard Prentice, 1952–2008. The rigor and intelligence he put into his tourism investigations will continue to inspire many, and influence our research agenda.

References

Boniface, P., & Fowler, P. J. (1993). *Heritage and tourism in 'the global village'*. London: Routledge.

Braun, B. M., & Soskin, M. D. (1999). Theme park competitive strategies. *Annals of Tourism Research, 26*, 438–442.

Brown, G., Chalip, L., Jago, L., & Mules, T. (2002). The Sydney olympics and brand Australia. In N. Morgan, A. Pritchard, & R. Pride (Eds.). *Destination branding: Creating the unique destination proposition* (pp. 163–185). Oxford: Butterworth Heinemann.

Burgan, B., & Mules, T. (1992). Economic impact of sporting events. *Annals of Tourism Research, 19*, 700–710.

Chee, F. (2009). Star-studded affair off the track. *Straits Times*. 27 September.

Dybedal, P. (1998). *Tourism in peripheral areas of Europe*. Bornholm, Denmark: Bornholms Forskningscenter.

Florida, R. (2003). *The rise of the creative class* (new ed.). New York: Basic Books.

Foo, A. (2008). City's image will be the big F1 winner. *Straits Times* 19 September.

Green, B. C., & Chalip, L. (1998). Sport tourism as the celebration of subculture. *Annals of Tourism Research, 25*, 275–291.

Hall, D. (1999). Destination building, niche marketing and national image projection in Central and Eastern Europe. *Journal of Vacational Marketing, 5*, 227–237.

Harmaakorpi, V., Kari, K., & Parjanen, S. (2008). City design management as a local competitiveness factor. *Place Branding and Public Diplomacy, 4*, 169–181.

Kim, H., & Jamal, T. (2007). Touristic quest for existential authenticity. *Annals of Tourism Research, 34*, 181–201.

Knox, D. (2008). Spectacular tradition Scottish folksong and authenticity. *Annals of Tourism Research, 35*, 255–273.

Koh, L. (2005a). MM Lee voices 2 regrets. *Straits Times*. 17 April.

Koh, L. (2005b). Two new icons for the city state. *Straits Times*. 18 April.

Lanfant, M. -F. (1995). International tourism, internalization and the challenge to identity. In M. -F. Lanfant, J. B. Allcock, & E. M. Bruner (Eds.). *International tourism: Identity and change* (pp. 24–43). London: SAGE Publications.

Lee, K. Y. (2005). Why old virtues are not enough. *Straits Times*. 20 April.

Lim, I. L.P. (2008). Singapore grand prix. Singapore Infopedia, National Library Singapore, (accessed on 2.10.09) at URL http://infopedia.nl.sg/articles/SIP_1353_2008-12-02.html.

Lim, J. (2009). F1 fuels brisk sales for most outlets. *Straits Times*.

Lim, L. (2009). SM: F1 good for Singapore branding. *Straits Times*.

Loh, S. (2009). *Singapore roars into racing games*. 27 September.

McIntosh, A. J., & Prentice, C. (1999). Affirming authenticity: consuming cultural heritage. *Annals of Tourism Research*, *26*, 589–612.

MICA (2005). *Why Integrated Resorts?* Singapore: MICA Publicity Brochure.

Mossberg, L., & Getz, D. (2006). Stakeholder influences on the ownership and management of festival brands. *Scandinavian Journal of Hospitality and Tourism*, *6*, 308–326.

Nilsson, Å, P. (2007). Stakeholder theory: the need for a convenor. The case of billund. *Scandinavian Journal of Hospitality and Tourism*, *7*, 171–184.

Oakes, T. S. (1993). The cultural space of modernity: ethnic tourism and place identity in China. *Society and Space*, *11*, 47–66.

Ooi, C. -S. (2002). *Cultural tourism and tourism cultures: The business of mediating experiences in copenhagen and Singapore*. Copenhagen: Copenhagen Business School Press.

Ooi, C. -S. (2004). Brand Singapore: The hub of New Asia. In N. Morgan, A. Pritchard, & R. Pride (Eds.). *Destination branding: Creating the unique destination proposition* (pp. 242–262). London: Elsevier Butterworth Heinemann.

Ooi, C. -S. (2005). Sate-civil society relations and tourism: Singaporeanizing tourists, touristifying Singapore. *Sojourn – Journal of Social Issues in Southeast Asia*, *20*, 249–272.

Ooi, C. -S. (2007). The creative industries and tourism in Singapore. In G. Richards, & J. Wilson (Eds.). *Tourism, creativity and development* (pp. 240–251). London: Routledge.

Oprah Winfrey Show. (2009). Oprah on Location: The Happiest People on Earth. 21 October. (http://www.oprah.com/dated/oprahshow/oprahshow-20091021-happiest-people, (accessed 4.11.09).

Prentice, R. (2004). Tourist familiarity and imagery. *Annals of Tourism Research*, *31*, 923–945.

Prentice, R. C., Witt, S. F., & Hamer, C. (1998). Tourism as experience: the case of heritage parks. *Annals of Tourism Research*, *25*, 1–24.

Pretes, M. (1995). Postmodern tourism: the santa claus industry. *Annals of Tourism Research*, *22*, 1–15.

Richards, G. (1996). Production and consumption of European cultural tourism. *Annals of Tourism Research*, *23*, 261–283.

Ritzer, G., & Liska, A. (1997). 'McDisneyisation' and 'post-tourism': Complementary perspectives on contemporary tourism. In C. Rojek, & J. Urry (Eds.). *Touring cultures: Transformation of travel and theory* (pp. 96–109). London: Routledge.

Singapore Parliament Hansard (2004). Vol. 77, Session 1, Parliament sitting March 13, 2004.

Slater, J. (2004). Brand Louisiana: Capitalizing on music and cuisine. In N. Morgan, A. Pritchard, & R. Pride (Eds.). *Destination branding: Creating the unique destination proposition* (2nd ed, pp. 226–241). London: Elsevier.

Smith, M. F. (2004). Brand Philadelphia: The power of spotlight events. In N. Morgan, A. Pritchard, & R. Pride (Eds.). *Destination branding: Creating the unique destination proposition* (2nd ed, pp. 261–278). London: Elsevier.

STB. (2010). Singapore gets personal: uniquely Singapore evolves into Your Singapore. Press release URL https://app.stb.gov.sg/asp/new/new03a.asp?id=11383, (accessed October 2, 2009).

Straits Times. (2009). *F1 not just about revenue*. Iswaran *Straits Times,* 20 October.

Tan, D. W., & Lim, W. C. (2008). F1 event drives retail profits up. *Straits Times.* 5 October.

van Miriah, C. (2009). And Singapore partied. *Straits Times.*

Weaver, A. (2005). The Mcdonaldization thesis and cruise tourism. *Annals of Tourism Research, 32,* 346–366. 29 September.

Useful website

http://www.yoursingapore.com

CHAPTER

15

Branding a 'new' destination: Abu Dhabi

Sheena Westwood

INTRODUCTION

The brand new 'Brand Abu Dhabi' was launched in 2007. This was not a re-branding or the extension of an existing brand, but the strategic creation of a totally new holistic destination brand for a place that, although controlling the world's largest sovereign wealth fund (Davidson, 2009), until 2007 had very low global awareness in the majority of markets into which it was diversifying. To be sustainable a destination brand requires the investment and commitment of organisations, communities, and stakeholders, and branding Abu Dhabi is part of the government's overall vision and long-term strategy for economic diversification and the positioning of the Emirate as an 'outstanding, globally recognised, sustainable tourism destination' (Abu Dhabi Tourism Authority, 2010). In using the case of Abu Dhabi, this chapter considers the strategic development and growth of a brand for an emergent destination that, unlike many developing economies, is not hindered by lack of financial or governmental support. To appreciate the progress of the brand strategy to date, it is however crucial to consider the phenomenal and ongoing economic, social, and physical development of Abu Dhabi within a history and time context. The chapter therefore

* Considers the strategic creation of a totally new holistic destination brand for a place with low global awareness in its target markets;
* Uses the case of Abu Dhabi to illustrate the strategic development of an emergent destination brand.

© 2011 Published by Elsevier Ltd. All rights reserved.
DOI: 10.1016/B978-0-08-096930-5.10015-1

CONTEXTUALISING ABU DHABI

Geography and history

Abu Dhabi is the capital of the United Arab Emirates (UAE), a federation of seven sheikhdoms, comprising Abu Dhabi, Dubai, Sharjah, Ras Al Khaimah, Umm Al Quwain, Ajman, and Fujairah. Formally established on December 2, 1971, the UAE occupies 83,600 km² in the east of the Arabian Peninsula and is bordered by the Sultanate of Oman to the east and north, and the Kingdom of Saudi Arabia to the south and west, with coastline on the Gulf of Oman and the Arabian Gulf. Today the UAE is predominantly renowned for the oil wealth which has enabled the nation to develop its infrastructure and its global stature.

Covering over 80% of the total land mass of the UAE (approximately 67,340 km²), Abu Dhabi holds the majority (approximately 90%) of oil reserves (Tabler, 2007). Historically the economy of the sheikhdom was based on trading, fishing, date agriculture, and pearling. After suffering heavily from the combined effect of the economic depression of the 1920s and the production of Japanese cultured pearls in the 1930s, the Indian government's taxation on imported pearls struck the final blow to the formerly thriving and highly lucrative pearling industry. For the three decades before the commercial production of oil in the mid-1960s, the inhabitants of Abu Dhabi lived at subsistence level in the desert and the coast without paved roads, hospitals, or proper schools (United Arab Emirates, 2007). Even after the discovery and subsequent exportation of oil, Abu Dhabi remained cautious in terms of development and diversification, particularly when compared with its geographically close neighbour Dubai, located 124 km to the north east.

Dubai (covering an area of approximately 3885 km², 5% of the UAE's total landmass (Iranian Business Council Dubai, 2008)) is without doubt the most internationally well-known place brand in the region. As such it vastly overshadows the other emirates, with its phenomenal growth and development in the last three decades having done much to raise awareness around the world of the UAE as a place of strategic and economic significance, as a place to work, to invest, and as a tourism destination. Dubai began its development in the 1970s and has already secured a worldwide brand reputation for business, 'super fast urbanism' (Bagaeen, 2007), architectural attractions, glamour, and predominantly '4 S' tourism – sand, sun, sea, and shopping, which currently accounts for approximately 17% of its GDP (Davidson, 2009).

Government and administrative framework

It was much more recently that Abu Dhabi took on a new impetus in expansion and economic diversification. In 2004, power passed to HH Sheikh Khalifa bin Zayed Al Nahyan, ruler of Abu Dhabi and president of the UAE, and HH Sheikh Mohammad Bin Zayed Al Nahyan on the death of their father, Sheikh Zayed bin Sultan Al Nahyan, founder and first president of the UAE. Tourism was identified as a key development area in the drive to diversify the economy, not only to increase foreign earnings but to promote the international profile of the emirate. Major barriers to destination development and branding, particularly those in developing economies, are a lack of adequate finance, insufficient government support, and lack of expertise (Hall, 2004). As an emergent destination, Abu Dhabi is almost unique in the fact that it has full government support in the form of funding and policy, while expertise is provided by growing numbers of qualified Emirati nationals working alongside experienced expatriates.

As part of the economic diversification strategy, Abu Dhabi Tourism Authority (ADTA) was launched as a statutory body in 2004 by Abu Dhabi Government. The authority's responsibilities include the development, growth, and promotion of tourism in Abu Dhabi which has a very clear positioning statement as 'a world class destination of distinction ... an upmarket destination with an uncompromising determination toward sustaining and preserving its natural environment and treasured heritage and traditions' (Abu Dhabi Tourism, 2010). The select, key target markets are business tourism (which currently accounts for 75% of tourism arrivals) and high-end leisure, sport, adventure, and 'cultural seekers'. Abu Dhabi sees cultural tourism as pivotal to its development as a world capital, and also as a particularly important means to encourage intercultural discourse and understanding (Gerson, 2008). Despite the economic downturn, hotels in Abu Dhabi received 1.6 million guests in 2009, a 2% rise when compared to 2008, with a 10% and 15% increase forecast for 2011 and 2012, respectively; however, due to the downturn the original aim of attracting 2.7 million tourists by 2012, as stated in the ADTA 5-year plan for 2008–2012, has now been revised to 2.3 million (Franklin, cited in Sekhri, 2010).

Collaboration with public and private sector industry stakeholders is a priority for ADTA, whose remit also includes industry licensing and industry professional development. The government's high level of involvement and commitment to tourism-related development is evidenced by the ambitious and extensive projects, some which are nearing completion or completed, whilst others are in the early stages of construction or in the planning stage. Much of the tourism-related development is under the control of ADTA's tourism development arm, the Tourism and Development Investment Company (TDIC) which was formed in 2006 as the governmental organisation mandated to 'develop the emirate's tourism assets and help Abu Dhabi become a premier international destination' (TDIC, 2008).

Abu Dhabi's primary assets include its strong Arabian heritage and culture, its spectacular landscape with huge expanses of desert and sand dunes, fertile oases and magnificent coastline, climate, political stability, tolerance, safety, and its accessibility. Its geographical location equidistant between Europe and much of Asia means that London is approximately 7 hours and Hong Kong 8 hours away by air. Both Abu Dhabi and Dubai have major international airlines. Etihad Airways (which won the 2009 'World's Leading Airline' award at the World Travel Awards in London) is Abu Dhabi's flagship carrier serving over 60 destinations, while Emirates Airways fly to over 100 destinations from Dubai. The UAE has six international airports at Abu Dhabi, Dubai, Al Ain, Fujairah, Ras Al Khaimah, and Sharjah. Abu Dhabi International Airport is currently undergoing a £254 million expansion, while the new Al-Maktoum International Airport at Jebel Ali 35 km southwest of Dubai and (approximately 50 km from Abu Dhabi International Airport) is due to be completed in 2015, and will have capacity to handle over 120 million passengers (uaeinteract.com. 2005).

Abu Dhabi is extending tourism development beyond the city and its immediate environs to historically important Al Ain in the east, the western region of Al Gharbia, and several of the surrounding islands. Qasr Al Sarab, a luxury resort overlooking the Rub Al Khali opened in 2009, and two of the recently opened major projects in the $40 billion Yas Island development are the Yas Marina Circuit, home to the first Abu Dhabi Grand Prix in November 2009, and a links golf course. Other attractions under development include waterparks, a marina, and a Ferrari theme park (opened in October 2010). 'Eco' and wildlife tourism are high on the development agenda, with a $110 million eco-spa resort, and a complex of six nature reserves spread across eight islands, predicted to attract approximately 250,000 visitors when the first phase is complete in 2010. When fully operational visitor numbers are forecast to reach over 1 m, generate $333 million tourism revenue annually, and create 6500 jobs. By 2012, Abu Dhabi will see the number of hotel rooms increase from 9000 in 2008 to 25,000. A significant facility in the positioning of Abu Dhabi as a world class business tourism destination is Abu Dhabi National Exhibition Centre. Phase two became operational in October 2008 and with 55,500 m² of space it boasts the largest air conditioned concourse in the world. The exhibition centre forms the nucleus of Capital Centre, a 'micro-city' of commercial, residential, accommodation, and leisure facilities, which will include a 10,000 capacity conference centre (Everden, 2008). Arguably the most ambitious and prestigious project in Abu Dhabi is Saadiyat Island. 'The aim of Saadiyat Island must be to create a cultural asset for the world. A gateway and beacon for cultural experiences and exchange. Culture crosses all boundaries and therefore Saadiyat will belong to the people of the UAE, the greater Middle East and the world at large' (HH Sheikh Mohammad Bin Zayed Al Nahyan, quoted in TDIC, 2008). In keeping with its positioning and policy of attracting high-end and cultural tourists, Saadiyat Island Cultural District will house a unique cluster of cultural facilities including the Guggenheim, Louvre, Maritime and National Museums and a Performing Arts Centre, designed by world class architects including Frank Gehry, Jean Nouvel, Tadao Ando, Sir Norman Foster, and Zaha Hadid. In addition to the Cultural District, Saadiyat Island will have 29 hotels, including a seven-star resort, three marinas, two golf courses, as well as a range of commercial, civic, and residential properties. The first of the planned golf courses opened in 2010, with the remainder of the three-phase $100 billion project being due to be completed in 2018.

However, although some developments are now complete, any destination promotion strategy has to take into account the fact that as yet, Abu Dhabi is still very much the promise of the future. With the majority of attractions and resorts incomplete, the risk of damaging its reputation by being unable to meet visitor expectations is a key consideration in the destination marketing and brand roll out. As an emergent destination, a significant challenge that Abu Dhabi and other emirates face is the lack of international awareness and understanding about the geography and relationship of the emirates that make up the federation. Abu Dhabi is often identified through its proximity to Dubai, but even Dubai, despite the prominence of its global brand, suffers from geographical confusion, a common misconception being that it is a country in its own right (Bundhun, 2009). Although FutureBrand's 2009 Country Brand index (FutureBrand has recently opened an office in Abu Dhabi) identified the UAE as the top country brand in the Middle East and North Africa region, and 29th overall in an index of 102 countries, based on data from business and leisure travellers (FutureBrand, 2009), there is currently no unified federal body that oversees 'Brand UAE' with each emirate autonomously developing its individual brand. Regarding the tourism sector, although currently each tourism authority likewise develops its own brand and marketing strategy without collaboration between other emirates, in December 2009 it was announced that the National Council of Tourism and Antiquities will play a role in promoting the tourism sector at a national level (ameinfo.com 2009).

CREATING BRAND ABU DHABI

Under the directive of His Highness Sheikh Mohamed bin Zayed Al Nahyan, Crown Prince of Abu Dhabi and Chairman of the Executive Council, two government organisations – The Executive Affairs Authority and the ADTA – were tasked with developing a brand that would build on the legacy of the highly revered visionary, the late Sheikh Zayed bin Sultan al Nahyan, and 'capture and define the brand identity of the Emirate of Abu Dhabi' .... together with 'a comprehensive strategy to ensure that this brand is applied consistently and appropriately by the public and private sectors when they represent the Emirate' (Office of the Brand of Abu Dhabi, 2010 n.p.) With long-term sustainable growth as the policy mainstay, Abu Dhabi released its strategic 'plan 2030', a blueprint for the staged expansion of the urban environment in 2007, a key element of which was the ongoing development and guardianship of the Abu Dhabi brand. Consequently, the Office of the Brand of Abu Dhabi (OBAD) was formed in 2007 to develop and manage the implementation of the brand, its dual mandate being

1. *The creation of a brand that captures the essence of the Emirate of Abu Dhabi in an identity that is visual, literal, and behavioural, and*
2. *To act as the guardian and patron of this brand identity.*

The OBAD is a government entity, established in 2007. OBAD is responsible for delivering a compelling and consistent brand for Abu Dhabi which embraces the Emirate's vision for the future and respects the culture, heritage, and traditions of its past. OBAD acts as the guardian and patron of the brand, providing guidance to the public and private sectors on its application in all activities that may have an impact on the reputation of the Emirate of Abu Dhabi – from tourism, to inward investment to the service industry (Office of the Brand of Abu Dhabi, 2010).

As this quote illustrates, consciousness of potential socio-cultural erosion, the preservation of traditional values, culture and heritage, and community involvement are major considerations in Abu Dhabi's development strategy.

The increasing concerns about the threat of diminishing local identity and the need for preservation of the national character in the face of increasing multiculturalism are well founded when the demographic balance is considered. According to the 2005 census, the population of Abu Dhabi was less than 1.5 million, only 20% of whom were Emirati. The population is projected to increase to 3.1 million in the next two decades (Hope, 2010), not including the potential 2.7 million visitors (Oxford Business Group, n.d.). Indeed, such socio-cultural anxieties are cited as a reason for the significant lack of investment in infrastructure development during the period following the discovery of oil (Davidson, 2009). In creating a brand for Abu Dhabi it was therefore imperative to support it with a strategy that would engage and create a sense of ownership among government and industry stakeholders, the national and multicultural international resident communities and businesses, in addition to the wider global audience: 'The ultimate outcome of this initiative is a clear and defined brand for the Emirate of Abu Dhabi, and a comprehensive strategy to ensure that this brand is applied consistently and appropriately by the public and private sectors when they represent the Emirate' (Office of the Brand of Abu Dhabi, 2010).

Successful, sustainable brands enter into the psyche of consumers and other stakeholders, and engender emotional reactions such as loyalty, commitment, and symbolic attachment. While the functional destination attributes such as access, infrastructure, and facilities form the tangible core of the brand, a brand has many layers of meaning. It is the richness of emotional and psychological associations created through the character and imagery, and that are developed over time, which captivate minds and hearts. Establishment of the core values and development of the brand identity are the foundational stages of destination brand building (Morgan & Pritchard, 2004). Understanding of the international perceptions of Abu Dhabi, and how the local community understood their own identity, was high on the research agenda, thus the extensive research that was carried out internationally and among the local community crucially informed the brand architecture which was created by drawing on several recognised destination brand frameworks such as brand personality, and the destination brand pyramid (Morgan & Pritchard, 2004).

Research in the major source markets (UK, Germany, France) identified the key target audience as 'Cultural Seekers', that is, affluent early adopters who seek unique, meaningful, and high-quality experiences, and can afford to pay for luxury and exclusivity. The combination of tangible and intangible associations with Abu Dhabi, identified during the research include authenticity, tradition, culture, being warm and human, open to new ideas, oil wealth, business, high tech, modern, and connected to its roots (Office of the Brand of Abu Dhabi, 2010). In addition to the physical attributes such as the beaches, coastline, desert, oases and the modern, cutting-edge architecture, its unique Arabian heritage, culture, and inherent sense of hospitality were also considered primary assets in the brand development.

Although Abu Dhabi brand is intended to be a brand for the Emirate across all sectors, tourism was the primary sector for the brand development and implementation, with ADTA being the first government entity to adopt the brand at its launch in 2007. The brand identity was developed by ADTA,

OBAD, and senior government officials in collaboration with creative agency M&C Saatchi, and built around word 'respect' which was identified as the brand essence. 'Respect' communicates the intangible aspects such as experience, feelings, uniqueness, and hospitality, and the characteristics of heritage and culture combined with the primary physical characteristics in the development and design of the brand assets. Figure 15.1 shows how the research findings were fed into the inverted brand benefit pyramid that was used to provide the functional and emotional and value development framework for brand Abu Dhabi.

The broader key features and benefits include historical elements such as the Bedouin heritage, Sheikh Zayed's legacy, and falconry and the tangible, physical characteristics such as the sea, desert and climate, economy and business, narrowing down to the intangible, experiential, and emotional elements and values such as authenticity, relaxation, tolerance, individuality, uniqueness, and adventure. A key aspect in the creation process was that of brand personality which refers to the personification of brands in the belief that brands, like people have symbolic characteristics. Personality traits associated with a brand personality can influence consumer attitudes, with consumers purchasing brands in part, based on the attractiveness of the brand's personality (Martineau, 1957; Morgan & Pritchard, 2004; Westwood, 2006). Personality traits identified as being associated with Abu Dhabi included 'wealth' and 'legacy', and also 'considered' and 'understated'. Distilling all this into just one word that can encapsulate the spirit of a destination is highly challenging, yet the OBAD identified 'respect' as the word that has since become accepted as the essence of brand Abu Dhabi.

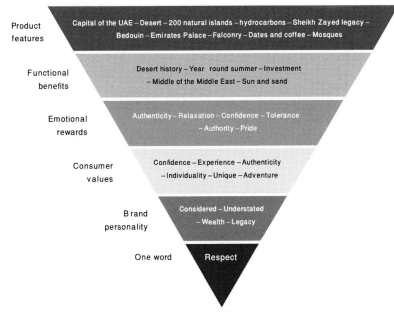

Figure 15.1 The inverted destination brand benefit pyramid. Source: Office of the Brand of Abu Dhabi, 2010.

The visual identity

A significant component of the brand identity is the visual identity. To ensure consistent reinforcement of the brand identity the OBAD developed five key elements: the brand mark, the frame, the colour palette, the typeface, and the photographs, all of which reflect the Emirate's tradition, heritage, and vision. 'We are proud of our Islamic heritage. Of Sheikh Zayed's legacy. Our identity should reflect this. To that end we propose a design which combines Islamic tradition with contemporary design based on an Arabic calligraphy of Abu Dhabi' (Office of the Brand of Abu Dhabi, 2010). The brand mark is the shape of the dhow sail (the traditional Arabic sailing vessel) and is usually filled with 'Abu Dhabi' in Arabic text (Figure 15.2). The Arabic and English typeface was created specially, inspired by the Arabic Nazanin typeface, with the Arabic text always coming before the English (Figure 15.3).

The frame which is widely used as a border on publications and advertisements was inspired by the designs used on the bisht, the Arabic mens' traditional outer cloak which is usually worn by royalty and other dignitaries during formal and state occasions, and during the cooler winter months (see Figure 15.4). Commensurate with the identified personality traits 'considered' and 'understated', the master and sub-brand colour palettes

Figures 15.2 The development of the brand mark in the shape of the dhow sail (Source Office of the Brand of Abu Dhabi, 2010) (two images).

Figure 15.3 The Arabic Nazanin-inspired brand typeface (Source Office of the Brand of Abu Dhabi, 2010)

reflect the natural colours of the sea, sky, sand, and Bedouin heritage, the colours having names such as heritage red, calligraphic gray, sand dune, Arabian sky, desert sun, glittering sun, Bedouin night, and oasis among others.

The visual identity is further significantly supported with imagery through photographs. Four different collections of photographs that reflect different aspects of life in Abu Dhabi and form part of the Abu Dhabi brand identity were taken by the renowned photographer William Huber (Figures 15.5 and 15.6). Other collections of brand photographs were taken by the finalists of the 2009 and 2010 'Abu Dhabi Through Your Eyes' competition that is now an annual event. Organisations involved with the destination promotion of Abu Dhabi may apply to OBAD to use the photographs.

Figure 15.4 The gold bisht border embroidery inspired the frame design (Source Office of the Brand of Abu Dhabi, 2010)

Figures 15.5 William Huber photographs used for posters placed in underpass tunnels during the F1 Abu Dhabi Grand Prix (Source Office of the Brand of Abu Dhabi, 2010)

Figure 15.6 William Huber 'Red Girls' from the photograph collection (Source Office of the Brand of Abu Dhabi, 2010).

Brand launch, adoption, and protection

Although the brand was initially launched with ADTA, the foundational concept was to encourage other governmental organisations to adopt it in whole or in part so as to communicate a consistent representation of Abu Dhabi. However, although the OBAD offer guidance and assistance to both public and private sectors, safeguarding the reputation of the Emirate is paramount, thus they carefully control the use of the brand. The role of OBAD is that of a 'hands on' brand consultant, and it maintains a close link with partner organisations, fostering a team relationship in advising, reviewing, and supporting the brand application and alignment through, for example, help with design and communications, and giving practical advice on working with agencies (OBAD personal interview, 2010). Rather than being a 'one size fits all' brand, the brand of Abu Dhabi is carefully customised for each partner, under the guidance of OBAD. Applications have to be made to OBAD adopt the brand, with use restricted primarily to selected Government departments and foundations that are involved with the promotion of Abu Dhabi as a tourist or investment destination, and the protection and promotion of the cultural identity of Abu Dhabi (OBAD personal interview, 2010). OBAD emphasise that this is to ensure constant representation and encourage shared understanding, rather than being a brake on creativity or individuality, 'this brand is much more than a logo or slogan, it defines how we should project

ourselves to the outside world and how we should interact as an Emirate'
(Al Shemari & Pearce, 2007).

Outreach and community engagement

Education and buy-in by public and private organisations and the community
were key considerations during the brand rollout. Following the launch in
November 2007, several workshops were held by OBAD for public and private
sector organisations and agencies to educate them about the brand and enable
understanding of its application in their particular organisations. Ongoing
local education and awareness initiatives include a series of workshops at
Abu Dhabi universities and colleges in 2009 designed to widen students'
perceptions about the role of the Abu Dhabi Brand, to explore their personal
insight about the Emirate and to engage them, as future leaders.

Other activities that OBAD are using to develop the brand and its local
adoption include the annual 'Abu Dhabi Through Your Eyes' photographic
competition. The high-profile photographic competition invites local amateur
and professional photographers to submit pictures that capture the spirit of
the Emirate. The main aims of the competition are threefold: to engender
a feeling of belonging and involvement among the wide community; to
encourage local talent; and to gain insights into the way people feel about Abu
Dhabi. The 2009 competition promotion included display stands and drop
boxes in locations such as coffee shops, petrol stations and shopping malls,
advertisements in Arabic and English press, editorials and radio interviews,
direct marketing, educational visits, website (where hits increased by 70%
during the competition), and social media through Facebook. In total 4066
entries were received from 77 different nationalities, 30% of which were
Emirati nationals (2009 Abu Dhabi Through Your Eyes Summary Report).
The competitions have yielded some extremely high-quality and insightful
photographs, which in addition to attracting several thousand dollars in
prize money for the finalists, have become widely used additions to the brand
photographic library. Following the 2009 competition, a tourism photography
exhibition road show brought the winning images to various local venues,
assisted by over 90 young national volunteers from Takatof (a social program
aiming to encourage a culture of volunteering throughout the UAE) who, as
Abu Dhabi Ambassadors, ensured that visitors understood the purpose of
the exhibition, and encouraged visitors to take part in a research survey. The
survey was completed by 45 different nationalities, of which 75% were under
the age of 39 years. The findings of the survey indicate that people feel positive
about the holistic nature of the brand for the Emirate, with perceptions of Abu
Dhabi as a welcoming, multicultural place, a good place to live with growing
opportunities (2009 Abu Dhabi Through Your Eyes Summary Report).

The reach and awareness of the brand has expanded significantly, largely
as the result of consistent investment and brand reinforcement through the
promotional activities of government organisations and initiatives. To date,
OBAD have been involved with over 300 enterprises which include hosting
high-profile international events such as the FIFA World Cup UAE, and the
Formula 1 Grand Prix, and brand creation for events such as the UAE President

of the UAE Cup (Arabian horse race series) and the Abu Dhabi Film Festival (ADFF), as well as smaller initiatives. Governmental organisations that have adopted the brand include the Department of Transport who are using the colour palette and bisht frame to provide a distinctive livery for the cabs in the new taxi fleet. For visitors, the most visible locations for the brand are at Abu Dhabi's international and domestic airports. 'Branding the Gateways' ensures that the brand communicates with travellers through the colour blue to reflect the Arabian sky (which is standard across all), and through each airport's customised identity echoing the brand mark. An aligned identity was developed for Abu Dhabi International Airport which adopted the brand mark in the 'Arabian Sky' colour together with the typeface across its airport portfolio. For the national carrier, Etihad Airways, the brand essence 'respect' forms the core for their service proposition. The brand is embedded in their product and service by drawing on the colour palette in the livery, décor, and uniforms to give the customer a sense of place, in the quality of the service experience, through to the HR policies and practise. Other initiatives for extending the brand include the recent launch of beach merchandise using the colour palette which, developed by the Municipality of the City of Abu Dhabi in collaboration with OBAD, is distributed through specific kiosks near beach entrances.

Regional branding

Incorporating the brand identity into the wider regions of Abu Dhabi is a key part of the strategy, with the purpose of ensuring consistency and connection between the government, community, and other stakeholders. Recently two of Abu Dhabi's municipal regions, Al Ain and the newly branded Al Gharbia (Western Region) have adopted the identity. The Western Region of Abu Dhabi covers 60,000 km², and is rich in Bedouin culture and heritage; it also has 350 km of coastline including a range of islands and is home to some of the most spectacular desertscapes in the world. Although it is part of Abu Dhabi, the region has its own economic and social policies and agendas, and it has received significant public and private funding for infrastructure, tourism, and economic development projects – several of which such as the Sir Bani Yas Island and Qasr Al Sarab resorts are now operational (Welcome to Al Gharbia, n.d.). In 2008 the region was launched as a tourism and investment destination that, while remaining strongly linked to Abu Dhabi master brand, holds its own unique positioning and offering. The Arabic brand name 'Al Gharbia' which translated means 'western region' was chosen, along with a bespoke brandmark with landscape colours from the master palette and the Arabic and English typeface.

Abu Dhabi Tourism Authority

As a primary force in the brand's development and early adoption, ADTA remains the most prominent and extensive promoter of the brand. The international unveiling of the brand was at the 2007 World Travel Market in London. To ensure a high visual and emotional impact at the event, ADTA used all the brand elements combined with communication of traditional culture and heritage through the welcome and hosting of visitors to the stand. Alongside the positioning promise 'Travellers Welcome', signage-incorporated images from the William Huber photographic 'essence collection', alongside consistent and prominent use of the brand mark and typeface. Collateral and VIP gifts also included brand elements such as calligraphy, colour palette, frame, and photographs (OBAD Case Study, n.d.).

With full government support and funding, ADTA's ongoing strategic and focused marketing efforts involve consistent reinforcement of the brand through its corporate identity, and promotional activities including prominent participation in international exhibitions and trade shows, sponsorship of regional and international events, the website and the high-quality marketing collateral, the brand mark, colours, typeface, and photographs. Combinations of the visual elements of the brand identity are used across all promotional material and artefacts including publications, stationery, business cards and marketing collateral. The positioning line 'Travellers Welcome' which was originally created for the international brand launch at the 2007 World Travel Market in London has endured and become synonymous with the message and promise that destination Abu Dhabi is promoting to the rest of the world:

> *It's not just a tourist line. This is a broad claim to the rest of the world. It is as relevant to the business traveller as the holidaymaker. Born out of the past it recognises our place in the world today. We are a peaceful nation with strong connections throughout the world. We are host to many people from other nations. Our wealth means that we aren't desperate to make money from tourism (Office of the Brand of Abu Dhabi, 2010).*

Events and festivals

Events and festivals play a strategic and significant role in building brand awareness and positioning Abu Dhabi as a world class destination, with international and regional events and festivals spanning arts, culture, and sport as well as significant trade exhibitions and conferences already becoming regular fixtures. Although it takes a long time for events to become firmly associated with a particular destination and it is still early days for Abu Dhabi, the portfolio of events is growing year on year as new venues and facilities become available, and the potential for events in attracting a worldwide destination reputation together with benefits such as increasing visitor numbers, employment, and community engagement is beginning to be realised. Formula 1 motor racing is televised in 188 countries and has a potential 600 million individual viewers who watch during live broadcasts, and when the first F1 Abu Dhabi Grand Prix was held in the Yas Marina Circuit in November 2009, 50,000 spectators watched the event live, many of them visitors from neighbouring Gulf countries as well as from further afield.

Other arts and sports events hosted in 2009–2010 include the Art Abu Dhabi, Abu Dhabi Film Festival, World of Music and Dance (WOMAD), Abu Dhabi International Book Fair, Gourmet Abu Dhabi, Red Bull Air Race Mubadala World Tennis Championship, FIFA Club World Cup, Abu Dhabi

Golf Championship, F1 Powerboat Racing, and the Abu Dhabi International Triathlon. In May 2010 Office of the Brand Abu Dhabi launched an events website specifically to promote this growing portfolio of events and festivals (www.abudhabievents.ae). Regionally, both Al Ain and Al Gharbia are building their brand image and tourism destination awareness by hosting events such as the Al Ain Classical Music Festival, organised by ADTA and Abu Dhabi Authority for Culture and Heritage (ADACH), while cultural and sporting festivals in Al Gharbia include Al Dhafra Festival of Camels, Liwa Date Festival, and Al Gharbia Water Sports Festival.

CONCLUSION

Brand Abu Dhabi is a new brand for a new destination. Abu Dhabi is one of the wealthiest economies in the world, and unlike the vast majority of places, it has the financial prowess to create spectacular venues, resorts, and other tourism infrastructure and the physical space in which to do it, combined with complete government commitment and investment in the strategic promotion and holistic branding of the Emirate. Yet, it operates in a highly competitive global market, with increasingly confident, discerning, and information literate consumers. Regionally it is not alone in including tourism in its economic diversification plans, and along with several of the other emirates, wealthy GCC countries such as Bahrain, Qatar, and Oman are also investing heavily in tourism, and are at similar stages of infrastructure and brand development.

As tourist destinations, in the short term they have the allure of the exotic and new, but these countries have similar geographical locations, climates, physical landscapes, and culture, and are building comparable attractions and facilities. For Abu Dhabi, differentiation will be created by its landmark developments and attractions, notably the cluster of architecturally remarkable branded museums and facilities in the Saadiyat Island Cultural District. Sustained differentiation will be achieved through the maintenance of a coherent, identifiable brand that reaches, connects, and because of its meaning for them, remains salient with target consumers, the marketplace, the stakeholders, and the local community – and has the ability to adapt and evolve as the destination matures. The Office of the Brand Abu Dhabi was established in 2007 to develop and protect a brand that would define the identity of Abu Dhabi. Still in the growth stage, brand Abu Dhabi's development is measured and synergistic with the tourism infrastructure development that is taking place. The brand strategy is carefully considered and managed collaboratively by OBAD, with consciousness not only of the need to engage external consumers and markets but that awareness, understanding, and commitment by the local multicultural community is essential for its prolonged success. Working closely with the government-sponsored ADTA as its flagship, and with other government entities, in just over 3 years it has successfully created a recognisable, value-laden brand that has achieved remarkable awareness and engagement locally while continuing to increase its international saliency.

ACKNOWLEDGEMENT

Our sincere thanks to The Office of the Brand of Abu Dhabi for their support.

References

Abu Dhabi Tourism, (accessed 2/03/10), Available at: http://www.abudhabitourism.
ae/en/main/about-adta.aspx

Abu Dhabi through your eyes summary report (2010) Abu Dhabi Office of the
Brand.

Al Shemari, R., & Pearce, S. (2007). The journey begins, Abu Dhabi brand
briefing, presentation, December. (accessed on 1.4.10) at: Available at:
http://brand.abudhabi.ae/Sites/OBAD/Content/EN/PDF/dec-briefings-english,
property=pdf.pdf

Bagaeen, S. (2007). Brand Dubai: The instant city; or the instantly recognizable
city. *International Planning Studies*, *12*(2), 173–197.

Bundhun, R. (2009). National tourism office set to open. The National, 15
November. (accessed on March 6, 2010) at Available at: http://www.thenational.
ae/apps/pbcs.dll/article?AID=/20091115/BUSINESS/711159956/1057/rss

Davidson, C. M. (2009). *Oil and beyond*. London: C.Hurst & Co.

Dubai to make Jebel Ali world's largest airport, (2005), *UAEinteract*. (accessed
on 2.12.09) Available at: http://www.uaeinteract.com/docs/Dubai_to_make_Je
bel_Ali_worlds_largest_airport/18682.htm

Everden, K. (2008). The bold and the beautiful. Buying Business Travel,
September/October 23.

FutureBrand (2009). (accessed on March 23, 2010) at: Available at: http://www.
futurebrand.com/think/reports-studies/cbi/2009/rankings/

Gerson, J. (2008). Cultural tourists are key to the economy. The National, 24
September, p. 8 accessed 27/12/10, http://www.thenational.ae/business/
travel-tourism/cultural-tourists-key-to-economy.

Hall, D. (2004). Branding and national identity: the case of Central and Eastern
Europe. In N. Morgan, A. Pritchard, & R. Pride (Eds.), *Destination branding*
(2nd ed., pp. 111–127). Oxford: Elsevier.

Hope, B. (2010). Abu Dhabi raises its profile. The National, March 30.

Iranian Business Council Dubai (2008). (accessed on 4.04.10) Available at:
http://www.ibcuae.org/2008073165/resources/about-uae/introduction.html.

Martineau, P. (1957). *Motivation in advertising: Motives that make people buy*.
London: McGraw Hill.

Morgan, N., & Pritchard, A. (2004). Meeting the destination branding challenge.
In N. Morgan, A. Pritchard, & R. Pride (Eds.). *Destination branding* (2nd ed.,
pp. 59–78). Oxford: Elsevier.

OBAD Case Study (n.d.). Abu Dhabi Tourism Authority launches International
outreach for the new Abu Dhabi brand identity. (accessed 24.03.10)
Available at: http://brand.abudhabi.ae/Sites/OBAD/Content/EN/PDF/case-study-
adta, property=pdf.pdf

OBAD personal interview (2010) with representative of Office of the Brand of
Abu Dhabi

Office of the Brand of Abu Dhabi (2010). (accessed 2.04.10) Available at:
http://brand.abudhabi.ae/Sites/OBAD/Navigation/EN/the-brand-strategy.html

Office of the Brand of Abu Dhabi (2010). (accessed 3.04.10) Available at: http://brand.abudhabi.ae/Sites/OBAD/Navigation/EN/SupportingElements/Typogr aphy/primary-font, did=88374.html

Oxford Business Group (n.d.). (accessed 30.03.10) Available at: http://www.oxfordbusinessgroup.com/country.asp?country=36.

Sekhri, R. (2010). Abu Dhabi sees double digit visitor growth. Maktoob News, Assessed on 23 February at: http://business.maktoob.com/20090000438922/Abu_Dhabi_sees_double-digit_visitor_growth/Article.htm

Tabler, L. (2007). We are targeting high-end tourists: TDIC chief. *The Business Weekly, 4* November, 18–19.

TDIC (2008). (accessed on September 30, 2008) Available at: http://www.tdic.ae/en/article/about-us/about-tdic.html

ameinfo.com (2009) UAE Tourism Council holds first meeting in Dubai (2009). Available at: http://www.ameinfo.com/218492.html, retrieved April 12, 2010 (accessed on December 12)

United Arab Emirates (2007). London: Trident Press, p. 14.

Welcome to Al Gharbia (n.d.). (accessed on April 12, 2010 Available at: http://www.algharbia.ae/en/

Westwood, S. (2006). What Lies Beneath? Using creative, projective and participatory techniques in qualitative tourism inquiry. In I. Ateljevic, N. Morgan, & A. Pritchard (Eds.), *The critical turn in tourism studies: Innovative research methodologies* (pp. 293–316). Oxford: Elsevier.

Yas Marina Circuit. (Accessed on March 22, 2010) Available at: http://www.yasmarinacircuit.com/en/content/41/abu-dhabi-grand-prix.html

Useful websites

Abu Dhabi Authority for Culture and Heritage (ADACH) http://www.aacf.ae/en/index.html

Abu Dhabi Events http://www.abudhabievents.ae

Abu Dhabi Music and Arts Foundation (ADMAF) www.admaf.org

Abu Dhabi Tourism Authority:http://abudhabitourism.ae

Al Ain Municipality: http://am.abudhabi.ae/English/index.php

Al Dhafra Festival of Camels: http://aldhafrafestival.ae/en

Al Garbia Festivals: http://www.algharbiafestivals.com

Al Gharbia Water Sports Festival: (http://www.algharbiafestivals.com/water sports/

Office of the Brand of Abu Dhabi: http://brand.abudhabi.ae

Tourism Development and investment Company (TDIC):http://www.tdic.ae

Visit Abu Dhabi: http://visitabudhabi.ae

Yas Marina Circuit: http://yasmarinacircuit.com

CHAPTER

16

City brands and special interest tourism: Macau

Cindia Lam and Clara Lei

INTRODUCTION

Not so long ago Macau was a small city with a weak international image – and then in 2002 its gaming industry was liberalised from a 60-year monopoly (Siu, 2006). From then until the international financial crisis broke in 2009, the city experienced an increase of more than 150% in Gross Domestic Product (GDP) per capita – with tourism and gaming leading this growth (Statistics and Census Service Macau, 2009). By 2006 its gambling revenue had surpassed that of Las Vegas, making Macau one of the world's richest economies by 2007 (Anonymous, 2008). Today, Macau is widely seen as a casino city, the Las Vegas of the Far East. However, this positioning does not tell the full story of a city which also boasts UNESCO heritage status, whose MICE (meetings, incentives, conferences, and events) industry is rapidly developing and which has a unique and appealing cultural blend of East and West. Macau is much more than simply a casino city and having recently become one of the players in international tourism, the government of Macau is strongly promoting the diversification of its core industries, so as to ensure long-term sustainable growth.

This chapter examines a possible alternative special interest positioning for Macau – that of a destination for medical tourism. Specifically the chapter

- Examines the possibilities of special interest or niche tourism for destination brands;
- Discusses a case study of Macau to illustrate the particular possibilities of medical tourism.

The chapter begins with an overview of medical tourism, followed by an analysis of demand–competitor–supply and the prospects for medical tourism from different tourism segments, according to the region of origin. Three major competitors are identified based on geographic proximity, namely Hong Kong, Singapore, and Thailand. The strengths and weaknesses of each

© 2011 Published by Elsevier Ltd. All rights reserved.
DOI: 10.1016/B978-0-08-096930-5.10016-3

of these major competitors is compared to Macau in terms of (i) accessibility; (ii) availability of hardware (infrastructure) and software (human resources) for medical tourism; (iii) level of government support; (iv) appeal to potential customers; and (v) degree of differentiation in terms of medical tourism.

This demand–competitor–supply analysis is followed with an evaluation of Macau's readiness for medical tourism development. The chapter argues that this special interest tourism holds considerable potential for the city. Macau, as a Special Administrative Region (SAR) of China, enjoys the privilege of the support of the Central Government of China, has access to the large mainland Chinese population, and has the capability to practise Chinese and Western medicine. If it is to develop a strong reputation for this type of tourism, however, more effort has to be made to support it through investment and legislative change.

THE MEDICAL TOURISM CONTEXT

Medical tourism has emerged as a newly identified form of special interest tourism in recent decades, although there is no consensus on its definition and commentators use the terms medical tourism and health tourism interchangeably. Clearly, we can say that medical tourism involves people travelling to a place outside their usual place of residence for medical or health care services or treatment (Shaywitz & Ausiello, 2002). And, in fact, long before academics discussed the emergence of medical tourism, people (particularly wealthy ones) were accustomed to travel for advanced medical services particularly to more economically developed countries (MEDCs).

During recent years, a new list of medical tourism destinations has emerged, including Argentina, Brazil, Cost Rica, Philippines, India, Thailand, Korea, and South Africa, just to name a few (Paradise & Fox, 2007). Most of the hospitals in such places have received accreditation from either the Joint Commission International (JCI) or the Trent International Accreditation Scheme or even both, which has helped to improve their professional reputation as well as their trustworthiness for consumers. Moreover, most of these places have packaged their medical services with tourism, prominent examples being Thailand and South Africa, with the former having developed 'hospital resorts' and the later 'medical safaris' (Seth, 2006; Wagner, 2006). It seems that medical tourism holds much development potential, particularly for less economically developed countries (LEDCs). Indeed, the Asia region is predicted to see a double digit annual growth rate in its medical tourism industry between 2009 and 2012 and research by RNCOS Industry Research Solutions (International Medical Travel Journal, 2009) expects medical tourism income in the region to exceed US$5 billion by 2012.

This burgeoning medical tourism market is a by-product of globalisation (Anderson, 2007; Connell, 2006), affordable international transportation, and ageing populations, who are heavy consumers of health and medical services (Byron & Newman, 2006; Smerd, 2006; World Health Tourism Congress, 2007). In MEDCs, patients often encounter the high cost of local health care and long-waiting times for both straightforward and more complex procedures. In many MEDCs, faced with the heavy medical financial burden, health administrations classify patients according to their level of sickness and schedule their treatment accordingly. In such circumstances quality medical services at competitive prices then becomes an alluring option. If this treatment is overseas, then there is also the option of combining the medical treatment with a vacation so that it becomes even more blurred with tourism and leisure activities. This is not to suggest of course that medical tourism is risk-free or uncontroversial. Patients run the risk of complications after their medical treatment due to travelling soon after surgery and infectious diseases in LEDCs, while in countries such as India medical tourism has provoked hostility as it has exacerbated the disparities in local medical provision (Gentleman, 2005; MacReady, 2007).

THE POTENTIAL MARKET OF MEDICAL TOURISM IN MACAU

Macau is a small city of 538,000 people and occupies a geographic area of 29.2 km^2. The liberalisation of its gambling industry in 2002 transformed the city and brought in more than 30 million tourists by 2008, while the Individual Visit Scheme (IVS) recently introduced by China has further boosted tourist arrivals. Today over half of Macau's tourists are from China, most of whom are interested in medical tourism (Lam, du Cros, & Vong, 2009). Table 16.1 shows the dominance of mainland Chinese and Hong Kong tourists to Macau (together totalling over 80%). The city's remaining tourists are composed as follows: different regions of East Asia aside from China and Hong Kong 7.98% (Taiwan and Japan); South Asia 0.48% (India); Southeast Asia 6.73% (Malaysia, Singapore, Indonesia, Philippines, Thailand); America 1.37% (Canada and United States); Europe 1.41% (Germany, France, Italy, Portugal, United Kingdom); Oceania 0.58% and others.

The fifth of tourists who come from the range of regions beyond China and Hong Kong are so diverse that the cost-effectiveness of targeting them with medical tourism-related marketing activities is doubtful. In addition, Hong Kong, which makes up Macau's second largest tourist segment, has such a well-developed health care system that it is one of the healthiest places in the world (Government of Hong Kong SAR (HKSAR), 2003). Thus, there is little likelihood that tourists from Hong Kong will visit Macau for medical tourism.

Table 16.1 Potential medical tourism to Macau

Region	Tourist distribution %	Interest in medical tourism?	Potential medical tourism to Macau
China	50.61	Yes	Yes
Hong Kong	31.07	Yes	No
Others	18.32	N/A	N/A

Source: Statistics and Census Service Macau (2009).

In contrast, tourists from China, which make up more than 50% of all incoming tourists of Macau, are potential customers for medical tourism due to four major reasons: their increase in disposable income; their rising concern for health care (Shanghai Medical Tourism & Health Services Conference & Fair (SMTHSCF), 2009); inadequate health insurance coverage (Ozaki, 2007); and China's underdeveloped food and drug safety. As a result of these four factors, people from mainland China are more likely than ever before to seek good quality medical services outside China.

China's rising disposable income and concerns for health care

In last quarter of the century, China has experienced an average annual increase of more than 8% in GDP and even achieved a double-digit increase between 2003 and 2008, before the international financial crisis broke. This has resulted in a substantial increase in personal disposable income, especially in China's growing urban centres (Mocan, Tekin, & Zax, 2004) which has fuelled the demand for good quality medical services. In addition, this increasing demand has been accompanied by the transition to a more market-oriented health care system. In 1980 the State Council approved a report on the provision of private medical practise submitted by the Ministry of Public Health and since then China has seen a significant growth in its private medical market. However, with a total population of more than 1.3 billion, China faces considerable challenges to its medical system, especially in regard to the quality of its medical staff and medical services (Ozaki, 2007). Adding to this burden is China's Family Planning Policy, introduced in 1979 as a form of population control. Under the policy, each married couple in the urban areas can only give birth to one child (Information Office of the State Council of the People's Republic of China (IOSC), 1995). This has resulted in a situation where the single child has become the focus of most families and is provided with the best of resources, especially in terms of food, entertainment, and health care.

China's health and food scares

The trend for mainland Chinese to seek better health care services and products has been further accelerated by the growth in fake and adulterated medicine and foodstuffs, which has resulted in serious sickness and even death (Blanchard, 2008; Merrett, 2007). In one high profile incident 13 babies died from malnutrition as a result of being fed fake milk powder in the eastern province of Anhui in 2004 (Blanchard, 2008). In the wake of this horrifying story of melamine-contaminated milk power, it is understandable that mainland Chinese tourists became interested in purchasing medical and personal care goods outside of China, particularly in destinations with strict food and drugs regulations. Since this incident, the Chinese government has invested considerable resources to improve the regulation and inspection of food production, but given the size of the country, a perfect system is still some years away.

Given these issues on the mainland, Hong Kong would seem the obvious choice for Chinese medical tourists with its well-developed health care system. However, in recent years there have been increasing concerns about its lack of medical staff, the outbreak of fatal diseases such as SARS and H1N1 Influenza A, and the increasing incidence of medical blunders and negligence, including inaccurate drugs prescribed for patients, the misidentification of newly born babies, and the loss of deceased babies (Yao & Lei, 2009). All of these incidents and concerns have undermined Hong Kong as a medical tourism destination and added further burden to its already limited medical resources. At the same time under the IVS, introduced by China in 2003 to help the economic development of Hong Kong and Macau, Chinese citizens from approved areas of China (47 prefecture-level regions and two municipalities) can visit Hong Kong or Macau on an individual basis. During the first 6 months of implementation, the Scheme brought in around 1.7 million tourists (Macau Government Tourism Office, 2004).

Thus, this easing of individual travel restrictions (plus the above-mentioned inadequate medical system and underdeveloped food and drugs safety policy) has created a strong potential medical tourism market amongst China's huge and increasingly affluent population. Indeed, Chinese tourists have been increasingly spending on medicine and personal care products since 2004. The average personal spending of a Chinese tourist on medicine has been escalating from MOP56 in the last quarter of 2001 to MOP90 in 2008 (one US$ is equal to approximately eight MOP), peaking at MOP132 in 2007 (Macau Statistics and Census Services, 2009). Moreover, there have been cases of pregnant women travelling from mainland China to give birth in Macau and Hong Kong at a cost of US$5,000 for a 3-day, 2-night labour package (Li, 2007). It is reasonable to expect that mainland Chinese who have high disposable income will increasingly seek better medical products and services overseas, particularly in cities like Macau where Chinese is the official language.

MACAU'S MEDICAL TOURISM COMPETITORS

There are three cities or countries which constitute Macau's major competitors in terms of medical tourism, namely Hong Kong, Singapore, and Thailand. The chapter will now discuss their comparative strengths and weakness in six areas: (i) location and accessibility to China; (ii) availability of infrastructure for medical tourism (hardware); (iii) availability of adequate medical staff for medical tourism (software); (iv) government support for medical tourism; (v) existing tourism links to China (active tourism market); and (vi) factors that make the city different in regard to medical tourism (differentiation). These are summarised in Table 16.2.

Hong Kong

Hong Kong enjoys similar comparative advantages to Macau. Both are Special Administrative Regions (SARs) of China, enjoy the privileges of the

Table 16.2 Differentiation between Macau's medical tourism competitors

City/country	Macau	Hong Kong	Singapore	Thailand
Location	√	√	x	x
Hardware	√	√	√	√
Software	x	x	√	√
Government support	√	x	√	√
Active Tourism market?	√	√	x	√
Differentiation	Chinese medicine	Luxury hospitals	High-end medical services	Plastic surgery

IVS policy, are located only a short distance from mainland China, and have similar cultural backgrounds, with Cantonese as their native language. The major difference between the two cities lies in their degree of development and medical capability. In 2009 Hong Kong had 13 private and 44 public hospitals (The Department of Health (DHHK), 2009), with 11 of the private hospitals having already been accredited by the United Kingdom's Trent Accreditation Scheme (one of the most reputed international accreditation systems for medical care services). In addition, Hong Kong has also hosted medical fairs in 2006 and 2008 and The Health & Medical Tourism Pavilion (The Pavilion) which began in 2009.

Against this background, Hong Kong seems well equipped to outmuscle Macau in attracting medical tourists. However, there are also factors which militate against Hong Kong becoming a major medical tourism destination and its private and public hospitals have not marketed themselves in this way. This may be partly due to Hong Kong's lack of trained medical staff as the increasing demand on medical services and the heavy workload in most public hospitals have led to the resignation of significant numbers of medical staff (Moy, 2009). Taken together with the health challenges posed by the city's ageing population (Census and Statistics Department Hong Kong SAR, 2007), the outbreaks of SARS and H1N1 Influenza A in 2003 and 2008 respectively and a number of high profile cases of medical negligence, all these circumstances have hindered the development of medical tourism in Hong Kong and presented an opportunity for Macau.

Thailand

Thailand is a keen competitor amongst South-east Asia's medical tourism providers and has marketed itself as a medical tourism destination for some time with some hospitals and travel agents cooperating on medical tourism packages. The country has a number of internationally accredited hospitals (accredited, e.g., by the Joint Commission International) which serve tens of thousands of patients annually, many of them international patients. In recent years Thailand moved beyond basic body check-ups and has developed a reputation for expensive packages such as health screening and plastic surgery, especially sex reassignment therapy (Pfafflin & Junge, 1998).

Thailand's strength in medical tourism is its competitive pricing – thus, for example, the price of a comprehensive health screening package in Thailand is only one-third of the price of one in Macau or Hong Kong, at around US$390 (Bumrungrad Hospital, 2009). In addition, reputable hospitals in Thailand often offer translator services, including Chinese, Japanese, and Arabic, and the Thai government has recently waived the visa fee for Chinese citizens which is likely to increase the flow of Chinese tourists into the country (China Hospitality News, 2009). Overall then, Thailand represents a keen competitor for Chinese medical tourists, although Macau has the capability to offer Chinese medical treatment and can thus offer combinations of Chinese and Western medical treatment.

Singapore

Singapore is Macau's third major competitor destination for medical tourism in Asia; it offers a wide range of top-quality health care services and is on a par with Thailand in terms of its reputation for such services. Although Singaporean medical treatment and surgeries are more expensive than in other Asian medical tourism destinations, they are still considerably cheaper than in many Western countries. In addition, Singapore's world renown cleanliness gives it a major advantage over cities such as Bangkok with its air pollution and hectic traffic, while English and Chinese are among the four official languages of Singapore, making it attractive to both Western and Chinese medical tourists, who can talk to medical practitioners in a familiar language.

Singapore also has a further major strength as a medical tourism destination – the support of the Singaporean government, which has implemented several different schemes in order to boost the city-state's medical tourism sector. These include the WSQ Programme in Medical Tourism, whereby the government sponsors Singapore-based businesses in the travel and health care sectors that support their staff to pursue a career in medical tourism (Singapore Government Online, 2009). In addition 'Singapore Medicine' is a biomedical science development taking place in Singapore, the objectives of which according to the Minster of Health, Dr. Lam Pin Min are to attract patients to Singapore for treatment and to contribute to medical research to seek solutions to global health care problems (Ministry of Health Singapore, 2009). However, although Singapore possesses these strengths as a medical tourism destination, it focuses on high-end medical services and thereby targets a different customer segment from that of Macau. In addition, Chinese tourists require an entry visa for Singapore, which also creates a further barrier in this market.

POSITIONING MACAU AS A MEDICAL TOURISM DESTINATION?

There seems a clear demand for medical tourism in South-east Asia and Macau has the potential and maybe the incentive to develop as one of these destinations. A recent study conducted by Lam and Vong (2009) revealed that gaming was only one of the five top attractions for tourists visiting Macau and the city's casinos are largely seen as sight-seeing attractions rather than as the major incentive to visit. Moreover, around 37% of tourists visit with their family, making this the second largest tourism segment, behind those who visit with friends (39% of all incoming tourists). Thus, although Macau may be known as the Las Vegas of the Far East, this might not be a long-term brand position for the city, particularly when the casinos lose their novelty with tourists.

The IVS has boosted the numbers of tourists from mainland China to Macau, so that by 2008 over half of the city's 30 million tourists in 2008 were from the mainland. The enormous demand in mainland China for trustworthy medical products and services discussed above and the development of Macau's new medical service providers following the gambling liberalisation of the city create opportunities. However, the level of Macau's private and public medical services is not yet equal to those of Thailand and Singapore. Although there has been a continuous increase of private clinics in Macau from 499 in 2000 to 706 in 2008, there are only 15 public health service establishments in Macau and local demand still outstrips health service provision (Macau Statistic and Census Department, 2009). More worryingly, the Macau Government Tourist Office (MGTO) and Legislative Assembly (LA) of the Macau Special Administrative Region have done little to support the development of medical tourism.

There are, however, some signs that the private sector is recognising the medical tourism potential of the city with the development of two large-scale private clinics – the Malo Clinic-Spa (MCS) and the University Hospital of Macau University of Science and Technology (MUST). The MCS is located at the Venetian, one of Macau's new mega-resorts and claims to be the largest facility of its kind in Asia offering a wide range of medical and spa services with a team of over 50 medical doctors and 100 spa therapists. The MUST hospital offers both Western and Chinese medicine and in our interviews with its medical staff, is reportedly targeting both local residents and tourists.

Such developments could enable Macau to emulate the successful medical tourism destination models of Thailand and Singapore. However, government support and a strategic development plan are necessary to enable this to happen and Macau must develop a higher quality of provision and more trained staff. The Macau government may wish to implement a scheme similar to 'Singapore Medicine' in order to facilitate the sector's development or pursue policies such as government-subsidised training programs for careers in the medical field.

CONCLUSION

This chapter has demonstrated the market potential for Macau to diversify its current positioning as a casino city to include a reputation for medical tourism. Although the city is currently enjoying tremendous prosperity with high numbers of incoming tourists, such diversification of its destination reputation would certainly offer further opportunities for its already flourishing tourism industry. It would make sense, however, to avoid direct competition with more established neighbouring destinations by focussing on areas such as Chinese medicine, dental procedure, and health screening. Macau as a prime Chinese-speaking travel destination for mainland Chinese tourists could take full advantage of its Chinese culture and proximity to the mainland to position itself as a credible and more convenient alternative to Thailand or Singapore. We have suggested that Macau should not miss the potential to develop medical tourism and to this end, investment in sufficient medical services together with government support and enabling tourism policies are essential to capture the increasing number of tourists seeking medical services.

References

Anderson, J. L. (2007). Adventures in medical travel. *Kiplinger's Personal Finance*, *61*(9), 101–102.

Anonymous (2008). Macau richest place in Asia [Electronic Version]. iGamingBusiness.com. Retrieved on April 4, 2009, from http://www.igaming business.com/article-detail.php?articleID=16796

Blanchard, B. (2008, March 3). *China reports big rise in food-poisoning deaths*. [Online version, Reuters (Beijing)]. Retrieved from http://www.reuters.com/article/idUSPEK11273

Bumrungrad Hospital (2009). Health screening program. Retrieved on September 1, 2000, from http://www.bumrungrad.com/package/health-screening-center/index.aspx

Byron, Y., & Newman, O. D. (2006). Medical tourism. *Journal of the American Optometric Association*, *77*(12), 581.

Census and Statistics Department Hong Kong SAR. (2007). *Projections of population distribution 2007–2016*. Hong Kong SAR: Planning Department.

China Hospitality News (2009). Thailand waives visa fee for Chinese tourists. Retrieved on 8 September 8, 2009, from http://www.chinahosp italitynews.com/en/2009/02/24/10706-thailand-waives-visa-fee-for-chinese-tourists/

Connell, J. (2006). Medical tourism: Sea, Sun, Sand and…. surgery. *Tourism Management*, *27*, 1093–1100.

Gentleman, A. (2005, December 2). Controversy in India over medical tourism. Retrieved on August 29, 2009, from http://www.iht.com/articles/2005/12/02/news/india.php

Government of Hong Kong SAR (HKSAR) (2003). Hong Kong health indices among world's best (Press Release No. 28 January). Hong Kong: Hong Kong Special Administrative Region. Retrieved on December 2, 2009, from http://www.info.gov.hk/gia/general/brandhk/0128005.htm

Information Office of the State Council of the People's Republic of China, IOSC (1995, August). Family planning in China. Retrieved August 27, 2009, from http://www.fmprc.gov.cn/ce/celt/eng/zt/zfbps/t125241.htm

International Medical Travel Journal (2009). ASIA: Asian medical tourism income to exceed $5 billion by 2012. Retrieved on September 8, 2009, from http://www.imtjonline.com/news/?EntryId82=141968

Lam, C. C., & Vong, T. N. (2009). Macau: The gambling paradise. Profiling the roles and motives of customers. *Journal of China Tourism Research*, *5*(4), 388–400.

Li, J. (2007). Hong Kong curbs entry of pregnant mainlanders. China Daily. Retrieved September 1, 2009, from http://www.chinadaily.com.cn/china/2007-01/17/content_785174.htm

Macau Government Tourism Office (2004). More mainlanders can visit individually. Retrieved on August 28, 2009, from http://cn.macautourism.gov.mo/en/ezone/mttdetail.php?lan=cn&id=1494

Macau Statistic and Census Department (2008). Health statistics. Retrieved on September 2, 2009, from http://www.dsec.gov.mo

MacReady, N. (2007). Developing countries court medical tourists. *The Lancet*, *370*(9), 318.

Merrett, N. (2007, April 19). Mass poisonings highlight China food safety concerns. AP-Food. Retrieved from http://www.ap-foodtechnology.com/Formulation/Mass-poisonings-highlight-China-food-safety-concerns.

Ministry of Health Singapore (2009). Update on medical tourism in Singapore. Retrieved on September 18, 2009, from http://www.moh.gov.sg/mohcorp/parliamentaryqa.aspx?id=23054

Mocan, H. N., Tekin, E., & Zax, J. S. (2004). The demand for medical care in urban China. *World Development*, *32*(2), 289–304.

Moy, P. (2009, December 15). Public nurses exodus sparks care level fear. [Online version, The Standard newspaper]. Retrieved from http://www.thestandard.com.hk

Ozaki, H. (2007). *Chinese health care system reform at a crossroads*. Tokyo, Japan: Japan Center for Economic Research (JCER).

Paradise, A., & Fox, L. (2007). Global medical networks make medical travel a viable option. *Benefits & Compensation Digest*, *44*(4), 40–43.

Pfafflin, F., & Junge, A. (1998). Sex reassignment: Thirty years of international follow-up studies: A comprehensive review, 1961–1991. Retrieved on December 27, 2009, from http://www.symposion.com/ijt/

Seth, R. (2006). Medical tourism: Hidden dimensions. Retrieved August 29, 2009, from Express Hospitality, http://www.expresshospitality.com/20060630/market08.shtml

Shanghai Medical Tourism & Health Services Conference & Fair (SMTHSCF). (2009). *Supplementary information*. Shanghai: Shanghai International Exhibition Co., Ltd.

Shaywitz, D. A., & Ausiello, D. A. (2002). Global health: A chance for western physicians to give – and receive. *The American Journal of Medicine*, *113*, 354–357.

Singapore Government Online (2009). WSQ Programme in medical tourism. Retrieved on 18 September 2009, from http://www.business.gov.sg/EN/Industries/TCMPractices/ProgrammesNAssistance/gp_wsqMedTourism.htm

Siu, R. C.S. (2006). Evolution of Macau's casino industry from monopoly to oligopoly: Social and economic reconsiderations. *Journal of Economic Issues*, *40*(4), 967–990.

Smerd, J. (2006). A ticket to lower care costs. *Workforce Management*, *85*(22), 1–31.

Statistics and Census Service Macau (2009). Statistics. Retrieved on December 27, 2009, from http://www.dsec.gov.mo/e_index.html

The Department of Health (DHHK) Government of the Hong Kong Special
Administrative Region (2009). Registered hospitals. Retrieved on August 30,
2009, from http://www.dh.gov.hk/english/main/main_orhi/main_orhi.html

Wagner, M. (2006). Medical tourism: what are your options?. *Employee Benefit News*, *20*(13), 60–61.

World Health Tourism Congress (2007). Health tourism 2.0. Retrieved on
August 29, 2009, from http://www.medtrotter.com/publications/WHTC_2007

Yao, Y.Z., & Lei, Z. O. (2009, August 30). The fourth medical blunder in public
hospital during the month (□□□□□□4 □□□□□). Wen Wei Po (□□□).

CHAPTER

17

Repositioning city brands and events: Milan

Manuela De Carlo and Francesca d'Angella

INTRODUCTION

According to the literature on place competition (Dwyer & Chulton, 2003; Gordon & Buck, 2005; Markusen & Shrock, 2006), cities and territories have to work hard to distinguish themselves from other destinations and to create a positive, distinct, and sustainable image in order to attract different targets, government funding, and corporate inward investment. In this context, place branding, based on core values of the destination, makes it possible to build a positive image (Hunt, 1975; Morgan, Pritchard, & Pride, 2004; Tapachai & Waryszak, 2000) to both external audiences and to the different internal stakeholders who contribute to the process of creating the place experience – thereby overcoming the disparities that may arise among identity, image, and experience (Govers & Go, 2009, pp. 254–267).

Although empirical observations demonstrate that place branding is a key factor in the strategic repositioning and development of a destination (Trueman, Cook, & Cornelius, 2008), there is little consensus about the role and nature of city branding and there remains a significant gap in the literature in terms of city branding processes and their link with destination strategies (Kavaratzis, 2009; Kavaratzis & Ashworth, 2006). In comparison to product and service branding, *place branding* has distinct features that are linked to the unique characteristics of destinations: a noticeable dependence on macro-environmental factors and geographical constraints; the complex decision-making process of tourism consumption (Woodside & Dubelaar, 2002); the presence of a range of stakeholders with differing interests; the importance of the political dimension and of seeking consensus; the greater complexity of brand loyalty, and finally, the presence of small budgets and a lack of top-down implementation control (Hankinson, 2005; Morgan & Pritchard, 2004; Pike, 2005). For these reasons, the success of the destination branding process is closely connected to the presence of strong governance roles within the destination which are able to express a vision of the

© 2011 Published by Elsevier Ltd. All rights reserved.
DOI: 10.1016/B978-0-08-096930-5.10017-5

positioning objectives and to mobilise partnerships among public and private actors in order to generate a unique and sustainable experience for visitors.

The complex and multi-stakeholder nature of place branding is highlighted in the literature on the subject, and especially seen in that on place image evaluation (Beerli & Martin, 2004; Echtner & Ritchie, 2003; Gallarza, Saura, & Garcìa, 2002; Padgett & Allen, 1997; Tapachai & Waryszak, 2000;) and logo design (Blain, Levy, & Ritchie, 2005). However, some recent studies have moved away from conventional brand elements of design by integrating branding at the destination strategy level (Balakrishnan, 2009; Hankinson, 2007; Kavaratzis, 2009; Trueman et al., 2008). The starting point is to apply basic principles and methodologies of corporate branding to place branding, thus emphasising the similarities between these two concepts (both deal with multiple identities, multiple groups of stakeholders, multidisciplinary roots and both require long term development). This may prove to be a promising approach as long as it is emphasised that the managerial criticalities of city branding are even greater than those of corporate branding due to the relative lack of hierarchical control mechanisms, the multifaceted nature of tourism consumption, and the complex system of vested interests that underlie the running of a destination (Marzano & Scott, 2009).

To avoid a simplistic interpretation, this approach should be developed through in-depth comparative case studies of a range of destinations of differing geographical size (Caldwell & Freire, 2004), market positioning, phase of life-cycle, and so on. Milan is one such case study and provides an interesting example of a mature destination engaged in a broader repositioning strategy. In particular, the city illustrates the complexity involved in place branding and the various components of an integrated approach to managing mature city brands. In the last 25 years, Milan has undergone significant development despite the absence of a deliberate destination strategy. This growth has largely been due to its trade fair activity and a vibrant business environment. In this setting, isolated strategies have often been carried out in different operating sectors (such as the Milan Trade Fair, hotels, cultural organisations, entertainment operators, service suppliers, and merchants), each according to management policies aimed at maximising short-term results, with weak coordination mechanisms. This fragmentation has led to various problems of positioning and image that have hampered the development of the city, making it less able to compete with its major European destination rivals (De Carlo, Canali, Pritchard, & Morgan, 2009). In 2007, however, the awarding of Expo 2015 to Milan forced the city into a process of planning and strategic repositioning that is still underway, and in which the process of brand building plays an essential role.

This chapter explores these broad issues and specifically, it:

- Explores how a mature destination engages in a broader repositioning strategy;
- Examines a range of positioning and image problems which hamper the development of a city destination;
- Discusses the example of Milan, host of Expo 2015 to illustrate the argument.

MILAN'S POSITIONING CHALLENGE

Located in Western Lombardy, Milan is Italy's largest city, with its metropolitan area accounting for a population of 7.4 million. It also occupies a significant position in the country's tourism sector and boasts several strong points as a tourist destination. Indeed, in Simon Anholt's (2006) City Index, Milan is highly rated (in the top 20) as a city of fashion, design, shopping, and designer lifestyles, even out-ranking Paris for these features. The city is the second most important Italian destination in terms of overnight stays, with a tourism capacity superior to the 'stars' of Italian heritage tourism such as Florence and Venice. In 2008, Milan and the surrounding area attracted 5.1 million tourists, which generated 10.6 million overnights.

Clearly, tourism is a strategic activity for Milan given its weight in the city's economy as well as its potential for development. However, until now the main driver of tourism has been trade fair activity and a lively business environment, rather than any deliberate destination strategy that is part of a wider plan of international development for the city. Milan continues to invest significant resources into improving its offer and developing structures and infrastructures that increase its competitiveness in relation to other important European destinations. Nevertheless, Milan has not been able to convert these efforts into success factors for the city's image. The city fails to attract events of great international appeal, which means that its existing structures (theatres, sports stadiums, etc.) are not sufficiently utilised. In short, the city has not yet achieved its full potential for tourism development despite its wealth of resources and attractions.

The reasons for these weak points can be traced to Milan's entrepreneurial nature. Being lively and active, it generates numerous isolated initiatives; however, each one has its own objectives, sometimes contradictory. This situation reflects an absence of effective coordinating mechanisms among the different actors in the tourism system, a lack of shared strategic objectives and no clear definition of the priorities for action and long-range planning. Indeed, upon closer examination, Milan's current positioning reveals four crucial weaknesses.

1) First, Milan's positioning depends strongly on trade fairs, which leads to considerable problems of weekly and monthly seasonality. Indeed, Milan's tourist trend is shaped mostly by trade fair activity, with vertical drops in occupancy levels in the months of April, August, and December, as well as at the weekends. In addition, the annual rates of hotel occupancy and the average stay in Milan are both lower than in other European benchmark destinations. This situation is exacerbated by the fragmented character of tourist development based on the strategies of single operators who are intent on exploiting business opportunities linked to the Milan Trade Fair, and by the city's lack of a unified destination strategy.

2) Second, despite the city's undoubted cultural and entertainment appeals, the customer mix is markedly skewed towards business clients. Thus, analysis of a semi-structured questionnaire of 120 city hotels (reflecting

the city's hotel mix in terms of level of quality, size and location) shows that the business market constitutes the primary target for Milan, representing 72% of total annual room occupancy. The trade fair alone accounts for 32%; in contrast the leisure segment accounts for only 20% and the congress segment amounts to 4%, with a further 4% coming from other segments. Apart from the inconsistent occupancy rates, the dominance of the business segment leads to two other negative effects. First, the business segment is less 'manageable' from the standpoint of the destination since this market is closely linked to the vitality of the diverse economic sectors of the city and less likely to be managed or directed with tourism policies. Secondly, this dominance negatively influences perceptions of the city in other segments by bringing to mind typical problems associated with business destinations (such as traffic, pollution, lack of greenery, etc.).

3) The third positioning challenge relates to the disparity between Milan's cultural resources (it is estimated that 11% of Italy's artistic heritage can be found in Milan) and 'the offer' actually publicised by public agencies such as the Lombardy Region, the Province of Milan, and the Milan City Council. Less than a quarter (24%) of the city's cultural resources are mentioned in the communications of those organisations that are responsible for promoting Milan. This finding emerged from an analysis conducted during January–March 2006, which mapped and classified the artistic resources of Milan by type (buildings, monuments, museums, etc.) and by historical period. At the same time, a parallel mapping exercise (analysing both digital and paper-based material) was conducted of the artistic-cultural resources promoted by public agencies. This failure to transform heritage into a distinctive marketing asset springs from the lack of coordination between the city's heritage management organisations and those responsible for destination promotion and management as well as the lack of an all-encompassing destination strategy.

4) The fourth issue is the lack of coordination between Milan's tourism offer and the natural, cultural, and gastronomic attractions of the surrounding territory. These latter elements could play a decisive role in boosting the perceived image and the quality of the visitor experience, and thereby increase the leisure component of the tourist mix and reduce seasonality in the city.

MILAN'S PERCEIVED IMAGE

The weaknesses in Milan's positioning discussed above are reflected in the perceived image of the destination and in the quality of the experience as discerned by those who visit the city. As part of the preparations for hosting 2015 Expo, the Milan Chamber of Commerce and the Milan Municipality commissioned an analysis of the city and its perceived image and a study of its position in the major international rankings in comparison to its major worldwide competitor destinations. To examine the perceived image and personality of the city, two surveys were conducted between December 2007 and April 2008 (De Carlo & d'Angella, 2009). The first was based on a face-to-face questionnaire ($n = 1285$) to determine the image of Milan held by tourists who have visited the city. The second was a web survey ($n = 600$) centred on the perceptions of potential tourists from the city's three main incoming markets: Japan, Russia, and the UK.

Milan is a well-known destination, and one of Italy's most famous cities. However, among potential tourists, there is a significant gap between knowledge of the city ('I've heard others speak about Milan' 95%) and actual intention to visit the city ('Milan is an interesting place to visit' 53%, with the highest gap registered among British respondents) that is not found in the perception of other Italian destinations, such as Venice or Rome. Although the city is seen as beautiful, dynamic, and a 'capital of business', it is also viewed as polluted, expensive, and not very safe. Equally, despite its recognition as a city of high fashion, European football, and shopping, Milan is not identified with 'historical attraction' and 'food', which are the pillars of Italy's image in the world. Furthermore, the perceived separation of the city from its surrounding territory is confirmed in the survey, which reveals that 70% of tourists who visit the city do not travel to other smaller destinations nearby.

Tourists who have already visited the city expressed a generally positive opinion about their experience in Milan, with 66% stating that they intend to return to Milan for leisure, and 64% saying that they would advise a friend to visit the city. Although the city meets the tourists' expectations, it does not exceed them, as 66% of the interviewees confirm that their experience as a visitor to Milan is exactly what they thought it would be. If we analyse tourists' satisfaction according to the motivation for the journey, business tourists are the most satisfied. This is in line with the traditional strength of the city as a business destination and underlines the challenge to increase its attractiveness amongst potential leisure travellers.

If we compare the perceptions of those who have visited the city and those of potential tourists, it emerges that people who have already visited Milan have a better image of it than potential tourists. Perceptions of Milan's cultural offer and entertainment shows the widest perception gap, especially shopping, heritage, museums, and galleries; food, events, and night life, which are points of strength of the city. In all these areas, Milan is much more appreciated by people who have visited it than by those who have not.

This research therefore reveals an interesting and challenging position for the city. First, despite Milan's high international reputation, the perceived image of the city has several weaknesses that make it relatively less attractive as a travel destination. Second, the experience of tourists in the city is more positive than the image of the city expressed by potential visitors; this shows a discrepancy between the product offered on the one hand, and the perceived identity of the city on the other. It appears that the image is strongly influenced by clichés associated with traditional business positioning; and furthermore that the city's broad range of cultural and leisure attractions is only marginally appreciated by potential visitors.

A second area of investigation focuses on Milan's position in the international ranking of attractiveness. Table 17.1 shows the relative positioning of Milan compared to seven competing destinations (Barcelona,

Table 17.1 The positioning of Milan with respect to its competitive set

Barcelona – Berlin – Brussels – London – Madrid – Paris – Rome	
Indicators by sectors	Milan average rank (out of 8)
Exhibition industry	2.8
Tourism services	4.9
Transport	5.1
Economic and cultural environment	5.7
Telecommunications	6.0
Governance	7.0
Meeting industry (congress venues)	7.4
Quality of life and sustainability	8.0
Milan's total average ranking	5.4
Indicators by object	Milan average rank (out of 8)
Cost	3.7
Demand	5.7
Offer	6.0
Quality of the experience	6.4
Milan total average ranking	5.4

Berlin, Brussels, London, Madrid, Paris, and Rome) with respect to different sectors of activities (indicator categories) and different areas of assessment, including the perceived place quality experienced by the visitors.

The analysis shows that Milan compares poorly with competing destinations, particularly in terms of: quality of experience perceived by different target visitors; attractiveness as a venue for international congresses; quality of life; and sustainability. In contrast, a very positive assessment of the city is evident in terms of the exhibition industry and Milan holds second or third place for all indicators considered, confirming its strong position as a business destination. In short, the city is well known, and respondents expressed positive associations, but they do not value the variety of the city's attractions or its diverse character. It therefore follows that Milan's image needs to be enhanced and broadened to include the attributes, benefits, and offers that are most relevant and motivating for the desired target audiences (Anholt, 2007).

THE EXPO 2015 CHALLENGE

In October 2006, the mayor of Milan presented the official bid dossier for Expo 2015 to the Italian government. It was approved 10 days later and Milan became an official candidate for the international exposition with the leading theme 'Feeding the Planet, Energy for Life'. In Paris on March 31, 2007, it was announced that Milan had won Expo 2015, gaining 86 votes and beating Izmir in Turkey into second place with 65 votes. It is anticipated that the event will bring 21 million visitors, 27% of them from abroad, who will generate 29 million visits. To achieve these goals, a total of €3,228 million will be invested as follows: to build the exhibition site and the necessary facilities €1,253 million; to improve connections between the site and the surrounding area €1,780 million; to improve the accommodation capacity €135 million; and for other technological infrastructure €60 million. In turn, it is expected that Expo 2015 will create 70,000 new jobs during 2010–2015 and (as stated in recent research by the Chamber of Commerce of Monza e Brianza) generate about €6.7 billion through tourism economic impact in Milan's province and €9.4 billion in the whole Lombardy region.

The decision to bid for Expo 2015 highlighted certain questions about Milan's identity and positioning but following the successful bid, the need for a clear destination strategy became even more urgent. The wealth of literature on strategic management of large events (Berridge, 2006; Bramwell, 1997; Getz, 1992, 2007) emphasises how the presence of strong governance roles and a shared vision of desired positioning are essential if the event is to strengthen the image of the destination and its long-term competitiveness. Moreover, the experience of several European destinations, which over the last 20 years have focused on major events as drivers of development and repositioning, endorse the notion that a clear destination strategy is needed if a place is to maximise the value generated by the event and ensure sustainable development.

In virtually all major European destinations, the management of the tourism sector is entrusted to bodies usually termed Destination Management Organisations (DMOs) which represent the interests of different categories of stakeholders. In contrast, Milan had no such organisation when it was awarded Expo 2015 and the upcoming event increased the urgency to formulate a tourism development strategy for the city which was shared by the main public and private stakeholders (city, county, state, trade fair, chamber of commerce), and a government body responsible for its delivery. A benchmark analysis conducted in 2006 by the City of Milan on the strategic plans of 16 cities worldwide also revealed that 14 of them used tourism as a primary driver of image development and of relaunching or repositioning. Given this and taking into account the problems of the city's positioning and perceived image, the City Council established the Department of Tourism, Territorial Marketing, and Identity in 2006 by merging previously distinct areas of expertise into a single management body. This decision was based on the conviction that tourism is a powerful means to communicate shared values and traditions that underlie the identity of the city, and a strong driver of territorial development. Furthermore a DMO – the Tourism System of the City of Milan – representing the interests of different categories of stakeholders including the City Council, the Chamber of Commerce, and the main trade associations was created in 2008.

The second move towards beginning the process of repositioning Milan was the launch of a strategic planning process that led to the formulation of the first marketing plan of Milan in 2007. The plan, while identifying inadequacies in the offer and pointing out single issues that required action, focused specifically on initiatives to increase knowledge of the territory in the international market and among its prospective clients. Starting from the drivers of territorial development described by public planning documents,

10 issues were identified: (i) environment and sustainable development health; (ii) security, social welfare; (iii) economic development; (iv) human capital; (v) internationalisation; (vi) tourism; (vii) simplification; (viii) culture; (ix) leisure; (x) activities. All of them are linked to the overall objective of building the image of Milan as a city of knowledge, innovation, and creativity. For each issue, the plan identified the target audience where specific actions should be directed, the positioning to be sought, and an overall strategy in terms of actions in the supply system as well as in the areas of promotion and communication.

Tourism was identified as a high priority issue because of its strong potential for building Milan's perceived image. In this context, youth, talent, and cultural tourists are referred to as priority target groups, whereas the objectives to be pursued include reducing seasonality, lengthening the average stay of visitors, increasing the attractiveness of the city as a leisure destination, developing new target segments (especially youth and talent), and reaffirming Milan's claim as a high-level conference capital.

BRAND DEVELOPMENT AND STRATEGIC REPOSITIONING

Brand building has been a crucial step for Milan on the path of strategic repositioning. The analysis of the competitive environment and the perceived image by visitors described above revealed the inadequacies of the city's positioning. Moreover, the sense of urgency created by the deadline of Expo 2015 fostered willingness to change, and engendered higher levels of cooperation amongst the various stakeholders of the destination. At the same time, it was recognised that the development of the brand was a unique opportunity to stimulate dialogue among the different stakeholders and to reach consensus of what constitutes Milan's identity. In 2008, the first step in brand building was to define the city's core values and then connect them to Milan's resources and identity (Figure 17.1). Innovation, creativity, and knowledge were identified as central values to the strategic positioning of Milan, values which link to factors crucial to the development of the city, namely tradition, internationalisation, entrepreneurship, sustainability, social cohesion, solidarity, and quality of life. The identification of values was the result of an in-depth historical study with the objective of recognising those features that over the centuries have made Milan an ideal context for artists, designers, entrepreneurs, and scientists to work and express their genius. Milan's historical ability to attract and develop talent holds great emotional significance, has a great conversation value, and implies high anticipation for potential tourists (Morgan & Pritchard, 2004). In addition, this quality is difficult to imitate because it is ingrained in the city's history.

In the next phase, an international benchmark analysis made it possible to explore the different types of brand and marketing communications strategies used by competing cities. As a result, Milan's coat of arms was chosen as a starting point for designing the city logo; in addition, an analysis was carried out of destination brands that originate from a historical-heraldic symbol. Finally, a separate study investigated the evolution of Milan's symbol over the centuries, highlighting its strong link with the city's history. The next step

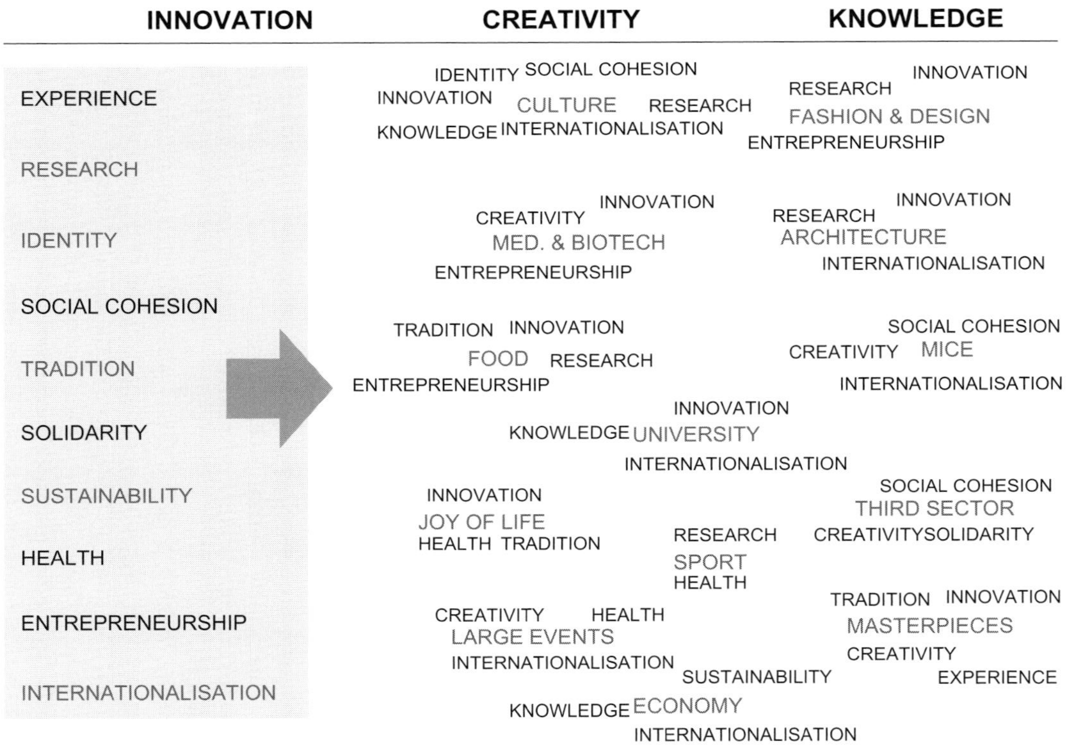

INNOVATION CREATIVITY KNOWLEDGE

EXPERIENCE

IDENTITY SOCIAL COHESION
INNOVATION   CULTURE   RESEARCH   RESEARCH   INNOVATION
KNOWLEDGE INTERNATIONALISATION   FASHION & DESIGN
ENTREPRENEURSHIP

RESEARCH

IDENTITY

CREATIVITY   INNOVATION   RESEARCH   INNOVATION
MED. & BIOTECH   ARCHITECTURE
ENTREPRENEURSHIP   INTERNATIONALISATION

SOCIAL COHESION

TRADITION

TRADITION INNOVATION   SOCIAL COHESION
FOOD   RESEARCH   CREATIVITY   MICE
ENTREPRENEURSHIP   INTERNATIONALISATION

SOLIDARITY

KNOWLEDGE UNIVERSITY   INNOVATION
INTERNATIONALISATION   SOCIAL COHESION
THIRD SECTOR

SUSTAINABILITY

INNOVATION   CREATIVITYSOLIDARITY
JOY OF LIFE   RESEARCH
HEALTH TRADITION   SPORT
HEALTH

HEALTH

CREATIVITY   HEALTH   TRADITION INNOVATION
LARGE EVENTS   MASTERPIECES
INTERNATIONALISATION   CREATIVITY
SUSTAINABILITY   EXPERIENCE

ENTREPRENEURSHIP

KNOWLEDGE ECONOMY
INTERNATIONALISATION

INTERNATIONALISATION

Figure 17.1 The core values of Milan and its brand

Figure 17.2 Milan's brand

was to define the logo of Milan (Figure 17.2) as described in the brand guides: 'A white shield with a red cross surrounded by a garland of laurel leaves. Above the shield rests a ducal crown that symbolises the city's fortress,' The choice of the coat of arms as an emblem links the brand to the city's origins and its history; the intersecting red line crossing the white field calls to mind the common thread that links the different facets of the city and suggests its openness to the future.

In 2009, the introduction and launch of the brand took place through a sequence of communication activities and tourist development projects, aimed at targets previously identified by the marketing plan. Consistency among all messages and initiatives was ensured by following a brand design style guide. In particular, traditional advertising and promotions took place in parallel with main-licencing and co-marketing activities in partnership with public and private entities. In addition, a digital marketing campaign was started using social media. The creation of a geo-referenced calendar of events and places and the launch of a new tourism portal gave impetus to a new information system for tourism. Numerous projects were created to enhance visitors' experience such as the creation of a Summer Campus Programme, the introduction of the Tourist Card, the creation of the project '100 Milan' proposing new thematic routes that connect Milan's most famous historical events and icons to lesser-known attractions, and the enhancement of traditional fairs and festivals. Finally, new tourism packages were designed with the involvement of major industry players (low-cost carriers, airlines, tour operators, tourism companies, etc.).

At the end of 2009, a second survey was conducted on a sample of 1,032 tourists to measure the evolution in the perception of the city compared to the 2007 survey, and to get a clear picture of the initial results of the new brand communication activities. Adopting the approach of the previous analysis, the investigation focused on tourists' expectations of the city, the perception of the tourism experience in terms of resources, facilities, and services; the likelihood of a return visit; and the willingness to recommend the city to others as a tourist destination. The survey revealed that the overall assessment of the city ('I would return to Milan for a vacation') had significantly improved (+27% of affirmative answers). In addition, by the 2009 survey, entertainment was more appreciated (65% of respondents) although cultural awareness (35% of respondents) still lags behind and the city has recently started to address this issue. The survey also confirms that the perception of Milan improved for those respondents who have already visited the city ('I found the city improved' – 48% positive responses from those who 'know the city well'; 12% from those who 'don't know the city very well') as well as for those who have returned to visit and know their way around ('I would recommend Milan as a tourist destination': 92% positive responses from those who have visited more than 3 times; 83% from those who have come for the first time). The comparative results confirm a shift in perception and the ability of the city to reinforce this image by creating a more meaningful experience for Milan's visitors.

CONCLUSION

This analysis of the Milan case study makes it possible to appreciate the close relationship between the process of brand development and the strategic repositioning of a mature destination. In particular, the analysis reveals that some essential components of destination branding emphasised in the literature, intertwine with the process of formulating a strategy for a destination, and form the basis for improving the image and perception of its attractiveness to potential new markets.

The starting point for Milan's brand development process was the city's candidacy as the site of Expo 2015. In 2005, despite the difficulties linked to the striking imbalance of the tourist mix in favour of the business segment, Milan was an established international business destination, with vigorous tourist activity that allowed the industry operators to achieve satisfactory levels of profitability, even in the absence of strong government roles or a strategy for the city. Expo 2015 has been credited with breaking down the resistance to change by entrepreneurs, business, and public institutions, by conveying a sense of urgency to redefine Milan's positioning and improve its international image. The candidacy process helped to create a strong, visionary leadership by the Municipality which, in turn, guided the formulation of strategy and brand building of the city through a series of relationships with a broad network of separately managed service organisations, both public and private.

The first step in brand building was the definition of a strategic vision that guided the city's repositioning. It is interesting to note that the vision grew out of an analysis of Milan's deeper identity by focussing on internal and external perspectives. From an internal perspective, the identification of Milan's core values and its historical and cultural heritage facilitated a 'vision assimilation' and a common feeling by the internal stakeholders and the local community. This is a key point because the delivery of brand promises depends on how residents and operators of the tourism system can translate the vision into a product offering and into a way of communication that suit the true identity of the place (Govers & Go, 2009, p. 71). From the external perspective, the vision aimed at overcoming some of the negative perceptions on the part of external stakeholders, namely, the international rankings of attractiveness and the image perceived by different segments of current and potential customers (Leisen, 2001).

This latter perspective was crucial to the sharing of specific objectives for enhancing the perceived image, and to directing the efforts of all the actors in the destination to achieving them. This common effort resulted in the noticeable improvement of perception as shown in the second survey conducted in 2009. In the second phase of brand building, the vision and the city's marketing plan drove the subsequent process of defining the brand architecture, following a path that was firmly grounded in Milan's core identity and therefore, unique and difficult to imitate. It is interesting to observe that Milan has given greater weight to symbols of its culture and heritage, (the coat of arms and the red line crossing the white field, to suggest openness to innovation and development) rather than to functional attributes associated with activities and facilities. This choice has served to enhance the brand personality (Hosany, Ekinci, & Uysal, 2006) and create an effective positioning that moves customers up the brand value pyramid, from tangible and functional benefits to emotional ones that can evolve over time (Morgan & Pritchard, 2004).

ACKNOWLEDGMENTS

The analysis mentioned in this chapter are part of detailed series of connected research studies conducted from 2005 to 2010 by IULM University on behalf of Milan's Municipality, Province and Chamber of Commerce, which led to a series of discussions and meetings with numerous institutions and individuals who contributed to the repositioning strategy of the city. To all of them, the authors extend their grateful thanks.

References

Anholt, S. (2006). City brands index (CBI) the Anholt city brands index: how the world views its cities (2nd ed.), Retrieved from: www.futuremelbourne.com.au/wiki/pub/FMPlan/S3Resources/Anholt_City_Brands_Index_cbi2006-q4-free.pdf (accessed on December 2, 2008).

Anholt, S. (2007). Competitive identity: the new brand management for nations, cities and regions. London: Palgrave Macmillan.

Balakrishnan, M. S. (2009). Strategic branding of destinations: a framework. *European Journal of Marketing, 43*(5/6), 611–629.

Beerli, A., & Martin, J. D. (2004). Tourists' characteristics and the perceived image of tourist destinations: a quantitative analysis – a case study of Lanzarote, Spain. *Tourism Management, 25*, 623–636.

Berridge, G. (2006). *Event design*. Oxford: Butterworth-Heinemann.

Blain, C., Levy, S. E., & Ritchie, J. R. B. (2005). Destination branding: Insights and practices from destination management organizations. *Journal of Travel Research, 43*, 328–338.

Bramwell, B. (1997). Strategic planning before and after a mega-event. *Tourism Management, 18*, 167–176.

Caldwell, N., & Freire, J. R. (2004). The differences between branding a country, a region and a city: applying the brand box model. *Brand Management, 12*(1), 50–61.

De Carlo, M., Canali, S., Pritchard, A., & Morgan, N. (2009). Moving Milan towards Expo 2015: designing culture into a city brand. *Journal of Place Management and Development, 2*(1), 8–22.

De Carlo, M., & d'Angella, F. (2009). Assessing the international image of an urban destination: the case of Milan. In A. Fyall, M. Kozac, L. Andreu, J. Gnoth, & S. S. Lebe (Eds.), *Marketing innovations for sustainable destinations: Operations, interactions, experiences*. Oxford: Goodfellow Publishers Ltd.

Dwyer, L., & Chulton, K. (2003). Destination competitiveness: determinants and indicators. *Current Issues in Tourism*, *6,*(5), 63–75.

Echtner, C., & Ritchie, J. R. B. (2003). The meaning and measurement of destination image. *The Journal of Tourism Studies*, *14*(1), 37–48.

Gallarza, M. G., Saura, I. G., & Garcìa, H. C. (2002). Destination image: toward a conceptual framework. *Annals of Tourism Research*, *29*(1), 56–78.

Getz, D. (1992). Tourism planning and destination life cycle. *Annals of Tourism Research*, *19*, 752–770.

Getz, D. (2007). *Event studies: theory, research and policy for planned events*. Calgary: Elsevier.

Gordon, I., & Buck, N. (2005). Introduction: cities in the new conventional wisdom. In N. Buck, I. A. Gordon, I. Harding, & A. Turok (Eds.), *Changing cities: Rethinking urban competitiveness, cohesion and governance* (pp. 1–10). Basingstoke: Palgrave MacMillan.

Govers, R., & Go, F. (2009). *Place branding*. London: Palgrave MacMillan.

Hankinson, G. (2005). Destination brand image: a business tourism perspective. *Journal of Services Marketing*, *19*(1), 24–33.

Hankinson, G. (2007). The management of destination brands: Five guiding principles based on recent developments in corporate branding theory. *Brand Management*, *14*(3), 240–254.

Hosany, S., Ekinci, Y., & Uysal, M. (2006). Destination image and destination personality: an application of branding theories to tourism places. *Journal of Business Research*, *59*, 638–642.

Hunt, J. D. (1975). Image as a factor in tourism development. *Journal of Travel Research*, *13*(3), 1–7.

Kavaratzis, M. (2009). Cities and their brands: lessons from corporate branding. *Place Banding and Public Diplomacy*, *5*, 26–37.

Kavaratzis, M., & Ashworth, G. J. (2006). City branding: an effective assertion of identity or a transitory marketing trick? *Place Branding*, *2*(3), 183–194.

Leisen, B. (2001). Image segmentation: the case of a tourism destination. *Journal of Services Marketing*, *5*(1), 49–66.

Markusen, A., & Shrock, G. (2006). The distinctive city: divergent patterns in growth, hierarchy and specialisation. *Urban Studies*, *43*(8), 1301–1323.

Marzano, G., & Scott, N. (2009). Power in destination branding. *Annals of Tourism Research*, *36*(2), 247–267.

Morgan, N., & Pritchard, A. (2004). Meeting the destination branding challenge. In N. Morgan, S. Pritchard, & R. Pride (Eds.), *Destination branding: Creating the unique destination proposition* (2nd ed.). (pp. 59–78) Oxford: Butterworth-Heinemann.

Morgan, N., Pritchard, S., & Pride, R. (Eds.), (2004). *Destination branding: Creating the unique destination proposition* (2nd ed.). Oxford: Butterworth-Heinemann.

Padgett, D., & Allen, D. (1997). Communicating experiences: a narrative approach to creating service brand image. *Journal of Advertising*, *26*(4), 49–62.

Pike, S. (2005). Tourism destination branding complexity. *Journal of Product & Brand Management*, *14*(4), 258–259.

Tapachai, N., & Waryszak, R. (2000). An examination of the role of beneficial image in tourist destination selection. *Journal of Travel Research*, *39*(1), 37–44.

Trueman, M., Cook, D., & Cornelius, N. (2008). Creative dimensions for branding and regeneration: overcoming negative perceptions of a city. *Place Branding and Public Diplomacy*, *4*, 29–44.

Woodside, A. G., & Dubelaar, C. (2002). A general theory of tourism consumption systems: a conceptual framework and an empirical exploration. *Journal of Travel Research*, *41* November, 120–132.

Branding and the opportunities of movies: Australia

Bill Baker

INTRODUCTION

It has long been recognised that films can play a positive role in the tourism marketing of destinations, and the nation of Australia has proven to be no exception. For decades, films and television programs have successfully projected the outstanding beauty, adventure and character of Australia to international audiences. Australia experienced a tremendous surge in interest in the late 1970s and 1980s following the international success of the films *Picnic at Hanging Rock, Mad Max, Crocodile Dundee,* and the television mini-series *The Thorn Birds* (filmed in California and Hawaii). Despite the success of *Crocodile Dundee* in particular and Australia's innovative tourism marketing during the 1980s, there was very little integration of the two, yet both contributed enormously to Australia's appeal as a desirable place to visit. Australia's *Shrimp on the Barbie* campaign, starring Paul Hogan, aired in North America in January–April 1983; whilst there was no direct "link" to the movie *Crocodile Dundee,* which also starred Hogan and was released in 1986, they clearly had a symbiotic relationship. Subsequent campaigns featuring Paul Hogan played on the Dundee persona and leveraged the film's extraordinary success.

Branding and marketing destinations is challenging at any time, but none more so than in the unprecedented 2008 business environment. A highly competitive media marketplace, the increase of new destinations, rising oil prices, a strong Australian dollar, and a global economic crisis and recession were major issues confronting Australia's tourism industry. Due to the worsening global economic backdrop in 2008, Tourism Australia believed it would be more difficult than ever to convince people around the world to take a holiday to Australia. During a time when there were dozens of practical reasons for people choosing not to travel, it was critical to appeal to their emotional desire to take a break and get away. Tourism Australia felt that there was no more powerful emotional tool than film, and film-makers are

© 2011 Published by Elsevier Ltd. All rights reserved.
DOI: 10.1016/B978-0-08-096930-5.10018-7

masters at emotional storytelling. The production and release of the film *Australia* in 2008 and the prospect of having Australian Baz Luhrmann, an Oscar-nominated director, create the advertising represented a unique and timely opportunity. It would enable Tourism Australia to showcase the country in a way that had not occurred before and expose little known aspects of the country's geography and history to an international audience.

An integrated marketing program was developed to link the film's themes of adventure, romance, and transformation through multiple projects and a variety of media to enhance Australia's approach towards experiential branding. The film was set for release in 70 countries from October 2008, with the DVD release to follow in March 2009. Importantly, the wide international release represented excellent coverage of Tourism Australia's 22 priority regions. While the film release and associated tourism marketing campaign was global, the specific examples included in this chapter relate to the integrated marketing conducted in the UK. Thus, the chapter:

* Briefly outlines the powerful role of film in the tourism marketing of destinations;
* Illustrates through the example of the movie *Australia* how an integrated marketing program can be developed to link a film's themes to enhance a destination's approach towards branding.

FILM-INDUCED TOURISM

The study of film tourism is relatively new in tourism research. Sometimes called movie-induced or film-induced tourism, film tourism can be defined as tourist visits to a destination or attraction as a result of the destination being featured on television, video, or the cinema screen (Hudson & Ritchie, 2006). In some cases the tourism potency of a major motion picture can extend far beyond its initial launch. In their 1998 study, Riley, Baker and van Doren discovered that growth of 54% in visitation of featured destinations was evident at least 5 years after release of the 12 movies in their study. Additionally, the continual screening of a movie over decades can influence the disposition of many generations of film-goers towards the location. A good example of this is the 1953 classic *Roman Holiday* starring Gregory Peck and Audrey Hepburn, filmed on location in Rome. Today it is frequently in the program lineup of cable television channels and reproductions of the original movie posters are still widely available at souvenir and market stalls in Rome's most popular tourist areas. *Roman Holiday* has been a perennial ambassador for Italian tourism without having had any ties to a destination marketing organisation (DMO). Yet, the film's irresistible backdrop of Rome has drawn untold thousands to visit and explore the Eternal City.

In the 57 years since the release of *Roman Holiday*, DMOs and the tourism industry have played far more proactive roles in capitalising on the awareness, celebrity, and marketing power of films to promote their destinations. Audiences would not have been so aware of the fact that the *Lord of the Rings* trilogy was filmed in New Zealand had there not been very close collaboration between the New Zealand Government; the New Zealand Tourism Board; and the film's production, publicity, and distribution companies.

New Zealand-born director Peter Jackson filmed the three movies in various locations around New Zealand. Jackson's special effects team turned New Zealand's already impressive landscape into a magical Middle Earth (New Zealand Tourism). The New Zealand Government created a special cabinet level position, appointing Peter Hodgson as Minister for the Middle Earth to capitalise on the opportunities that would arise from the trilogy's New Zealand roots. 'This film will really put us on the map,' Hodgson said on his appointment. 'Not many people knew that *Star Wars* was filmed in Morocco, but everyone will know that Middle Earth is in New Zealand,' he added. The destination marketing associated with the movie *Australia* also demonstrates the benefits of close collaboration between the marketing of a high profile movie and a well-known destination.

AUSTRALIA THE MOVIE

Produced by Bazmark Films (Luhrmann's production company) and Twentieth Century Fox, Australia is a romantic action adventure set in Northern Australia in the late 1930s and early 1940s. The story centres on an English aristocrat (Nicole Kidman) who travels to the Australian Outback where she meets rough-hewn stockman (Hugh Jackman) and a mixed-race Aboriginal child (Brandon Walters). Joining forces to save the cattle station she inherited, the three embark on a transforming journey across hundreds of miles of beautiful yet unforgiving terrain, only to face the Japanese bombing of the city of Darwin.

Australia was filmed on location in Western Australia, the Northern Territory, Queensland, and New South Wales. The outback scenes were shot in the Kimberly region of Western Australia, while other scenes were shot at Bowen on the Queensland coast, at Vaucluse on Sydney Harbour, and in the historic NSW town of Camden. In addition to the inspiration that came from these locations, Luhrmann became fascinated with what he refers to as 'the naturally occurring collisions of characters and imagery created by the juxtaposition of the Anglo administration, Aboriginal cowboys, Chinese pearlers, crocodiles, palm trees, and other contrasting elements' (Fox Filmed Entertainment, 2008).

THE OPPORTUNITY EVOLVES

Tourism Australia approached Twentieth Century Fox in 2006 about a film in production called *Australia*. This was followed by further discussions with director Baz Luhrmann and the production team at Bazmark Inq. Tourism Australia Managing Director Geoff Buckley said the unique opportunity created by the production of Luhrmann's epic film *Australia* was one that the organisation could not let pass. 'We knew that this film would create a wave of publicity that would put the country in the spotlight around the globe,' he said. 'And we found that the film's story had a remarkable resonance for what we do in marketing the country as a travel destination. The challenge was always going to be how to ride the power of the film, but with a stand-alone and self-reliant tourism campaign. Getting Baz Luhrmann and his team on board to make that campaign was simply the best result we could have hoped for' (Tourism Australia).

Mr. Luhrmann said, 'When Tourism Australia came to us, we were reticent at first because we did not want to confuse the promotion of the film with a tourism campaign. The more we talked, the more I realised that we both had the same aims; to celebrate the truly unique and transformative power of this ancient and extraordinary continent. With this in mind, we agreed to put our team into the conception and realisation of a contemporary campaign which, while not aping the film, reflects this singular and attractive truth' (Tourism Australia, 2008a).

Like their counterparts in the fast-moving consumer goods category, destination marketers need to periodically introduce ways to supplement or replace conventional marketing practises that are losing their effectiveness. This philosophy led Tourism Australia to consider alternate approaches to the traditional communication and media channels such as radio, television, direct mail, and print advertising in order to cut through the clutter and resonate with key audiences. The Australian tourism industry was confronted with a highly competitive media marketplace, the rise of new destinations, the introduction of low cost carriers, a strong Australian dollar, and a rapidly unfolding global economic crisis. Australia needed a paradigm shift to successfully address these challenges.

Partnering with Twentieth Century Fox for the launch of *Australia* the movie offered Tourism Australia a unique and timely opportunity to address these challenges and break through the 'noise' of competitors, expand exposure for the country, and reach new audiences on an emotional level. Despite the enticing benefits of the project, Tourism Australia executives carefully considered a variety of factors to ensure that it would be a viable marketing proposition for Brand Australia and the Australian tourism industry. These considerations included the following:

- Alignment of the film's theme, locations, storyline, characters, and depiction with the core values of Australia's destination brand.
- The likelihood of resonating positively with target markets, given the need to communicate with culturally diverse audiences in many countries.
- The willingness of Twentieth Century Fox to work with Tourism Australia to the extent needed for optimal tourism benefit.
- Whether Tourism Australia could develop cooperative programs that would appeal to tourism partners and be acceptable to the movie's stakeholders.
- Ensuring that the essence of Australia's brand, as well as its visual and verbal identity would be retained in the collaboration.
- The opportunity to feature key tourism experience themes in an environment that will likely be dominated by the brand messages of the movie.
- The risk of failure that could be associated with the movie and the chance that it may not be seen by a large audience.

In 2007, Tourism Australia and Baz Luhrmann agreed that Bazmark Inq would produce a special, stand-alone campaign and that the best way to ensure synergy between the movie and Tourism Australia's advertising was for Luhrmann himself to conceive and produce the ads and link the campaign to the movie. The campaign would highlight the movie's 'essential truth' and its link to the country's tourism brand. To achieve this, Tourism Australia and Bazmark Inq identified those aspects of the movie's story which captured the country's tourism brand. Those themes were adventure, romance, and the transformative power of an Australian experience (Tourism Australia, 2008b).

While there was the consideration that the movie, like all movies, ran the risk of commercial failure, the decisions by Tourism Australia were made on the basis that success would not be measured on the result of box office returns. The primary focus of the campaign was to ride the wave of marketing and publicity to intensify a viewer's desire to visit Australia. The first, and in many respects most important, benefit was the opportunity to capitalise on the estimated one hundred million dollar marketing investment by Fox. It was anticipated that hundreds of millions of people globally would be exposed to the movie's publicity and tens of millions were likely to see the movie. The marketing strategy of positioning the word 'Australia' as meaning adventure and romance would reach a global audience. The buzz created by the Twentieth Century Fox marketing campaign for the movie offered an unprecedented opportunity to engage prospective visitors on an emotional level and link to enticing travel products. It was considered that every moviegoer was a prospective visitor to Australia who was paying to be immersed in the country for more than 2 hours. An added bonus was that the movie created a positive perception of Australia as a romantic place and a place that will change the visitor for the better. It was this expanded perception that was expected to enhance Australia's current brand position and make it more enticing to a wider global audience.

BRAND AUSTRALIA

Tourism Australia, and its predecessor the Australian Tourist Commission, have been vigorously marketing Australia internationally as a tourist destination for more than 40 years. During this time, Australia has established a reputation as an innovator in tourism marketing and has built one of the world's most successful and desirable destination brands. Overall, the nation performs well in global studies such as FutureBrand's Country Brand Index (number 1 for 2 years running) and the Anholt-GfK Roper Nation Brands Index (top 10 since 1995). Impressively, Australia also ranked first out of 104 countries in the 2008 Legatum Prosperity Index that found that the conditions that drive both economic prosperity and personal well-being are currently stronger in Australia than any other nation.

Australia's Brand Platform

Australia's Brand Platform provides the foundation which guides all aspects of the brand: its visual and verbal identity, communications, product and experience development, partnerships, and organisation and stakeholder behaviour. The positioning statement that encapsulates Australia's Brand Platform is:

> *The people of Australia are unique. Their friendly, straight talking and open attitude make visitors feel welcome. The Australian people make it easy for you to enjoy adventures you could never have imagined. They turn the wide open landscapes, pristine oceans and vibrant cities into a vast yet accessible adventure playground.*

Australia's Brand Platform is underpinned by a set of five global tenets that influence all brand communications. These represent the qualities, benefits, and value the brand presents target audiences. Transformation – A holiday in Australia gives a fresh perspective.

- Welcoming – Australia is a welcoming holiday destination.
- Immersion – Holidays in Australia are about participating in life, not observing it.
- Adventure – Australia is an adventure holiday destination.
- Nature – Australia offers engaging experiences in the natural environment.

Experiential branding

To link the Brand Platform with its target audiences, Tourism Australia employs an experiential branding approach. It presents Australia's immersive experiences in ways that connect with them on a sensory and emotional level to increase preference for Australia. Using their extensive research, Tourism Australia worked with the State Tourism Organisations and the tourism industry to develop an experiential framework based on the tenets that underpin the Australia brand and provide its competitive edge. This framework provides industry partners with strategic, consistent, and meaningful ways to align with Australia's overall tourism brand and their marketing and product development efforts.

Through its consumer research, Tourism Australia is able to match the experiences which best meet the motivations and behavioural needs of specific audiences, and highlight those which differentiate the country from competitors. This strategy increases visitor dispersal throughout the country and ultimately, higher visitor spending. Importantly, it motivates target audiences to move from preference to intention to travel. To accomplish this, Tourism Australia and its industry partners emphasise seven key Australian Experiences. These are:

- Aboriginal Australia
- Aussie Coastal Lifestyle
- Australian Major Cities
- Australian Journeys
- Food and Wine
- Nature in Australia
- Outback Australia

Tourism Australia's General Manager UK/Europe Rodney Harrex highlighted the priority that Australia places on experiential branding when he said, 'The success of Brand Australia is not conveyed by our advertising alone, but through all encounters and experiences with Australia and its people. To achieve this we are transforming the brand from being presented as a trip, vacation or destination to becoming a wholly immersive, aspirational and engaging experience' (Baker, 2007, p. 154).

GLOBAL EXPERIENCE SEEKERS

Tourism Australia has undertaken extensive global psychographic research to identify the ideal visitor segment for Australia. This research has identified a group of travellers who, regardless of their culture or background, are looking for the type of experiences that Australia offers. This target audience has been termed Global Experience Seekers. The studies examined how these travellers think and feel in order to determine their likely travel preferences and behaviour.

Experience Seekers were identified across different cultures in all international markets, except New Zealand and Australia. They are well travelled and have a unique set of values, attitudes, and motivations that extend beyond typical holiday behaviour. Experience Seekers are long haul travellers and can be found among all age groups, income levels, and occupations; however, there are commonalities in their attitude towards travel, personal development, and everyday life.

Experience Seekers want to encounter cultures and lifestyles different from their own and are more inclined to travel off the beaten path to interact with local people and develop personal relationships. They welcome the opportunity to learn and to challenge themselves. The research revealed that this group can best be reached through internet communications, cable television, lifestyle channels and programs/documentaries, digital media, and cinema (Tourism Australia). Some of the words describing what they want from their travel and which they strongly identify Australia as offering are:

- Active/energetic
- Adventure/daring
- Carefree
- Letting go
- Lose inhibitions
- Natural
- Spontaneity/playful
- Vital/alive

'Come walkabout' marketing campaign

The advertising created by Baz Luhrmann was designed to encapsulate Australia's brand tenets and core experiences in a campaign named *Come Walkabout*. The goal was to encourage movie goers, especially Global

Experience Seekers, to get excited about Australia, research the destination, and ultimately book their Australian holiday. While developing the concept for the 'Come Walkabout' campaign, Luhrmann and his team faced the additional creative challenge of ensuring that the tourism advertising was capable of standing alone as a brand campaign for the destination, and not be about the movie. While the advertising does not mention the movie, it does reflect the themes of the movie by capturing the transformational qualities of an Australian holiday or vacation.

The advertising tackles head-on the stress that Australia's target markets feel due to life's pressures. It follows a harried couple escaping their everyday pressures in a metropolis to their self-discovery and rejuvenation in the Australian wilderness. This mirrors Luhrmann's film, which tells the story of a woman who has lost her sense of self but finds adventure, romance, and her true self when she comes to Australia. He achieved this by creating engaging, short film-styled advertisements for Tourism Australia using the movie's core themes of adventure, romance, and transformation by using the uniquely Australian concept of 'walkabout' – a tradition steeped in the Aboriginal culture. The term, 'walkabout' involves a person returning to the bush for a short period to reconnect to the land and their traditional way of life. For the majority of Australians, their 'walkabout' takes the form of a holiday – a time to refresh and reconnect.

The campaign was based around the notion that exploring Australia can transform your life. The idea that Australia is a place to experience, not just to see, is central to Australia's tourism brand. This is expressed by the words 'Sometimes we gotta get lost to find ourselves. Sometimes we gotta go walkabout,' which are key lines in the advertising.

An important linking device to connect the *walkabout* theme across all applications was the tagline, *Lose yourself in the movie. Find yourself in the country*. Although, in the North American market the approved tag line was *Lose yourself in the movie. Find yourself in Australia*.

The meaning and outcome of an Australian *walkabout* reinforces Tourism Australia's experiential branding strategy and touches on all of the key motivational themes at its core. By encouraging people to 'come walkabout' in Australia, Tourism Australia retained the tradition that it had set in past advertising by issuing a warm invitation. On this occasion, the welcome was again extended in an innovative, yet authentic way. *Australia* star Brandon Walters, a young Aboriginal boy, issued the invitation to come walkabout in each of the television and cinema advertisements.

Two television advertisements were created in a variety of formats from 30 to 90 sec for the international markets, one for eastern regions and one for western markets. They were aired in 22 regions which included the UK, US, Canada, Ireland, the Nordic countries, Germany, France, Netherlands, Switzerland, Italy, the Gulf countries, Malaysia, Thailand, India, Singapore, Taiwan, China, Hong Kong, South Korea, Japan, New Zealand, and Australia.

Integrated marketing strategy

In order to simultaneously leverage the movie's capacity to gain attention and Fox's huge marketing budget, an integrated global strategy was developed by Tourism Australia to convey Australia's tourism messages through a variety of methods, partners, and channels. Because the campaign was to be screened predominantly in cinemas with rich digital media and television as the secondary channel, Luhrmann developed short film-styled advertisements. Tourism Australia's newly appointed creative agency DDB Worldwide produced the print, online and outdoor versions, all based on Luhrmann's inspiration.

Of vital importance to the integration of the campaign was the need to ensure broad reach and engagement of target audiences across a variety of media and channels. The strategy called for extensive cinema and television advertising that would build excitement and emotion to provide a link to the movie, while print and rich digital channel executions would allow the 'walkabout' theme to be fully revealed and connected to Australia's key tourism experiences and products.

Through the partnership with Twentieth Century Fox, the Australian tourism industry was presented with opportunities to develop dimensions to marketing programs not previously possible. These opportunities included participation in Fox promotional activities, access to Fox marketing assets relating to *Australia* the movie and opportunities to reach and convey messages to new audiences.

In the UK, the campaign rolled out from October 2008 and in all markets in which Tourism Australia is active. It was scheduled to coincide with the most critical decision-making period for holidaymakers, while overlapping with both the launch of the movie and the DVD release several months later. The budget allocated by Tourism Australia for this worldwide investment in conjunction with the movie including the Twentieth Century Fox campaign and the Fox partnership was approximately AU$40 million (£23 million).

1. Consumer marketing

Building upon the momentum of the movie and communicating directly with consumers enabled Tourism Australia to expand the Australian tourism story and encourage consumers to learn more about its travel experiences and travel opportunities. Critical to this was extensive cinema, television, print, and online advertising, as well as custom produced magazines, high profile consumer events, and competitions in priority markets. The themes of romance, adventure, and transformation are delivered through stunning imagery and short messages such as:

> *'Arrived with a thousand things on our minds. Departed without a care in the world.'*

A select group of industry partners including tour wholesalers, Aussie Specialist travel agencies, and airlines were encouraged to work cooperatively on movie-related projects. The objective was to find beneficial methods to leverage the release of *Australia* and in doing so, inspire people to see the movie, motivate them to visit Australia, and point them in the right direction to book their travel.

One of the most prominent cooperative marketing programs in the UK was with Emirates Airlines featuring a national television and cinema advertising campaign designed to encourage Brits to travel to Australia for a rejuvenating holiday experience. The campaign included print, online, and outdoor activity in London rail stations.

Additionally, in the UK, 1 week before the premier of the movie, a cinema promotion in partnership with Emirates Airlines and Tourism Western Australia was launched. The advertising saturated key cinemas in the UK. Posters in cinema foyers and washrooms directed consumers to branded postcard racks in the foyers stocked with themed postcards which comprised a fold out film experiences map and a 24-page booklet containing motivating images and information about Australia. Movie-goers were also invited to enter an online competition to win a 2-week holiday to Western Australia and experience some of the movie's locations first hand.

2. Trade marketing

Developing enthusiastic support among wholesalers and travel agent staff was considered a priority in order to satisfy consumer demand for Australian travel experiences arising from the media attention associated with the movie. To achieve this, a range of programs were designed to increase trade awareness and encourage them to develop travel products and promotions related to the movie.

Tourism Australia and 13 partners exhibited at the 2008 World Travel Market in London. Tens of thousands of travel professionals attended the event where Australian tourism operators met with the trade, travel agents, and media to discuss opportunities to promote Australia. The booth decor featured both print and television creatives from the campaign along with *Australia* the movie images and video trailer. The trade marketing activities included exclusive screenings and training for Aussie Specialist Travel Agents in major cities.

Tourism Australia encouraged their industry partners (including tour wholesalers, travel agents, and airlines) to align their marketing to the key messages and themes of the movie. Tourism Australia secured permission from Twentieth Century Fox for the partners to actively participate in the campaign and use the movie promotional artwork in their individual marketing activities. This step provided yet another level of marketing that fused the movie with Australian travel opportunities for consumers. The Tourism Toolkit materials and templates included the following:

- Print advertisements
- Posters and banners for window displays/offices and themed events
- Postcard templates to send clients
- Advertorial templates
- Direct mail template for postal or electronic distribution
- Invitation templates to enable agents to host movie screenings for their clients
- Folder template for itineraries and tickets
- Tour shell template for itinerary productions and special packages
- Online templates for advertising and special package promotion

3. Media relations

Movie and campaign messages were extended through media liaison programs, which resulted in wide exposure in some of the world's leading print, online, and broadcast media. Assistance was given to leading journalists and travel programs to visit Australia so that they could experience and report on locations in Australia relevant to the movie and core experience themes. Importantly, Tourism Australia worked in conjunction with Fox to encourage the stars and the director of the movie to tell their stories of filming in the outback as a way of inspiring Experience Seekers to travel to Australia.

4. Digital marketing

Tourism Australia's digital marketing strategy continued to be highly innovative. Australia was the first country to enter the MySpace community and is currently social networking worldwide with 250,000 people online. This internet strategy facilitates the distribution of tourism messages through high traffic consumer and social media sites including Australia.com, YouTube, Facebook and Flickr, and a variety of country specific platforms.

5. Affinity partners

Working with a range of like-minded brands, Tourism Australia strengthened the distribution of tourism messages via editorial, merchandising, competitions, and direct marketing. As exclusive wine partner of Australia the movie, Jacob's Creek Wines launched the most prominent affinity partner campaign with consistent media and outdoor advertising, and in-store promotions. The company launched an on-pack promotion offering the chance to win prizes ranging from a luxury Jacob's Creek Wines hamper to cinema tickets to the ultimate Australian holiday experience.

CONCLUSION

Australia had been seen by over 23 million people worldwide as of April 2009 and had grossed over US$211 million by the end of that year. This makes it the second highest grossing Australian movie of all time, trailing Crocodile Dundee (US$ 328 million). In the US, *Australia* sold almost two million DVDs in one month, 80% of what the studio predicted it would sell altogether. Since being released in Australia, the DVD has sold double what the studio expected (Box Office Mojo). The critical reviews for the movie were mixed to positive with the general consensus that it was a good, but not great movie.

Tourism arrivals for all of Australia's competitor destinations were negatively impacted by the global recession which coincided with the launch of the movie and Tourism Australia's marketing programs. Results for Australia were also below expectations; however, this cannot be attributed to the results of the film's marketing or Tourism Australia's strategy. The campaign generated an unprecedented level of exposure for Australia among target audiences worldwide, generating an estimated US$ 440 (£270) million worth of publicity for Australia (Tourism Australia). A record 155 million people were exposed to Tourism Australia's marketing, including 1,200 Aussie Specialist agents who completed the movie-related destination training program.

While the economic climate has suppressed results from the campaign in the short term, Tourism Australia research indicates that people who have seen advertising campaigns for Australia are 22% more likely to visit the destination. Tourism Australia executives are confident that the high profile campaigns in conjunction with the movie will result in increased visitation in the medium term.

References

Austrade, Fact sheet: Austrade national brand project – Better positioning Australia.

Baker, B. (2007). Destination Branding for Small Cities. Creative Leap Books

Fox Filmed Entertainment (2008). Australia: Production Information.

Hudson, S., & Ritchie, J. R. B. (2006). Promoting destinations via film tourism. *Journal of Travel Research,* 44, May, 387.

New Zealand Tourism Guide, http://tourism.net.nz/lord-of-the-rings.html

Riley, R., Baker, D., & van Doren, C. S. (1998). Movie induced tourism. *Annals of Tourism Research*, 25(4), 919–935.

Tourism Australia (2008a). Press Release 29 July 2008.

Tourism Australia (2008b). Tourism Australia's destination campaign By Baz Luhrmann – Campaign Strategy 2008.

Tourism Australia, Global Tourism Seekers Fact Sheet

Tourism Australia, www.tourism.australia.com

Useful websites

New Zealand Tourism Guide, http://tourism.net.nz/lord-of-the-rings.html
Tourism Australia, www.tourism.australia.com

CHAPTER

19

Branding, stakeholders, and integration: Namibia

Tom Buncle

INTRODUCTION

How did a country that was little known for anything other than its turbulent political past emerge into the spotlight as one of Africa's most popular tourism destinations? This is the story of the development of the Namibian brand and its impact, under the auspices of the European Union Tourism Development Programme (EUNTDP). Until 2003, Namibian tourism promotion had been largely confined to Germany and South Africa – countries where, for reasons of historical connection and proximity, awareness of Namibia was reasonably developed. But this had taken place without the strategic underpinning of a destination brand and was therefore largely tactical; similarly any promotion of Namibia outside these markets was limited and largely tactical (e.g., attendance at trade shows, ad hoc advertising, etc.) with no consciously consistent theme that attempted to unite Namibia's messages in a way that would make the country standout from its competitors.

The development of a Namibian brand in 2003 not only focused Namibia's tourism marketing on promoting Namibia's core values, but it also challenged long-held perceptions and united the Namibian travel industry and other important stakeholders behind the way Namibia presented itself internationally and to visitors. Namibia experienced significant tourism growth in the first decade of the 2000s. It is now Africa's fifth most visited destination. But it was not always on the tourism map for travellers from the large outbound tourism-producing countries in Western Europe. It has propelled itself into the consciousness of potential long-haul travelers, particularly in Europe, in a relatively short space of time.

Outside Germany, Namibia was relatively unknown, or merely a name from the political news pages of the late twentieth century – somewhere that was, unfortunately and inaccurately, probably lumped together in the European mind with other unknown African countries in the box marked 'conflict, violence, corruption, disease, famine, and insecurity'. To move from

© 2011 Published by Elsevier Ltd. All rights reserved.
DOI: 10.1016/B978-0-08-096930-5.10019-9

such a position of oblivion and prejudice to become an established tourism destination – and a particularly aspirational one – required a significant transformation.

As evidence of the distance travelled, in 2007 Namibia outperformed its big, well-established, high-spending neighbour, South Africa, with a 17% increase in tourism from Europe compared to South Africa's modest 2.3% growth from Europe. So what happened? This chapter aims to explain how this transformation took place, which relied primarily on three important steps:

1. A clear focus on developing a strong and distinctive destination brand.
2. Buy-in to the brand by destination stakeholders.
3. An unwavering commitment to implement the brand and use it as the basis for all external promotion of the country; it had to run through all marketing communications like words in a stick of rock, as the destination's DNA.

This was not rocket science. These are three simple but fundamental steps in the marketing of any destination. But destinations often fail to achieve them, or to align them effectively. This is usually to do with the plethora of stakeholders and political pressures, which can get in the way and prevent destinations from maximising their potential.

Difficulties that destinations experience in following these three steps usually stem from: failure to agree on a destination's core characteristics, which comprise its essence; failure to truly understand how visitors and potential visitors perceive the destination; lack of courage to adopt the focus necessary to distinguish the destination from competitors in the eyes of potential visitors for fear of not being sufficiently representative of some constituents, regions, or businesses; failure to commit to the long-term implementation of the brand; or failure to integrate the destination's core brand values effectively and creatively in all marketing communications.

Such pressures can frustrate the development of a powerful brand, and therefore compromise the destination's ability to stand out from its competitors in international markets – a fundamental first step, and one in which such failure would be almost unthinkable in the world of consumer goods, where success is highly dependent on the creation and nurturing of powerful brands. What is therefore remarkable is that Namibia managed to achieve this where so many other destinations fail.

The case of Namibia is also particularly instructive because it was possible to track the growth in awareness and business from scratch: after developing a branding strategy where there had been none before; and in at least one market (UK) where awareness of Namibia was very low and Namibian marketing had been practically nonexistent. In other words, the branding of Namibia took place in almost 'pure laboratory' conditions, which made it possible to identify the factors that contributed to its success. This is a rare situation in tourism marketing, as most countries start with a certain degree of awareness amongst their target markets, as well as a history of marketing in them, which makes it difficult to establish a baseline against which to judge the impact of branding and marketing campaigns. This also makes it particularly difficult to isolate the factors that contribute towards awareness and sales.

THE DESTINATION AND THE CHALLENGE

When God made this country he must have been angry

–Bushman saying.

Namibia is a photographer's dream – it boasts wild seascapes, rugged mountains, lonely deserts, stunning wildlife, colonial cities and nearly unlimited elbow room…. Namibia is one of those dreamlike places that make you question whether something so visually orgasmic could actually exist. Time and space are less defined here. Landscapes collide. Experiences pile up.

–*Lonely Planet* (http://www.lonelyplanet.com/namibia)

Namibia is a large, but sparsely populated, country in southwest Africa. With 825,418 km^2 of land inhabited by only 1.8 million people, it is the second least densely populated country in the world (after Mongolia). Until the middle of the first decade of the twenty-first century, Namibia was largely unknown as a tourism destination outside its former 'mother state' and neighbour, South Africa, and its former 'colonial godmother', Germany. It achieved independence from South Africa in 1991 after a war of independence. It is, for the most part, hyper-arid, hot, and characterised by a stark, and apparently inhospitable and inaccessible, desert landscape.

Creating and maintaining an infrastructure necessary to accommodate visitors, particularly in reasonable comfort, is expensive; distances are great; and travel is mostly on sand roads, or requires a 4 × 4 off-road vehicle, or by small plane or private charter. In short, Namibia does not, at first glance, appear to offer the most conducive conditions in which to develop a thriving tourism industry.

But it has one major thing going for it – most people who have visited Namibia are extremely passionate about the country. The challenge was therefore to identify what inspired this surprisingly emotional reaction in visitors, capture and 'bottle' its essence, and find a way of articulating it, so that it could form the basis of all future marketing communications and inspire people to visit.

THE VISITOR PERSPECTIVE: SEEING THE DESTINATION THROUGH THE EYES OF POTENTIAL VISITORS

Asking the right people the right questions

Failure to see the world through the eyes of others is one of the commonest business mistakes. When those who want to encourage visitors to their country are unable to see their own country through their visitors' eyes, they are almost always doomed to failure. If they cannot understand what appeals to their visitors, as well as what their visitors find unremarkable or even repellent, and how they compare to their nearest competitors in their visitors' eyes, their marketing will miss the mark and they will not attract as many visitors as their country deserves.

The first step was therefore to establish how Namibia was perceived. This involved talking to previous visitors and, importantly, people who had never been to Namibia. It was important to understand what previous visitors thought about the country; but it was equally important to understand why people who enjoyed African travel and had the means to visit Namibia had never considered it for a holiday. This was not just about establishing what they liked and disliked about the country. It was about understanding their deeper motivation for travel: What did they want out of a holiday? What did they find appealing or unappealing about Namibia? What other destinations had they considered? Why? What similarities, differences, and competitive advantages did they have over Namibia? Where did Namibia sit in their holiday choice hierarchy in relation to these other countries? Above all, what sort of emotional experience were they seeking from a holiday and how did they feel different countries talked to this motivation and how did they satisfy it? And ultimately, how did Namibia satisfy it?

Clearly, asking these questions directly would not yield helpful results. That is because, at face value, they appear quite crass to interviewees; such direct questions also tend to elicit superficial and product-related responses, which provide little insight into how people really feel (e.g., they tend to elicit a list of likes and dislikes, such as the food, the weather, friendly people, wildlife-watching, rather than any critical or comparative analysis of these experiences and how they might have contributed to respondents' overall perception of the country and the way they perceived it in relation to other destinations that offer similar experiences). Consequently, the questions needed to be framed in such a way, and set in such a context, that would elicit the required depth of emotional response in order to reveal peoples' deeper motivation for travel and feelings about the destination. This is something that people are not always consciously aware of, or able to express articulately. But it can be elicited by a skilful interviewer. For this reason, professional branding/research agencies with extensive experience of in-depth interviewing in the travel industry were recruited in the UK, Germany, and South Africa to undertake this research in key markets.

Local perceptions and stakeholder buy-in

But first, in order to provide a starting point for this research, inbound tourism operators in Namibia and Namibia Tourism Board (NTB) employees were consulted. The primary aim was to establish what they thought Namibia's key appeals were; why they believed people visited Namibia; and how they considered Namibia performed in relation to its key competitors. This would establish a basis from which to explore perceptions of Namibia in international markets; and it would be enlightening to compare the views of those who delivered the service (Namibian tourism operators) with those of international consumers (visitors and potential visitors), particularly if, as happened, there was any discrepancy between stakeholders' and visitors' perceptions of Namibia.

A significant by-product, which was nevertheless an intended consequence of this approach, was the achievement of stakeholder buy-in: by involving key Namibian stakeholders at an early stage, this ensured their understanding of the process, its aims, and how it might benefit them in the future. They then became active participants in the development of the Namibian brand. This is possibly one of the single most important lessons in developing a destination brand: if people do not like the way in which their country is promoted internationally, whether to attract tourism or inward investment or for diplomacy or trade, then there is a risk that the messages visitors receive from residents when they get there will not gel with those that they expected; the visitor's experience will not live up to the marketing promise.

Getting residents and key stakeholders on-side, and ideally eventually recruiting them as enthusiastic brand ambassadors who reflect the brand in the way they interact with visitors, is very important. This has to be built in from the start, with stakeholders being treated as active participants in formulating the brand, rather than passive bystanders who are presented with a fait accompli after the process has been completed. Otherwise, they will not feel they own the brand, reflect it in their behaviour, or promote it with enthusiasm – all of which can make the difference between a modest brand and a really powerful brand.

In addition to Namibian tourism operators, other Namibian stakeholders were consulted in outward-facing industries and organisations in the diplomatic, export, manufacturing, trade, food, drink/brewing, creative, and financial sectors. The rationale was both to engage them and achieve their understanding of the notion of branding Namibia, as well as eventually to encourage them to reflect some of Namibia's brand values, when developed and where appropriate, in their own marketing communications. If Namibia's brand values could be adopted and promoted consistently by a range of different stakeholders who talked about Namibia outside the country, the resultant synergy could achieve an impact for Namibia that would not be achieved through the promotion of the country as a tourism destination alone.

Similarly, this impact could be magnified, and the brand reinforced, if those who provided goods and services to visitors above and beyond the tourism industry reflected Namibia's brand values wherever they communicated with people when they were in Namibia (e.g., other businesses, such as financial services, food producers, and manufacturers). For this reason too, advertising and creative/design agencies in Namibia were also involved – so that they might understand and reflect Namibia's brand values, where appropriate, in the work they did for other, particularly non-tourism, clients.

Segmenting the market

Once these local perceptions had been established, a plan was then drawn up to undertake research amongst consumers and outbound tour operators in Namibia's key markets (Germany and South Africa) and in a major potential, but largely untapped, market (UK). In order to elicit the deeper psychological responses that would reveal peoples' underlying motivation for travel, qualitative research was considered essential. This was undertaken in focus groups amongst consumers and through in-depth interviews with outbound tour operators in source markets.

Outbound tour operators were interviewed first in order to begin complementing the picture already built up through the interviews with Namibian stakeholders. They provided a broad picture of the Namibian tourism products sold and travellers' preferences in each country. But they were not considered as a proxy for the views of travellers themselves, as they could not answer the deeper psychological questions about personal travel motivation that only consumers themselves could answer. Nevertheless, they provided some useful insights into general trends in African travel, and an indication of Namibia's main competitors, as well as obstacles to selling Namibia, which could be fed back to inbound tourism operators and the Namibia Tourism Board to be addressed.

Target groups of consumer interviewees in these markets were selected according to demographic segmentation criteria that reflected Namibia's current visitor profile, as well as others who might have a propensity to travel to Namibia on the basis of their demographic profile. These could broadly be defined as a mix of younger people (double-income-no-kids = DINKS; and single-income-no-kids = SINKS), and middle-aged/older people without children or whose children had left home (empty-nesters), all of whom were relatively affluent regular travellers who had previously visited at least one sub-Saharan African country. The South African market was segmented further, because of the size of the market and its familiarity with Namibia, to cover residents of Johannesburg and Cape Town, as well as both English-speaking and Afrikaans-speaking people. In all countries, care was taken to achieve a balance between people who had previously visited Namibia, and people who had never visited Namibia but who had been to sub-Saharan Africa before.

The aim was to discover the following:

- People's underlying holiday motivation.
- Their destination decision-making criteria.
- Their perceptions of Namibia.
- Who they considered as Namibia's key competitors when thinking of a holiday.
- Their deeper emotional attitudes to Namibia and other destinations.

This was done through group discussion about their normal holiday patterns and their views on a number of developing countries in Africa, Asia, and South America, which they were then asked to group together according to whatever criteria they felt appropriate. They were then asked for their views on Namibia. Only at this point were they informed that Namibia was the country they were there to discuss. Stimulus boards, in the form of mock advertisements promoting different aspects of Namibia, had been developed to assist in probing people's'' deeper feelings about Namibia; these included a headline, a selection of pictures, and a strapline that reflected each different characteristic quite starkly. These are outlined in Table 19.1, along with responses from interviewees.

Table 19.1 Summary of stimulus boards (Namibia)

Namibian characteristic	Headline	Strapline	Response
Dramatic, stark wilderness landscape: showing sand dunes, empty landscape and desert elephants	'Touch the Untouched'	'I wonder if anyone has ever stood here before me'	Loved by previous visitors and non-visitors who thought Namibia would be appealing. Considered intimidating by people who would never consider Namibia appealing.
Tranquil empty spaces: showing room to escape, space to reflect on life	'Where the Silence Speaks to You'	'I felt my place in the universe; it put me in touch with my soul'	Ditto
Strange, primeval environment: showing petrified forests, shipwrecks on the Skeleton Coast and abandoned ghost towns	'Like Nowhere You've Ever Seen Before'	'It's like a different planet here on earth'	Ditto
Culture: showing Himba and Herrero tribal heritage, German colonial legacy, and modern, postapartheid Namibia	'The Ancient Spirit of Africa'	'I felt the ancient spirit of Africa breathing life into the nation's future'	Considered appealing by those who had not been to Namibia. But ... relegated to the status of a secondary appeal to the landscape by previous visitors.
Adventure activities: showing sand-boarding, off-road 4 × 4, quad-biking, dune-biking, ballooning, hiking	'Not for the Faint-Hearted'	'It took me to the edge of somewhere I'd never been before. I found a courage I didn't know I had.'	Not seen as a significant reason for travelling to Namibia
Quality standards of a modern tourism destination: showing accommodation, food transport, accessibility	'All the Thrills without the Spills'	'Planning an expedition in Namibia removes the uncertainty, but not the comfort or the thrill'	Considered a 'hygiene factor' – quality, comfort, and accessibility are expected as the norm in a holiday destination; they are not a reason to visit anywhere.

THE VISITOR PROFILE: WHO ARE THEY AND WHAT DO THEY WANT WHEN THEY TRAVEL?

Travel motivation

The research clearly identified two overriding interests amongst people who travelled to sub-Saharan Africa. These were:

1. a desire to experience African nature, particularly wildlife, but also the atmospheric appeal of scenic landscapes;
2. an interest in African people and tribal culture.

It was also important that their destination was relatively undiscovered, gave visitors a feeling of freedom and escape and, exclusively for those who liked Namibia, offered an experience that they found challenging and had to think about and possibly work at in order to feel rewarded and fulfiled (e.g., where there was a sense of physical and mental challenge – as a result of the rugged landscape, climate, and wildlife, which required an element of planning, and engendered a frisson of excitement and a feeling of intrepid, expeditionary travel – a feeling of 'safe/manageable danger').

Consequently Namibia was measured against its nearest competitors in terms of its ability to deliver on the following axes:

- Nature and culture
- Mass tourism vs. undiscovered places
- Frenetic vs. soulful, liberating
- Easy versus raw, challenging

Namibia's strengths

Respondents' views on Namibia's strengths were, fortunately, remarkably similar to those expressed by Namibian stakeholders (but with a significant difference in emphasis on the appeal of culture). These were:

- Surreal, extreme, majestic landscape
- Silence, tranquillity
- Uncongested, space
- People expressed a view that the wildlife was more 'natural' in Namibia than in other African destinations. On probing, this turned out to be an expression of the feeling that people could get close to animals in the national parks and possibly be the only person there, as a result of the ease of self-driving in Namibia and the lack of tarmac roads. Self-driving was not considered either safe or advisable in most other sub-Saharan African countries (apart from South Africa), which resulted in visitors travelling in tour buses to see wildlife, often on tarmac roads, and competing with other busloads of visitors for wildlife photos. This made the wildlife experience all the more intimate, personal, and authentic or 'natural' in Namibia.

- Previous visitors waxed emotionally lyrical about the personal relationship they felt with the environment, because of the feeling of space, scale, and tranquillity
- No mass tourism
- Safe, no hassle from people
- Self-drive was possible

The following were the themes that consistently presented themselves:

- The closeness and variety of the wildlife: 'You see them (animals) in their habitat, not in parks you have to visit with buses' (German visitor).
- A feeling of independence: 'No human trace for hours – it knocks you out. And you know you depend entirely on yourself' (German visitor).
- The sensory experience – in relation to the vast wilderness landscape: 'You have to experience the vastness and space: nothing can prepare you for it' (older British visitor).
- The spiritual experience – in relation to the vast wilderness landscape: 'It gives you a sense of proportion – you are so insignificant – you forget everything else' (younger British visitor).

Visitor profile: Ayes to the right, nos to the left

The consumer research revealed some very valuable insights. Firstly, like Marmite, people either love or hate Namibia. Namibia provokes extreme reactions in people. The research split respondents starkly between those who loved Namibia with a passion (previous visitors), or to whom it appealed (amongst non-visitors), and those to whom it was an anathema and who would never consider visiting such a place. People loved Namibia's dramatic, stark wilderness landscape, its tranquil empty spaces, and its strange primeval environment, or they felt intimidated by them. It emerged that visitors want to experience more than just 'a Himba (tribal people), a (desert) elephant and a dune,'[1] as one tour operator intimated. The research identified Namibia's majestic, rugged, wilderness landscape – and its associated sense of escape, tranquillity, and spirituality – as the country's strongest asset and its most distinctive competitive differentiator in relation to other African destinations that also offer wildlife, scenery, culture, and adventure.

The research demonstrated that, while people are generally interested in African tribal culture, this was not perceived to be as great a strength as the landscape in Namibia. Those who had *never been* to Namibia saw culture as being of major interest. But those who *had visited* Namibia talked of the risk of intruding on indigenous people's lives and of patronising them on sightseeing tours. They also suggested that this made indigenous culture less accessible to visitors than in some other African countries and therefore not a primary reason for visiting. On the other hand, they extolled the landscape and the intense emotions that its scale, emptiness, and scenic drama inspired. This

---

[1] Namibia has some of the largest and most spectacular sand dunes on earth at Sossusvlei. The main feature of the Namibia Tourism Board logo is a massive sand dune.

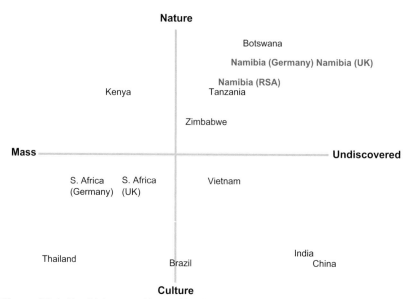

Figure 19.1 Namibia's competitive position (nature and undiscovered)

enabled the Namibian Tourism Board and Namibian tourism operators to re-prioritise their marketing to emphasise the landscape and the opportunities it offered for escape, reflection, and emotional regeneration, and to introduce culture as a supporting appeal (if handled responsibly), rather than leading with it, which they had been doing before.

Finally, the consumer research highlighted Namibia's ability to deliver against visitors' desire for wildlife, nature, scenic drama, escape and for a physically challenging holiday (in terms of planning itineraries and expeditions – for self-drive car rental visitors), as well as for an indulgent, high-quality African lodge experience. It also identified Namibia's competitors and Namibia's competitive position in relation to key drivers of tourism to sub-Saharan Africa (e.g., Botswana, Tanzania, Zambia, Kenya, South Africa) in each of its key source markets (Germany, UK, South Africa), as Figures 19.1 and 19.2 illustrate.

However, as a word of caution, the consumer research clearly showed Namibia which types of people it should target in its marketing and which it should ignore:

Namibia is for people who are:

- Self-reliant
- Resourceful
- Independent-spirited
- Keen to be challenged (e.g., in terms of planning expeditions and itineraries)

For people who say: 'It's a privilege to experience this type of place'

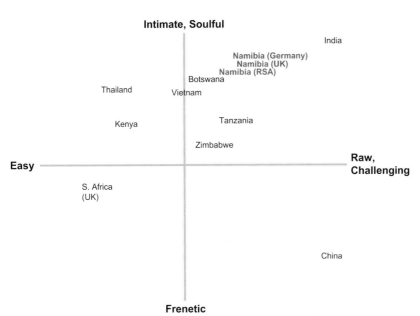

Figure 19.2 Namibia's competitive position (intimate/soulful and raw/challenging)

Namibia is *not* for people who are:

- Timid, cautious
- Gregarious, to the extent that they constantly need the company of others and are uncomfortable spending much time on their own or just with their partner
- Culture vultures, whose main motivation for travelling is to experience other cultures
- Mass tourists
- Passive
- Agoraphobic, or uncomfortable in a sparsely populated environment with great distances between visitor facilities

Not for people who say: 'What is there to do in the evening?'

In short, Namibia inspired passionate responses amongst its advocates about the space, scale, and majesty of its wilderness landscape, while those who would never visit such a place found these same aspects intimidating and potentially risky – a clear division between those who would, and those who would never be in Namibia's target market. Even though tourists might participate in adventure activities, such as quad-biking, off-road driving, etc. while on holiday in Namibia, this was not considered a reason for visiting Namibia. Adventure activities had the status of 'nice to do,' but not a reason for going. Ballooning was not considered an adventure activity, but a fabulously tranquil way of seeing the landscape in a way that was in keeping with the soulful experience associated with Namibia. High standards of comfort, service, product quality, and accessibility were considered as the norm, and certainly not a reason for visiting – and therefore as a 'hygiene factor.'.In fact, a destination that did not offer appropriate quality and service standards would not be considered by many people in these market segments.

Respondents were also asked three ethical questions about the extent to which the policies and behaviour of a destination or a tour operator would have on their decision to travel to that destination or to book/not book with a particular tour operator. These related to:

- Environment: policies and behaviour
- Political regime: nature of government (repressive or liberal)
- Community benefit: empowerment, or the extent to which communities benefited directly from tourism.

Most respondents were surprisingly unconcerned or felt powerless about ethical issues, at least when it came to influencing their choice of destination or tour operator. They felt that good behaviour by government and tour operators in these areas was 'nice to have', but would not influence their choice of destination or tour operator either way, for example:

On environmental issues:

- 'You have to be tolerant. Other countries see environmental issues differently from us – that's the way it is' (German respondent)

On community benefit:

- 'It would make no difference to my choice, and anyway I wouldn't believe them (tour operators)' (German respondent)
- 'I can't do anything about it – and they still get jobs' (German respondent)

On political regime:

- 'I want to go to Myanmar. I know the regime is unpleasant and the people are oppressed but I still want to go' (British younger respondent)

Although they spoke passionately about the emotional impact Namibia had on them, people expressed a resistance to being told in tourism marketing campaigns that this is how they would feel. They wanted to find this out for themselves and found it patronising for tourism officials or tour operators to tell them how they would feel ('What do they know about me?'). This poses a continual challenge for the Namibia Tourism Board and Namibian tourism businesses to convey a sense of the potential emotional impact of the relationship between the holidaymaker and the environment – which is Namibia's strongest asset – without talking about it. The conclusion was that it probably has to be communicated visually, which requires stunning photography.

BUILDING THE BRAND

Key insights

The rich textural information that this research yielded was distilled to produce the key insights that would form the core of the Namibian brand. The most powerful concepts: were 'untouched,' 'infinite,' 'spiritual,' and 'mystical.' Key words were 'pristine', 'untouched', 'vast', 'infinite', 'natural beauty' (physical – destination) and 'soul', 'spiritual', 'raw', 'intimate', and 'liberating' (experiential – personal). Namibia is a profound, deeply emotional experience. This is a powerful asset, which is evident to those who have visited, but it is but hard to communicate in marketing materials to people who have never been before. This is a tough marketing challenge for the Namibia Tourism Board and Namibian tour operators. Namibia is not a passive exhibit that is viewed from a distance. Namibia happens to you, it engulfs you; Namibia is an experience, the result of each individual's relationship with the vast, dramatic landscape, and wildlife.

'You have to be comfortable with yourself and your partner to visit such a place' was one comment that summed up the emotional impact of Namibia's greatest impact, its vast, lonely, tranquil landscape.

These findings led to the fundamental insight, which would underpin the brand: *Namibia is an experience rather than a place*. This led to a definition of Namibia's visitor profile as 'confident escapers,' rather than 'cautious socialisers' – cumbersome descriptions, but nevertheless useful for the Namibia Tourism Board, Namibian tourism operators and others responsible for promoting Namibia, by defining Namibia's prospects both in terms of their psychographic profile/mindset/values-based lifestyle ('confident escapers') – rather than just in demographic terms – and in terms of the antithesis of the Namibian visitor ('cautious socialisers').

The Namibia brand pyramid and Namibia's core essence

These insights were then used as the basis for developing the Namibian brand. The Namibian brand pyramid (Figure 19.3) shows how the core elements of the brand were built up, starting with Namibia's rational attributes and ascending towards its brand essence.

Namibia's brand essence and core brand values were established by looking at three things (Figure 19.4):

1. *The place* (destination): What was its physical nature?
2. *The relationship* that visitors had with the destination: How did it make them feel when they were there? How did they connect with the destination?
3. *The visitor benefit*: What benefit did they feel a holiday in Namibia gave them? This flowed from the relationship they had with the place. It was about their emotional take-out from a visit to Namibia – how it had affected them emotionally by the end of their holiday.

STAKEHOLDER BUY-IN AND ADVOCACY

The need to involve stakeholders in developing the brand from the outset has been articulated above. But they need to be involved at *every* critical stage. Stakeholder workshops were held in Namibia to discuss the research findings.

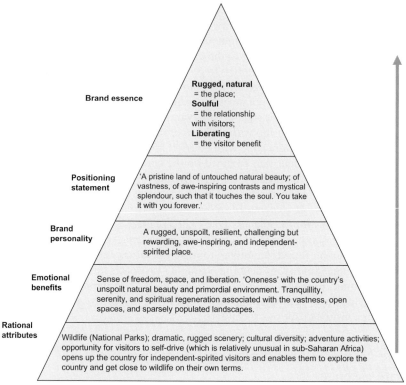

Brand essence

Rugged, natural
= the place;
Soulful
= the relationship
with visitors;
Liberating
= the visitor benefit

**Positioning
statement**

'A pristine land of untouched natural beauty; of
vastness, of awe-inspiring contrasts and mystical
splendour, such that it touches the soul. You take
it with you forever.'

**Brand
personality**

A rugged, unspoilt, resilient, challenging but
rewarding, awe-inspiring, and independent-
spirited place.

**Emotional
benefits**

Sense of freedom, space, and liberation. 'Oneness' with the country's
unspoilt natural beauty and primordial environment. Tranquillity,
serenity, and spiritual regeneration associated with the vastness, open
spaces, and sparsely populated landscapes.

**Rational
attributes**

Wildlife (National Parks); dramatic, rugged scenery; cultural diversity; adventure activities;
opportunity for visitors to self-drive (which is relatively unusual in sub-Saharan Africa)
opens up the country for independent-spirited visitors and enables them to explore the
country and get close to wildlife on their own terms.

Figure 19.3 Namibia brand pyramid

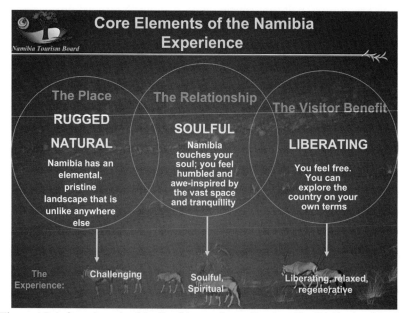

Figure 19.4 Core elements of the Namibia experience. (Courtesy: Namibia Tourism Board)

The key insights discovered during the international consumer research were discussed in these workshops. The core elements that would form the basis of the Namibian brand were then elicited through debate with stakeholders. This ensured that stakeholders could challenge any assumptions with which they felt uncomfortable and interrogate the research findings. But, most importantly, they were able to understand the process of building the brand by hearing the views of people who mattered – potential visitors who could choose wherever they wanted to travel on holiday – and they played an active role in developing the brand framework. At this stage it was important to try to bring potential visitors' views (as expressed in the consumer research) and Namibian stakeholder views as close together as possible. Fortunately, as identified above, these views were largely similar. Had they been poles apart, it could have proved difficult to develop a powerful brand. If there had been a significant discrepancy between what motivated visitors and how Namibians saw their own country, there would have been a serious risk of brand dissonance, whereby the visitor experience might not live up to the marketing promise. Involving stakeholders from the start was important – not just to ensure they understood the brand, but also to encourage them to become enthusiastic brand advocates.

IMPLEMENTATION: BRINGING THE BRAND TO LIFE

Having developed the core elements of the brand, it was then important to explain how to apply the brand. The Namibian tourism industry and others who would talk about Namibia in external markets, as well as those who provided services for visitors in Namibia, needed to know how they could use and reinforce the Namibian brand. How could they reflect 'Namibian-ness' in their own activities and behaviour? This was crucial step that would bridge the gap between branding theory and marketing practise. This involved two key steps, the development of a brand toolkit and a series of brand seminars.

The brand toolkit

Destination brands often fail to achieve impact, and particularly fail to convince stakeholders to adopt them, because no one understands how to apply them. Merely establishing a brand essence or values is insufficient. Destination Management Organisations (DMOs) and stakeholders need to understand what steps to take to reflect the brand in their own marketing communications. To this end a brand toolkit was developed (Figure 19.5). It contained three main elements:

1. *Branding concept*: It explained the role of the brand in simple terms, as people would need to be convinced of its role and importance. This involved explaining what the values meant and how they had been conceived.

2. *Application of the brand*: It contained guidelines on how to reflect the brand in marketing communications: for example, in design style, tone

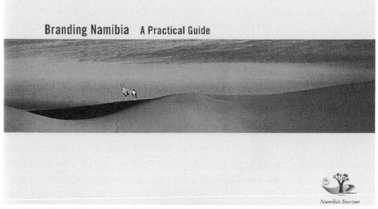

Figure 19.5 Namibia brand Toolkit. (Courtesy: Namibia Tourism Board)

Figure 19.6 Core brand value illustrations (Namibia). (Courtesy: Namibia Tourism Board)

of voice, visual imagery, colur palette, image texture, and typeface. For instance, one of the insights was that a destination, whose appeal lay in the vast, majestic scale of its wild landscapes, lent itself much more to a landscape – rather than portrait – orientation in its photography.

3. *Technical specifications*: It contained technical specifications for those authorised to use the Namibia logo, plus further contact details.

Quite simply, the aim of the brand toolkit was to help people understand how they could 'look more Namibian.'

Each core brand value was illustrated and reinforced with powerful, genuine quotes from participants in the consumer research (Figure 19.6).

The toolkit was endorsed in branding seminars, led by the Namibia Tourism Board as the drivers and guardian of the Namibia brand. These were organised throughout the tourism industry and other sectors in Namibia to explain the role of the brand and how to apply it.

CONCLUSION

This chapter has provided several key insights into the crucial role stakeholders play in creating a powerful destination brand and the overall process of destination brand development. Firstly, we have seen how qualitative research will yield the in-depth psychological insights required to build a destination brand. It is useful to start by obtaining destination stakeholders' views, followed by perceptions of outbound tour operators in key source markets, to help frame questions for later research amongst consumers. Non-visitors should be interviewed as well as previous visitors, as long as they are sufficiently well-profiled to be potential visitors (e.g., as previous visitors to sub-Saharan Africa). This can yield significant insights as to why they have never considered the destination (e.g., because they found Namibia's wilderness landscapes intimidating, in spite of the wildlife and cultural appeals that they might otherwise have found attractive).

Traditional assumptions and 'sacred cows' should be challenged through consumer research, because they might not be based on evidence or market knowledge (cf. the discovery that culture should play a supporting, rather than leading, role to Namibia's dramatic landscape as the top appeal). Some elements, which consumers consider important, might be significant only as 'hygiene factors' (e.g., standards of quality, service, comfort and accessibility), or as supporting attractions (e.g., adventure activities), but are not considered as reasons for visiting. They should therefore not be factored into the development of the brand. They may, however, need to be communicated for the sake of customer reassurance at a later, and more appropriate, stage in the marketing process, such as in websites, brochures and PR. The hierarchy of importance – between what distinguishes a destination from its competitors and acts as a real hook in attracting visitors, versus things people just like to do or expect to have in any holiday – has to be understood.

In this case, Namibia appeals to a mindset: it is an experience rather than a place. Understanding who might be – and who will definitely never be – potential visitors to Namibia, demands a sophisticated market segmentation process. This requires a value-based, not just a demographic, segmentation approach. Income and education are no definer of taste. But an 'experiential' destination is hard to communicate. People do not want to be patronised by being told how the destination will make them feel. This will probably have to be created visually and through creative marketing techniques (e.g., stunning photography, testimonials from previous visitors, PR, user-generated website content, and social media) and a dramatically scenic destination such as Namibia lends itself to landscape-oriented, not portrait-oriented, photography.

It is important to accept that some people might never find your destination appealing (e.g., those who found Namibia too intimidating). In this case, ignore them in your marketing and focus ruthlessly on core market segments, which are your destination's best prospects (e.g., 'confident escapers'). Of course commitment from the very top is essential. The most powerful brand strategy is unlikely to be widely adopted where it counts – in marketing by stakeholders – if it is not enthusiastically endorsed by respected opinion leaders. In Namibia's case, the NTB Chief Executive, Head of Marketing, and heads of various travel industry bodies, such as the Federation of Namibian Tourism Associations (FENATA), became instant and vocal advocates of the brand from the beginning of the brand development process. This had significant influence on the brand's adoption throughout NTB marketing activities and stakeholder marketing communications, both within and beyond the tourism industry.

In this chapter we have seen how stakeholder understanding, buy-in, and adoption of the brand in their own marketing communications are fundamental. This requires stakeholder involvement in developing the brand from the outset, as well as an ongoing program to encourage them to become brand advocates and ambassadors once it has been developed. Bridging the gap between a brand strategy and its implementation requires a toolkit. This should explain clearly and simply how to apply the brand in marketing communications. It should be aimed primarily at tourism board staff and stakeholders.

Namibia is a profound, deeply emotional experience, but hard to communicate in marketing materials, especially to potential visitors who have never been there. This is a marketing challenge, which relies on stunning photography and creative communication. However, the results speak for themselves: stakeholder take-up of the brand was widespread and Namibia's growth rate from Europe outperformed South Africa's (2007: Namibia + 17% vs. South Africa + 2.3%).

A rational, transparent, and inclusive brand development process can inspire stakeholder confidence and encourage their adoption of the brand. On being thanked for his role in developing the brand by some Namibian tour operators 2 years after the brand was developed, the author replied that most Namibian tour operators knew their country's brand values so well that they already intuitively reflected them in their brochures and websites, to which the response came 'But you gave us the confidence to know that we were right'. Sometimes it is the small things, and their consistent application, that make a big difference.

CHAPTER

Branding, destination image, and positioning: San Antonio

Jonathon Day

INTRODUCTION

The lazy San Antonio River runs through the centre of one of America's most popular tourism cities. On its banks, the San Antonio River Walk is a popular retail and dining area that attracts locals and visitors from across the United States and around the world. Close by, the Alamo stands as a reminder of the bravery of Bowie, Travis, Crockett, and the other defenders who stood against overwhelming odds for their ideals. This chapter will examine how brand strategists for San Antonio have used these images and others to create a destination brand campaign for one of America's iconic destinations.

San Antonio is home to almost 1.3 million people according to the US census bureau and is a growing and prosperous city. Tourism is an important component of the San Antonio economy. According to the 2008 San Antonio Hospitality Industry Economic Impact study, hospitality contributes over US\$11 billion to the economy and employs over 106,000 people, one in every eight workers from the San Antonio metropolitan area. Each year the city welcomes over 11 million overnight leisure visitors and another 5 million visitors for conventions, meetings, and other business purposes (Butler and Stefl, 2008). It is popular destination for the people of Texas and also attracts visitors from across the United States. In addition, San Antonio has become a popular international destination.

This chapter addresses the issues associated with effective destination branding and looks at some of the models that can be applied to the process. In developing the new brand, the team at San Antonio Convention and Visitors Bureau (SACVB) has addressed many of the key issues confronting destination marketers. The chapter examines the brand development process and addresses the following issues:

- Destination image – a 'natural resource'
- Alignment of the brand to strategic objectives

© 2011 Published by Elsevier Ltd. All rights reserved.
DOI: 10.1016/B978-0-08-096930-5.10020-5

- Stakeholder engagement
- Leadership and other roles
- Identity creation

The case study will also examine the role of the creativity in the process of successful brand development and address issues of brand strategy implementation. It analyses San Antonio's positioning and the importance of an integrated, all-inclusive marketing approach to developing the brand. The case will also examine the brand alignment of marketing activity within the destination and opportunities to extend the destination brand to other markets. Finally we study the issues of brand measurement and how the destination can measure the impact of the branding activity.

SAN ANTONIO: IMAGE AND BRAND HERITAGE

San Antonio is a destination that conjures up a variety of images. San Antonio is an important part of the mental collage that represents 'Texas' in the minds of many Americans. In school, literature, and movies, Americans learn of the bravery and determination of the men of San Antonio's Alamo. Those who know Texas know that San Antonio is a gateway to the Texas Hill Country. It is renowned for arts, food, and culture and considered by many people to be the centre of Tejano culture. Image studies of San Antonio indicate that visitors consider the destination a safe place to visit, good value for money, and a location with pleasant weather and friendly people as well as a welcoming atmosphere. The River Walk appeals to Texans and non-Texans alike with historical sites and the image of the city adding to the desirability of the destination for out-of-state visitors (SACVB, 2010). Like its tourism competitor, New Orleans, San Antonio is a destination that combines history and a vibrant culture into an appealing destination experience. San Antonio has an abundance of attractions: theme parks, the nation's third largest zoo, and a SeaWorld, but all these attractions are value added to the core experiences of San Antonio itself.

These images of San Antonio are created by a wide range of inputs and can be considered San Antonio's 'image capital' (Tasci & Gartner, 2007). A deep understanding of the destination image and the image capital of the destination is useful for the destination brand strategist as they are the foundation on which all marketing must be based. Nevertheless, destination image is a complex phenomenon and several authors have noted that it is often poorly defined (Echtner & Ritchie, 1991; Pike, 2002; Tasci & Gartner, 2007). Most definitions of destination image refer to the 'associations, impressions, and beliefs' or 'mental constructs' of a destination held by an individual. Echtner and Ritchie (1991), in their assessment of destination image studies, note that a destination can be considered in terms of functional characteristics and psychological characteristics, as well as specific attributes and the destination as a whole – elements that are common with other destinations and elements that are unique. More recently, Tasci and Gartner (2007) have developed a model that includes image components that incorporate both the common and the unique; the attributes of the destination; the cognitive, conative, and affective images of the destination; and the holistic or overall image of the destination. Destination image is clearly more than just a set of attributes and brand strategists frequently incorporate 'feel' or mood of the destination (Pritchard & Morgan 1998) as well as function or attribute-based components. Destination image is in the 'eye of the beholder'; different groups will understand the destination in different ways based on their previous experiences. In developing destination brands, the brand strategist must consider the variety of ways destination image is created in order to determine the best ways to position the destination with specific groups.

Over the years SACVB has contributed to the tourism image of San Antonio with campaigns and other marketing activities. Previous campaigns for San Antonio have attempted to incorporate cultural messages into their strategies. 'Beyond the Alamo,' a campaign launched in July 2000 (Anon, 2000), endeavoured to showcase cultural aspects of San Antonio and broaden the consumer awareness of city's features. In the years immediately prior to the new brand program, the SACVB had run the campaign 'Find yourself in San Antonio' based on discovery of features of the destination. Advertising in this campaign included headlines such as 'find that everything does taste better outdoors' (River Walk image), 'find the right setting for a soak, rinse and spin' (water park image), and 'find the soul of Texas in the Heart of Downtown' (Alamo image). This campaign was developed as a tactical activity designed to drive sales and destination awareness but not as a part of a brand strategy. From this base, a new brand was developed.

STRATEGY AND BRAND

Brand development is a strategic activity that should be undertaken in the context of a broader strategic plan. The destination experience itself is an important way the brand is developed in the minds of consumers; the brand strategy needs to reflect that experience today and in the long term. San Antonio undertook an extensive strategic planning process (SACVB, 2006) to establish the key determinants of visitor industry growth in San Antonio. The first two objectives of the strategic plan included enhancing the attractiveness of the destination to both visitors and residents and protecting and enhancing the unique cultural and historical characteristics of San Antonio. Recommendations of the plan include protecting the authenticity of the destination and investing in infrastructure tied to themes incorporating the River Walk, the Alamo, and other prominent city features. The third objective of the plan was to enhance the ability of the visitor industry to create significant economic benefits for the residents of San Antonio. This objective tied directly to the development of a brand strategy to 'raise the image of San Antonio as a desirable destination.' These objectives fundamentally address how the San Antonio experience is delivered to consumers and are core to the brand experience itself. In other words, the strategic plan shares the same core values as the brand. The brand development process is informed by the strategic planning process and the two activities work together to achieve long-term goals.

Branding is the positioning of specific elements of a destination identity in the minds of specific target markets (Aaker, 1996). In most communities, the development of destination branding for tourism is the responsibility of Destination Marketing Organisations (DMOs). DMOs undertake branding because it supports their mission to create economic and social benefits for their communities. In some ways, the brand strategists working to develop the brand San Antonio are building an asset just like the extension of the River Walk or new public infrastructure tied to themes that is included in the strategic plan. These physical assets, like the intangible brand asset, will be used by many groups in the community and will create long-term value for the destination. Brand assets can be substantial. According to Interbrand (2009), a leading brand valuation consultancy, the value of the 'Coca Cola' brand is estimated to be over $68 billion and the value of the Disney brand is $28 billion. Brand strategists find it challenging to provide values for these intangible assets in the commercial sector. There are a variety of methodologies used, none of which are easily transferable to the destination branding context. Nevertheless, many stakeholders in the tourism system can leverage the brand assets to great advantage.

Traditionally, brand equity has been examined from the benefits it creates for either the firm or the consumer. The benefits to the firm, in this case the DMO, include increased efficiency and effectiveness of marketing programs, brand loyalty, less vulnerability to marketing crises, more inelastic consumer responses to price increases, trade leverage, trade cooperation and support, and the ability to extend the brand and competitive advantage (Aaker, 1991; Keller, 1993, 1998). Indeed, competitive advantage (Baker & Cameron, 2008; Hall, 2004; Morgan & Pritchard, 2002; Murphy, Benckendorff, & Moscardo, 2007) is cited most frequently as the rationale for tourism destination branding. Competitive advantage can be best described in terms of the roles of branding for the consumer that Keller (1998) describes as a 'risk reducer, signal of quality, an identification of source of the product and a promise, bond or pact with the maker of the product.' However, this traditional view of brand equity, focused solely on the company and the consumer, significantly underestimates the value of branding for a destination as it fails to recognise the composite nature of the destination. Destinations are 'amalgams of tourism products' (Buhalis, 2000) and, thus brand benefits extend to each of the products and services within the destination. Indeed, even beyond the destination itself, the destination brand is leveraged by stakeholders like tour wholesalers or convention planners creating benefits for them in their marketing efforts. In one study of a branded destination, the top three benefits of destination branding identified by destination products and tour wholesalers were the ability to focus on product sales knowing the 'destination message' had been covered; direct or indirect tactical sales as a result of brand campaigns; and easier introduction of new products to market because of the destination brand (Day, 2005). In developing the brand for San Antonio, the SACVB set out to create an asset that will provide a foundation for effective marketing efforts over the long term. The organisation committed to developing a world-class brand that would be an asset for San Antonio for years to come.

Brand development also supports growth and yields goals of the destination. San Antonio destination strategists determined that growth objectives would be achieved through visitor growth from major markets on the east and west of US coasts. They particularly wanted to reach affluent members of households from those areas who stay for a longer period of time and spend more money. San Antonio also determined that it would broaden its visitor portfolio by attracting more international visitors who tend to have higher expenditures at the destination. SACVB research identified that while San Antonio was a very strong regional brand, it lacked consumer awareness in these markets (White, 2010). As Scott White, the Executive Director of SACVB, states 'We knew that national branding would not only help us elevate the destination to attract a larger diverse leisure audience, but it would also help us with targeting meetings and conventions as well. Launching a new brand was imperative for San Antonio to compete effectively on both national and international levels.'

DESTINATION BRAND LEADERSHIP

As leaders in the branding process of a destination, DMOs undertake the tasks required to develop the brand identity: understanding and analysing the existing image capital of the destination; developing the strategic brand identity that the destination wants; and determining the key elements of the brand identity that will maximise benefits to the destination in the short term. These activities require extensive consultation and engagement with a variety of stakeholders. As Kotler, Haider and Rein (1993, p. 37) note, 'Images aren't easy to develop or change. They require research into how residents and outsiders currently see the place; they require identifying true and untrue elements, as well as strong and weak elements; they require inspiration and choice among contending pictures; they require elaborating the choice in a thousand ways so that residents, businesses, and others truly express the consensual image; and they require a substantial budget for the (brand) image's dissemination.'

The SACVB recognised its role in the development of the brand and the importance of the brand to other stakeholders in the tourism community and elsewhere. As Scott White, the Executive Director of SACVB, states:

> The CVB had the lead role and coordinated all efforts in conjunction with the agency. It was critical that stakeholders and clients involved in the process understood this was not a new marketing campaign, but a true brand evolution for the destination with a goal to be around for a very long time. In order for San Antonio to grow and evolve, the brand must be adopted and embraced by the majority of our local stakeholders.

The effectiveness of the DMO in leading this process is a function of its management's leadership skills. The introduction of the destination brand can be seen as a major change program in the destination system and, as such, it requires active participation from the most senior management of the DMO (Kotter, 1996). As Baker (2007, p. 57) states, 'The president or executive director of the DMO must be actively engaged in every aspect of the brand's development and breathe vitality into the assignment. We have found that the only way for the brand to take off is when the CEO "gets it" and has passion, energy, skills and vision to make it work.' In 2006, Scott White joined the SACVB as Executive Director after successful senior management positions at Greater Phoenix CVB and committed to lead the project, advocating 'The CEO must be very active in this process and be the leader driving the initiative forward. It was imperative that the CEO's face and voice was front in centre at all aspects of the process' (White, 2010).

While Executive Director White remained closely involved throughout the process, SACVB's Brand Team expanded to include Sandy Smith and Jeff Miraglia. Sandy Smith who is the Director of Marketing at the SACVB was charged with executing a brand strategy. Jeff Miraglia, of Mindset Inc. and Bromly Communications, contributed to the strategy and provided creative direction. Both Smith and Miraglia came from outside the San Antonio tourism industry and were immediately immersed in the consultation process. Their approach supported a new look at the image that was respectful of marketing heritage but was able to see the brand from a newcomer's perspective.

DESTINATION BRAND ARCHITECTURE

Brand architecture can be described as 'an organising structure of the brand portfolio, the brand roles and the relationship among brands and different product market brand contexts' (Aaker & Joachimsthaler, 2000, p. 134). Brand architecture is an important consideration for destinations as consumers often have strong associations with destinations at several geographic levels. For instance, San Antonio is both part of Texas and the United States. The relevance of this architecture changes with different target markets. A domestic market with shared cultural identity will find the national destination brand less important than state- and city-based positioning. For the local domestic market, these image associations may be quite inconsequential, but in target markets such as Chicago or Los Angeles, the association with Texas may be more important. In certain international markets, San Antonio evokes associations with both Texas and the United States. The brand architecture strategy will determine the use of different branding elements in various markets while maintaining core positioning for brand identity development.

Texas has a strong and distinct image, very much American but also very independent. It is 'big sky' country with an attitude all of its own. 'Don't mess with Texas,' a common catchphrase from the Lone Star state, relates to the frontier spirit and 'Western' characteristics of the state. The Texas Department of Tourism has invested significant resources in their tourism branding 'Texas – It's like a whole other country,' leveraging Texas image capital to focus on a positioning designed to encourage visitation to the state. San Antonio benefits from the association with Texas and can focus its marketing on the points of differentiation with other competitors, including other Texas cities such as Dallas, Fort Worth, and Houston, to name a few. These cities share attributes based on their Texas heritage, but each city has a unique identity and separate brand goals. Indeed, San Antonio is so secure in its association with Texas that it does not directly reference it in its logo or tagline. The San Antonio brand also consciously embraces its American heritage. The brand 'illuminates San Antonio as an "Authentic American" city with historical significance, unique charm and a rich cultural tapestry of the population' (SACVB, 2008). As with the association to Texas, these brand ties are largely implicit with copy and imagery leveraging associations with America without necessarily explicitly referring to them.

TARGET MARKET: WHOSE BRAND IS IT?

A critical component of the branding process is determining the target market. San Antonio is protecting its core while expanding into new markets. SACVB has identified two primary markets. The first priority is a national group of affluent travellers with annual household incomes above $100,000. This target group is 35–64 years of age and resides in major metropolitan areas. The second primary market is the local Texas market with a broader age group between 25 and 54 years and a lower household income threshold of $50,000. The group has been San Antonio's core market in recent years. While San Antonio's identified primary market is critical, its brand positioning must adapt to meet the needs of additional markets. Destinations with broad appeal like San Antonio often proactively work to attract visitors from a broad range of markets. For instance, San Antonio also targets a series of 'niches,' such as 'foodies' or the 'golf market,' from within its two primary markets. As noted previously, the meetings and convention market is also an important market for San Antonio. Development of the brand identity accounted for the positioning needs of this market as well. To add complexity to this process, San Antonio markets internationally for the leisure market. It actively promotes to leisure travellers in Mexico, Latin and Central America, Canada, Europe, and China.

A daunting task exists for a relatively small organisation such as a DMO to develop marketing plans for so many markets, both domestically and internationally. Brand identity provides a core-organising framework, adjusting positioning to the specific needs of individual markets. The challenge is to use brand identity to create images that appeal to the consumer and stimulate action to ensure the brand image resonates with the consumer. Congruity is important between the self-image of the person receiving the message and the brand image (Chon, 1992; Ekinci, 2003; Sirgy & Su, 2000) and the brand positioning must match destination image with the consumer's self-image.

BRAND AND THE DESTINATION SYSTEM

Several researchers (Hall, 2004; Morgan & Pritchard, 2002; Ryan, 2002) have noted the political nature of destination branding. Clearly, the process of destination branding differs significantly from the traditional fast-moving consumer product branding where only company insiders need to agree on strategy and execute brand campaigns, although it would be misleading to suggest that the destination branding process is unique in the level of consultation it requires. Destination image is a community resource and it is common to include significant community consultation when community resources are developed. There are at least two specific groups that should be considered in development of the destination – the local destination system and the residents and their representatives.

Similarly, the members of the destination system – hoteliers, attraction managers, restaurant operators, and others – must recognise the value of the brand and its ongoing development. Destination branding, while accruing some benefits for the DMO, is undertaken primarily to support the marketing efforts of the tourism destination system. As beneficiaries of the brand tourism industry, participants are expected to be actively engaged in the process. In developing the new branding, the SACVB conducted over 100 interviews with key stakeholders in the tourism industry and local business leadership. In addition to hoteliers and tourism industry partners, the SACVB interviewed people involved in conservation and historical preservation of San Antonio.

The role of residents in destination branding is complex. They are consumers of the brand and stakeholders in the brand. They are 'brand' element mediums through which the brand is communicated. Destinations are perceived differently by locals, returning visitors, and potential first-time visitors. Each of these groups has different levels of familiarity with the destination. Marketing communication requires clear and often simple messaging that appeal to the intended target market. Often markets use stereotypes and clichés to communicate their message as these elements are already imbued with positive association. From the visitor's perspective, the use of generic stereotypes can be useful for potential visitors, but it conveys little information to returning visitors and, at best, may be only a means of reinforcing previously held views. Nevertheless, many of these locals recognise that stereotypes fail to convey the richness of the community. The creative challenge becomes one of conveying that richness in a simple, easy-to-understand manner. In identifying the key images and messages to appeal to visitors, the brand strategists identified a range of elements – the attributes of the destination, the River Walk, the Alamo, the local people who 'personify' life in San Antonio, and 'the feeling' of the destination. These components tapped the sources of local pride and reinforced the positive self-image of the residents of the city. To be sustainable, the destination image must appeal to not only target markets but residents as well; destination brands must resonate with the locals as well as address the needs of target market.

San Antonio has also realised that stakeholder engagement is not a 'one-off' exchange. The brand is a strategic asset that will be honed and developed over the long term. The DMO will lead that process and facilitate the brand conversation, but the stakeholder engagement process must continue throughout the process.

BRAND IDENTITY AND BRAND ELEMENTS

As noted previously, while destination image is created through a wide variety of inputs, branding is a deliberate process undertaken by marketers. Aaker and Joachimsthaler (2000, p. 40) describe brand identity as the 'cornerstone' of this process. They define brand identity as 'a set of associations the brand strategist seeks to create or maintain.' SACVB has developed its brand identity through four key 'brand pillars' that capture the essence of their destination. These brand pillars are People, Pride, Passion, and Promise. According to brand launch documents (SACVB, 2008), People 'embody the power and spirit of the city,' Pride is 'drawn from deep-rooted history, fuelled by the progress of tomorrow,' Passion is the 'passion of the people for what they do and roles they play in the life of the city,' and Promise is the 'promise of the experience.' These 'brand pillars' are the touchstones for all marketing decisions and inform the SACVB on creative decisions regarding the brand.

While some destination brand strategists are careful to emphasise that destination branding is more than a logo or a tagline (Knapp & Sherwin, 2005), these brand elements can be important tools in the development of brand execution. The SACVB has developed a series of tools that provide symbolic representation of their brand. They include a` carefully crafted tagline, symbols that immediately convey the essence of the brand, and specific colours that are associated with the brand.

San Antonio chose 'Deep. In the heart.' as its tagline, borrowing words from a popular song and adding new context and dimensions to their meaning. The song 'Deep in the heart of Texas' was written in 1941 and first recorded by Perry Como; Gene Autrey made the song famous, and today it is an 'unofficial' anthem for Texas that is sung at baseball and football games – with its catchy, familiar chorus, the song is even taught to young children and is part of the cultural fabric of the United States. In adopting 'Deep. In the heart.' for San Antonio, the SACVB co-opts the easily recognisable statement that adds value to the campaign. The statement itself provides a springboard to explore deeper meanings associated with 'deep' and the 'heart.' 'The branding pays tribute to the heartfelt connection among both residents and visitors to San Antonio, a connection that differentiate the city… through the campaign's copy, the river is repositioned as a "bloodline" that "links key attractions in the downtown corridor and throughout the entire San Antonio region" (SACVB, 2008).

Symbols and graphic identities are used by marketers to represent the brand and create immediate mental connections to deeper association. San Antonio has adopted as their brand symbol a specially stylised quatrefoil (Figure 20.1). The symbol, immediately reminiscent of the Spanish influences of San Antonio's past, has deeper meaning in the context of the destination brand development. The SACVB describes the symbol in the following way:

> Its origins combine world lore, legend and legacy in much the same way as San Antonio itself. Historically, structurally, symbolically, spiritually and artistically, the shape carries significance and meaning. It is most recognised as the shape of a four leaf clover. According to legend, each leaflet of the four leaf clover represents a specific area of good fortune for the finder: hope, faith, love, and luck. By adopting the quatrefoil as the shape of the San Antonio brand, we honour (and intrinsically celebrate) the four specific pillars of the brand: People, Pride, Passion and Promise (2008).

Figure 20.1 The San Antonio quatrefoil logo

The SACVB also determined a colour palette that represents the brand. The primary colour for the logo is 'corazon,' a rich red that was chosen to show the 'heart' of San Antonio. Other program colours reflect land, architecture, and vibrant colours that are indigenous to San Antonio. These symbolic elements – the quatrefoil, the colour, and the tagline 'Deep. In the Heart' – provide immediate context to all other marketing elements and differentiate imagery through the associations to the brand.

In creating the advertising that would lead the brand roll-out, the SACVB found that using local people in the executions best conveyed the brand's four pillars – People, Pride, Passion, and Promise. These people, chosen as representatives of the destination, are either prominent in the local community or have national recognition in their chosen fields. These brand 'ambassadors' have connections with travel experiences or benefits sought by the traveller when visiting the destination; their stories endorse brand messages (Figure 20.2). People in the advertisement include Gini Garcia, a glass artist; Dave Stewart, director at the Alamo; Jorge Cortez, a successful local restaurateur; and Bill Rogers, a golf professional, to name a few. These people personify the brand and highlight key aspects of the brand messaging.

IMPORTANCE OF THE BRAND 'CREATIVE'

San Antonio's primary target market, affluent urban dwellers from major metropolitan cities in the United States, is the focus for many consumer products – all competing for the same discretionary dollars. No matter if their annual marketing budget is $10,000 or 10,000,000, marketers for these products face the same challenge – generating sales from their target market. In the meantime, consumers are overwhelmed by the messages and increasingly looking for ways to 'tune out' the messages that bombard them. Given this competitive environment, San Antonio – with a relatively modest marketing budget – must not only have its strategy right but creative executions of the brand strategy to capture the attention of these sophisticated consumers and stimulate behaviour.

While focus on the planning and strategy issues associated with destination branding is easy, one must recognise the importance of the 'art' of branding. The creative executions of the San Antonio brand were designed to convey the 'feeling' of San Antonio. It is relevant to note that many consumer brands are built on the emotional associations to the brand as well as attributes and functional benefits. As Jeff Miraglia, creative director for the brand, states, 'Destination branding requires the perfect marriage of strategy and creative execution. The brand creative interprets the brand visually and helps the consumer place the brand in the "mind's eye". The brand creative develops the "sense of place" through look, feel, tone and storytelling. Brand creative reveals the personality of the destination. It shows what is unique and builds emotional connections with the destination' (Miraglia, 2010). Great creative executions for marketing communications that resonate with consumers and other stakeholders are a critical success factor for effective brand strategies. Such executions breathe life into strategies, stimulate behavioural responses

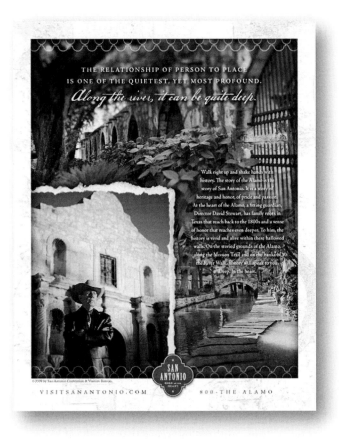

Figure 20.2 Advertisements based on the new branding. These advertisements show executions of the campaign used for the US leisure market.

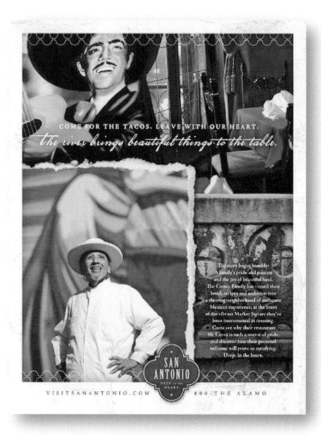

Figure 20.2   Cont'd

from markets, and help stakeholders see the vision for the future. Few brand strategies survive poorly received brand creative executions.

POSITIONING THE BRAND: MARKETING COMMUNICATIONS

In addition to being strategists, DMOs are the primary drivers of the brand positioning. They develop marketing materials and campaigns designed around the brand identity and lead the destination by example. Brand identity provides the DMO with a solid foundation for destination marketing decisions designed to position the brand. From the foundation, the destination marketing team can determine which elements of the identity will have the greatest impact on the chosen target market. Positioning is the process of establishing select brand elements in the mind of the consumer. Ries and Trout (2001), the authors recognised for creating the term, describe 'positioning' as 'what you do to the mind of the prospect. That is, you position the product in the mind of the prospect.' The strength of this foundation allows the destination to remain true to the core values/brand pillars while adapting specific campaigns to select target groups.

In considering the possible tools available to marketers to position their destination, one must consider the ways in which image is created. Image creation takes place as the result of a number of image creation agents. Gartner (1993) provides one of the most commonly used frameworks for examining how image is created. His model identifies three distinct types of image formation agents: induced agents, autonomous agents, and organic agents. Within the 'Induced' category, he identifies the traditional form of advertising (Overt Induced 1), information such as brochures received from distribution channel members (Overt Induced 2), personal endorsements delivered by traditional advertising (Covert Induced 1), and endorsements received through travel/lifestyle media as a result of marketing activity undertaken by the destination (Covert Induced 2). Within the 'Autonomous' category, he notes that both news and popular culture impact destination image formation. The 'Organic' category includes information sought from friends and relatives (solicited organic) and their unsought opinions (unsolicited organic) as well as the experience of the actual visitation to the destination (organic). The combined effect of these image formation agents on a given consumer creates the destination image.

Complicating the issue is the interaction of the image formation factors. Most obviously, if a consumer has visited the destination and experienced it first hand (organic image factor), he or she will interpret other image development factors differently from someone who has not visited the destination. As with other consumer products and services, the customer experience itself strongly influences perceptions of the brand. Destination image impacts behaviour previsit, during the visit and postvisit (Tasci & Gartner, 2007). The brand strategist must balance positioning designed to introduce the destination and stimulate visitation with messages designed to support loyalty and repeat visitation. The brand strategist also must ensure that there is congruence between the brand as it is projected and the actual destination experience.

A challenge for destination marketers is that little research reflects the relative importance of these image creation factors. As Hanlan and Kelly (2005) note, 'it is a significant limitation to our understanding of destination image formation that there has been little research on the relative importance of the various factors associated with image formation.' Nevertheless, there is ample evidence that consumers trust advertising claims least and that 'word of mouth' has a high level of consumer impact. From the brand strategist's perspective, that means that the image creation factors they have most control over have the least influence. With limited budgets, DMOs have traditionally embraced marketing that limits their control but maximises their reach. Public relations, for instance, has long been a staple of the marketing mix of DMOs and has been shown to be an effective use of marketing resources (Dore & Crouch, 2003). Like many DMOs, the SACVB has a communications department focused exclusively on influencing stories by travel journalists and other media representatives. SACVB has also begun marketing activities in social networks and websites that encourage user-generated content. Brand-related content has been included on YouTube, TripAdvisor, Flicker, and Twitter with positive initial responses.

As evident from the image creation factors, there are many image creation agents. The DMO's brand positioning is only one contributor to the consumer's perception of the destination. As such, the DMO must use its resources in the most effective manner. As a result, SACVB integrates the San Antonio branding in all marketing communications. The consistency of messaging across a wide variety of media reinforces the core brand pillars. San Antonio launched their marketing communication with a series of magazine advertisements in travel and lifestyle magazines including *Condé Nast Traveller*, *Travel + Leisure*, *Bon Appétit*, *Gourmet*, *Food + Wine*, *Travel and Leisure Golf*, *Departures*, *Architectural Digest*, *Southern Living*, *Midwest Living*, *Texas Monthly*, and AARP magazine. Subsequent phases of the campaign included similar magazines and added Texas newspapers to the media mix.

In conjunction with brand advertisements, the SACVB sponsored 'advertorial' in several of these magazines. 'Advertorial' applies a magazine article style to paid messaging in a way that consumers are able to receive detailed information on the destination in a format that supports the brand messaging. Most magazines will note 'special advertising section' on the page, but the page is formatted to be read as an article. The SACVB also placed television advertisements in the Denver metropolitan area and aired the destination video 'The San Antonio Story,' in conjunction with televised San Antonio events. This paid advertising provides the destination brand strategist greatest control over the message projected to consumers. The SACVB also produces a number of marketing tools that provided targeted mediums to reach information-seeking consumers. The SACVB website, the 'opt-in' newsletter, the Travel and Leisure Guide, and the 'Lure' brochure each enable the SACVB to communicate the brand identity.

As the internet and social networking have increased consumers' ability to communicate their experiences to large audiences, creating the so called 'e-WOM' effect, at least two things are becoming more important. First, DMOs must embrace the fact that if their brand positioning is aligned with the brand experience, they stand to gain much by losing 'control' of their messaging and encouraging visitors to share their experience online. Second, it is increasingly clear that DMOs must ensure that their brand position reflects their brand experience so that any third party e-WOM supports the brand. A viral video that contradicts the positioning can be a serious detriment to the brand.

POSITIONING THE BRAND: THE BRAND EXPERIENCE

Marketing communications is important but time at the destination will strongly impact beliefs about the brand. The destination itself is a critical part of brand image development. The experience at the destination must support and reinforce brand messaging. Destination branding requires an integrated approach to marketing, utilising not only marketing communications but product issues as well. This comprehensive marketing approach includes marketing communications as well as activities that impact the destination experience itself. Issues such as workforce development, urban planning, and investment strategies to name a few become 'brand-related' actions. San Antonio has recognised that for the brand to resonate with consumers, the brand positioning must be completely aligned with the visitor experience. The SACVB recognises that all components of the marketing mix can be used to support the branding experience. For this reason, SACVB hosted a series of meetings to explain the brand and how organisations can integrate it into their marketing and their company culture. The SACVB team also provides advice and support materials to individual companies to encourage the adoption of brand elements.

The destination is an important medium to reinforce brand messaging. With 25 million visitors to the city each year and learning first hand about the San Antonio brand, SACVB uses the city itself to reinforce brand messages. Brand banners are hung along main thoroughfares and, with support from the city and merchants, San Antonio branding is placed in empty shop fronts and other prominent locations across the city itself. In an innovative use of otherwise unused space, San Antonio is using empty shop fronts as a canvas to display brand communications.

ALIGNING DESTINATION MARKETING TO SUPPORT THE BRAND DEVELOPMENT

DMOs are only one agent within the destination system that undertakes destination marketing activities. To varying degrees, many of the actors in the destination promote the destination to consumers. Those destination actors include organisations such as attractions, lodging operators, and tour operators. Airlines, rail, and other travel providers also may take an active role in marketing the destination. In addition, tourism marketing organisations such as travel wholesalers, travel agents, and other distribution channel members promote the destination as well. The sum of the expenditure by these other agents on these destination marketing may greatly exceed the marketing resources of the DMO. It is clearly an advantage to the DMO's positioning goals if these destination marketing goals can be aligned with brand positioning.

San Antonio has recognised the opportunity and actively engages with destination partners to encourage adoption of the branding materials. This process takes place in two key ways: (1) internal destination marketing communications designed to encourage participation in the brand promotions efforts and (2) creation of marketing materials designed to encourage use of the brand elements in a way that is consistent with the brand identity.

One should note that the SACVB uses these tools to influence destination partners' activities but cannot direct them to do so. These organisations use brand elements because they see the value in communicating a consistent positive message. The SACVB 'markets' these benefits to the destination stakeholders through regular communication and interaction. Kotler, Bowens and Makens (2003, p. 666) define internal marketing as 'marketing by a service firm to train effectively and motivate its customer contact employees and all supporting service people to work as a team to provide customer satisfaction.' The DMO is undertaking internal marketing to the destination system or internal destination marketing to encourage the destination actors to 'work as a team' to meet the goals of the destination. In some ways, the inclusive approach of the brand development incorporates elements of internal marketing in that stakeholders receive regular communication of the brand creation process.

The SACVB recognises that it cannot control all marketing communication generated by tourism organisations associated with its destination and so they make brand materials available to third parties. In so doing, they significantly extend their ability to influence the marketing of these third parties. The brand toolbox created by the SACVB and available to its stakeholders includes a wide range of high-quality images, banner ads for websites, and descriptive text. The SACVB also partners with stakeholders providing resources and

Figure 20.3 Advertisements for the American meetings market in the United States and the Mexican leisure market.

Figure 20.3   Cont'd

guidance for incorporating San Antonio branding into their own marketing materials.

BRAND EXTENSION

The first phase of the branding campaign was developed for the core domestic tourism markets. Following the roll out to the domestic market, the campaign was adapted to the American meetings market and then the Mexican leisure market (Figures 20.3 and 20.4). In each case, brand executions were modified slightly to meet the needs of the target market.

As noted previously, the meetings market is an important part of San Antonio's visitor portfolio and that market was a key driver for the development of the new branding. The lack of consumer awareness in key markets on the West Coast and along the East Coast corridor was seen to be an impediment to growth in the meetings market. Research conducted by the SACVB showed

Figure 20.4 Adapting the logo for different markets. The quatrefoil logo is flexible for use in a variety of contexts. The examples show the quatrefoil design used for the United States leisure market, the meetings market, and the Mexican leisure travel market.

Table 20.1 Destination brand extension matrix

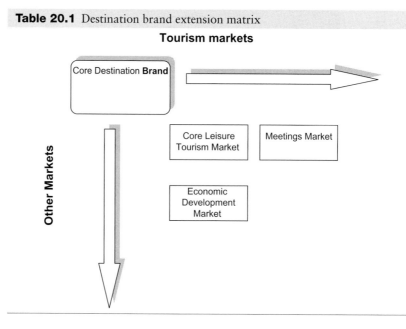

that weakness in consumer awareness impacted the group business as most decision-makers are based in New York, New Jersey, Philadelphia, Chicago, San Francisco, and Los Angeles (White, 2010). Unlike the consumer market, the meetings market is best characterised by a business-to-business sales process. Recognising the needs of the business decision-maker, the SACVB has developed specific marketing materials to meet the information needs of this market yet nevertheless retain the elements of the brand.

Similarly, SACVB has adopted the branding to meet the needs of international markets. Mexico is San Antonio's largest international market, and advertisements have been developed for magazine placement using imagery and story copy designed to appeal to the Mexican market. In addition, the tagline was modified to recognise San Antonio's Texas heritage and accentuate that aspect of the brand architecture.

As is often the case 'success breeds success' and that has been the case with the San Antonio destination brand. Many stakeholder groups have been closely associated with the development of the brand. That familiarity with brand development reduces the barriers to adopting the brand that are often seen by other San Antonio government departments. In addition, recognising the extension of the brand reinforces the overall brand strategy. The SACVB devotes internal resources to support the brand extension process to other government departments. This support ensures the brand is used in ways that are aligned with the SACVB strategy. Successful destination branding can be extended beyond tourism markets to a variety of other markets that impact community life (Table 20.1).

MEASURING DESTINATION BRANDING ACTIVITY

It is a management maxim that 'you can't manage what you can't measure.' Clearly, brand marketers must have a set of metrics to determine the effectiveness and efficiency of their brand marketing. If branding is the deliberate development of specific associations based on a predetermined plan within the minds of the target market, then the measurement of brand development effectiveness is straight forward. Brand marketers must measure the level of awareness of key brand elements within the chosen targets and then track changes in those levels as the brand marketing progresses. Destination branding measurement incorporates several key components including a clear understanding of destination image, specific brand identity elements that are being actively communicated, and longitudinal measures of the change in market perception of the brand against those elements. Additionally, changes in behavioural responses to the image are also tracked. SACVB's brand tracking incorporates measures that gauge impact at several points in the branding process. DMOs rarely undertake marketing activities that are purely brand building. Most destination brand campaigns must achieve tactical objectives, such as generating responses to specific offers, while contributing to the brand development. One of the key benefits of branding is the increased efficiency the branding provides marketing communication. In this respect, destination marketers must measure campaign return on investment and look to increase campaign efficiency based on the growth of the brand.

The SACVB tracks key elements of the destination image and notes changes in perceptions of elements that are part of the brand positioning. Based on this research significant improvements were noted in destination features including 'a relaxing or romantic atmosphere, unique atmosphere and experience, many attractions within easy walking distance.' In addition, awareness of the destination increased and the appeal of San Antonio improved in all but one market where the brand marketing took place. Finally, SACVB conducts regular conversion studies of marketing campaigns to determine the number of consumers who have requested information and then decided to travel to the destination.

CONCLUSION

The San Antonio branding case study provides a comprehensive examination of the components of effective branding campaigns. In developing the campaign, the SACVB tied brand goals to strategic destination goals, engaged extensively with stakeholders and took into consideration not only the target market but also local businesses, government, and residents. The SACVB tapped sources of local pride and identity and developed a communication strategy and creative execution that appealed to both locals and visitors. Scott White, the Executive Director of the SACVB, recognised the leadership role of the SACVB and the personal commitment required of him as the brand champion. The brand identity was developed with flexibility to allow brand positioning in many target markets: domestic and international, leisure, and meetings/conventions. The result was a brand identity, described in the four brand pillars of People, Pride, Passion, and Promise that have become the foundation of an effective campaign.

In executing the brand campaign, the SACVB recognised that it was competing with the world and ensured that their creative executions of the brand were world class. Every element of marketing communication was integrated with the brand to ensure maximum impact by the marketing budget. The SACVB recognised that by creating tools and relinquishing some control it could extend the reach of the campaign. Perhaps most important, the SACVB recognised that destination branding is far more than marketing communication and worked to ensure the destination itself was aligned with the brand. Finally, the SACVB set in place a comprehensive set of measures to ensure that results of destination branding could be assessed. Today, the current campaign is approaching its third year and the destination brand strategists for San Antonio continue to work to ensure the campaign continues to deliver for the tourism industry and people of San Antonio.

ACKNOWLEGDMENTS

The author gives special thanks to the San Antonio Convention and Visitors Bureau, particularly Scott White and Sandy Smith, for their cooperation in the writing of this case. Thanks are also extended to Jeff Miraglia of Mindset Inc. for his insights into the development of the brand elements

References

Aaker, D. (1991). *Managing brand equity: Capitalizing on the value of a brand name*. New York: Free Press.

Aaker, D. (1996). *Building strong brands*. New York: Free Press.

Aaker, D., & Joachimsthaler, E. (2000). *Brand leadership*. United Kingdom: Simon and Schuster.

Anon. (July 18, 2000). City of San Antonio office of cultural affairs previews cultural tourism campaign. *Business Wire*.

Baker, B. (2007). *Destination branding for small cities*. Oregon: Creative Leap Books.

Baker, M., & Cameron, E. (2008). Critical success factors in destination marketing. *Tourism and Hospitality Research*, *8*(2), 79–97.

Buhalis, D. (2000). Marketing the competitive destination of the future. *Tourism Management*, *21*, 97–116.

Butler, R., & Stefl, M. (2008). *San Antonio: The economic impact of San Antonio's hospitality industry*. San Antonio: SAHLA, AAHA, SACVB.

Chon, K. S. (1992). Self image/destination image congruity. [Research Note], *Annals of Tourism Research*, *19* pp. 360–376.

Day, J. (2005). *Branding nations as tourism destinations in the USA: The Australian experience*. Unpublished PHD Thesis Australia: James Cook University Townsville.

Dore, L., & Crouch, G. (2003). Promoting destinations: an exploratory study of publicity programs used by National Tourist Organizations. *Journal of Vacation Marketing*, *9*(2), 137–151.

Echtner, C., & Ritchie, J. (1991). The meaning and measurement of destination image. *Journal of Tourism Studies*, *2*(2), 2–12.

Ekinci, Y. (2003). From destination image to destination branding: an emerging area of research. *e-Review of Tourism Research (eRTR)*, *1*(2), 21–24.

Gartner, W. C. (1993). Image formation process. *Journal of Travel and Tourism Marketing*, *2*(2/3), 191–215.

Hall, J. (2004). Branding Britain. *Journal of Vacation Marketing*, *10*(2), 171–185.

Hanlan, J., & Kelly, S. (2005). Image formation, information sources and an iconic Australian tourist destination. *Journal of Vacation Marketing*, *11*(2), 163–177.

Interbrand. (2009). *Best global brands 2009: The definitive guide to the world's most valuable brands*. London: Interbrand.

Keller, K. (1993). Conceptualizing, measuring and managing customer based brand equity. *Journal of Marketing*, *57*(1), 1–22.

Keller, K. (1998). *Strategic brand management*. New Jersey: Prentice Hall.

Knapp, D., & Sherwin, G. (2005). *Destination brandscience*. Washington DC: IACVB.

Kotler, P., Bowen, J., & Makens, J. (2003). *Marketing for hospitality and tourism: International edition*. New Jersey: Prentice Hall.

Kotler, P., Haider, D., & Rein, I. (1993). *Marketing places: Attracting investment, industry and tourism to cities, states and nations*. New York: Free Press.

Kotter, J. (1996). *Leading change*. Boston, MA: Harvard Business School Press.

Miraglia, J. (2010). President – Mindset Inc. In J. Day (Ed.). (Interview ed.) San Antonio.

Morgan, N., & Pritchard, A. (2002). Contextualising destination branding. In N. Morgan, A. Pritchard, & R. Pride (Eds.), *Destination branding: Creating the unique destination proposition* Oxford: Butterworth Heinemann.

Murphy, L., Benckendorff, P., & Moscardo, G. (2007). Linking travel motivation, tourist self image and destination brand personality. *Journal of Travel and Tourism Marketing*, *22*(2), 45–59.

Pike, S. (2002). Destination image analysis – a review of 142 papers from 1973 to 2000. *Tourism Management*, *23*, 541–549.

Pritchard, A., & Morgan, N. (1998). Mood marketing – the new destination branding strategy: a case for wales the brand. *Journal of Vacation Marketing*, *4*(3), 215–229.

Ries, A., & Trout, J. (2001). *Positioning: The battle for your mind*. New York: McGraw Hill.

Ryan, C. (2002). The politics of branding cities and regions: the case of New Zealand. In N. Morgan, A. Pritchard, & R. Pride (Eds.), *Destination branding: Creating the unique destination proposition*. Oxford: Butterworth-Heinemann.

SACVB. (2006). *Destination SA: Strategic planning for visitor industry growth in San Antonio*. San Antonio: SACVB.

SACVB. (2008). San Antonio brand launch publication. San Antonio San Antonio Visitors and Convention Bureau.

SACVB. (2010). *2010 San Antonio visitors and convention bureau business development plan*. San Antonio San Antonio Visitors and Convention Bureau.

Sirgy, M., & Su, C. (2000). Destination image, self congruity and travel behavior: toward an integrative model. *Journal of Travel Research*, *38*, 340–352.

Tasci, A., & Gartner, W. (2007). Destination image and its functional relationships. *Journal of Travel Research*, *45*(4), 413–425.

White, S. (2010). CEO In J. Day (Ed.).

C H A P T E R

21

Country brands and identity: Slovenia

Maja Konecnik Ruzzier

INTRODUCTION

Destination or country branding is becoming an increasingly topical issue that has gained considerable importance in recent years (Cai, 2002; Konecnik, 2004; Konecnik & Gartner, 2007; Morgan & Pritchard, 2002; Pike, 2009). The theoretical approach of country branding has its roots in approaches designed for product brands. Although there has been considerable debate on the issue (O'Shaughnessy & O'Shaughnessy, 2000), a consensus has emerged that the fundamentals of branding approaches and ideas can also be applied to destinations (Cai, 2002; Konecnik & Gartner, 2007). However, considerable care is required in transferring product brand knowledge to other types of brands (de Chernatony & Dall'Olmo Riley, 1999), and this is especially important in the context of destination brands, which developed and have to be managed differently from other brands (Hankinson, 2007; Konecnik & Go, 2008; Pike, 2005). Destination brands are often seen as similar to corporate brands (Hankinson, 2007), although more complex particularly due to the large number of stakeholders influencing them (Buhalis, 2000; Buncle, Chapter 19 in this volume; Konecnik & Go, 2008; Morgan, Pritchard, & Piggott, 2002, 2003; Ryan, 2002).

After declaring independence in 1991, Slovenia sought to position itself in the world, but its early uncoordinated tactical brand building steps were taken without a brand plan. This chapter discusses the development of the country brand 'I Feel Slovenia,' which was undertaken in 2007 as the first systematic branding approach in the country (Konecnik Ruzzier, Lapajne, Drapal & de Chernatony, 2009). The process of developing the brand was complex and consisted of four phases, which are discussed in turn. During Slovenia's brand development, all relevant stakeholder groups were involved, which is a vital but often overlooked and under-researched aspect of the complex process of country branding.[1]

---

[1] The author contributed to the 'I feel Slovenia' brand development as an external brand consultant and this chapter draws on that involvement

© 2011 Published by Elsevier Ltd. All rights reserved.
DOI: 10.1016/B978-0-08-096930-5.10021-7

In fact, one of the biggest challenges in destination branding lies in the ability to include different influential stakeholders in the building process and the brand implementation. The literature argues that truly powerful destination brands are linked with internal stakeholders who have a clear idea of what their destination represents and how it differs from other destinations (Morgan & Pritchard, 2002). In this chapter, destination brand building is approached primarily from an identity perspective, and I discuss how a brand is perceived by its internal stakeholder groups (Konecnik & Go, 2008; Konecnik Ruzzier & Ruzzier, 2009) – although when building a brand, internal stakeholders must also keep in mind the perceptions of external stakeholders (Konecnik & Gartner, 2007). Country branding involves numerous internal stakeholder groups, from country managers and marketers employed at the governmental level to the local residents who live the brand, and I consider these different stakeholders in the following pages. The chapter therefore:

- Discusses the development of the country brand for Slovenia as an example of the first systematic branding approach of a newly independent country;
- Examines the ability of a destination brand group to include different stakeholders in the building process and the brand implementation.

SLOVENIA AND ITS ATTEMPTS TO BUILD A COUNTRY BRAND

Slovenia is a relatively young European country which declared its independence in 1991, previously having been one of the Yugoslav republics. Having appeared on the world map as an independent country, it was faced with the need to introduce itself to the world with an appropriate marketing strategy that would differentiate it from the crowd of its competitors. Slovenia lies in the heart of Europe, where the Alps face the Pannonian plain and the Mediterranean meets the mysterious Karst. Its neighbouring countries are Austria, Hungary, Croatia, and Italy. Encompassing just 20,256 km^2 and a population of a little less than 2 million, it is one of the smallest countries in the world. But although small, Slovenia is distinguished by extreme diversity in terms of both geography and history as well as with regard to its culture.

Since its history as an independent country is less than two decades old, Slovenia can be characterised as one of the so-called young countries. Nevertheless, the short post-independence period brought forth several important events. To mention but a few, Slovenia became a member of the United Nations Organisation and in 2004 joined the European Union and NATO. It was one of the first new accession members to introduce the European currency (Euro) in 2007 and successfully held the European Union presidency in 2008. In terms of development, Slovenia ranks close to older European Union members.

Despite a relatively short official history, the country's cultural and historical background is extremely rich. Over the centuries, Slovenia always belonged to larger empires or countries but has nonetheless continually preserved and pursued its identity, as is still evident in Slovenian life today. Thus, the two aspects which distinguish Slovenia and have played a role in the development of its brand are first its history (which poses major challenges as a 'new' country) and second its rich geographic, historical, and cultural diversity, which has emerged over the centuries leaving a deep imprint on Slovenia's identity and citizens.

Slovenia's previous marketing activities can be discussed in terms of three-time periods (Table 21.1). The first campaign, 'Slovenia – my country' centred primarily on fostering the self-confidence of Slovenians in relation to country development and marketing, and by the time it was replaced in 1996 it had found its way into the hearts of Slovenians. In contrast, the slogan 'Tourism is people' encouraged residents to implement the Slovenia brand in the domestic market, while the slogan 'On the sunny side of the Alps' was aimed at the foreign market. The entire campaign was accompanied with a linden leaf logo that represented a symbol of Slovenian identity. Launched more than 20 years ago, this still remains the most memorable country marketing campaign in Slovenia.

In 1996, the linden leaf was replaced by a bundle of flowers, which was in use until 2006. The flowers logo was accompanied by at least five slogans, none of which were as memorable as the first campaign's slogans. The most frequently used one was 'Slovenia – The green piece of Europe'. In 2004, with Slovenia's accession to the European Union, the slogan 'Slovenia invigorates' was chosen, and this campaign constituted the first attempt to establish a uniform brand and slogan not only in the field of tourism (which had been the case in previous two attempts), but also in other areas. The campaign was discontinued in 2006, since foreigners as well as Slovenians had many difficulties understanding the campaign and the slogan.

All these campaigns aimed at building the brand of Slovenia and strove to present the country by focussing on visual elements (slogan and logo). However, none of them were founded on a credible narrative of the country,

Table 21.1 Marketing activities regarding the brand of Slovenia from 1991 (1986) to 2006

Period	Marketing activities	Field	Slogan	Logo
1986–1996	Marketing campaign 'Slovenia – my country'	Tourism	'Tourism is people' – domestic market 'On the sunny side of the Alps' – foreign market	Linden leaf
1996–2004	Separate marketing activities	Tourism	More slogans; 'Slovenia – the green piece of Europe' used most commonly	Bundle of flowers
2004–2006	Marketing campaign 'Slovenia invigorates'	All fields	'Slovenia invigorates'	Bundle of flowers

nor were they based on a strategic plan for the long-term brand management and marketing of Slovenia. Furthermore, such frequent slogan changes were met with opposition and negativity, as Slovenian residents felt that future attempts of brand development would fail to be successful.

In addition to these attempts to build the brand of Slovenia, several additional marketing activities were prepared for specific purposes and aimed at specific media although they were not designed in line with an overall brand direction. One of these was the advertisement for Slovenia by the Slovenian Tourist Board on CNN Europe in 2006. The advertisement was accompanied by a slogan 'Slovenia, a diversity to discover,' which was used as a 'one-off' in this campaign and the bundle of flowers, Slovenia's official logo at the time, was replaced by the Slovenian flag. The failure to include the logo that had accompanied the country's marketing campaigns since 1996 provoked a broad discussion on how to systematically present the country in the future. The Slovenian government recognised that the country did not just need a new slogan and logo, but a systematic branding strategy to guide future management and marketing activities.

'I FEEL SLOVENIA': THE FIRST SYSTEMATIC BRANDING PROCESS IN SLOVENIAN HISTORY

In 2007 a large-scale project for building the Slovenia brand began. Throughout the process, the latest thinking in country brand development and marketing was followed (Cai, 2002; Morgan et al., 2002, 2003), with the one exception that the government chose and confirmed the slogan I feel Slovenia, which was supposed to be used in the new Slovenia brand the year before launching the process.

Since the process of developing the country brand Slovenia was complex, it is useful to discuss its development in four phases (Figure 21.1), which were systematically followed during the process:

- Phase 1: review and choice of relevant country brand development model(s).
- Phase 2: review of secondary data relevant in identity building for Slovenia.
- Phase 3: collection of primary data following a three-step approach to identity building. During this phase, consideration was given to which stakeholder groups should contribute and all relevant stakeholders who would live the brand were invited.
- Phase 4: development of brand identity based on the findings of the previous phases.

Phase 1: Identification of a country brand identity model

Given the lack of a widely accepted model for country identity building, we found de Chernatony's (2006) model to be best suited to our purpose as it is

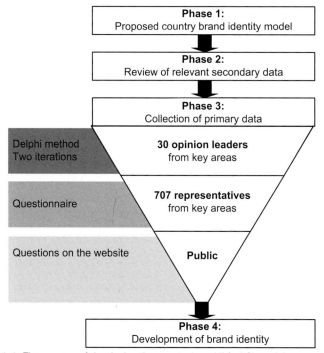

Figure 21.1 The process of developing the country brand 'I feel Slovenia'

easy to communicate, can be understood by diverse stakeholders, and captures the core elements of brand identity. We did, however, expand and revise this to encompass other research in place branding (Buhalis, 2000; Hankinson, 2007; Konecnik & Go, 2008; Morgan et al., 2003; Pike, 2005; Ryan, 2002). We concluded that place identity components include the following brand elements: vision, mission, values, personality, benefits, and distinguishing preferences. These elements constantly interact with each other to fulfill brand promises at the functional, emotional, and experiential level (Keller, 1993; Park, Jaworski, & MacInnis, 1986).

Phase 2: Review of relevant secondary data

We then reviewed all relevant information about Slovenia that might play an important role in its brand building. Starting with a review of the previous efforts to build Slovenia as a brand (outlined above), we considered the internal aspects of brand building. Next, we collected relevant information about the external perspective of the Slovenia brand by reviewing Slovenia's brand equity to outsiders (e.g., Brezovec, Brezovec, & Jancic, 2004; Konecnik, 2004). Finally, we reviewed current and historical strategic documents impacting on Slovenia 'the country brand.'

This phase also included a review of selected country brands, which provided insights into good and bad practises. When selecting the country brands to examine, we considered the following criteria: systematic country brand building, diversity in approaches to developing the country brand, and countries with similar characteristics and circumstances to Slovenia. As the most relevant and best case, we considered the brand of New Zealand (Morgan et al., 2002, 2003), as well as the brand-building practises for Austria, Germany, Switzerland, and Ireland.

Phase 3: Brand research

Having reviewed models of brand building, relevant secondary data and examples of global good practise, we began to consider which of Slovenia's many stakeholder groups to involve in developing the country brand. It was essential to invite the most important stakeholders in the fields of the economy, tourism, culture, science, sports, state, and the civic sphere to take part in defining the Slovenia brand identity. We decided to canvas the opinions of opinion leaders from these key areas and continued widening the circle of participants so that the final phase of brand identity building included the views of its largest stakeholder group – the residents of Slovenia. Therefore, our approach to building the Slovenia brand identity was holistic, as various stakeholders involved in implementing the Slovenia brand were invited to participate in its creation on different levels. In this way, we ensured that the process of Slovenia's identity branding involved as many of its future implementers as possible, since only a brand that is accepted among those who live it has the potential to develop into a strong brand that will add value to the country and thus increase its competitiveness.

A three-step approach was employed to target three different groups of respondents:

1. A Delphi method – a qualitative study with opinion leaders from key areas.
2. A questionnaire – a quantitative study with representatives from selected areas.
3. A web-based questionnaire – a quantitative study for the general public.

The basic elements of a brand identity for Slovenia were developed by means of a Delphi method. We targeted the most relevant opinion leaders and received feedback from 30 opinion leaders. The study was undertaken in two iterations, in each a questionnaire with open-ended questions was sent to respondents via e-mail. The first questionnaire included questions covering the spectrum of all brand elements proposed in the model adopted from de Chernatony (2006). The questions required opinion leaders to express their views about the vision, mission, benefits, and distinguishing preferences of the country of Slovenia, as well as values and personality of Slovenians. At least one question was posed with regard to each proposed brand element. In order to really capture respondents' opinions, some elements were covered by a larger number of more indirect questions. After the results of the first round of the Delphi study were reviewed, the same participants received a second questionnaire. This attempted to harmonise respondents' views in areas where there had been disagreement and to expand their reflections on issues that had not been thoroughly discussed in the first phase.

The second target group of our respondents were representatives from key sectors. We prepared a questionnaire which included closed questions for proposed brand identity elements as well as the socio-demographic characteristics of respondents. The questionnaire comprised two types of questions. The first type evaluated brand identity characteristics by ranking them on a scale from one to five (one being of least importance and five the most important). Several questions required respondents to select one or more answers; some addressed the proposed brand elements and others were based on results from the Delphi interviews. In total we received 707 questionnaires.

While the questionnaire was directed at representatives from key sectors, we also conducted a web-based consultation to obtain perspectives, views, and suggestions from the public. In addition, public opinion was monitored by analysing media publications on the Slovenia brand, reviewing opinions posted on blogs and responses received via e-mail. Such an approach provided additional insights into how the public perceived the branding process itself and the elements that are/should be part of the Slovenia brand identity.

Phase 4: Development of brand identity

The first draft of the brand identity was based on the outcomes of the first three phases outlined above. The draft was sent out to stakeholders in the key sectors for consultation and following incorporation of the feedback, the final brand identity for Slovenia emerged.

NEW BRAND 'I FEEL SLOVENIA'

The Slovenia brand was thus developed very much in conjunction with a range of key stakeholders who largely determined the foundations on which the brand identity elements were built. The general consensus was that the Slovenia brand should convey nature and therefore a range of natural concepts served as a starting point for developing the story of the Slovenia brand (Figure 21.2).

The distinguishing attributes that are seen to differentiate Slovenia from other countries include unspoiled nature, a 'crossroads' of various natural and cultural impacts in an exceptionally small space, safety, and the importance and diversity of the Slovene language. The consultation exercises identified the Slovenian personality as typified by a desire for recognition and tenacity – hardworking individuals who like to receive praise for their work. The Slovenian people self-identified their values as based around family and health, attachment to their local environment, and responsibility toward the environment and fellow human beings. These features provide a foundation for the benefits that Slovenia offers to its residents and visitors: it is accessible and characterised by a quality of life that is more easily attainable than elsewhere. A typical Slovenian lifestyle promotes activity and the wish to contribute and make a difference, plus the benefits of Slovenia also include being in touch with nature and the consequential awareness of environmental responsibility.

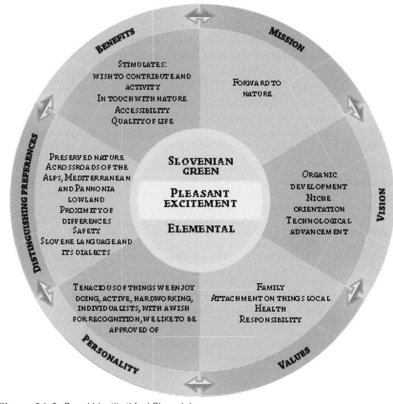

Figure 21.2 Brand identity 'I feel Slovenia'   Source: The brand of Slovenia, 2007.

Indeed it is this continuous contact with nature that forms the cornerstone of Slovenia's mission, inherent in the phrase 'forward with nature.' Slovenia's vision builds on preserving nature through niche-oriented economy and technological advancement. Slovenia will thus move forward with nature and transfer this mission to other countries and regions. The 'Slovenian brand experience' relates to the elemental, communicated through a limited number of 'elemental' symbols that are widely perceived as typically Slovenian. This return to the elemental can be observed as values and as functional promises and the promised experience is strengthened by the emotional promise. Slovenians hold dear personal qualities of activity, diligence, and individuality; embrace life with excitement; and feel a powerful connection to nature. These are the values encapsulated in the core of the Slovenian identity brand. It can be said that the typical experience of Slovenia is best described as 'green' or so-called Slovenian green; the concept of green thus refers to Slovenia's natural features, Slovenian attitude toward nature and life, and the balanced development that Slovenia is to pursue in the future.

The story of the brand is visualised by the slogan 'I feel Slovenia,' which as I mentioned above was chosen in advance of the branding process. The final visualisation of the 'I feel Slovenia' logo draws from the brand's identity characteristics and although the slogan (and partially the logo) was unusually

Figure 21.3 'I feel Slovenia' logo Source: The brand of Slovenia, 2007.

developed before the identity branding process, both resonated well with Slovenians' perceptions of their country (Figure 21.3). The logo's green colour evokes the typical experience of the Slovenian brand, and its inclined sides convey the sense that opposites create excitement and drive us 'forward with nature.' The slogan itself reflects the main functional promise of an elemental experience for visitors, while at the same time promotes an internal message of patriotism and connection with one's country.

The Slovenian story created from the individual elements bears more significance than the elements themselves and while some elements of the Slovenia brand are similar to those of other nations and countries, it is the combination of these elements and their role in the story that makes Slovenia special and constitutes its brand. The story of Slovenia serves as a basis of the Slovenian experience and should dictate the development of the country so as to provide a consistent, different, and recognisable Slovenian experience. During the 'I feel Slovenia' brand development, considerable efforts were made to tell the Slovenian narrative and ensured that the core message, which was to be communicated at home and abroad, would be clear and simple. We also strove to develop a brand and marketing strategy that would be considerably different from branding strategies applied in other countries, particularly. Above all, the brand values are captured in the experiential promise of the Slovenian green – more than simply a colour, this conveys the entire experience that one enjoys in Slovenia. This identity story is then narrated visually through the slogan and logo which is an enhancement of the brand.

CONCLUSION

Slovenia only gained independence in 1991 and in the initial post-independence period often failed to be recognised abroad or was characterised in ways that did not reflect the actual situation (Konecnik, 2004). Given this situation, it is not surprising that the idea of building Slovenia's brand quickly gained traction. At first, Slovenia attempted to market the country to the best of its abilities, even though there was a considerable lack of knowledge among internal stakeholder groups about how to approach strategic country marketing. The initial development of the country brand was aimed primarily at communicating its visual elements through slogans and logos. Moreover, after the first successful campaign, 'Slovenia – my country,' frequent changes to the marketing strategy, reflected in several slogan changes created much confusion in both Slovenia and abroad.

Recently, however, there has been a concerted effort to comprehensively market the Slovenia brand and a systematic approach to country branding and the development of long-term brand guidelines began in 2007. The outcome is a Slovenian branding approach which stresses the emotional and experiential attractions of the country and not merely the functional attractiveness created by the natural environment (see http://www.slovenia.info/). The Slovenia brand identity development took account of the opinions of the most influential stakeholders in the country, who constitute and form the country brand. Thus, we strove to build the Slovenia brand in a way that would also ensure its future. However, the establishment of the 'I feel Slovenia' brand did not signify the end of work, but its beginning. To ensure the appropriate communication and long-term coordination of the story, the brand needs a manager who can work to improve the Slovenia brand's equity in the eyes of its target groups. This function has been entrusted to the Government Communication Office, while the Slovenian Tourist Board also has an important role in maintaining the new Slovenia brand.

In addition to coherent brand implementation activities on the management level, the Slovenia brand must also be lived by the local people as a country brand can remain strong on a long-term basis only when residents believe in it and consistently live it. It is therefore crucial to ensure that residents are familiar with the Slovenia brand and the indications are that most Slovenian residents have responded well to the initiative. A survey conducted only 6 months after its launch reported a good recognition of the slogan and highly favourable attitudes toward it. On the other hand, the survey also revealed a lack of familiarity with the brand story or the identity characteristics of the new brand, with the exception being the so-called Slovenian green (Petek & Konecnik Ruzzier, 2008).

The Slovenia brand identity is clearly a work in progress. In other words, if 'I feel Slovenia' is to be successful, it needs (1) continuing internal and external communication of the Slovenia brand, (2) political support for the Slovenia brand and its development, and (3) the continued support from Slovenian residents and a commitment by them to endorse and 'live' Slovenia brand elements. Whether the brand of Slovenia does indeed succeed in leading Slovenia on its desired path (as consensually defined by key stakeholders in the new branding process) does not simply depend on Slovenian residents living the brand on their own initiative, however, but also depend on the management of its brand and the ongoing rise of Slovenia's reputation as an appealing place to live, work, and play.

References

Brezovec, A., Brezovec, T., & Jancic, Z. (2004). The interdependence of a country's general and tourism images. In S. Weber (Ed.), *Reinventing a tourism destination: Facing the challenge* (pp. 115–129). Zagreb: Institute for Tourism.

Buhalis, D. (2000). Marketing the competitive destination of the future. *Tourism Management, 21*(1), 97–116.

Cai, L. A. (2002). Cooperative branding for rural destinations. *Annals of Tourism Research*, *29*(3), 720–742.

de Chernatony, L. (2006). *From brand vision to brand evaluation*. Oxford: Butterworth-Heinemann.

de Chernatony, L., & Dall'Olmo Riley, F. (1999). Experts' views about defining service brands and the principles of services branding. *Journal of Business Research*, *46*(2), 181–192.

Hankinson, G. (2007). The management of destination brands: five guiding principles based on recent developments in corporate branding theory. *Journal of Brand Management*, *14*(3), 240–254.

Keller, K. L. (1993). Conceptualizing, measuring, and managing customer-based brand equity. *Journal of Marketing*, *57*, 1–22.

Konecnik, M. (2004). Evaluating Slovenia's image as a tourism destination: a self-analysis process towards building a destination brand. *Journal of Brand Management*, *11*(4), 307–316.

Konecnik, M., & Gartner, W. C. (2007). Customer-based brand equity for a destination. *Annals of Tourism Research*, *34*(2), 400–421.

Konecnik, M., & Go, F. (2008). Tourism destination brand identity: the case of Slovenia. *Journal of Brand Management*, *15*(3), 177–189.

Konecnik Ruzzier, M., Lapajne, P., Drapal, A., & de Chernatony, L. (2009). slCelostni pristop k oblikovanju identitete znamke I feel Slovenia. *Akademija MM*, *9*(13), 51–62.

Konecnik Ruzzier, M., & Ruzzier, M. (2009). A two-dimensional approach to branding: integrating identity and equity. In L. A. Cai, W. C. Gartner, & A. Munar (Eds.), *Tourism branding: Communities in action, bridging tourism theory and practice* (Vol. 1, pp. 65–73). Bingley: Emerald.

Morgan, N., & Pritchard, A. (2002). Contextualizing destination branding. In N. Morgan, A. Pritchard, & R. Pride (Eds.), *Destination branding: Creating the unique destination proposition* (pp. 10–41). Oxford: Butterworth-Heinemann.

Morgan, N., Pritchard, A., & Piggot, R. (2002). New Zealand, 100% pure. The creation of a powerful destination niche brand. *Journal of Brand Management*, *9*(4-5), 335–354.

Morgan, N. J., Pritchard, A., & Piggott, R. (2003). Destination branding and the role of the stakeholders: the case of New Zealand. *Journal of Vacation Marketing*, *9*(3), 285–299.

O'Shaughnessy, J., & O'Shaughnessy, N. J. (2000). Treating the nation as a brand: some neglected issues. *Journal of Macromarketing*, *20*(1), 56–64.

Park, C. W., Jaworski, B. J., & MacInnis, D. J. (1986). Strategic brand concept-image management. *Journal of Marketing*, *50*(4), 135–145.

Petek, N., & Konecnik Ruzzier, M. (2008). slUvajanje znamke "I feel Slovenia" ali "Slovenijo Čutim": Odziv prebivalcev Slovenije. *Akademija MM*, *8*(12), 49–60.

Pike, S. (2005). Tourism destination branding complexity. *Journal of Product & Brand Management*, *14*(4), 258–259.

Pike, S. (2009). Destination brand positions of a competitive set of near-home destinations. *Tourism Management*, *30*(6), 858–866.

Ryan, C. (2002). The politics of branding cities and regions: the case of New Zealand. In N. Morgan, A. Pritchard, & R. Pride (Eds.), *Destination branding: Creating the unique destination proposition* (pp. 66–86). Oxford: Butterworth-Heinemann.

Useful websites

http://www.majakonecnik.com/konecnik/dokumenti/File/brandbook_
ifeelslovenia.pdf
http://www.slovenia.info/

CHAPTER

Destination branding and the urban Lexicon: London, New York, and Barcelona

Rosanna Vitiello and Marcus Willcocks

INTRODUCTION

The notion of branding a place – one where we live, work, or visit for pleasure – does not sit happy with many people. As citizens, rather than branding professionals, we tend to understand places as being 'ours' or 'theirs,' belonging to people and with strong emotional connections. By contrast, when we speak of branding, it often implies a personality applied by 'the invisible other.'

When people talk about a place, they talk of its character, rather than its brand, as if it were a person – a friend or acquaintance rather than a conceptual entity created in a boardroom far away. For example, you could describe Paris as 'charming' and 'romantic' and San Francisco as 'laid-back' or 'cool.' Our Urban Lexicons street workshops (Vitiello & Willcocks, 2010, based on the research project undertaken in 2007–2009) saw that people associate all manner of personal attributes to urban spaces and details, including how 'loving,' 'welcoming,' or 'full of life' a place may be. Like people, some were seen as more 'charming' than others, from a garden 'jammed full of personality and off-the-wall kookiness' to a station that was 'soulless and slightly alienating.' [1]

If most of us see a place as a living character more than a brand, one of the first ways we get to know that character is through its streets – specifically, through the urban details that make up that streetscape: a well-placed bench, a tended flowerbed, a cracked pavement, and a vandalised door. These urban details are the ways in which a physical environment reveals its personality. While every city shares roads, crowds, and buildings in common, what differentiates one place from another are the details that define these structures; the clothes a place is dressed in, perhaps, more than its physique.

---

[1] The Urban Lexicons 2008 street workshop results can be found in more detail via the project website: www.urbanlexicons.com and the project report at http://issuu.com/marcus willcocks/docs/urbanlexicons.

© 2011 Published by Elsevier Ltd. All rights reserved.
DOI: 10.1016/B978-0-08-096930-5.10022-9

These tangible elements become synonymous with a place and inform an 'Urban Lexicon,' a vocabulary by which we read, understand, and react to our environment. In this chapter, we explore how the details that dress our public spaces inform people's real perceptions of a place and how place brands can be informed by and contribute to this process.

Place branding often centres on promoting an image of a given destination, elsewhere. A great logo, a memorable slogan, and a quality imagery are all worthwhile. For the perception to hold any meaning as a brand, however, it must emerge from the reality of the place; what is *actually* there. To avoid references to the 'Emperor's New Clothes,' a destination needs a distinct wardrobe that people will recognise, more than a logo on an otherwise invisible outfit. So clearly, to brand a destination it is important that the place have a physical personality to draw from, rather than a conceptual image applied to a lackluster space, as a starting point.

In light of this, we propose a dual call for destination and branding professionals to draw from the character-filled fabric of the city, to define the 'projected brand,' but importantly also to ensure there is significant character-filled fabric to draw upon, to define the 'perceived personality' of a place. The latter of these two helps to establish the character of the location, and the former – the projected brand – conveys and accentuates that perception. The better the city fabric combines and communicates its unique urban details (Unique Urban Details (UUDs) instead of the Unique Selling Proposition (USP)), the better these can be identified and inform the brand personality, which can in turn inspire future details and public spaces of a city. This ensures that the fabric of a place projects a distinct identity in keeping with the brand and establishes a symbiotic relationship between the bottom-up physical character and the top-down brand; each helping to define and develop each other. This chapter therefore:

- explores the 'signs' and urban fabric that influence our feelings about different parts of the city. We reference the *Urban Lexicons* project, initiated in London in 2007, and compare London with New York and Barcelona, cities we have come to know well;
- examines how these cities have succeeded and failed in working with those characteristics to develop and communicate their place brands. We also observe Southampton's *Legible City* project which has made positive steps toward connecting the content of the city and its brand.

THE SIGNS OF A CITY: URBAN LEXICONS AS 'PERCEIVED' PLACE BRANDS

Elsewhere we have argued for the forgotten potential of human-scale urban elements in influencing our impressions of a place and explored how designed and incidental details combine to develop our attitudes toward a place, affecting how we connect emotionally and how we behave toward it (Vitiello & Willcocks, 2006). When walking through a London street, for example, 'one might encounter the crunch of leaves, a whiff of a local greasy spoon, or a brightly painted door.' Such collections of details communicate much to us about the identity of a place. In the words of social ethnographer William H. Whyte (1980) 'The designer sees the whole building – the clean verticals, the horizontals … and so on. The person sitting on the plaza may be quite unaware of such matters. He is more apt to be looking in the other direction: not up at buildings, but at what is going on at eye level.' It is those small elements and daily encounters 'at eye level,' that act as signs that help people build their own picture and opinions of a place. We could say these urban details are like the different words spoken by a city, which associated together form a comprehensible sentence about what it is really like, an 'Urban Lexicon.'

The first strand of the *Urban Lexicons* project (Vitiello & Willcocks, 2010) tested this thinking, aiming to understand what these details might be and unravelling how they make us feel about urban places. Our participants took part in street workshops, visiting four different areas of London. Through in-depth post-workshop interviews, they fed back their emotive reactions toward each space and reported details they picked up on that contributed to these impressions. In each location, the participants looked at particular parks and green spaces, underground stations and travel interchanges, residential streets and housing estates, and street markets and commercial spaces – representative of typical spaces one might encounter in any urban area.

What came back resoundingly were interpretations of *groups of details*, as specific 'signs' of a place's identity. Participants' responses repeatedly alluded to a collection of signs which influenced their reading of each place; the basis for an Urban Lexicon. These included signs of 'character,' 'life,' 'welcome,' 'security,' and 'love' – positive personality traits that appeal to the people visiting and using these places. Our participants also identified the contrasting negatives: signs of 'blandness,' 'lifelessness,' 'exclusion,' 'fear,' and 'neglect.'

To follow, we start to unpack these Urban Lexicons and associated 'signs,' as revealed through our London participants' feedback, plus our own experiences of New York and Barcelona. These insights offer a framework to consider perceptions of place in two ways. First, it reveals one way in which people read their cities – a tool to define the character of a place and inform a place brand. Secondly, it provides examples of urban details that hold positive associations and can communicate a place brand back on the city's streets.

London

Signs of character and blandness

Details that conveyed a sense of 'heritage' were identified as a distinct sign of London's character. Examples include street signs using 'old case and design' that 'say you're in high class central London'; individually cast ceramic tiles with unusual patterns as a 'historical reference' and suggestive of 'a lot more effort involved'; and intricate iron railings which were seen as 'more interesting than modern railings, not because they're decorated, but because they're less utilitarian.' These were seen as clues that tell of the people who live, work, or play in an area, which create a sense of independent character that gives 'no sense of Great Britain plc you get in every town in Britain.' Others include a traditional market cart engraved 'Hiller Bros,' a shop window displaying wigs to suit a particular ethnic style, house doors painted in different colours that 'express the character of the people who live in them. No two people are the same.' Yet at the same time as places evoked character, numerous sites visited in London were seen to suffer from a blandness connected to utilitarian details, such as galvanised metal railings and non-descript street furniture. People described some spaces as 'totally anonymous,' 'lacking any personality whatsoever' stating that they 'could have been anywhere-land.'

Signs of life and welcome

Details that encouraged street life and evidence of London's diverse population were resoundingly appreciated. People were enlivened by the variety of smells, cuisines, and displays in street markets that were 'a mess of personalities rather than some hideously organised thing ... not branded.' Streets that housed 'a real mish-mash of different people' were 'vibrant.' Welcome was seen through details that encouraged public engagement, such as the following recollection in Covent Garden: 'Outside the coffee shop, they've got a bench for people to sit on ... Inside Neal's Yard you've got fridge magnet poetry which invites everyone to participate ... Those are really friendly and inviting details.' Low fences and few road barriers allowed clear lines of sight, inviting people in. In residential areas, such openness allowed parks to be seen as 'an extension of people's front gardens.'

Signs of fear and security

'Security features' were the very elements that communicated a sense that a place was unsafe (Figure 22.1). High steel fences, locked down shutters, and 'no entry' signs instilled a sense of fear, eliciting responses such as 'Steel shutters that are there for security purposes actually create an environment where it doesn't feel safe or friendly or attractive so you don't want to be there as a person' (*Steve*) and 'there was this pole with ... a thousand CCTV cameras ... It made me feel it was a purely utile zone where you're not meant to stay more than half a minute' (*Jon*).

Encountering areas where people were relaxing, finding easily comprehensible spaces, and noting personal touches and elements of trust were details that combated this fear, acting as signs of security. A notable reaction to a public community garden was: 'it was like someone's garden. I felt like it was a place of trust, there were things hanging on the trees. I thought, the place is open, they trust you not to run off with stuff and they're respecting you and you end up respecting them.'

Signs of love and neglect

Signs of love make us fall for a place because they show someone else has loved it first. Personal touches told of going the extra mile. Participants described how 'loads of plants, loads of green things show that people really care about that area' and noted when 'somebody had taken the trouble' to paint a mural to brighten up a space. They picked up on details that had been looked after such as old 'care-worn' benches without 'a speck of graffiti on them; people obviously care.' In contrast, details that showed neglect act as deterrents. Litter dumped in residential areas was described as 'a total disregard to your living environment' and smashed windows were 'soul destroying.'

Figure 22.1 London signs of fear/security: Steel shutters

New York City

Many of the details articulating New York's character are distinctly non-architectural: the ever-present street food vendors, for example, suggest a restless and informal city on the move. Signs of life are revealed through community notice boards in corner delicatessens, laundromats advertising private French lessons, and dog-walking services. The city's efforts to enhance its welcome include the recent formal 'friendlification' of Times Square, seen through the addition of seating and this time it is moveable (read interactive), and outdoor chess tables, synonymous with Washington Square Park, which invite intellectual engagement with strangers (Figure 22.2). In the summer the same can be said of chalk sidewalk notices hand-drawn by locals, which inform passers-by of neighbourhood stoop-sales. Signs of security in New York also come through a sense of trust, such as the pumpkins and chrysanthemums with which homeowners decorate their brownstone stoops (house entrances) in the autumn.

Despite these positive readings of its character, New York's City Commissioner admits years of neglect: 'Until now, [we have] not embraced a broad strategy for developing and caring for the public realm ... Indeed, despite so much change for the better during the city's renaissance of the past several decades, our streetscape remains broadly utilitarian' (NYC DOT, 2009a). This manifests itself in poorly patched-up roads, potholes, and tired street furniture. Yet, the recent program of landscaping plazas, delineated

Figure 22.2 New York City signs of welcome: Times Square has been revived at a human scale

with details such as flower planters, and café style seating and tables are pure signs of love. The thought involved in gearing these spaces toward pedestrians expresses the authorities' new attitude toward caring for public space and the people who use it.

Barcelona

An important part of 'Barcelonés' character is reflected in the chamfered (non-square) corners of the city blocks, most typical to the Eixample area. These create public gathering spaces at each corner plot and importantly act as a strong metaphor for the myriad of social places to stop throughout the city (Figure 22.3). Signs of life can be seen via the 'street armchair' style benches, juxtaposed to create intimate scenarios and encourage positive interaction. These are a clue to people taking more time to pause in public spaces. For pedestrians, Barcelona flings welcoming arms open via its multitude of 'rambla' tree-lined avenues. Wide central spaces are allocated to walkers and cyclists, with narrower lanes divided either side for lower priority motor traffic. Such elements act as simple ways to extend hospitality to a wider range of users in a place. The city's energetic street life maintains a sense of security through natural surveillance, facilitated by seating outside cafes open late into the night. Flexible spaces, such as open plazas with robust but adaptable furniture, encourage a timetable of positive activities throughout the day, linking signs of life and security; one might encounter a game of street football, tourists people-watching or a couple having a neighbourly chat. One sign of Barcelona's love is seen in the effort required to craft the artistic graffiti covering the city's walls. The authorities have shown some

Figures 22.3 Barcelona's signs of character

love back in the lenient attitude toward quality large-scale graffiti and the creative identity it portrays.

Nonetheless, the image of Barcelona is not all positive. Residents in the Ciutat Vella district use their balconies as public soapboxes and flying banners that read 'we want a dignified neighbourhood.' Such signs indicate frustration 'in face of the lack of solutions on the part of the administration' (Raval per Viure, 2009) and the neglect shown to their 'barrio.' Paradoxically, such details in themselves act as signs of love and show community life in striving for a habitable neighbourhood 'where residents can walk without fearing for their security' (Raval per Viure, 2009). Other evident signs of neglect include rows of bent and broken bike carcasses, suggesting remnants of attempted bicycle robberies or poor bike parking provision. In addition, dumped and split rubbish bags that spill out on the streets appear to add an atmosphere of fear; in spite of being part of the municipal waste collection schemes, it can suggest that nobody cares.

Learning from Urban Lexicons

Signs of life, love, welcome, security, and character indicate places treated well and respected by others. Through starting to unravel this urban vocabulary, we can pick up on the human presence of individual personalities and wider communities. These signs are the connection; the clues to local society and culture told through the environment. The identity of a place is, ultimately, defined by the people who inhabit it. But what they do there and how they respond to the location seem inextricably linked to the tangible makeup of formal and informal details and what these signify.

How can place branding learn from this vocabulary of signs? Consider these details of the urban fabric when defining the identity of a place and shaping a place brand. Details tell of London's heritage, New York's hustle and bustle, and Barcelona's social street life – all characteristics core to our image of these cities. These details communicate a city's identity and its most positive activities, through its streets and spaces, and a city keen to promote its welcoming nature might instill 'friendly' details that encourage public involvement. For example, seating outside cafes which enhance street life, park signage that promotes activities rather than prohibits, and moveable or adaptable street furniture flexible enough to be interpreted for various uses – all these allow people to make the city spaces their own.

THE IMAGE OF A CITY: 'PROJECTED' PLACE BRANDS

Signs as icons: The basis for a place brand

Through the Urban Lexicons workshops, we discovered how details as diverse as fences, flowerbeds, curtains, cars, and Closed Circuit Television (CCTV) cameras act as mediums of communication, relaying a message about the destination's identity. Some details are so unique and pervasive that they become synonymous with a place; New York City's (NYC) yellow taxicabs and hot-dog stands; London's Routemaster buses; and Barcelona's hexagonal *modernista* paving slabs and armchair-style benches. Trail the souvenir shops of La Rambla in Barcelona, and one finds chocolate bars, soaps, and wallets imprinted with the distinct paving pattern from the famed Paseo de Gracia. In London, one can pick up a Routemaster keyring, and in New York a miniature yellow cab. 'Detail' icons have not replaced Statue of Liberty lighters, Big Ben watches, and postcards of La Sagrada Familia, though their place as mementos on the mantelpiece back home reinforces the status of these details in representing a destination. Such urban elements hold power because they are everyday and everywhere: they are real. New York's streets fill with cabs that locals and visitors experience throughout their day (NYC, 2008); Londoners made 2.2 billion bus journeys in 2008 alone (Transport for London, 2008/09) and Barcelona's Paseo de Gracia constantly streams with strolling Catalans and exploring tourists.

Branding and tourism are often concerned with authenticity of experience. In 'A call for authenticity,' branding agency, Saffron Consultants (2009) warn against the dangers of brands that 'are manufactured; they have nothing to do with what the company is really about – and too much to do with hyperbole and wanting to impress.' The difference between a brand for tourists and a brand for insiders is shrinking. Consider that 'The tourist is an actual person, or real people are actually tourists' (MacCannel, 1999). New York, London, and Barcelona's rich cultures and leisure landscapes offer locals and tourists the chance to continually re-discover the city. Websites such as nycgo.com are designed to appeal to locals and visitors alike, to find out what is on in NYC. Outsiders also now have great access to 'inside' information about destinations, thanks to the explosion of sites such as Tripadvisor, Flickr, Twitter, and travel forums (see Chapter 11). The tourist's views are rapidly merging boundaries with the '*real* city.'

Has a true Londoner visited Big Ben, or a real New Yorker, the Empire State? Often the answer is no, or at least not for a long time. Yet in most towns, tourists, business people, and residents cross paths in the same streets, taking in many sights, sounds, smells, and sensations from within a few feet of each other. These streetscapes are the places to really start defining a destination's brand. With this approach how can one capture and project an image of a city destination? To address to this, we can look further at cases from Barcelona, New York, and London and also to Southampton as an emerging model with a different approach.

Barcelona: Transforming public space to build a brand

Barcelona is recognised to have 'landed' on the international destination map following its hosting of the 1992 Olympics. As the city prepared and followed up the surge of Olympic attention, not only did the marketing concepts change but vitally the urban fabric was radically reformed. This transformation at both large and small scales gave the location a new springboard with real characteristics to promote through destination marketing.

Barcelona engaged a citywide approach, opening streets and transforming details, to promote moving around, socialising, and many other activities in public spaces. The success of these initial efforts to transform the city and its reputation, under what has become known as the 'Barcelona model,' is almost undisputed worldwide. Recently, however, the city has come under critical attack, for its apparent desire to repeat the explosion in international status and investment, with attempts to re-promote or re-position via initiatives it hoped would have a similar impact to the '92 Olympics. These include the 2004 'Forum of Cultures' and the ongoing '22@' program of 'regeneration' around the ex-industrial Poble-Nou district. Such efforts have brought large-scale change in the city's urban contexts but have largely missed out on revitalising the details that impact so positively on people's daily city experiences.

Urban anthropologist, Manuel Delgado in his 2007 book, whose title translates as 'The Lying [untruthful] City' insists that the recent urban interventions in Barcelona have now 'constructed a stage built on fraud and failure.' He suggests that this has emerged from an evolved model, now centred only on tourism, commercial trade, and property – a model that forgets the smaller, local elements that originally facilitated the city's 'community spirit.'

Fransesc Muñoz's (2008) *Urbanilización* also cites Barcelona as having fallen into the 'global' trap of now creating urban spaces that are distinctly un-unique, shaping itself with cityscapes that are increasingly similar to other cities worldwide, following similar economic and political drivers.

However, the city is fighting hard to shake off such criticisms. Through an endeavour to promote its sustainable ambitions and environmental profile in 2009–2010, for example, the city has re-branded its cleaning and waste management sector; the department that was until autumn 2009, called 'BCNeta' (literally, 'BCN-clean'), has now become 'Barcelona pel Medi Ambient – i tu,' as in 'Barcelona for the environment – and you'. Central to the re-launch of the campaign are containers, for the citizen to do their bit, in participation with the city (Bcn.cat/neta, January 2010). These containers mark an increased presence of details that will help to transmit the notion of a 'sustainable' and 'collaborative' Barcelona. In addition, a 'caring' visual identity has replaced the punchy 'BCNeta' brand with an image of a smiling face within Barcelona's 'B' logo.

New York: 'There is only one New York City'

New Yorkers are famously straight talking and the city's brand is equally direct. NYC & Company – the city's official marketing and tourism organisation – ran a 2008 campaign, in part bowing to the challenges of branding such a diverse place, with their tagline 'There is only one New York City. But there is no one New York City.' Branding agency Wolff Olins (2008), commissioned to develop the city's brand, also appreciates that 'within the mind of every single New Yorker resides a different version of New York City.' In defining the brand, they describe a walk through New York City: 'Imagine what you'd see peering in a masonry façade ... the NYC brand is a transparent pane of glass that offers a view of real New Yorkers and real NYC neighbourhoods.' Brand-focused blog *brandnew (2007)* describes how the logo is representative of New York City in more ways than one: 'In its adherence to the grid it reflects that of the city ... in its shoulder-to-shoulder tightness it is a painful reminder of how little space there is here, but how much we enjoy and thrive in our proximity to each other.'

There are further links between the New York City brand and its city spaces. NYC & Company's 2009 campaign features bright illustrations of New York icons, many drawn from the streetscape (Figure 22.4). Rather than the Empire State Building, the hot dog and the taxi (among others) represent the *real* New York City and its on-the-go energy. The campaign features prominently on street banners to 'build the NYC brand and generate excitement for events and attractions throughout the five boroughs' (NYC & Company 2009). By focussing on details abundant daily in the city's streets, the brand works for tourists and connects with New Yorkers.

The taxi deserves special mention. NYC-based Design Trust for Public Space (2005) cites the importance of the taxi as a New York icon; 'Hailing a cab – with its promise of freedom, power, and anonymity – is the quintessential New York act. So deeply rooted is this notion, that visitors count hailing a cab among top tourist attractions.' The taxi is also a billboard for the city's brand. The

Figure 22.4 The NYC & Company 'Ask New York City …' campaign is prominent throughout the city's streets.

NYC logo appears on many of the city's communication pieces, but its most prominent placement is on every one of New York City's 13,000 taxicabs.

Alongside communication of the NYC brand, the Bloomberg Administration is revitalising the streetscape and, it hopes, the day-to-day reality of the city. Thus, once neglected streets are given new life through consistent and uniquely designed details as the introduction of the Department of Transport's Street Design Manual in 2009 guides usage of materials and street furniture to create quality urban environments that communicate a specific character and a sense of place. These improvements are being implemented in part 'to capture the city's uniqueness or character in a single frame … from the most basic human point of view – that of the pedestrian walking down the street' (NYC DOT, 2009a).

London: 'A vast and disparate city'

In the words of its Mayor, London is a 'vast and disparate city' (Mayor of London, 2009). To compare, New York comprises 5 boroughs, while London hosts 32. The city's brand is inconsistent and much of its public realm is incoherent. Each borough has jurisdiction over its own streetscape, resulting in broad variations in quality across the city, except perhaps the roadways, being among the only elements with a consistent (if exclusively 'utilitarian') identity. Where Barcelona established a strong identity through fluent and connected public spaces, London's street furniture, paving, and many other spatial details are not co-coordinated and communicate little about specific location. Responses from the Urban Lexicons workshops revealed the impact of bland streetscapes on London's identity:

- 'There was no sense of unity apart from the unremitting dullness of the road.'
- 'The street furniture is out of a catalogue. The local authority's got a bit of money and has bought some furniture for that section but there's nothing that says "this is London." '
- 'It's totally anonymous. It could be anywhere in the country.'

London suffers a dilemma. The city's personality is characterised by the diversity of its people and its neighbourhoods, and clearly should preserve this. Certain boroughs have created pockets of thriving spaces, full of details distinct to each neighbourhood; notable examples include the City of London, Barking & Dagenham, or the revival of people-focused spaces such as Trafalgar Square and the South Bank. But how successful are these programs if such 'pockets' are not connected by wider design principles to build a clear image of the city and to correspondingly afford (in the sense that Donald Norman (1988) uses affordance) diverse, positive 'activity support'?

Many brands are devised in an effort to corepresent aspects of London. The logo of one, Totally London, is based on the City of Westminster street sign. Its connection to London's urban fabric was positive, yet the brand's very purpose was all but lost among a myriad of simultaneous brands: Visit London, Think London, and London Unlimited, to name a few. Standing out from these, Transport for London (TfL) is often cited among the capital's strongest brands. The familiar roundel logo and typeface has been little changed since 1913, and 'over time it has become a symbol of the city' (Guardian.co.uk, October 9, 2008). The presence of the brand is strong throughout the streets of every borough; its sweep across London is seen from buses and tubes, to stops, shelters, stations, posters, memorabilia, and more. Though surely London is more than its transport department, isn't it?

Mayor Boris Johnson was spurred to act by the city's identity crisis in late 2009. He initiated a re-brand, to be 'promoted with one, all encompassing, single-vision,' conscious that 'the eyes of the world will turn to London as we host the greatest sporting event in the world and it's appropriate that we brand ourselves accordingly' (Mayor of London, 2009, legacy.london. gov.uk). Simultaneously, under the Mayor's 25-year 'London Plan,' he has communicated a vision to create 'a city that delights the senses and takes care over its buildings and streets' (Mayor of London, 2009). The connection between both visions is still tenuous, but if London has the foresight to link the development of its brand and public realm, it must realise both in unison.

CONCLUSION

We have learnt that the everyday urban detail, be it chewing gum or a mass of red buses, can say more about a place and its society than the monumental icon. Streetscape details shape our understanding and image of a place and can be channelled to determine and project a place's identity. A considered approach between place and brand affords a stronger encounter between the bottom-up physical and perceived character of the urban fabric and the projected brand, helping to define and develop each other. A new attitude is emerging, exemplified by Southampton, to 'align place marketing and place making agendas' (Rawlinson, 2009). Outside London, Southampton is the largest city in southeast England, yet has long lacked a clear image. A fractured urban structure disconnected the waterfront and centre, resulting in a city difficult to understand as a whole. The Southampton Legible City initiative is transforming the user experience of the city, promoting a clear, positive image of the place, by connecting the real everyday experience of those that use it with the promotion and marketing of that place.

In 2005, Southampton City Council began a program to transform the city centre's image by promoting legibility and creating a recognisable identity. The new brand was delivered through a visual identity but also guidance on the design of the public spaces, transport infrastructure, and wayfinding systems (Figure 22.5). The approach, led by City ID, was pioneering in developing a 'holistic response to [design and] place branding that would improve the totality of the city and its image,' informed by 'the literal signs and communicated messages that collectively shape our reading of place' (City ID, 2008).

The visual identity developed for Southampton Legible City was inspired by the urban environment to reinforce a sense of place, underpinned by brand values. Unique typefaces echo the strong graphics of the city's shipping industry.

Figure 22.5 Southampton legible city: A unique set of pictograms designed to work in combination with the Southampton typography

Figure 22.6 Southampton legible city: Signage.

Colour palettes link to the light, water, and other fabric of the city. Small details support the image of an 'active' Southampton; signage and maps show walking distance between points, time to destination, and calories burned, highlighting routes suited to strolling, skating, cycling, and jogging (Figure 22.6).

The suite of city products and services may be delivered through web, mobile, print, signs, streets, and people. City ID argue that the newly holistic approach 'could influence the "look and feel" of thousands of products and services across the city, from the design of information centres at the airport and ferry terminals, through to bus tickets, timetables, route maps, liveries and uniforms, as well the design of the city's streets and spaces.' They are intended to represent 'the continuity that will be experienced by residents and visitors from the start of their journey through to their destination and return home' (City ID, 2008).

The understanding that a place should match the 'branding process with on-the-ground improvements that enhance the everyday experience of using the city' (Rawlinson, 2009) can help bring the *real* city, the urban fabric, and the people that use it back into the picture. Many look to Barcelona as a model of success in developing a destination brand and detailing public spaces, and justly so in many respects. We must be aware though, of what has been described as 'meaningless megalomania' (Vives, 2007), leading, in some cases, to a rigid top-down approach to creating and controlling public space. This attitude has been criticised for stripping cities of authentic character and pandering to tourists over locals. The *Urban Lexicons* project showed that while 'love' from the authorities is important, allowing space for individual personalities communicates that 'this place belongs to people,' and tells of their enormous contribution to local character. Designing-in participation, allowing people to shape and care for their city, brings human character and authentic identity into the streets and quashes references to the 'trap of empty symbolism' (Vives, 2007) or 'the Emperor's New Clothes.'

New York has recently begun to invest more attention and creativity into its streetscape, tying together the business and environmental agendas to improve the public realm. Mayor Bloomberg is still a step away from intertwining the city's branding and the public spaces, but to his credit, he acknowledges that 'in a city as large and richly varied as [New York], one size does not fit all … We have been working especially hard to tailor the streets to best fit the needs of individual neighbourhoods and communities' (NYC DOT, 2009b).

Figure 22.7 Will London's desire for Olympic legacy be sustained by its 'crown jewel' constructions in allocated pockets of the city?

Image credits: Urban Lexicons Participants; Marcus Willcocks; Rosanna Vitiello; Luciano Vitiello; CityID; Mark Hillary (Flickr); London 2012

London's brands may be confused, but clearly 'those communicating London to the world will not be painting its image onto a blank canvas'(Tims 2007). On the cusp of the 2012 Olympics, what can London learn from these other cities, as it develops its 'all-encompassing' vision? The development of Olympic sites, public spaces, and transport systems is the perfect opportunity to reconsider the design of the streets with a holistic view. Urban details must now be designed from an emotional rather than a purely utilitarian perspective, to weave 'signs of love' and society back into the identity of London. To communicate a consistent brand, London should take advantage of its new opportunity to communicate its universal values citywide. But it needs to find a balance. The character of its many and diverse boroughs, and the personalities that make up London's population, should be reflected not suppressed through the public realm. There is much talk around London's present Olympic Legacy Masterplan, but what legacy will this really leave, if it cannot be found in the streets around many parts of the city? The greatest test for its 'legacy' brand will lie not in the recognition of a logo, but in the ability of London's many streetscapes to afford, define, defend, and communicate the city's true character (Figure 22.7).

References

BrandNew, Opinions on Corporate and Brand Identity Work (2007). I 'heart' Wolff Olins'. Available at: http://www.underconsideration.com/brandnew/.

City ID and Southampton City Council. (2008). Direct/Guide/Show, Southampton Legible City. Available at www.cityid.co.uk/Images/CityID_Southampton_Legible_City.pdf. City ID and Southampton City Council authored and self published a publication called Direct/Guide/Show, Southampton Legible City.

Delgado, M. (2007). *esLa ciudad Mentirosa, Fraude y Miseria del 'Modelo Barcelona'*. Madrid: Catarata Publishing.

Design Trust for Public Space. (2005). Designing the taxi: Rethinking New York City's Moveable Public Space. New York City.

MacCannel, D. (1999). *The tourist: A new theory of the leisure class*. Berkeley, Los Angeles, London: University of California Press.

Mayor of London (2009). The London plan, spatial development strategy for London. Available at: http://www.london.gov.uk/shaping-london/london-plan/docs/london-plan.pdf.

Muñoz, F *Urbanilización, Paisajes Comunes, Lugares Globales*. Barcelona: Editorial Gustavo Gil.

Norman, D. (1988). *The psychology of everyday things*. New York: Basic Books.

NYC & Company. (2008). Annual Report 2008. New York City.

NYC & Company. (2009). Annual Report 2009. New York City.

NYC Department of Transportation. (2009a). *World class streets*. New York: Remaking New York City's Public Realm.

NYC Department of Transportation. (2009b). Street design manual. New York.

Raval per viure. (2009). Available at: http://ravalperviure.blogspot.com/2009/07/volem-un-barri-digne.html

Rawlinson, M. (2009) *Re-imaging Southampton: City ID, Place and Sustainability*, 2, 42–43. Available at: www.rudi.net/files/file/required_file/03placesustain.pdf.

Saffron Consultants (2009). Authenticity = success. Available at: http://saffron-consultants.com/2009/10/26/authenticity-success/.

Tims, C. (2007). Barcelona, Diffuse Factory Vs. Model 22@. In: Joost Beunderman, Melissa Mean, Joan-Anton Sánchez de Juan, Fundació Ramon Trias Fargas, & Demos (Eds.), Quaderns de Pensament 24, BCN LDN 2020. Barcelona.

Transport for London. (2008/9). Annual Report and Statement of Accounts 2008/9, London.

Vitiello, R., & Willcocks, M. (2006). The Difference is in the detail: the potential of detail as a place branding tool and its impact on our perceptions and responses. *Journal of Place Branding*, 3(2), 248–262.

Vitiello R., & Willcocks, M. (2011). Unravelling the urban lexicons of our everyday environments. Lulu. Based on the research project undertaken in 2007–2009.

Vives, A. (2007). Barcelona, diffuse factory vs. Model 22@. In: Joost Beunderman, Melissa Mean, Joan-Anton Sánchez de Juan, Fundació Ramon Trias Fargas, & Demos (Eds.), Quaderns de Pensament 24, BCN LDN 2020. Barcelona.

Whyte, W. H. (1980). *The Social Life of Small Urban Spaces*. New York: Project for Public Spaces.

Wolff Olins. *NYC One for many*. Available at: http://www.wolffolins.com/nyc.php2008.

Useful websites

Bcn, 2010Bcn.cat/neta, January 2010 http://www.bcn.cat/neta/es/novedadesservicio-anuncios.html

Bcn, 2010Bcn.cat/neta, January 2010 http://www.bcn.cat/neta/es/index.html

Jnd, 2004Jnd.org, Affordances, 2004 http://www.jnd.org/dn.mss/affordances_and.html

Mayor of London, Mayor of London, Mayor unveils new Council to promote and rebrand London June 2009 http://legacy.london.gov.uk/view_press_release.jsp?releaseid=22398

Guardian, 2008Guardian.co.uk, A century of the London Underground logo, October 2008 http://www.guardian.co.uk/artanddesign/gallery/2008/oct/03/design.london

City ID: www.cityid.co.uk

Branding a post-conflict destination: Northern Ireland

Michael Gould

INTRODUCTION

In 2006 research was published which examined the ability of Northern Ireland to be able to brand itself as a nation in the United States without an agreed national identity (Gould, 2006). The research focused on the use of place branding as a method of promoting a positive image of Northern Ireland as a post-conflict society in the United States in the absence of an agreed single national identity on which to build a brand. The results showed that Northern Ireland had adopted a 'Janus' strategy when marketing Northern Ireland internationally – marketing Northern Ireland as 'Irish' in Ireland-friendly markets and 'British' in Great Britain-friendly markets. The research examined nations as social constructs, either real (Gellner, 1997) or imagined (Anderson, 1983), which contain individuals bound together by a collective sense of national identity. Quelch and Jocz's (2005) work makes the point that strong national images matter for both 'powerful' and 'weak' countries if they are to enjoy the rewards of positive place branding. However, since its establishment in 1921, Northern Ireland has not had one single identity upon which to build a place brand, neither has it had a positive national image internationally due to many years of civil unrest.

Gould and Skinner (2007) made the point that Northern Ireland, at just under 90 years old, is a relatively young nation and whether the nation is real (Gellner, 1997) or imagined (Anderson, 1983), it has experienced a great deal of conflict during its short history. They believed that it is, at least in part, due to its history that no one single shared sense of national identity exists among its people. Gould and Skinner's findings show that although Northern Ireland may be seen, at least in some target markets, as having a

© 2011 Published by Elsevier Ltd. All rights reserved.
DOI: 10.1016/B978-0-08-096930-5.10023-0

strong national image that this image is troubled and is not bringing about the positive effects of place branding identified in the literature (Quelch & Jocz, 2005).

One of the issues adding complexity to the practise of place branding is the sheer number and type of stakeholders involved in creating and communicating messages about the place to various target audiences. Skinner (2005) has already identified some of the problems faced by place branders in managing consistent messages; however, the respondents in Gould's (2006) work were universally unsupportive of any formal attempt being made to control these messages, believing that message consistency was not always a worthwhile goal. Another matter, over which the respondents also agreed, was that there is some element of consistency in the way communications from many stakeholders in Northern Ireland are attempting to overcome the country's negative image, noting that the country is a place in transition and changing away from its past troubled image. This concurs with the work of Endzina and Luneva (2004), Viosca, Bergiel & Balsmeier (2004), and Dzenovska (2005) who believe that without such attempts people from outside the country will generate their own perceptions of the place that may not be a true reflection of the positive changes that are happening.

So, although negative country images may be overcome (Niss, 1996), this needs consensus and a consistent effort by all the managing agents of the country brand (Viosca, Bergiel, & Balsmeier, 2004). In 2005–2006 tourism stakeholders in Northern Ireland did not believe this consensus and consistent effort was happening in any meaningful way for the country's image, although they all concurred with Hall (2004) that there was some need to do this when marketing Northern Ireland as a post-conflict place. Gertner and Kotler (2004) offer practical solutions – the use of honesty (to contextualise the negative issue), making a positive out of a negative, the use of iconic figures (if available and willing), and the removal of the negative – to places suffering negative images and the challenge remained for Northern Ireland to overcome these impeding internal factors and to deliver a positive and dynamic image of a post-conflict Northern Ireland. In 2007, Northern Ireland was presented with an ideal opportunity to do this through its participation at the Smithsonian Institution's Folklife Festival and with the Rediscover Northern Ireland Programme in Washington DC. This chapter, therefore, uses the example of Northern Ireland to explore:

- The use of place branding as a method of promoting a positive image of post-conflict societies;
- The issues confronting Destination Marketing Organisations (DMOs) in the absence of an agreed single national identity on which to build a brand;
- The challenge facing destinations suffering from negative images;
- The complexities of place branding created by the sheer number and variety of stakeholders involved in creating and communicating messages about the place.

REDISCOVER NORTHERN IRELAND: THE OPPORTUNITY TO BUILD A NATION BRAND WITHOUT 'TRADITIONAL/LOCATION' ELEMENTS

The Smithsonian Institution was created by the US Congress in 1846 following the donation to the American nation from James Smithson, a British immigrant, to create 'an establishment for the increase and diffusion of knowledge.' Today the Smithsonian Institution consists of 19 museums, 9 research centres, and the US National Zoo (Smithsonian Institution, 2009). Headquartered in Washington DC the Smithsonian Institution is one of the most prestigious US organisations and is very highly regarded internationally. Each year the Smithsonian Institution organises the Smithsonian Folklife Festival which is an outdoor, professionally curated exposition of living cultural traditions featuring the US states, countries, or regions of the world or specialised themes.

The Folklife Festival takes place at the National Mall in the heart of Washington DC between the White House and the Capitol Building and as such has one of the most significant locations on the 'world stage.' The Festival lasts over 10 days in late June and early July and encompasses the US's Fourth of July celebrations in Washington DC. Each year the Folklife Festival attracts over one million visitors and significant media coverage in the United States and beyond.

Northern Ireland accepted an invitation from the Smithsonian Institution to participate in the 2007 Folklife Festival and the importance of this opportunity to participate in such a prestigious internationally acclaimed festival cannot be underestimated. It was an opportunity to be present on the 'front lawn' of the US Congress and to have a physical presence which could demonstrate that the two communities in Northern Ireland can come together and celebrate their uniqueness through culture, heritage, food, tourism, and trade. However, to understand the full significance of what was achieved in 2007, it is important to understand something of the history of the Northern Ireland conflict.

Historical context of the conflict in Northern Ireland

The Celts are believed to have arrived in Ireland between 1000 and 400 BC, although evidence exists that Ireland was inhabited as long ago as 7000–6500 BC (Bardon, 1992). The Vikings and the Normans invaded between 800 and 1300 AD, disrupting the very well-developed Christian Gaelic society which had flourished when the rest of Europe was in the 'Dark Ages' (McKernan, 2002). The Norman integration into Irish society continued and by the sixteenth century the Tudor rulers of Britain had declared themselves Kings of Ireland (McKernan, 2002). Under the reign of James I, a deliberate policy of settlement known as the 'Plantation of Ulster' resulted in an influx of Protestant colonists (Bardon, 1992). This led to the establishment of two separate cultural, political, and religious identities in the north of Ireland: the native, mainly Catholic population holding allegiances to Ireland, and the

Protestant settlers who considered themselves loyal to the English crown. An Irish Parliament was established in Dublin in 1782, but due to the 'Penal Laws' that effectively kept Catholics from having any power or influence, power was retained by the 'English Ascendancy.'

Revolution in France and America inspired a group known as the United Irishmen to lead a rebellion in Ireland in 1798. It was easily put down and the leaders executed but the rebellion gave support to the proposition that Ireland should no longer have its own parliament and in 1801 the Act of Union ended the Parliament in Dublin. However, in the late 1880s the issue of a Dublin parliament was raised again with demand for a policy known as 'Home Rule.'

The outbreak of the World War I put the Home Rule question on hold but Irish nationalism surfaced again in 1916 when a Republic of Ireland was declared in Dublin in what became known as the 'Easter Rising.' The Rising was quashed and the leaders executed, but the methods used in putting down the rebellion left a deep sense of animosity in the native population and led eventually to the Irish 'War of Independence' which lasted until 1921. The Government of Ireland Act was passed in 1920 which effectively established two parliaments in Ireland and divided the country, with 6 northern counties forming Northern Ireland and the remaining 26 counties becoming the 'Irish Free State.' The Free State was named Eire and remained a member of the Commonwealth of the British Empire until 1949 when it left the Commonwealth and became the Republic of Ireland.

Inspired by the civil rights movements in the United States in the 1960s, a number of organisations were formed to campaign for equal rights for Catholics in elections, housing, and employment. The civil unrest known as the 'Troubles' began in Derry in 1969 when a public march was attacked as it passed through a loyalist area. Within days, violent rioting broke out all over Northern Ireland with Catholic homes being attacked and burned. By 1971 the Irish Republican Army (IRA) had organised and armed itself to defend nationalist areas. Their campaign of violence was countered by loyalist paramilitaries who attacked mainly the Catholic community. The 35-year period of unrest resulted in 3,600 deaths and more than 80,000 people being injured (McKittrick, Kelters, Feeney, & Thornton, 1999).

With the assistance of President Clinton and Senator George Mitchell, the British and Irish governments began a series of discussions with all the political parties in Northern Ireland which culminated in the 1998 Good Friday or Belfast Agreement. A referendum was held to ratify the public's support for the Agreement in both Northern Ireland and the Republic of Ireland and in 2000 the Assembly and Executive took over government of Northern Ireland. Political tensions existed in the 'forced coalition' and a lack of trust between the parties led to a number of occasions whereby the Assembly and Executive were suspended. The decommissioning of IRA weapons was announced by the Independent International Commission on Decommissioning in September 2005, although the removal of these arms and the end of the military campaign in itself did not restore devolution as the unionist parties wished to see Sinn Fein support the Police Service of Northern Ireland.

Discussions between the British and Irish governments and the Northern Ireland political parties continued in 2006 culminating in the St. Andrews

Agreement whereby devolution would be restored once all parties agreed to support policing and justice becoming a fully devolved matter. Elections to the Northern Ireland Assembly were held in March 2007 and resulted in the Democratic Unionist Party (DUP) and Sinn Fein being returned as the largest parties. The Northern Ireland Executive was restored in May 2007 with the DUP leader Ian Paisley as First Minister and Sinn Fein's Martin McGuiness as Deputy First Minister. Following a very cordial beginning the political environment became more hostile on the issue of devolution of policing and justice to the Northern Ireland Assembly. As a consequence devolution itself has brought into sharper focus the question of national image and national identity.

From its inception the population of Northern Ireland has been comprised of two groupings differentiated by religion. At the formation of the State the majority of the population were Protestants. Today the groups are more evenly balanced (51% Protestant; 43% Roman Catholic). The population is still divided around this issue of nationality and identity and the divisions also tend to be along religious grounds. The Protestant community is largely unionist and in favour of the link with the United Kingdom and the Roman Catholic community is largely in favour of a united Ireland – indeed, the divisions are now stronger than in the 1970s and 1980s (Hughes, 2003).

Northern Ireland is therefore a place in transition, seeking to reposition itself to both its citizens and the wider world, yet it is still troubled by its image following 35 years of civil conflict. Moreover, the place does not have a single agreed national identity that encompasses its two main communities. There is also an issue of conflicting stakeholder objectives where some organisations wish to use the past images of strife and conflict while others wish to portray Northern Ireland as a modern, successful, post-conflict society.

Northern Ireland and the United States

Northern Ireland and the United States enjoy a long and positive relationship. Many of the founders of colonial America were from what is now Northern Ireland, as were many of the soldiers and leaders of the American War of Independence and a few of the signatories of the Declaration of Independence. It is estimated that around one-third of the Presidents of the United States have ancestral links to Northern Ireland. The first emigration of the predominately Scots Irish in the mid-eighteenth centuries was supplemented by the mainly catholic immigrants in the mid- and late nineteenth centuries and together they have left diasporas which cover the continental United States. Perhaps for this and other reasons successive presidents and the Congress in the past 30 years have taken active roles in peace building in Northern Ireland, and this interest continues today. The United States has also been the largest source of Foreign Direct Investment projects, a major destination for exports of goods and services and an important source of tourists to Northern Ireland. It would seem natural that Northern Ireland would wish to build on these connections and to take the opportunity to portray itself as a modern, dynamic, post-conflict society that the United States would wish to 'do business with.'

The role of public diplomacy

'Diplomatic communication is no longer confined to government-to-government interaction, but includes also governments' communication with ordinary people in foreign countries' (Tuch, 1990). Governments in the developed and the developing world have found the need to use and refocus public diplomacy to establish, maintain, or enhance their nations' reputation with other governments, international bodies such as the International Monetary Fund and World Bank, and other nations' citizens. As Wang (2006) states 'An inherent goal of public diplomacy is to communicate and cultivate on behalf of a nation state a desired image and reputation and to build common ground and understanding among nations and people.' The decision of the Northern Ireland Government to support a presence at the Smithsonian Folklife Festival was one of its most ambitious attempts at public diplomacy. It was for the first time trying to present a coordinated message across a number of separate stakeholder organisations to enhance the international reputation of Northern Ireland. Three main organisations represent the interests of Northern Ireland in the United States: the Northern Ireland Bureau, Invest NI, and Tourism Ireland. Each has a distinct role and set of functions. The Northern Ireland Bureau is the diplomatic representation of the Northern Ireland Executive in North America; it has full diplomatic accreditation with the US Authorities through the British Embassy. The remit of the Bureau is to represent the whole of the Northern Ireland Executive and their 11 government departments in the United States. Invest NI is the economic development agency in Northern Ireland and its main role in the United States is to encourage foreign direct investment projects to locate in Northern Ireland and to develop exports of goods and services from Northern Ireland to the United States. Tourism Ireland is a cross-border body established by the Good Friday Agreement in 1998 with responsibility for developing tourism on the island of Ireland from international markets. The work of these three bodies is supplemented by four government departments and many agency and voluntary sector organisations to deliver the Rediscover Northern Ireland programme.

Scotland had exhibited at the Folklife Festival in 2003 and the diplomatic staff in the Bureau recognised the potential that such an opportunity could offer Northern Ireland – particularly given the history and shared cultural links with the United States. In 2004 the Department for Culture, Arts and Leisure in Northern Ireland decided to fund a post in the Northern Ireland Bureau to explore potential linkages on cultural issues with the United States and with the encouragement of the Bureau staff early contact by the Cultural Affairs Officer with the Smithsonian Folklife organisers resulted in an invitation to participate in the 2007 Folklife Festival.

'Rediscover Northern Ireland – see, feel, discover'

The authorising environment in the public sector can be intricate and a decision which requires interdepartmental agreement can become very complex. Throughout late 2004 and early 2005 the process of obtaining 'buy in' and securing approvals continued through senior officials, the Head of the

Civil Service, Ministers, and finally the Secretary of State for Northern Ireland. This work was largely 'behind the scenes' with the public announcement by the Secretary of State in Washington DC, heralding the move to a different level of organisation and activity.

Given its prestigious and unique nature, participation in the Folklife Festival was considered a 'once in a lifetime opportunity' (Wilson, 2008) and government and the other stakeholders set about devising and mounting a coordinated series of events that showed many additional facets of Northern Ireland life, in this respect, a 'focus on the culture and heritage of a place [links] to the wider issues of public diplomacy in affecting the perceptions of an entire nation' (Skinner, 2008). The coordinated program was branded 'Rediscover Northern Ireland – see, feel, discover' and was designed to maximise Northern Ireland's presence at the Festival by presenting aspects of Northern Ireland that would enlighten, educate, and entertain US citizens.

The overarching strategic message was:

> To present Northern Ireland as a creative, confident, outward looking region and to develop further strong relationships with the United States that would be mutually beneficial.

Supporting this overarching message were five core themes and multiple activities – all component parts of the overarching Rediscover Northern Ireland theme. They were as follows:

- *Arts and culture*: The creativity and confidence of Northern Irish artists was demonstrated through 66 arts and cultural events staged between March and July, involving 27 Northern Ireland-based organisations partnering with 21 Washington-based arts bodies and venues.
- *Trade and investment*: Three separate trade missions from Northern Ireland used the Rediscover Programme as a backdrop for their activities in promoting exports of goods and services into the large US Federal and State Government procurement market and to promote foreign direct investment prior to the major United States – Northern Ireland investment Conference in Belfast in May 2008.
- *Tourism*: An extensive promotional campaign was organised by the Northern Ireland Tourist Board and Tourism Ireland. The promotional activities included activities at the Folklife Festival and participation in the Smithsonian Associates Lecture Programme and their specialist magazine with a circulation of 85,000. A 'Titanic – Made in Belfast' exhibition was also hosted in Washington's iconic Union Station, highlighting the industrial heritage and redevelopment opportunities in Belfast.
- *Food and drink*: To highlight the food and drinks offering from Northern Ireland, the Department for Agriculture and Rural Development hosted a Masterclass featuring a group of Northern Ireland's best chefs to food writers and journalists. The British Ambassador Sir David Manning hosted a gala reception at his residence for 170 key people from food, tourism, and politics in the United States and the participants on the food export mission from Northern Ireland.
- *Higher education*: Both the Queens University and the University of Ulster contributed to the Rediscover Programme by promoting Northern

Ireland as a modern and progressive region with a world-class education system and a global leader in research and development activities. Events included a major poetry symposium exhibition of Northern Ireland artists and receptions which strengthened both the universities' academic links with US universities and also their Alumni across the United States.

Between March and July 2007, over 3,000 prominent influencers, business people, and politicians attended events on these key themes. 'Rediscover Northern Ireland' staged over 65 arts events, involving 40 US partner organisations with in excess of 200,000 people attending from Maryland, Virginia, and Washington DC. The Rediscover Northern Ireland Programme succeeded in raising US awareness of Northern Ireland as a good place to invest, visit, live, work, and study. The program culminated in the Northern Ireland presence at the Folklife Festival.

The Smithsonian Folklife Festival is regarded as prestigious and widely respected annual event that provides 'a professionally curated, outdoor museum exhibit of contemporary cultural traditions' and as such it offered more than a tourism or trade showcase. This is because those working in the cultural and trade exhibits were chosen from their specialist fields of expertise in Northern Ireland and in effect became an integral part of the 'living' exhibits and through real interaction they provided a unique insight into Northern Ireland for the Festival visitors.

It is always difficult to measure the value of such promotional activities and messages and while the evaluation of the events is still ongoing (Wilson, 2008), the 'headline figures' on the impact of the complete Rediscover Programme would indicate that this was a success for Northern Ireland. The figures are as follows:

- 1,006,195 visitors attended the 10-day Smithsonian Festival
- 97% of visitors rated their experience of visiting the Festival as excellent, superior, or good.
- 80% of visitors said they might visit or would consider visiting Northern Ireland
- 71% of visitors stated that they learned a lot or something about Northern Ireland from the Festival
- 112 million audience of Fox News Live, CBS, CNN, Channel 9, and Channel 5
- 87,929 visitors to the Rediscover Northern Ireland web site with 22.6 million page views.

Managing the stakeholders

Clearly given the large number of events and activities contained within the Rediscover Programme and the Folklife Festival, good management and governance of all the stakeholders was crucial. The design and delivery of the Rediscover Programme and the Folklife Festival was also unique in that for the first time it involved a significant partnership between the public and the private sector. Significant cash sponsorship and in-kind sponsorship were provided by the private sector in Northern Ireland amounting to approximately 20% of the overall costs. These monies helped offset the use of public funds and demonstrated great commitment from the private sector companies.

Management of the Rediscover Programme and presence at the Folklife Festival was through three main steering groups: the Leadership Group; the Coordinating Group, and the Curatorial Group. Each played a distinctive part and fulfilled a specific role. The Leadership Group was formed to help lever private sector support for the activities in Washington, to raise sponsorship, and to provide guidance on keeping public and private sector activities consistent and focused. The Leadership Group was cochaired by the Head of the Civil Service in Northern Ireland, Sir Nigel Hamilton, and by the then Chairman of the Ulster Bank, Dr. Alan Gillespie.

The Coordinating Group was formed from senior government and public stakeholders whose organisations were contributing to and involved in the events in Washington. The purpose of this group was to provide both governance and accountability and to assist in managing communication channels both internally and externally. The final group – the Curatorial Group – was the first group to be formed and consisted of representatives of the public and voluntary sectors. Their remit was to consider the ranges of cultural activities which could be used to portray a positive and representative image of Northern Ireland and to work closely with the curatorial staff of the Smithsonian Institution organisations to translate these concepts and ideas into reality for the Festival.

A subset of the Leadership Group, the VIP Group, was also established in virtual form. This Group consisted of individuals who agreed to lend their support to brochures, letterheads, web sites, and attendance at some events. The Group included Senator George Mitchell, Sir James Galway, Barry Douglas, Kenneth Branagh, Brian Friel, Brian Kennedy, and Geraldine Hughes.

Gaining political support

Given that civil servants advise on policy and Ministers take decisions, political support for the Rediscover Programme and the presence at the Folklife Festival was essential and in the hubris which was Northern Ireland politics that political support had to be gained twice. The first support was sought in 2004 during a period of suspension of the Northern Ireland Assembly when 'Direct Rule' Ministers were appointed to govern Northern Ireland by the Prime Minister in Westminster. The process of seeking political support had to be repeated again under the 'shadow arrangements' which operated in the Northern Ireland Assembly in the lead up to the restoration of devolution in May 2007. Thankfully, on both occasions when their support was sought the Direct Rule and local ministers endorsed the project fully.

The restoration of the political powers to the Northern Ireland Assembly occurred on May 8, 2007, 7 weeks before the Folklife Festival. Both First Minister, represented by Finance Minister and subsequent First Minister, the Rt. Hon. Peter Robinson MP MLA and Deputy First Minister, Mr Martin McGuinness MP MLA, attended the opening ceremony and set the tone for the exhibition and the mood of optimism which had entered Northern Ireland politics at the time. The Deputy First Minister said:

I have visited this city many times but today is different. Today I am here not just as a representative of one part of the Community. Today I am proud, honoured and humbled to speak to you as the joint leader of an administration which represents our entire society. A society not just in transition but in transformation; a society moving from division to one united in our celebration of diversity. When you meet our performers and participants you will see first hand the vibrancy, diversity and creativity of our cultural life and its influence here in the United States and I am sure you will be pleasantly surprised.

Mr. Robinson endorsed these sentiments, adding:

When you visit us – as I hope you will – you will be in no doubt about the astounding progress that is being made. Our two traditions are serving together in a new government. It is a government that is about change, about building, about progress, about promoting a confident and capable Northern Ireland and I can believe there is no limit to what we can achieve together. Over the next two weeks our common heritage can be explored and experienced here. You will see innovation is central to our development and will be the springboard for our future prosperity. As we look to the future with hope, expectation and realism, we need only reflect on our common heritage to realise the potential for future relationships between our two countries.

Keen political support and strong leadership from the most senior levels in the public and private sectors was a crucial factor in all the stakeholder organisations being able to deliver a consistent and coordinated message about Northern Ireland (Figure 23.1).

Figure 23.1 Congressman Richie Neal, Chair of the Friends of Ireland and Congressman Jim Walsh, Deputy Chair of the Friends of Ireland welcomes Martin McGuinness MP MLA and the then Finance Minister Peter Robinson MP MLA to Capitol Hill.
Photo courtesy of Smithsonian Institute

CONCLUSION

The use of 'spotlight' and world events to promote positive messages and to build nations' reputations is now widely accepted (Brown, Chalip, Jago, & Mules, 2004; Pride, 2004; Smith, 2004). However, the challenge still remains for DMOs to be able to deliver on the potential for such events, to create a strong and consistent message and to manage effectively a diverse group of stakeholders to deliver it (Skinner, 2005). Judged against these perspectives the Northern Ireland presence in Washington with the Rediscover Northern Ireland Programme was a success.

The invitation to participate in the Smithsonian Folklife Festival offered the opportunity to bring a positive message about Northern Ireland to a wider audience. The design and the development of the Rediscover Northern Ireland Programme, with its five distinct themes and comprehensive series of activities was innovative and very ambitious. It was significant as it provided separate promotional platforms for the different stakeholder groups to engage with their target audiences under one umbrella brand with a consistency of message. It was also significant in that it allowed Northern Ireland to differentiate itself from other countries and regions which had participated in the Folklife Festival in the past, and it provided Northern Ireland with a substantial public diplomacy campaign in one of the world's most international cities where making an impact is very difficult.

Clearly the whole management process was made easier with the support of the most senior civil servant, senior business leaders, and both the direct rule and the local politicians. Their vision and leadership provided direction and authority for both the private and public sectors. This was evident in the personal involvement of Dr. Gillespie in raising approximately £500,000 in corporate sponsorship and with Sir Nigel Hamilton who persuaded his senior civil service colleagues that the program was worth supporting for the 'greater good' and should be paid for out of their departmental finances. The presence of two of the most senior politicians from Northern Ireland at the opening ceremony of the Folklife Festival also sent a very powerful positive message about the new political administration in Northern Ireland and its hopes for the future.

Following the lessons learned by Scotland at the Folklife festival in 2003, greater emphasis was placed on communications for the Northern Ireland presence. One year before the event the Rediscover brand was created which tied all aspects of the program together and acted as an umbrella identity under which the individual stakeholders could still express their individual identities. The brand appeared on all publications and marketing materials in relation to the program. A dedicated web site was built and a small specialist communications unit established and a PR agency in Washington employed. The overall outcome was judged as positive with 386 press cuttings in the United States and Northern Ireland and an estimated audience in the United States of 112 million viewers (Wilson, 2008).

Unforeseen benefits of the Northern Ireland presence in Washington also arose. Many artists and participants commented on the increase in their own self-confidence as artists and specialists that occurred through their participation in the events. They believed that their exposure to such an international audience and the positive way in which they were received had done much to boost their self-esteem and professional reputation. Additionally, many had found the whole process of living and working with individuals from the 'other community' in Northern Ireland very positive and reconciling experience. Both these aspects of participation were largely unplanned but will help form part of the legacy to the Rediscover Northern Ireland Programme. All these factors bode well for Northern Ireland's presence at future world events such as the London Olympics in 2012.

Finally, in all of the success that the Rediscover Northern Ireland Programme represented at the time, there is a lesson for all those involved in place branding/destination marketing – 'you can't afford to take your eye off the ball.' The world has moved on significantly since 2007. At the time of writing we are in the midst of a global recession brought about by the collapse of the world's financial systems in 2008. This is inevitably going to have a negative impact on the global trade of goods and services, foreign direct investment, and tourism; 2008 tourism figures from the United States to Northern Ireland were down by 2% (D. Sellar, personal communication, 2009). Due to a weaker Sterling there has been a significant increase in shoppers, 26% (D. Sellar, personal communication, 2009) from the 'euro zone' (Republic of Ireland), and this has helped offset the worst effects of the recession for the retail trade in Northern Ireland. Within Northern Ireland itself the political environment has become more competitive with forthcoming elections to Westminster imminent and elections to the Northern Ireland Assembly expected before 2011. The years 2009 and 2010 saw the reappearance of extreme republican terrorist violence, and several large-scale bomb attacks have been thwarted by the police and security forces. All these events, be they global or local, have the potential to undermine and negate the work of DMOs, but they should also reinforce efforts to portray nations, countries, and regions as being places of quality to work, live, visit, and buy from while also being unique.

References

Anderson, B. (1983). *Imagined communities: Reflections on the origin and spread of nationalism*. London: Verso.

Bardon, J. (1992). *A history of Ulster*. Belfast: Blackstaff Press Ltd.

Breakwell, G., & Lyons E. (1996). Changing European identities, social psychological analyses of social change. Oxford: Butterworth-Heinemann.

Brown, G., Chalip, L., Jago, L., & Mules, T. (2004). Developing brand Australia: examining the role of events. In N. Morgan, A. Pritchard, & R. Pride (Eds.). *Destination branding creating the unique destination proposition* (2nd ed., pp. 279–305). Oxford: Elsevier Butterworth Heinemann.

Condor, S. (1996). Unimagined community? Some social psychological issues concerning English national identity.

Dzenovska, D. (2005). Remaking the nation of Latvia: anthropological perspectives on nation branding. *Place Branding, 1*(2), 173–186.

Endzina, I., & Luneva, L. (2004). Development of a national branding strategy: the case of Latvia. *Place Branding, 1*(1), 94–105.

Gellner, E. (1997). *Nationalism*. Great Britain: Weidenfield and Nicolson.

Gertner, D., & Kotler, P. (2004). How can a place correct a negative image? *Place Branding*, *1*(1), 50–57.

Gould, M. (2006). *Branding on ambiguity? Place branding without a national identity – marketing Northern Ireland as a post conflict society in the USA*: University of Glamorgan.

Gould, M., & Skinner, H. (2007). Branding on ambiguity? Place branding without a national identity: marketing Northern Ireland as a post conflict society in the USA. *Place Branding and Public Diplomacy*, *3*(1), 100–113.

Hall, J. (2004). Branding Britain. *Journal of Vacation Marketing*, *10*(2), 171–185.

Hughes, J. (2003). Attitudes to community relations in Northern Ireland: Grounds for optimism? Research Update Number 20. Available at: http://www.ark.ac.uk [accessed 10 September 2009].

McKernan, M. (2002). Editor. Northern Ireland Yearbook 2003: *A comprehensive reference guide to the political, economic and social life of Northern Ireland* (pp. 11–21). Lagan Consulting Moira: BMF Publishing.

McKittrick, D., Kelters, S., Feeney, B., & Thornton, C. (1999). *Lost lives*. Edinburgh & London: Mainstream Press.

Niss, H. (1996). Country of origin marketing over the product life cycle. *European Journal of Marketing*, *30*(3), 6–22.

Pride, R. (2004). A challenger brand: Wales, golf as it should be. In N. Morgan, A. Pritchard, & R. Pride (Eds.). *Destination branding creating the unique destination proposition* (2nd ed., pp. 159–168). Oxford: Elsevier Butterworth Heinemann.

Quelch, J., & Jocz, K. (2005). Positioning the nation state. *Place Branding*, *1*(3), 229–237.

Skinner, H. (2005). Wish you were here? Some problems associated with integrating marketing communications when promoting place brands. *Place Branding*, *1*(3), 299–315.

Skinner, H. (2008). The emergence and development of place marketing's confused identity. *Journal of Marketing Management*, *24*(9/10), 915–928.

Smith, M. (2004). Brand Philidelphia: the power of spotlight events. In N. Morgan, A. Pritchard, & R. Pride (Eds.). *Destination branding creating the unique destination proposition* (2nd ed., pp. 261–278). Oxford: Elsevier Butterworth Heinemann.

Smithsonian Institution. (2009). Available at: http://www.smithsonian.org/about/history.htm viewed October 22, 2009.

Tuch, H. M. (1990). *Communicating with the world: US public diplomacy overseas*. New York, NY: St. Martin's Press.

Viosca, R. C., Bergiel, B., & Balsmeier, P. (2004). Effects of the electronic Nigerian money fraud on the brand equity of Nigeria and Africa. *Management Research News*, *27*(6), 11–20.

Wang, J. (2006). Localising public diplomacy: the role of sub-national actors in nation branding. *Place Branding*, *2*(1), 32–42, (11).

Wilson, P. (2008). *Northern Ireland At the Smithsonian. Report on Participation in the 41st Smithsonian Folklife Festival, 2007*. Northern Ireland: Department for Culture, Arts and Leisure, June 2008.

CHAPTER

24

Repositioning destination brands at a time of crisis: Jerusalem

Yoram Mitki, Ram Herstein and Eugene D. Jaffe

INTRODUCTION

According to the US Department of State, transnational terrorist incidents that have caused injuries or deaths have numbered from 300 to 600 each year since the 1970s (US Department of State), while violent terror activities and the threat of additional forms of potential terror such as eco-terror, agro-terror, and bio-terror have been well documented. The upsurge of global terror of whatever form, which has been gaining in strength since the end of the twentieth century, has occurred in major cities that had previously escaped attack. This escalating phenomenon has direct impact on tourism in general and on the hotel industry in particular. The impacts of terrorism on destination places have been described as 'unpredictable and highly differential'; in other words, the effect on tourist (both inbound and domestic) demand may be short term or in other cases, sustained and long-term (Mansfield, 1999, p. 32). In order to cope with the impact of terrorist acts on destination places, crisis management guidelines and actions are necessary (Mansfield, 1999, pp. 35–36).

One city that has been inordinately affected by these events in the last decade has been Jerusalem. Jerusalem is the major tourist attraction in Israel. The Western Wall remains the most popular spot for visitors to the country, with 54% of tourists visiting the site. Ironically, the number is even higher among Christian visitors, with 64% of Christian tourists coming to the site. The many terrorist attacks that occurred in the city led to a sharp drop in the number of tourists visiting and staying at least one night. While a tourist's reasons for not visiting a place that has been subject to a terrorist act may not be entirely rational, it certainly is a powerful emotional one (Fleisher & Buccola, 2002, p. 1343).

The Israel Ministry of Tourism and the Jerusalem Hotel Association understood that without intensive marketing activities based on repositioning the city as an attraction for the domestic Israeli population, achieving a reasonable level of hotel occupancy in the city would be impossible.

© 2011 Published by Elsevier Ltd. All rights reserved.
DOI: 10.1016/B978-0-08-096930-5.10024-2

Accordingly, it was decided that the city's repositioning strategy would be based on two approaches: the city of three religions (for foreign tourists) and the city of David – the city of the Bible (for domestic tourism). While the three religions approach had been the foundation of the marketing efforts for the previous four decades and its objective had been to bring pilgrims and tourists from around the world, the city of David approach, which was developed and began to be implemented at the end of 2001, was intended to attract domestic tourists in order to increase hotel occupancy in Jerusalem and fill the gap caused by the decrease in inbound tourists.

This chapter discusses both marketing approaches, but largely focuses on the new positioning 'City of David – City of the Bible' theme. The attempt made in Jerusalem to build a double-branded model targeted at creating a holistic positioning is innovative and unique. Generally, this type of approach is usually implemented in the marketing of organisations and not of places (countries or cities). In particular, the chapter

- Describes the steps and contents of the process of constructing the repositioning campaign and then lays out the process results.
- On the basis of the successful Jerusalem experience, presents recommendations for hoteliers and others involved in the tourist industry who must continue working in periods of terrorism.

POSITIONING JERUSALEM AS A 'HOLY CITY' – 'THE CITY OF THREE RELIGIONS'

From the time of the establishment of the state of Israel up to the end of 2001 the positioning strategy of the city of Jerusalem was based on one primary concept 'Jerusalem, the holy city – Jerusalem, the city of three religions.' This concept developed from the fact that almost everyone brought up in the three largest monotheistic religions – Judaism, Christianity, and Islam – has heard about Jerusalem and nurtures deep feelings toward the city. Accordingly, all the marketing activities were directed toward believers, whomever they are, based on their historical-religious, emotional and spiritual bonds with the city. For Christian tourists, the obligation to come as pilgrims is embedded in the fact that Jerusalem is the cradle of Christianity and it is here that the Christian 'end of days' prophecy would be realised. The Israel Ministry of Tourism's appeal to Christian tourists has always been premised on the concept of the fulfillment of the prophecy and even as a new, personal Christian pilgrimage. Consequently, the typical visits to Jerusalem by individuals or groups focused primarily on a tour of the various magnificent churches spread out through the city. The most momentous tour for Christian tourists in Jerusalem is going through the 14 Stations of the Cross on the Via Delarosa, which according to Christian tradition was the path that Christ, carrying his cross, took on his way to the crucifixion.

In contrast to the advertising campaigns aimed at Christian tourists, the advertising and marketing campaigns directed at Muslim tourists underscored the Islamic importance of Jerusalem and the city's many holy places, the most famous of which is the Al Aqsa Mosque. For Jewish tourists worldwide, Jerusalem was showcased first and foremost as the site of the Holy Temple, the symbol of God's eternal presence in the city. Here too, similar to the importance of Christians and Muslims coming on pilgrimage to Jerusalem, the appeal to Jewish tourists around the world was based on the concept of pilgrimage, an act that has become a clear statement of Jewish identity.

The Israel Ministry of Tourism took advantage of the proximity of the places holy to all three religions to Jerusalem when promoting tourism and tours but while the focus of marketing activities until the beginning of 2000 was foreign tourism, the Israel Ministry of Tourism barely made any overtures to domestic Israeli tourists. Most local campaigns focused on presenting the city as the nexus of the three religions, pointing out the sites that are holy to all three, with emphasis on sites relevant to Israeli modern history such as the city after the Six Day War or as a site for commemorating the Holocaust. Due to the city's uniqueness as a top tourist centre, through the years tens of hotels were built, and by 1996 it had more rooms than any other city in Israel. Today, the city has more than 10,000 rooms in 74 tourist hotels, with an average of 2.5 beds per room.

TOURISM IN JERUSALEM IN THE SHADOW OF TERRORISM: THE COUNTRY IMAGE APPROACH

Whereas the threat of a terrorist attack in the world's major cities is a phenomenon of the last decade, Jerusalem has witnessed terrorism since the establishment of the state of Israel. Nonetheless, in the past 15 years the phenomenon has grown in intensity, reaching a climax in the years 2000–2001. During the first half of 2001, there were eight terrorist attacks that resulted in many deaths and wide destruction (Retner, 2002). This reality resulted in a 40% drop in foreign tourists coming to Israel in general, and to Jerusalem in particular (Figure 24.1). With the dearth of domestic tourism, this situation precipitated a severe crisis in the hotel industry, to the extent that the entire industry was on the edge of collapse.

In order to cope with the tourism crisis and prevent hotels going into bankruptcy and shutting down, the Ministry of Tourism worked on two levels, which together formed an emergency plan for revitalisation of the industry. First, hotels were offered financial aid including grants and loans, and second, the ministry initiated a campaign to market the city to the local population.

At the end of 2001 a strategy team from the Ministry of Tourism and the Jerusalem Hotel Association began to put together a plan to reposition the city. Based on the forecasts of terrorism experts and consultants in the area of tourism marketing, it was decided to establish a long-term repositioning strategy and give this plan priority over sporadic marketing activities. The strategy included massive support in promoting the marketing of Jerusalem throughout the world as the city of three religions (the present positioning) and additionally, to adopt an active marketing policy focused on domestic tourism and championing the new positioning of Jerusalem as 'the City of

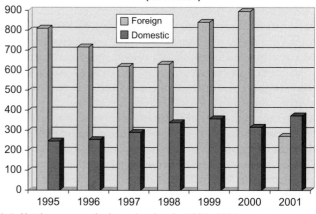

Figure 24.1 Hotel occupancy in Jerusalem hotels, 1995–2001

David – the City of the Bible.' This positioning was based on an approach to marketing known as 'country/place image.'

PLACE MARKETING

The question 'can a country, region or city be a brand?' is no longer as enigmatic as it was in decades past, since today most branding researchers and practitioners tend to market countries, cities, and regions as if they were products (Jaffe & Nebenzahl, 2006; Kotler & Gertner, 2002). In fact, today as is done with products, marketers evaluate the places where they market the product they are trying to promote in 'country (place) equity' terms (Shimp, Saeed, & Madden, 1993).

Over the last quarter of the century, countries, cities, and regions have started to be marketed and even branded as if they were products (Kotler & Gertner, 2002; Morgan, Pritchard, & Pride, 2004; Papadopoulos, 2004; Ward, 1998). It appears that this marketing approach is derived from the marketing realm of the 'country-of-origin effect' (national image), which presents very profound evidence that products bearing 'Made in Japan' (cars, cameras, and consumer electronics), 'Made in France' (wines, perfume, and clothing), or 'Made in Italy' (furniture, shoes, and sports cars) labels are commonly regarded as high quality, due to the reputation of these countries as top world manufacturers and exporters (Jaffe & Nebenzahl, 2006).

Although today marketers already realise that places should be marketed and should be treated as brands, there are still differences between marketing consumer products and marketing places. In contrast to consumer products, place products are considered to be more complex (Morgan, Pritchard, & Pride, 2002) and therefore require a much more holistic approach (Kerr, 2006). According to Ashworth and Voogt (1990) there are three main differences between these two types of products. First, places exist both as holistic entities or nuclear products and as collections of contributory elements or individual services and facilities. Therefore, a place such as city can have an overall reputation as an old industrial city, while individual elements (museums, sports facilities, universities, shopping centres) can have their own individual reputations for totally independent reasons. Second, the place product can be assembled uniquely by each visitor from their experiences of a chosen set of individual contributory elements. Third, places are multi-functional and each place can offer historical buildings, shopping facilities, sports facilities, and entertainment venues. These may all be consumed by the same consumer group such as residents or individually by different consumers with special interests. Moreover, while poor image products can be easily re-fashioned or dropped, places cannot. On the basis of these differences, Hankinson (2005) claims that the job of the destination marketer requires first to select a portfolio from the individual elements to form the basis of a destination product, second, to assure control, under the limitations, over the product experience, and third to appeal to different consumers' segments.

PLACE IMAGES

Today, marketers who cope with place branding are working hard to create a unique image to their place. Marketers define the concept of a 'place image' as the sum of the beliefs and impressions people hold about a place (Kotler, Haider, & Rein, 1993). A place image results from the place's geography, history, art and music, famous citizens, and other features (Kotler & Gertner, 2002). In order to attract tourists, factories, companies, and talented people and to find markets for their exports, many governments all over the world invest tremendous efforts in creating a real, competitive advantage over other nations and cities (Gilmore, 2001; Kotler, Jatusripitak, & Maesincee, 1997; Porter, 1989). In recent years, countries such as Thailand (Nuttavuthisit, 2007), Costa Rica, Moldova (Florek & Conejo, 2007), Ireland (Gould & Skinner, 2007; O'Leary & Deegan, 2003), Turkey (Kemming & Sandikci, 2007), Spain (Gilmore, 2001), Britain (Gilmore, 2001; Hall, 2004), Yugoslavia (Hall, 2002), Australia (Morgan & Pritchard, 1999), and New Zealand (Morgan, Pritchard, & Piggott, 2003) underwent processes to position themselves and promote a positive image.

Other nations that are also pursuing the same agenda include Wales (Pritchard & Morgan, 1998) and Western Australia (Crockett & Wood, 2000). Furthermore, cities such as Glasgow (Daskou, Thom, & Boojihawon, 2004), Manchester (Ward, 2000), Bradford (Trueman, Klemm, & Giroud, 2004), and London (Anholt, 2006; Hopper, 2003) have already completed the design of their new images and/or brands. Despite the fact that most research on place image focuses mainly on cities, regions, and countries, it seems that place image determination also applies lower down the spatial scale (Ashworth & Voogt, 1994), to leisure tourism places like museums, shopping centres, sport facilities, and so forth. According to Caldwell and Freire (2004) there are differences in the way that people perceive places. Countries, for example, are so functionally diverse that they are perceived in terms of the representational parts of their brand identity, whereas regions and cities, being smaller in scale, are perceived more from a functional point of view. Conversely to countries, regions, and cities, marketing a leisure tourism place is much more complex since the number of attributes (physical and human) associated with leisure tourism are very limited.

THE REPOSITIONING OF JERUSALEM: 'THE CITY OF DAVID – THE CITY OF THE BIBLE'

After studying the different approaches to location branding, a strategy team chose to adopt the Positioning Diamond model as the one to use for repositioning Jerusalem and promoting domestic tourism. This model was chosen for two reasons. First, the model served as a very successful framework for repositioning Spain. Branding Spain was very problematic, but in the end was successful. Second, as a result of what was learned from the case of Spain, the strategy team believed that the model could be applied to cities as well.

The Positioning Diamond model

According to the Positioning Diamond model there are four essential factors that need to be considered for each country: macro-trends, target audiences (stakeholders), competitors, and core competencies (Gilmore, 2001). In order to make this model suitable for positioning a city, and not a country, the strategy team decided to change the first factor from macro-trends (country) to micro-trends (city).

Micro-trends – It refers to socio-economic trends, political and legal status, emerging industries, population trends, and cultural and lifestyle trends such as integration and tolerance among religions and beliefs, entertainment styles, etc. By studying these micro-trends the strategy team would be able to place the current situation of the city into proper context and help highlight the present issues the city is facing and those that it could face in the future.

Target audiences/stakeholders – Each city has many relevant audiences such as present and future residents, local and foreign investors, students, local-national and foreign tourists, etc. By focussing on the relevant target audiences in the city's positioning process, the strategy team should be compatible and mutually supportive when taken together.

Competitors – When referring to competitor cities in the city positioning process, the team must ensure that the competitive city set would in turn depend on the target audience that the city brand sub-positioning is focused on.

Core competencies – It refers to physical and human assets. Physical assets mean historical sites, facilities, unique hotels, old buildings, etc. Human assets mean 'exceptional individuals' such as politicians, mayors, artists, celebrities, etc. Therefore, in order to ensure a powerful city branding, the strategy team should link these core competencies to the three other factors.

In order to implement the model vis-à-vis repositioning Jerusalem as a target for domestic tourism, the strategy team began raising different aspects of the city relevant to each of the model's four factors. This action was done

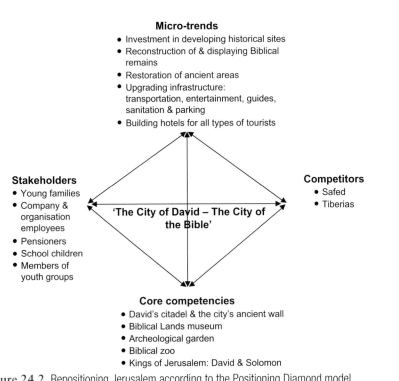

Micro-trends
- Investment in developing historical sites
- Reconstruction of & displaying Biblical remains
- Restoration of ancient areas
- Upgrading infrastructure: transportation, entertainment, guides, sanitation & parking
- Building hotels for all types of tourists

Stakeholders
- Young families
- Company & organisation employees
- Pensioners
- School children
- Members of youth groups

'The City of David – The City of the Bible'

Competitors
- Safed
- Tiberias

Core competencies
- David's citadel & the city's ancient wall
- Biblical Lands museum
- Archeological garden
- Biblical zoo
- Kings of Jerusalem: David & Solomon

Figure 24.2 Repositioning Jerusalem according to the Positioning Diamond model

through brainstorming and with the collaboration of experts from the field of tourism marketing. The objective was to find linkages between different components upon which the city's new image could be based. The selected aspects are presented in Figure 24.2.

Analysis of the different aspects that appear in Figure 24.2 clearly indicates that the issue with the strongest linkage to the model's four components is the 'City of the Bible' feature. In regard to micro-trends, it is plain to see that the issue of displaying and restoring archeological sites from the Biblical period together with improvement in infrastructure, transportation, services, and tourism facilities are among the most prominent in recent years. Concerning stakeholders, it was found that local audiences are increasingly showing interest in educational tours in Jerusalem. Among the stakeholders are labour unions, pensioners, schoolchildren, and members of youth movements. Regarding competitors, the analysis showed that Jerusalem is a city with deep-seated roots, which resonates with importance more strongly than Safad and Tiberias, especially in everything related to Biblical study and history. The core competencies such as David's citadel, the Biblical Lands Museum, and the Biblical Zoo are strongly interlaced with the world of the Bible from many angles: culturally, historically, educationally, learning-wise, and visually.

As mentioned above, the strategy team found that the concept 'City of David – City of the Bible' transmits the right marketing message, as expressed in the analysis of the Positioning Diamond model in the best and most significant manner. The idea behind the hyphenated name was to actualise for the target audiences the Biblical experience and allow them to feel close to and to identify with the most famous and admired of the kings of Israel.

The next stage in the strategy team's work was to find a way of putting the repositioning strategy into action. In order to do this the team surveyed the marketing activities of the city's hotels over the preceding four decades, when Jerusalem was being marketed as 'the city of three religions.' During this period the city's hotels operated on their own, with no collaboration among them. Most helped the many tourists who came from abroad and the few Israelis who stayed in their hotel to plan tours of sites holy to the three religions. The profile of the average tourist consisted of older families, sometimes travelling with older children, who stay in the city between four and seven nights. The foreign tourists combined their holidays with visits to museums, the promenade, shopping centres, and entertainment sites. A large number of the tourists had their visits arranged through travel agents and others came with organised groups.

Table 24.1 Past and present domestic tourism marketing strategies for the city of Jerusalem

Characteristics	'Holy City – City of the Three Religions'	'City of David – City of the Bible'
The positioning concept for the city	The meeting point of three religions and a stroll through layers of history	The story of the Bible: An educational and mystical experience
Main tourist attractions	Places that are holy to the three religions	Sites linked to the Bible
Entertainment culture	'Western culture': Museums, promenades, restaurants, shopping centres, and entertainment spots	'Israeli culture': Biblical exhibitions, ultra-Orthodox neighbourhoods, authentic marketplaces, and middle eastern restaurants
Hotel management style	Each hotel designed its own strategy and operated on its own in organising attractions for its clients	Joint strategy and presentation of tourist attractions
Essence of the holiday	Historical religious experience	Biblical historical experience
Target audience	Older tourists and pilgrims	Youth, young families, business organisations, and pensioners
Duration of vacation	Four to seven nights	Two to four nights
Marketing activities	Tourism magazines, global newspapers, travel agencies, tourism exhibitions, and conferences	Mass media (television, newspapers, radio, billboards), Ministry of Education, direct appeal to labor unions

In contrast to this approach, the strategy team chose to adopt the concept of 'the City of David – the City of the Bible' for promoting the city among the local population. Promotion of the concept was done through a collaborative effort of all the city's hotels, with the initiation and encouragement of the Ministry of Tourism and the Jerusalem Hotel Association. Advertisements of holidays in Jerusalem as 'the City of David – the City of the Bible' presented the central sites, which included a tour of David's citadel, the Biblical Lands Museum, the Archaeological Garden, and the Biblical Zoo. The figure that appeared as a motif in all the advertisements was that of King David who invited young families and their children to come experience a fascinating trip into the past. The aim was for a stay of two to four nights. Table 24.1 presents the two strategies for marketing the city of Jerusalem.

Moving from a marketing strategy based mainly on foreign tourism to a marketing strategy that encourages domestic tourism proves itself to be a necessary and effective step that allowed the city's hotels to survive the era of terrorism. From data collected by the Central Bureau of Statistics in Israel and the Hotel Association it appears that up to the year 2000 the number of nights foreign tourists spent in Jerusalem were 30% more than domestic tourists. However, beginning in 2001 and up to 2003, hotel occupancy deriving from domestic tourism constituted nearly twice the occupancy from foreign tourism (Figure 24.3). From 2004, even though hotel occupancy from domestic tourism continued to grow, the trend reversed with a significant increase in occupancy from foreign tourism owing mainly to an improvement in the security situation.

The repositioning of Jerusalem for domestic tourists turned into a success story for Jerusalem's hoteliers and ensured a turnover of 15% more than that of 2000. An additional indicator that highlights the success of tourist hotels in Jerusalem after the repositioning campaign was the employment of hotel staff. Each year from 2002 through 2005 there was a steady annual rise of an average of 5% in the number of hotel employees.

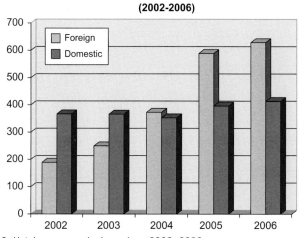

Figure 24.3 Hotel occupancy in Jerusalem, 2002–2206

CONCLUSION

Jerusalem's repositioning was a unique example of marketing activities characterised by a high level of creativity, which was targeted at stopping a decline in hotel stays in Jerusalem and constituted a growth impetus for future years following characterised by a continuation of terrorism. The uniqueness of the strategy was in the combination of its flexibility and reliance on the city's physical and spiritual resources. The repositioning of the city of Jerusalem indicates that a new identity does not have to replace an old one and that a benefit can certainly be generated resulting in a competitive edge gained from a combination and operation of dual images. The new image facilitates segmenting new markets and expanding business activities especially in troublesome periods, whether these are the result of terrorist attacks or ecological or other types of calamities. Countries and major cities in the world that find themselves under the continual threat of terrorism must be innovative in their thinking so that they can reposition themselves and hence better cope with new challenges. Likewise, the fact that terrorism does not distinguish between nations, nationalities, or states, justifies and necessitates transmission of the accumulated experience and lessons among countries.

The example presented here emphasises the fact that one can use the tools developed to measure the position of states also to measure the position of cities. These methodologies require more broadening, in-depth research, and improvement. The repositioning of Jerusalem may be used as a commercial-marketing model for many hoteliers in cities and locations that have been the victims of terrorism, such as New York, Madrid, London, Moscow, Kashmir, and Sharm a-sheikh, which can maintain tourism by marketing to the domestic population.

References

Anholt, S. (2006). The Anholt-GMI city brands index how the world sees the world's cities. *Place Branding and Public Diplomacy, 2*(1), 18–31.

Ashworth, G. J., & Voogt, H. (1990). *Selling the city: Marketing approaches in public sector urban planning.* London, UK: Belhaven Press.

Ashworth, G. J., & Voogt, H. (1994). Marketing and place promotion. In S. V. Ward, & J. R. Gold (Eds.). *Place promotion, the use of publicity and marketing to sell towns and regions* Chichester: John Wiley.

Caldwell, N., & Freire, J. R. (2004). The differences between branding a country, a region and a city: applying the Brand Box Model. *Journal of Brand Management, 12*(1), 50–61.

Crockett, S. R., & Wood, L. J. (2000). Brand Western Australia: a totally integrated approach. *Journal of Vacation Marketing, 5*(3), 276–289.

Daskou, S., Thom, C., & Boojihawon, D. K. (2004). Marketing a city: glasgow, city of architecture and design. *Global Business and Economics Review, 6*(1), 22–37.

Fleisher, A., & Buccola, S. (2002). War, terror and the tourist market in Israel. *Applied Economics, 34*(11), 1335–1344.

Florek, M., & Conejo, F. (2007). Export flagships in branding small developing countries: the cases of Costa Rica and Moldova. *Place Branding and Public Diplomacy*, 3(1), 53–72.

Gilmore, F. (2001). A country – Can it be repositioned? Spain – The success story of country branding. *Journal of Brand Management*, 9(4), 281–293.

Gould, M., & Skinner, H. (2007). Branding on ambiguity? Place branding without a national identity: marketing Northern Ireland as a post-conflict society in the USA. *Place Branding and Public Diplomacy*, 3(1), 100–113.

Hall, D. (2002). Brand development, tourism and national identity: the re-imagining of former Yugoslavia. *Journal of Brand Management*, 9(4–5), 323–334.

Hall, J. (2004). Branding Britain. *Journal of Vacation Marketing*, 10(2), 171–185.

Hankinson, G. (2005). Destination brand images: a business tourism perspective. *Journal of Services Marketing*, 19(1), 24–32.

Hopper, P. (2003). Marketing London in a difficult climate. *Journal of Vacation Marketing*, 9(1), 81–88.

Jaffe, E. D., & Nebenzahl, I. D. (2006). *National image and competitive advantage, the theory and practice of place branding, 2/e*. Denmark: Copenhagen Business School Press.

Kemming, J. D., & Sandikci, O. (2007). Turkey's EU accession as a question of nation brand image. *Place Branding and Public Diplomacy*, 3(1), 31–41.

Kerr, G. (2006). From destination brand to location brand. *Journal of Brand Management*, 13(4/5), 276–283.

Kotler, P., & Gertner, D. (2002). Country as brand, product, and beyond: a place marketing and brand management perspective. *Journal of Brand Management*, 9(4–5), 249–261.

Kotler, P., Haider, D. H., & Rein, I. (1993). *Marketing places: Attracting investment, industry, and tourism to cities*, *States and Nations*. New York: Free Press.

Kotler, P., Jatusripitak, S., & Maesincee, S. (1997). *The marketing of nations*. New York: Simon & Schuster Trade.

Mansfield, Y. (1999). Cycles of war, terror, and peace: determinants and management of crisis and recovery of the Israeli tourist industry. *Journal of Travel Research*, 38, 30–40.

Morgan, N. J., & Pritchard, A. (1999). Building destination brands: the case of Wales and Australia. *Journal of Brand Management*, 7(2), 103–118.

Morgan, N. J., Pritchard, A., & Piggott, R. (2003). Destination branding and the role of the stakeholders: the case of New Zealand. *Journal of Vacation Marketing*, 9(3), 285–299.

Morgan, N. J., Pritchard, A., & Pride, R. (2002). Introduction. In N. J. Morgan, A. Pritchard, & R. Pride (Eds.). *Destination branding* Oxford: Butterworth-Heinemann.

Morgan, N. J., Pritchard, A., & Pride, R. (2004). *Destination branding creating the unique proposition*   (2nd ed.). Oxford: Elsevier Butterworth Heinemann.

Nuttavuthisit, K. (2007). Branding Thailand: correcting the negative image of sex tourism. *Place Branding and Public Diplomacy*, 3(1), 21–30.

O'Leary, S., & Deegan, J. (2003). People, pace, place: qualitative and quantitative images of Ireland as a tourism destination in France. *Journal of Vacation Marketing*, 9(3), 213–226.

Papadopoulos, N. (2004). Place branding: evolution, meaning and implications. *Place Branding and Public Diplomacy*, 1(1), 36–49.

Porter, M. (1989). *The competitive advantage of nations*. New York: Simon & Schuster Trade.

Pritchard, A., & Morgan, N. (1998). "Mood marketing" – the new destination branding strategy: a case study of "Wales", the brand. *Journal of Vacation Marketing*, *4*(3), 215–229.

Retner, D. (2002). Research on terror in Israel. Haaretz, Israel.

Shimp, T. P., Saeed, S., & Madden, T. J. (1993). Countries and their products: a cognitive structure perspective. *Journal of the Academy of Marketing Science*, *21*(4), 323–330.

Trueman, M., Klemm, M., & Giroud, A. (2004). Can a city communicate? Bradford as a corporate brand. *Corporate Communications: An International Journal*, *9*(4), 317–330.

US Department of State. (various years). Patterns of global terrorism. Washington, DC: US Department of State.

Ward, S. V. (2000). *Selling places: The marketing of towns and cities. 1850–2000*. London: Routledge.

CHAPTER

Epilogue: Tourism and place reputation in an uncertain world

Annette Pritchard, Nigel Morgan and Roger Pride

INTRODUCTION

Three themes have run through this book. First, we have seen the importance of a place's reputational balance sheet in today's competitive globalised tourism marketplace. Growing recognition by governments and agencies that a place's competitiveness is significantly dependent on its reputation has highlighted the importance of country, city, and regional 'identity premiums,' and several of the book's case studies demonstrate the value of pursuing a holistic approach to place reputation management, projecting a place as an attractive place to live, visit, study, invest in and as an exporter of high-quality, value-added products and services. Secondly, many of the contributions have demonstrated how destination marketing organisations (DMOs) tend to be the most experienced and professional in a place's reputational management 'team' and how tourism 'leads' place reputation management strategies. And the final message – which we summarised in the virtuous circle of destination reputation management in Chapter 1 – is that those responsible for the stewardship of places and their reputations must embrace creativity, innovation, and sustainable ways of living. In this epilogue we return to this final point and reflect on the future of place reputation management, tourism, and tourism places. The chapter will:

* Briefly summarise the book's key points;
* Reflect on destination reputation management and tourism futures.

REFLECTIONS ON DESTINATION BRANDS: MANAGING PLACE REPUTATION

While most of the chapters in this collection focus on tourism and destination brands, many have also sought to reinforce that destination reputation management is not merely concerned with tourism but is intimately entwined

© 2011 Published by Elsevier Ltd. All rights reserved.
DOI: 10.1016/B978-0-08-096930-5.10025-4

with a broader public diplomacy agenda. If handled appropriately to the benefit of local communities (and of course that is an important caveat), tourism can enable communities, cities, regions, and countries to build their economic competitiveness, improve their residents' quality of life, and steward their cultural and linguistic traditions and their natural environment. In many countries (often but not exclusively less developed economies), however, the tourism industry itself is politically weak, lacks visibility, and is extremely fragmented. The real sources of power in such a vacuum are often the DMOs and a handful of major companies, particularly the airlines.

In these cases the DMOs must rise to the task of being the primary front-line promoter for any destination and as government financing continues to be squeezed as a result of the global financial crisis, it is critical that the roles performed by DMOs are valued and continued. Their role is to act as the guardian of the destination brand, ensuring it is delivered and not diluted or compromised. As destinations can no longer be everything to everybody, DMOs must be able to segment visitors by willingness to purchase against lifestyle and geographical location. In addition, they must ensure an easy and clear pathway for visitors in understanding the brand through the exploration of information, including the use of internet sites or other technology intermediaries that facilitate both exploration and purchase.

The success of many of the tourism brand strategies discussed in Part 3 shows that destinations can pursue activities which enhance their reputations and build brands with emotional appeal. That does not mean, however, that it is easy to build a strong destination travel brand or that DMOs can claim all or even most of the credit, given that they do not control the product, the message, or the media. Clearly, to maximise their influence and the message impact, DMOs must work on a collaborative and integrative basis outside traditional advertising. This is particularly true of niche destinations with a small share of voice but all destinations must be alive to alternatives to advertising and focus on leveraging the branding opportunities of sport, popular culture, and events. Obvious examples in this book include the release of the movie *Australia* in 2008, the 2010 Ryder Cup in Wales, the London 2012 Olympics, and Milan Expo 2015. All have or will provide worldwide interest and platforms for public relations and promotional campaigns. At the same time, however, destinations should also be alive to the opportunities provided by local initiatives. For instance, hosting a popular radio station's (Radio One) premier music event featuring Alicia Keys in North Wales gave the region a week's sustained coverage with audiences not usually targeted by the DMOs VisitWales. The success of the event and the subsequent viral buzz generated the kind of publicity that money simply cannot buy.

DMO must also look to the future and consider the opportunities offered by interactive media and the web. In the longer term, mobile communication will be more important than conventional PC-based communication and destinations should already be offering SMS, podcasts, and mobile website services and product listings to satnav service providers. These media cannot be ignored as not only do they interactively engage visitors pre-trip, they also provide direct marketing opportunities for relationship building, which can be resurrected and sustained post-trip. The web is an ideal platform for developing and projecting a destination brand in order to provide the industry with the best selling environment. Historically, the internet could not contribute much to brand-building, but that is no longer true. Broadband can convey rich imagery, personal time spent on web pages has increased hugely, and it is its seamless combination of information, contact, transaction, entertainment and relationship services that distinguishes the internet from the off-line world. It is what makes it so successful.

In addition, online social networks are a new and powerful arena for destination marketers as these networks, and the user-generated content which they stimulate, are central to those holiday decisions that are based on recommendation as they are excellent sources of word-of-mouth feedback about destination experiences. Destinations can and should actively encourage the creation of user-generated content about the destination, wherever it is published – equally, they should use it in their own communication channels, and integrate it with their own content. Blogs are particularly important for destination marketers because so many people include travel experiences and travel diaries in their blogs. Thus, blogs are ideal channels of conversations about places and blogging has grown exponentially in recent years – in 2010 there were over 126 million blogs, more than twice as many as there were in 2007 and more than triple the number in 2006. As has been underlined by several contributors in this book, DMOs are now engaged in conversations with individual consumers rather than mass market campaigns – which mean they will have to think and act differently in the future.

Those responsible for destination reputation management will have to think smarter and have tenacity. The examples from this book show that it takes patience to establish positive reputations and building a powerful destination reputation is a long-term effort. Certainly, the collection demonstrates that those destinations that have emerged as reputation winners do have a number of common features. They often have travel brands based on a vision which is founded on intensive stakeholder, consumer, and competitor research and which is expressed with care and discipline in everything that communicates the brand's personality. Once the brand personality has been identified, marketers must have the courage to stay with the brand's essence – while refinements may be made to how the values are expressed in the brand architecture, the essentials of the brand personality should remain consistent. The secret is to continually evolve and enrich the original brand personality, building on the initial strengths to strengthen their appeal and to broaden the market. Take the examples discussed here of Singapore and Wales, which have woven 'new' attributes (such as culture, heritage, and sports events) into their original brand personalities.

TOURISM AND PLACE FUTURES

As we said in our introduction to this book, the twenty-first century has been a tough one for tourism so far. Environmental disasters, financial and economic crises, political insecurity, war and terrorism, and epidemics have all made their mark in the last decade. The impact of such crises is particularly evident in our hyper-mobile, integrated world and in the ever-increasing number of places which are heavily dependent on tourism. To take just one example, the volcanic ash cloud from the 2010 Eyjafjallajokull eruption in Iceland is estimated to have cost the global airline industry US$1.7 billion after just one week of flight restrictions in European airspace, while the wider cost to European firms is estimated at around 2.5 billion Euros (see Hall, 2010). At the same time, the world is facing a number of long-term threats, including resource depletion, climate change, and food and water shortages. Arguably, the time has come for DMOs and the wider tourism industry to take account of these threats in future planning.

Of course, scenario planning is a key tool for many organisations in the tourism industry such as DMOs and the UNWTO (Chapter 13). In many of these scenarios the future seems bleak yet despite this growth predictions continue to dominate strategy documents in most countries. Tourism 2023, which considers a number of scenarios for the UK outbound tourism industry describes four distinct pictures, much of which makes for uncomfortable reading (Table 25.1). Close reading of the scenarios suggests that all those with a stake in the tourism industry need to take a step back to consider what kind of tourism future and strategic indicators are desirable, attainable, and sustainable. This is probably the greatest challenge facing the tourism industry precisely because it is a challenge that few wish to confront. Today's strategies are effectively wedded to short-term KPIs such as volume, value, foreign currency earnings, and profit and employment figures. Such growth models value expansion above all else and regard low or no growth as evidence of failure. Should such crude growth indicators continue to dominate our thinking or should we look at measures of success focused on 'mindful' development, linked to low carbon, sustainable growth, quality of life indicators, social benefits, community involvement and cohesion, and cultural and aesthetic values? Mindful development is not a turning away from progress; it is crucial to progress (see Pangilinan 2010).

We raised the possibility at the outset of this book that we are in the midst of a paradigm shift as agents of change transform human activity. Of course, no one can ever know what the future will hold but never before in human history have so many cultures, belief systems, and new scientific discoveries emerged and interacted so quickly. These transitional times are indeed exciting and challenging as our dominant ways of living and of understanding the world and old societal structures are increasingly stressed. Who knows what history will term this period? We do know that we are already seeing a shift from a mechanistic, manufacturing, industrial society to an organic, service-based, information-centred society, and increases in technology will only continue this shift to a globalised, connected world. The internet in particular has enabled or accelerated the creation of new forms of human interactions. But there are also signs of a trend towards more connected living across every area of human activity in a different sense. The growth of the knowledge economy and the tentative emergence of quality of life as a measure of societal progress are both fundamental changes in emphasis, which suggests humans may redefine (or be forced to redefine) the relationship between human and

Table 25.1 Tourism 2023 scenarios

Boom & bust	Divided disquiet
• Quest for new destinations	• Troubled world, travel less attractive
• Pressure on wilderness areas	• Protectionism and mistrust
• Overseas travel attractive and easy	• Closed borders
• Quick economic recovery	• Asymmetries of world order
• Growth of Brazil, Russia, India, & China	• Ideological wars
• Globalised world, more visitors and destinations	• Easy, safe, cheap travel over
• Advances in technology, other sectors make carbon cuts to allow growth	• Destinations struggle to attract visitors
• Overcrowding	• Safe destinations overcrowded
	• Virtual experiences replaces some travel

Price & privilege	Carbon clampdown
• Cost constraints lead to restructures	• Demand for overseas travel declines as ethical issues dominate
• Oil price super spikes	• Carbon regime
• More advanced economies struggling	• Individual carbon allowances
• Cheap mass air travel a thing of the past	• New technologies fail to deliver
• Once in a lifetime holidays	• Less travel, over capacity in the sector
• Low margins, poor wages	• Focus on domestic tourism or global business
• Fewer economic benefits for destinations	• Longer holidays
• Wealthy minority of elite travellers	• Staycations
• Right to fly movements	• Airships make a comeback
• Holiday credit schemes	
• Infrastructural change	

Source: Adapted from Tourism 2023: Visions for UK outbound tourism

material capital, between life and work, between the intuitive and the rational, between society, science, and ethics in the near future.

As with any regime change, there are opportunities as well as threats. As Dennis and Melewar (2010, p. 76) point out, 'the greater the chaos, the more the people seek security of the places that they know and trust – the place brands.' And there are opportunities for tourism to move from the margins to the centre of contemporary economies and societies. Johannesson and Huibens (2010) have commented how tourism has returned to the fore in Iceland as a direct result of its financial crisis so much so that it is increasingly being viewed as a creative and key sector of the economy. But as with any sector, tourism worldwide needs to focus on upskilling the employment opportunities which it provides to make these jobs more effective and rewarding and to secure its long-term role in the global social economy. At the same time, local tourism industries need to recognise that there is a growing demand for more ethically conscious brands, products, and services and that there are reputational gains to be made in this area.

Destinations which embrace such thinking could become renowned as truly creative and agenda-setting. The pressure of climate change and the predicted human pressures on resources will eventually lead to a shift in our consumption patterns, for if everyone on Earth lived as a typical American does today, we would need five planets to live on (http://www.oneplanetliving.org). Tourism creates huge pressures on urban and rural environments; for example, in dryer regions like the Mediterranean, the issue of water scarcity is of particular concern. Because of the hot climate and the tendency of tourists to consume more water when on holiday than they do at home, the amount used can run up to 440 litres a day. This is almost double what the inhabitants of an average Spanish city consume. We are already seeing a renaissance in local food growing, processing, and distribution. As we noted in the introduction, this may soon be followed by a shift to steady-state tourism, moves from more distant to 'slower,' localised holiday-taking and a demand for high-quality, locally sourced produce (Hall 2010). As we have seen, the Slow City movement founded in Italy in 1999 celebrates and supports the diversity of culture and the specialities of a town and its hinterland; its goals include improving the quality of life in towns while resisting 'the fast-lane, homogenised world so often seen in other cities throughout the world' (http://wwwslowmovement.com). While Italy remains its core with 69 communities, 14 countries have at least one officially accredited Slow City or Cittaslow community, including Sonoma Valley in the USA, Perth in Scotland, and Lens in Belgium.

Slow travel is in its infancy but similar socially driven, sustainable initiatives abound. There are currently Fairtrade Towns in Australia, Austria, Belgium, Brazil, Canada, Denmark, Finland, France, Ireland, Italy, Norway, Spain, Sweden, the Netherlands, Germany, the UK, and the USA. Wales became the world's first Fairtrade nation in June 2008, although it has yet to really build on this in its place reputation management strategies (www.fairtrade.org.uk). Carbon neutral regions or CNRs, such as Roanoke in Virginia, USA are developing initiatives to educate and engage the community towards the achievement of sustainable living. Roanoke has positioned itself as 'a proving ground for sustainable technologies' in a bid to attract new businesses, generate new jobs, and become a model community for sustainable living. The ultimate goal is for the region to be carbon neutral by 2030 (http://www.cnr2030.org/).

Moving beyond fair trade and carbon zero living to combine social and ecological goals, One Planet Communities are developments where not only are the buildings designed to be as energy efficient as possible, but where there are also the services, infrastructure, and design features to enable residents to reduce their ecological footprint to a One Planet level by 2020. The One Planet Communities program is an initiative for private and public property developers, which aims to help them to create mixed-use places where it is easy, attractive, and affordable for people to live within a fair share of the Earth's resources. There are four One Planet endorsed Communities – two in the UK (One Brighton and One Gallions), one in the USA, and one in Portugal, while there are five more applying the One Planet principles (Table 25.2) in Australia, China, South Africa, UAE, and the UK. The first endorsed community is Mata de Sesimbra, south of Lisbon in Portugal. This €1 billion integrated sustainable building, tourism, nature conservation, and reforestation 5,300 hectare site will eventually create a 4,800 hectare nature reserve and native pine and oak forest restoration project – the largest private forest restoration project in Europe. Alongside this is a 500 hectare tourism development comprising around 5,000 units. The reforestation project has been underway for a number of years, and final planning permission has now been granted for the development area. The development will go on to meet zero carbon and zero waste targets, while 50% of food will be sourced locally (http://www.oneplanetliving.org).

Table 25.2 The ten principles of One Planet Living

One Planet Guiding Principle	
Zero carbon	Our climate is changing because of human-induced build up of CO_2 in the atmosphere
Zero waste	Waste from discarded products and packaging creates disposal problems and squanders valuable resources
Sustainable transport	Travel by car and plane is contributing to climate change, air and noise pollution, and congestion
Local & sustainable materials	Destructive resource exploitation increases environmental damage and reduces local community benefits
Local & sustainable food	Industrial agriculture produces food of uncertain quality, harms local ecosystems, and may have high transport impacts
Sustainable water	Local supplies of freshwater are often insufficient to meet human needs, due to pollution, disruption of hydrological cycles, and depletion
Natural habitats & wildlife	Loss of biodiversity due to development in natural areas and over-exploitation of natural resources
Culture & heritage	Loss of cultural and linguistic heritage throughout the world due to globalisation, resulting in loss of local identity and knowledge
Equity & fair trade	Many in the industrialised world live in relative poverty and many in the developing world cannot meet their basic needs from what they produce or sell
Health & happiness	Rising wealth and greater health and happiness increasingly diverge, raising questions about the true basis of well-being and contentment

Source: http://www.oneplanetliving.org.

CONCLUSION

It is customary practise for books to conclude with a discussion of future research agendas. In the field of place reputation management and destination brands, however, these opportunities are particularly significant as more bridges need to be built between those who practise and those who write about destination reputation management. Such bridges would enrich the field of destination branding, strength its research base, and enhance both theory and praxis. We hope that the earlier editions of this book have been such bridges. However you have read this edition, whether from start to finish or simply by dipping into its individual parts or chapters, we hope it has been an enjoyable read and a useful resource. It is not intended to be all-inclusive. The subject has now become too large and too important to make such a claim but we hope that students and scholars of destination marketing will find enough of interest here to provoke further critical study and debate.

Destination reputation management deserves more attention from both academics and practitioners. It is an extremely complex and highly political activity that can enhance a place's economy, self-image, and identity. Many organisations and groups have vested interests in the promotion of particular identities (many of which may be in direct conflict with the interests of others) and we need much more work on how these interests intersect. In particular, there is a pressing need for study of the processes underpinning the support in the public and private sectors for place reputation management. Nation brands can encompass several regional sub-brands that require accommodation in the overall brand and, more complex still, may involve co-operation across several regions and countries as smaller, less well-known places attempt to gain a foothold in the international marketplace. While there is a rapidly expanding body of work on the process of destination reputation management or stewardship, we still do not understand the extent to which these processes impact on local communities. We also have little understanding of the extent to which place brand management is a collective activity embraced by residents and smaller trade operators. Research also needs to explore the relationship between culture and branding, given that it is their cultural differences that create place tone and give them a sense of place.

Above all, as indicated by Jeremy Hildreth's chapter, there is a pressing need for more study of the wider effectiveness of tourism marketing and promotional activity – which remains wide-open for examination. This book leaves a host of questions unanswered in connection with creative destinations. What do we mean by the term itself? How do we account for and categorise creativity; where are the creative hotspots; are cities inherently more creative than towns, villages and hamlets? What is the link between social/public policy (in the arts, culture, education, planning etc.) and the creative industries and a place's residents? How innovative, curious, talented, able and welcoming of new challenges are particular places' communities? This brings us back to the fundamental question of what is tourism's role in place creativity and innovation. How can it help places respond to the challenging times of today? Although place marketing has often been viewed as a pragmatic act, a response to the shift from industrial to post-industrial, largely city-based economies, it is inherently a political act, whether conducted at community, city, regional or national level (Eisenschitz, 2010; Pritchard, 2009). How place marketing and place reputation management develops and responds to the new global challenges of tomorrow remains to be seen.

References

Dennis, C., & Melewar, T. C. (2010). Guest editorial, special issues on place for people in a turbulent world. *Journal of Place Branding and Public Diplomacy, 6*(2), 76–78.

Eisenschitz, A. (2010). Neo-liberalism and the future of place marketing. *Journal of Place Branding and Public Diplomacy, 6*(2), 79–86.

Hall, C. M. (2010). Crisis events in tourism: subjects of crisis in tourism. *Current Issues in Tourism, 13*(5), 401–417.

Johannesson, G., & Huibens, E. (2010). Tourism in times of crisis: exploring the discourse of tourism development in Iceland. *Current Issues in Tourism, 13*(5), 419–434.

Pritchard, A. (2009). *Keynote: 'Destination branding. The key challenges'*. 3rd. International Conference on Destination Branding and Marketing Macau SAR, China: Institute for Tourism Studies.

Pangilinan, R. D. (Redefining the good life in a sustainable society. Philosophy for business. Available at: http://www.isfp.co.uk/businesspathways/issue60.html2010.

Useful websites

http://www.cnr2030.org
www.fairtrade.org.uk
http://www.oneplanetliving.org
http://wwwslowmovement.com

Index